SOVIET BOMBERS
OF THE SECOND WORLD WAR

SOVIET BOMBERS OF THE SECOND WORLD WAR

JASON NICHOLAS MOORE

FONTHILL

I dedicate this book to the brave women and men of the Soviet Union, both military and civilian, who sacrificed so much in their terrible war to defeat Nazi aggression.

Fonthill Media Language Policy

Fonthill Media publishes in the international English language market. One language edition is published worldwide. As there are minor differences in spelling and presentation, especially with regard to American English and British English, a policy is necessary to define which form of English to use. The Fonthill Policy is to use the form of English native to the author. Jason Nicholas Moore was born and educated in the United States, but prefers to write in British English; therefore, British English has been adopted in this publication.

Fonthill Media Limited
Fonthill Media LLC
www.fonthillmedia.com
office@fonthillmedia.com

First published in the United Kingdom and the United States of America 2019

British Library Cataloguing in Publication Data:
A catalogue record for this book is available from the British Library

ISBN 978-1-78155-716-7

Typeset in 10pt on 13pt Sabon
Printed and bound in England

Preface

Many of the Soviet-built Second World War bombers remain little known in the West, sometimes just as names, although they significantly helped the Red Army achieve its great victory over the forces of Nazi Germany and its allies. It is my hope to rectify that lack of renown with this reference work on these bombers. I will describe in detail the Soviet-built bombers in use from 1939 to 1945. This book will not describe in detail the Western Allied-supplied Lend-Lease bombers, as that will be covered fully in a later book. In addition, I will not describe in detail seaplanes and flying boats that were also used as bombers, as that will be dealt with in an upcoming book. I will examine both the design and history of the Soviet-built land-based bombers, including single-engined attack aircraft (such as the Il-2 Shturmovik) and multi-engined bombers (such as the Pe-8 and the Il-4).

A serious issue arises with some of these bombers in that only a few, or none (such as the Pe-8 or the Su-2), have survived the ravages of time (or the deliberate effort by the Soviet Union in the 1950s to scrap all aircraft considered obsolete). This means that the development and the construction of these aircraft have to be reconstructed from photographs, factory records, manuals, contemporary descriptions, or even still-existing wrecks, there being in some instances no existing complete aircraft to examine. Therefore, you will see me use a term such as 'apparently' or a phrase like 'unclear from the record' more than I would have liked; it is difficult to be completely certain about changes or additions to the airframe and exactly when they occurred due to gaps in the record and the lack of surviving airframes to check against.

Nonetheless, the major types (such as the Il-2, the Il-4, the Pe-2, and the Tu-2) will have their structures and systems described in some detail (examples of all these aircraft are still extant). Minor types (such as the Yak-4) will not be described in such detail as they were insignificant players in the war and no examples survive to this day. Bombers such as the TB-3 and SB, although significant at the time they were introduced and in the early part of the war, disappeared from front-line combat service during the war and will not be described in the same detail as the major Great Patriotic War types, such as the Il-2 and the Pe-2, for example. The Pe-8 will also not be described in the same detail as the Tu-2, as an example, partly because no examples exist today and partly because it was produced in such small numbers (perhaps only ninety-three), and although the few examples built saw quite a bit of combat, it had no great effect upon the war.

As with my previous books, a term you will not see me use in this book is 'Russia' to refer to the Soviet Union. Although this convention is still used in nearly every English-language war history (much to my chagrin), even those originally written by Russian (or Soviet) authors, it is inaccurate. Russia, or the Russian Soviet Federative Socialist Republic, was the largest and most populous Soviet republic, but still just one of the constituent republics that together made up the Soviet Union. Although ethnic Russians made up a majority of the military, both in the field and especially in the officer corps, millions of non-Russians also served in the Red Army during the Great Patriotic War (and died—1.5 million ethnic Ukrainian soldiers alone perished during the war). It should also be remembered that Josef Stalin, the head of the Soviet Union himself, was not Russian, but Georgian. In addition, most of the Soviet civilian casualties occurred in the non-Russian republics of Byelorussia and Ukraine, and these were the areas that bore the brunt of the initial German invasion. It is no more accurate to refer to the members of the Red Army (or the Red Air Force) as 'Russians' or to their country as 'Russia' than it is to refer to the British and Commonwealth forces of the Second World War as 'English', or to the UK as 'England'. When I use the term 'Russia' in this book, it is to refer to a specific geographic region in the Soviet Union, not to the Soviet Union as a whole, and 'Russian', if used, will refer to an ethnic Russian, not just any Soviet citizen.

Jason Nicholas Moore
Seguin, Texas
1 February 2019

Acknowledgements

I gratefully acknowledge the kind assistance of Viktor Kulikov and Gennadiy Petrov for the fine photographs they have provided. Without the help of these gentlemen, this book would have been much harder to complete. I would like to give a special thank you as always to Mike Williams of Britmodeller.com (a fine site), who introduced me to Jay Slater of Fonthill Media (a special thank you goes out to you, Jay, also, and to all the fine people at Fonthill Media for your hard work in turning the original manuscript into a presentable book). I also especially would like to thank Michal Sekula. Without Michal's excellent, painstakingly researched, and accurate work on the colour profiles, this book would have been much the poorer in both appearance and accuracy. As always, I thank my family for their moral support, financial assistance, and forbearance as I pursued this literary work. As with all my humble efforts, I hope that I have made them proud with it. Finally, any errors and inaccuracies in this work, either by commission or omission, are my own.

Contents

Glossary

AA: Anti-aircraft artillery, sometimes abbreviated to 'AAA' or referred to as 'triple-A'. Another name for this is flak, the German name for it (which is the name I will normally use throughout this book—see entry for *flak* further on). These were guns, ranging from rifle calibre guns to large cannons that were used against aircraft, including by the Soviet PVO (see entry further on).

ADD (*Aviatsiya Dal'nevo Deystviya*): 'Long-range Aviation', which was under the direct control of the *Stavka*, the Soviet High Command (see further on). The ADD was dissolved in late 1944 and its aircraft absorbed into the Red Air Force as the 18th Air Army.

AVMF (*Aviatsionniy Voyenno Morskovo Flota*): the Naval Air Forces. Generally, the AVMF used the same aircraft as the Red Air Force, including bombers such as the Il-2, the Pe-2, and the Il-4.

Axis: originally from the term 'Rome–Berlin Axis', which referred to the alliance between Nazi Germany and Fascist Italy (the Pact of Steel). It later grew to include those countries that were part of the Anti-Comintern Pact and the Tripartite Pact between Germany, Italy, and Japan. It is used in this book to refer not just to Germany and Italy, but to their allies and puppet states such as Finland, Romania, and Croatia, for example.

BAD (*Bombardirovochnaya Aviatsionnaya Divisiya*): Bomber Division. This referred to bomber aircraft divisions. A Guards division would be referred to as a GvBAD (in this case, the Gv stood for *Gvardeiyskaya*, the Russian adjectival variant of Guards).

BAK (*Bombardirovochniy Aviatsionniy Korpus*): Bomber Corps. This referred to bomber aircraft corps. A Guards bomber corps would be referred to as a GvBAK (Gv for *Gvardeiyskiy*, or Guards). This was the largest named bomber unit, there being no bomber aircraft air armies named as such (the 18th Air Army was composed solely of bombers and transports but was simply named as an 'Air Army', not a 'Bomber Air Army').

BAP (*Bombardirovochniy Aviatsionniy Polk*): Bomber Regiment. This referred to bomber aircraft regiments. A Guards regiment would be referred to as a GvBAP.

Bezant: a synthetic leather that was used by the Soviets, among other items, to cover seat cushions or portions of the landing gear.

Blitzkrieg: 'Lightning War' in German. This was the name given to the German method of war, whereby the enemy was to be overwhelmed by the speed of armoured columns striking deep through the enemy's lines, supported by infantry and the heavy use of aircraft, such as the dive-bombing Ju 87. It was this method of warfare that had worked so well in Poland and Western Europe, as well as initially against the Soviets during Operation Barbarossa (see entry further on).

Bort: tactical or aircraft number. Most Soviet warplanes bore some sort of aircraft number, on the tail or fuselage, or much more rarely, both.

CAS: close air support, often referred to as ground attack; this was the main duty of the Il-2 (see further on), but one in which bombers such as the Pe-2 and Tu-2 were also involved. This consisted of support for the Red Army ground troops and armoured divisions, which involved attacking the German units that the Soviet troops were engaged with. Fighters were used for protecting the bombers and Il-2s engaged in this activity. This and the terms ground attack or ground support are used interchangeably in this volume.

CMF: Black Sea Fleet. One of the Soviet naval fleets. Based originally in Sevastopol. The fleet was based at Batumi and Poti in Soviet Georgia during much of the Great Patriotic War after the fall of Sevastopol in 1942. Although the Soviets did not have aircraft carriers during the Great Patriotic War, ground-based aircraft units were attached to all the fleets. Sometimes you will see this as 'ChMF', from *Cherniy Morskovo Flota*, which is 'Black Sea Fleet' in Russian.

DBAP (*Dal'niy Bombardirovochniy Aviatsionniy Polk*): Long-Range Bomber Regiment. At first, part of the Red Air Force (VVS), these units became part of the ADD.

Eskadrilya: a squadron.

FAB (*Fugasnaya Aviatsionnaya Bomba*): 'General Purpose Aviation Bomb' in Russian. For example, a FAB-100 was a 100-kg aerial bomb. There were other acronyms used for bombs, such as BETAB, but FAB was the most common.

Flak: a contraction of the German term *Flugzeugabwehrkanone*, or 'Aircraft Defence Cannon'. This is the same as anti-aircraft artillery (AAA) and is the term I will use throughout this book.

Front: the Soviet equivalent of a German Army Group (like Army Group Centre), for example, the 1st Byelorussian Front.

Frontal Aviation: used to describe the aviation units that operated close to the front lines in support of the ground troops. This included fighter, ground attack, and bomber units, such as Tu-2 units.

GKO (*Gosudartsvenniy Komitet Oborony*): 'State Defence Committee' in Russian. The name of the supreme war council in the Soviet Union during the Great Patriotic War. Josef Stalin was its chairman.

Great Patriotic War (*Velikoiy Otechestvennoiy Voiyni* in Russian, or *BOB* in Cyrillic): the Soviet/Russian term for the war between Nazi Germany and the Soviet Union (22 June 1941–9 May 1945). This normally excludes the August 1945 campaign against the Japanese Kwantung Army in Manchuria (known by the Soviets as the 'Manchurian Strategic Offensive Operation').

Ground attack (support): see CAS. These terms will be used interchangeably.

Guards: a designation for units that had distinguished themselves in combat (*Gvardiya* in Russian). In addition to receiving higher pay than normal Red Army units, they also were the first units to receive new equipment. These were considered elite units. Some aircraft units, including bomber units, were designated as Guards units.

Heer: the official name for the German army under the Nazis. Seldom used, as the Wehrmacht (see further on) has supplanted it in common usage.

Hero of the Soviet Union: Often abbreviated to 'HSU', the highest military honour accorded to Soviet military personnel during the Great Patriotic War. Equivalent to the awarding of the American Medal of Honor and the British Victoria Cross. The medal that went with the title of Hero of the Soviet Union consisted of a simple golden star suspended from a small red rectangle.

Il-2: the main Soviet ground attack aircraft of the war and the single most important aircraft in the Soviet inventory (see *Shturmovik* entry further on).

Ilyushin, Sergey Vladimirovich—born in 1894, one of eleven children in a peasant family. He became the chief designer of the Ilyushin design bureau and was the designer of the Il-2 and Il-4. These aircraft were far from his only designs, and he enjoyed a long and successful career after the Great Patriotic War, designing, among other aircraft, civilian airliners and military transports. He passed away in 1977. His design bureau still exists in Russia, under the name of The Open Joint Stock Company 'Ilyushin Aviation Complex'.

Interdiction: in military terms, this refers to the interception of enemy men and materiel, such as ammunition and troops, behind the front lines. Various Soviet aircraft were used for this important operation.

Istrebitel': 'Destroyer' in Russian, this was the Soviet term for a fighter aircraft. Before the adoption of using the designer's initials for aircraft, 'I' was used for fighter designations, for example, the pre-war Polikarpov monoplane fighter was the 'I-16'.

Izdeliye: 'Object' in Russian. Aircraft (and other products) were assigned an *Izdeliye* number by the appropriate design bureau or *OKB* (see further on for a definition of 'OKB'); for example, the Tu-2 was initially the '103', '103' being the *Izdeliye* number. Thus, the first Tu-2 was '*Izdeliye* 103' or 'Object 103'.

KBF (*Krasnoznamyonniy Baltiskiy Flot*): 'Red Banner Fleet' (or Baltic Fleet). One of the Soviet naval fleets. Based in Leningrad, although during the siege of Leningrad its ships did not venture out into the Baltic Sea (other than submarines). The aircraft attached to the fleet, such as the DB-3Ts, Il-4Ts, Pe-2s, A-20s, and Il-2s did operate in the Baltic Sea against Axis shipping and Axis ports, as well as providing ground support for Red Army troops, with fighters providing protection for the ground attack and bomber aircraft such as the Il-2 and the Pe-2.

Kriegsmarine: the German Navy. Although the war was fought mainly on land, the *Kriegsmarine* was very active in the Baltic and Black Seas during the Great Patriotic War. Along with the *Heer* (Army) and the Luftwaffe (Air Force), it formed the Wehrmacht.

Lavochkin, Semyon Sergeyevich (1900–60): the chief designer of the Lavochkin design bureau, or OKB (see entry further on), and the designer of the Lavochkin fighters used during the Great Patriotic War, which along with the Yakovlev fighters (see entry further on) were the main fighters used by the Soviet Union during the war. One of the main duties of these fighters was providing escort for bombers and ground attack aircraft. They were also used for ground attack themselves.

LII: Flight Research Institute. From *Lyotno Isslydovatel'skiy Institut* in Russian. Based at Kratovo, which was renamed to Zhukhovskiy in 1946, outside of Moscow.

Luftwaffe: the German Air Force. It officially came into existence in 1935, in defiance of the Treaty of Versailles (1919). Unlike the Red Air Force or *VVS* (see entry further on) it was a separate service co-equal with the Army (*Heer*, although the term Wehrmacht is normally used) and Navy (*Kriegsmarine*).

NBAP (*Nochnoiy Bombardirovochniy Aviatsionniy Polk*): Night Bomber Regiment.

NII VVS: Scientific Research Institute of the Red Air Force. From *Nauchno-issledovatel'skiy Institut Voyenno-vozdushnykh Seel* in Russian. The testing facility for the VVS (Red Air Force), located at Kratovo, which was renamed Zhukhovskiy after the war in 1946.

NKAP (*Narkomaviaprom*; from *Narodniy Komissariat Aviatsionnoy Promishlinnosti*): Soviet Air Ministry (literally 'People's Commissariat of the Aircraft Industry'). This was the ministry responsible for aircraft development. During the Great Patriotic War, it was headed by Aleksei Ivanovich Shakhurin (1904–75).

NKVD (*Narodniy Komissariat Vnutrennik Del*): 'People's Commissariat of Internal Affairs', the ministry that included the security or secret police, in addition to normal police and border guards, including trained soldiers. It was this ministry that arrested Andrey Nikolayevich Tupolev (1888–1972) and other aviation specialists such as Vladimir Mikhailovich Petlyakov (1891–1942) and imprisoned them in a special prison, or *sharashka* (see entry further on). It later became the MVD in 1946, when the 'People's Commissariats' became 'Ministries'. This was the precursor to the KGB of Cold War fame.

OKB (*Opitnoye Konstruktorskoye Byuro*): 'Experimental Design Bureau', 'OKB' being the acronym. A state-run research institute that was something like an engineering company tasked with the design of prototypes. These organisations were not intended for mass producing the aircraft they designed. However, they usually had the facilities and resources to construct prototypes. Designs accepted by the state were then assigned to factories for mass production (see entry for *Zavod*, further on). A bureau was officially identified by a number or an acronym (such as 'TsKB') and later by initials from its head engineer's last name (such as 'Il' for Ilyushin).

Also known as a 'Design Bureau' they were a collection of Soviet designers grouped around a single head designer, with the bureau being under the name of the head designer (from mid-December 1940 onwards). In the case of the Tu-2 bomber, for example, the head designer was Andrey Tupolev. Design bureaux would respond to (or be directed to respond to) government specifications for aircraft. In contrast to Western aircraft companies, Soviet design bureaux did not own their own production facilities during the Second World War but factories were assigned to produce their designs as described above. The terms 'OKB' and 'Design Bureau' will be used interchangeably in the text.

Operation Barbarossa: this operation, named after a twelfth-century German king, was the name the Germans gave for their initial campaign against the Soviet Union. Opened on 22 June 1941, this operation was designed to defeat the Soviet Union by the end of 1941, but failed ultimately, although at a huge loss to both sides.

PARM (*Polevaya Aviaremontnaya Masterskaya*): 'Field Aircraft Repair Work Shop' in Russian. These repair shops, in addition to repairing damaged aircraft, sometimes rebuilt the often poorly constructed aircraft that came directly from the factories, before releasing them to front-line units. Ironically, one of the reasons the aircraft were often of poor manufacture is that the experienced machinists and mechanics were in the Red Army and not on the production lines, where their place was often taken by semi-skilled and unskilled labourers.

Para: a pair of aeroplanes, two of which composed a *zveno* (flight).

Pe-2: the main Soviet twin-engined light bomber and dive bomber during the Great Patriotic War, designed by Vladimir Petlyakov. It was sometimes known as the *Peshka* or 'Pawn' in Russian. Post-war, the Pe-2 was known as the 'Buck' by NATO.

Polk: Regiment. As used in this book it refers to an 'Air Regiment' (*Aviatsionniy Polk*) often shortened by the Soviets to *Aviapolk*.

RAF: Royal Air Force. The air force of the United Kingdom. Unlike the Red Air Force and the USAAF, it was an independent military arm like the Luftwaffe. The RAF was the first independent air force in the world, being formed in 1918 during the First World War. Some RAF aircraft—such as the Spitfire, Hurricane, Airacobra (an American design, but used for a short time by the RAF), and the Boston (another American design used by the RAF)—were sent to the Soviet Union via Lend-Lease.

RKKA: Red Army (taken from the Cyrillic acronym for the 'Workers and Peasants Red Army': *Rabochye-Krestiyanskoy Krasniy Armiy*—PKKA in Cyrillic). The Air Force was the 'VVS RKKA' (BBC PKKA in Cyrillic; see entry further on for a definition of the VVS).

Red Air Force: Also known as the *VVS*. This term will be used interchangeably with VVS in this book. Note that after the war, it was often called the 'Soviet Air Force', but the term Red Air Force continued to be used, as did the term VVS.

Red Army: the main fighting force of the Soviet Union, consisting of rifle (infantry), tanks, cavalry, and the Air Force (although not until 1944 the long-range bomber force, the *ADD*, which was until then under the direct command of the Soviet High Command: the *Stavka*—see entry further on). The name was officially changed to the Soviet Army in early 1946, although it was still commonly referred to as the Red Army until the end of the war and for a long time thereafter. The Soviet Navy (see entry further on) was a separate military arm from the Red Army.

SAP (*Smeshanniy Aviatsionniy Polk*): 'Combined Air Regiment'. This referred to regiments that utilised mixed types of aeroplanes, for example, 1-15bis and I-16 fighters with SB bombers.

SMF (*Severniy Morskovo Flot*): 'Northern Sea Fleet'. Based at Murmansk, it was responsible, among other things, for providing protection to Allied convoys bringing Lend-Lease equipment to the Soviet Union.

Serial number: applied at the factory, this number could consist of from six to ten digits and normally incorporated the *Zavod* number, such as '1660920', where *Zavod* 166 was the producing factory. Sometimes, this number is referred to as the construction number, or 'c/n'.

Sharashka: a prison organised by the NKVD for special prisoners, such as scientists and engineers. These prisons had better conditions than the run-of-the mill NKVD prisons and camps, and the prisoners were allowed (or coerced) to continue their work, under close NKVD direction and supervision. Andrey Tupolev designed the Tu-2 medium bomber in a *sharashka*, known as *Zavod* 156 or Z.156. Vladimir Petlyakov also designed his dive bomber, the Pe-2, in the same *sharashka* as Tupolev.

Shturmovik: Russian for 'ground attack aeroplane' (Штурмовик); it became synonymous with the Il-2 ground attack aircraft designed by Sergey Vladimirovich Ilyushin (1894–1977). Note that the accepted customary transliteration for this word into English is '*Shturmovik*', not 'Sturmovik', 'Stormovik', or other variations you will see. This was the standard Soviet ground attack aircraft for the Red Air Force throughout the Great Patriotic War. Normally it will be referred to as the 'Il-2' in this book. The Il-10, the Il-2's successor in service, was also a 'shturmovik' but will be referred to as the 'Il-10' in this book.

Soviet Air Force: another name for the Red Air Force. Both these terms (and 'VVS') will be used interchangeably in this work.

Soviet Navy: a separate military arm from the Red Army, unlike the Red Air Force, which was part of the Red Army. The Soviet Navy included the AVMF (Naval air forces, see previous AVMF entry).

Soviet Union: this term, the shortened version of the Union of the Soviet Socialist Republics, to give its full name translated into English, will be used throughout this book instead of the commonly used, but inaccurate, especially in the context of the Great Patriotic War, 'Russia'. Likewise, 'Soviet' will be used instead of 'Russian'.

Stavka: The Soviet High Command (*Shtab Glavno/Verkhovnovo Komandovaniya*). The *Stavka* had direct control over the ADD, the Soviet strategic bomber force, as well as control over the Soviet military forces.

TsAGI: The Central Aerodynamic and Hydrodynamic Institute—*Tsentralniy Aerodynamitskiy i Gidrodynamitskiy Institut*. This institute was the equivalent of the American NACA (the National Advisory Committee on Aeronautics—the precursor to NASA).

Top cover: one of the duties of the Red Air Force fighters was to provide 'top cover' for the Soviet bombers. This normally consisted of them flying above the bombers to protect them from Axis fighters.

Tupolev: this refers both to the man, Andrey Nikolayevich Tupolev, and the OKB that he founded. Andrey Tupolev was born in Pustomazovo, near Tver (Tver was called Kalinin during the Great Patriotic War), on 10 November 1888, and he died in Moscow on 23 December 1972. He was the most prolific and influential designer in Soviet aviation history, and some of his designs, such as the Tu-95 'Bear' strategic bomber, continue in use today. He was a pioneer in the use of all-metal aircraft, including all-metal bombers, such as the TB-1 and TB-3.

USAAF: United States Army Air Forces. Sometimes simply referred to as the 'Air Force' during the Second World War, this semi-autonomous arm of the US Army was the American equivalent to the Luftwaffe, RAF, and the Red Air Force. It was still technically a part of the US Army and not a fully independent military arm like the Luftwaffe and the RAF. In that respect, it was like the Red Air Force, which was a part of the Red Army. Many aircraft used by the USAAF found their way to the Soviet Union via Lend-Lease, including such bombers as the North American B-25 Mitchell and the Douglas A-20 Havoc (Boston), which both proved to be popular in Soviet service. The American Bell P-39 Airacobra fighter also proved to be very popular with the Red Air Force, indeed much more popular than it was in USAAF service.

VVS (*Voyenno-vozdushniye siliy*): the 'Military Air Forces' (Red Air Force), *BBC* in Cyrillic (Военно-воздушные силы). This acronym will be used interchangeably with the term '(the) Red Air Force' in this book. The head of the VVS from 1942 until after the war was Aleksandr Aleksandrovich Novikov (1900–76), who replaced Pavel Fedorovich Zhigarev (1900–63), who himself replaced Novikov after the war (1946).

Wehrmacht: the German Armed Forces under the Nazis, including the Kriegsmarine (Navy) and the Luftwaffe, in addition to the *Heer* (Army), although now often used to refer to the German Army alone. The actual German term for the army was *Heer*, but this is almost never used in historical books and will not be used in this work. Following convention, the term 'Wehrmacht' will be used to refer to the German Army, and the Kriegsmarine and Luftwaffe will each be referred to as such.

Yakovlev: refers to both the designer, Aleksandr Sergeyevich Yakovlev (1906–89), and the aircraft he designed. The Yakovlev fighters, often referred to simply as 'Yak' or 'Yaks', were the main Soviet fighters of the Great Patriotic War, along with the Lavochkin fighters. The Yak-1 through Yak-9 were produced in huge numbers, with more than 36,000 being produced. As with other Soviet fighters, one of the main duties of these fighters was providing escort for bombers and ground attack aircraft. In addition to the fighters for which he was justifiably famous, he also designed a twin-engined light bomber, the Yak-2, which was developed into the Yak-4, both being produced in small numbers.

Zavod (pl. *Zavodi*): Russian for 'Factory', sometimes also known as a *GAZ* (*Gosudartsvenniy Aviatsionniy Zavod* or 'State Aviation Factory' in Russian). These factories were owned by the state, and design bureaux would be directed by the NKAP to use a particular *zavod* for a particular aeroplane. *Zavodi* could and did change which aeroplanes they built, for example, *Zavod* 381 at Nizhniy Tagil in 1942 went from producing single-seater Il-2s to producing Lavochkin fighters (this was part of the same effort to produce more fighters that led to the cancellation of the first version of the Tu-2). I will use '*zavod*' and 'factory' interchangeably in the text.

Zveno: flight, composed of two *paras* (pairs or *pari* in Russian, plural) of aeroplanes, for a total of four aircraft. Copied from the Luftwaffe *schwarm* or 'finger-four' formation.

Note on transliteration: I have tried to use generally accepted norms for transliteration from Russian Cyrillic to English language Latin characters throughout this book. You will see the common Russian adjectival suffix 'ий', used both in proper names and adjectives, transliterated as 'ii', 'iiy', 'y', 'yi' or 'iy'; I have tried to consistently use 'iy'.

Timeline

The list below is a timeline of important or noteworthy occurrences in the development of Soviet/Russian bombers. It is in strict chronological order:

11 December 1913: First flight of the Ilya Muromets (the world's first four-engined bomber).
26 November 1925: First flight of the TB-1 (ANT-4, Tupolev's first all-metal bomber).
1929: The TB-1 enters service.
22 December 1930: First flight of the TB-3 (ANT-6, Tupolev's first production four-engined bomber).
1932: The TB-3 enters service.
7 October 1934: First flight of the ANT-40RTs (SB prototype).
June 1935: First flight of the TsKB-26 (ancestor of the DB-3).
1936: The SB enters Soviet service.
31 March 1936: First flight of the TsKB-30 (DB-3 prototype).
27 December 1936: First flight of the TB-7 (Pe-8 prototype).
1939: The TB-7 enters service.
1 September 1939: Beginning of the Second World War in Europe.
2 October 1939: First flight of the TsKB-55 (Il-2 prototype).
22 December 1939: First flight of the VI-100 fighter (was developed into the Pe-2).
1940: Creation of Tupolev OKB under NKVD control; first Myasishchev OKB founded.
14 May 1940: First flight of the Yer-2 (Er-2).
15 December 1940: First flight of the Pe-2.
29 December 1940: First flight of the TsKB-55P (Il-2 production prototype).
22 June 1941: Invasion of the Soviet Union by Germany begins (Operation Barbarossa).
1942: First flight of the Myasishchev DBV-102 (Myasishchev OKB's first bomber).
20 June 1944: First of three B-29s lands on Soviet territory (The B-29 was developed into the Tu-4, the Soviet's first post-war strategic bomber).

9 May 1945: Victory Day (Official end of the European War for the Soviets).
2 September 1945: Official end of the Second World War.
1946: The Petlyakov OKB is dissolved.
1948: The TB-1 is retired from civilian Arctic service.
Late 1940s: The Il-2 is retired from Soviet service.
1952: The Il-4T is retired from Soviet service.
1956: The Il-10 is retired from Soviet service.
1957: The Pe-8 is retired from civilian Arctic service.
Early 1960s: The UTB is retired from Soviet service.
1970s: The Il-10 is retired from Chinese service.
Late 1970s or Early 1980s: the Tu-2 is retired from Chinese service.

Introduction

This is not the first book on Soviet bombers of the Second World War, as the famous Soviet aircraft historian Yefim Gordon has already written an excellent book on these aircraft—a book that also includes twin-engined fighters. It is, however, the first time (as far as I know) that a comprehensive guide to Soviet-built bombers of the Second World War has been written by a native English speaker.

The basic layout of this book is simple enough: I will list, first by type, such as 'Strategic Bombers', then in alphabetical order by OKB (design bureau) under each type, the Soviet-built bombers that saw service in the Second World War. I shall also include, again in alphabetical order, an overview of the experimental bombers that were designed during the Second World War. The experimental versions of production aircraft will be described in that aircraft's section. I will not describe every experimental version of the production types, but only those that are the most interesting or important. I will not describe in detail the Soviet use of foreign-built aircraft (such as Lend-Lease types like the A-20 Havoc (Boston) and the B-25 Mitchell) because as mentioned previously these shall be dealt with in a separate book devoted to Lend-Lease aircraft under Soviet use. Although the Li-2 was based upon an American design (the Douglas DC-3), it is described in some detail as it was licence-built in the Soviet Union and appeared in a purpose-built bomber version (the Li-2NB) quite distinct from Western versions of the DC-3/C-47, which the Soviet Union also received under Lend-Lease.

Besides describing the genesis of each bomber, I shall describe their service use. The strategy and tactics peculiar to each type will be discussed, as will their use in the main Soviet campaigns of the war. The Soviet campaigns will be described in one section, as opposed to the combat service of each aircraft being described separately, as there would have been too much overlap and redundancy otherwise. However, some of the general combat use and even some specific use will be described for each aircraft in their appropriate section.

Colour profiles of each service bomber are also included in a colour plates section, to show typical camouflage and markings for each service type, as well as some experimental types.

1
Pre-War Bombers

Even before the creation of the Soviet Union in the early 1920s, bombers had been developed for the Russian Empire. Indeed, the first true strategic bomber in the world was Russian, the four-engined *Ilya Muromets* of the First World War. Bomber development continued under the Soviet Union, as both single and multi-engined types were developed for a multitude of tasks, from close air support to long-range strategic bombing.

R-5

Designed by Polikarpov as replacement for the R-1 (the Soviet unlicensed copy of the Airco DH.9A), the R-5 was a biplane light reconnaissance bomber, of the type then in some vogue in the 1920s and 1930s (such as the French Potez 25 and Breguet XIX, the Dutch Fokker C.V, and the British Hawker Hart family). The R-5 was produced in very considerable numbers (some 7,000 were built), seeing service throughout the 1930s. It first flew in autumn 1928, entering service in 1930. It was powered by the M-17 engine, which was a licence-built version of the German BMW VI twelve-cylinder inline liquid-cooled engine. The R-5 was a thoroughly conventional single-bay biplane of mainly wooden construction. Throughout most of the 1930s, it was the main Soviet light bomber and reconnaissance aircraft. In its ground attack or shturmovik version (the Polikarpov SSS), it saw use in the Spanish Civil War, and its light reconnaissance bomber version saw heavy use in the Winter War with Finland in 1939–40.

The R-5 continued to be used in the early and middle years of the Great Patriotic War as a front-line aircraft, despite its patent obsolescence. At least through the Battle of Stalingrad and as late as the Battle of Kursk, it saw use alongside the U-2 as a night harassment light bomber or nuisance bomber, along with its development, the R-Z. It also saw considerable use as a trainer throughout the Great Patriotic War. It was partly as a replacement for the only partially successful and clearly obsolete shturmovik version that the Il-2 was developed.

Polikarpov R-5 in black/green Great Patriotic War scheme. (*Viktor Kulikov's collection*)

R-5 in green camouflage with crudely applied black bands, probably in 1941. This aircraft appears to be a transport or ambulance version (note the slid-back partly transparent cover over the rear fuselage). The pilot's position also appears to be enclosed. (*Viktor Kulikov's collection*)

R-Z (R-Zet)

The R-Z, or R-Zet, was a considerably 'cleaned-up' and improved version of the R-5. It was similarly of mainly wooden construction, featuring a deeper and shorter semi-monocoque fuselage and an enclosed or semi-enclosed, extensively glazed cockpit for the pilot and the rear gunner. The lower wing was narrower in chord and some R-Zs featured spatted main wheels, although these were often removed in service. The M-17 engine of the R-5 was replaced by the more powerful Mikulin M-34 engine of 820 hp, designed by Aleksandr Aleksandrovich Mikulin (1895–1985), who had worked on the M-17. This gave the R-Z a top speed of 196 mph (316 kph) at 11,483 feet (3,500 m).

The R-Z flew for the first time in January 1935. It was selected by the Red Air Force over a competing design, the Kocherigin LR, which was itself a development of the R-5. The R-Z entered service in 1935 and supplemented the R-5, rather than supplanting it completely.

Like the R-5, the R-Z also saw action in the Spanish Civil War, the Winter War, and the Great Patriotic War. Like the R-5, in the Great Patriotic War, the R-Z saw use as a light night bomber. As with the R-5, it may have seen active service as a night bomber until as late as the Battle of Kursk in the summer of 1943.

The R-Z (R-Zet) prototype. Note the fully enclosed pilot's position. (*Viktor Kulikov's collection*)

An R-Z being serviced on the ground. This aircraft has the fully enclosed pilot's position. (*Viktor Kulikov's collection*)

A close-up of the crew's cabin on an R-Z. In this case, the pilot has a semi-enclosed canopy; the top part is no longer present in order to improve the pilot's view. The gunner has a ShKAS machine gun on a semi-circular mount. (*Viktor Kulikov's collection*)

2
Soviet Air Doctrine Before the Second World War

In Soviet military doctrine of the time, the Red Air Force (VVS) was subordinate to and under the control of the ground forces of the Red Army (RKKA). One of its most important jobs was to support these forces, operating close to the front and at low altitudes in the case of attack (close air support) aircraft. Long-range and high-altitude performance were not considered important factors for close air support aircraft. The ability to operate from rough airfields near the front was considered an important factor.

With the introduction of the four-engined TB-3 in the early 1930s, the Red Air Force possessed the first truly effective strategic bomber in the world, capable of carrying a useful load over a long range, and strategic bombing became an integral part of Red Air Force doctrine. However, the lack of success of level bombers (such as the Tupolev SB during the Spanish Civil War) led the Red Air Force to move away from the idea of strategic bombing to a doctrine that placed almost full emphasis on achieving air superiority over battlefields through the use of fighters. Once the fighters had achieved this air superiority, the bombers and attack aircraft could then function in support of the ground forces. Bombers were used not for long-range strategic purposes but mainly for missions against targets not far from the front lines (tactical or direct targets, as opposed to strategic or indirect targets).

Perhaps a short discussion of what constitutes strategic bombing as opposed to tactical bombing is in order here. In short, strategic bombing involves bombing strategic targets while tactical bombing involves bombing tactical targets. That is a bit of a circular explanation, so a more in-depth explanation is needed. The shorthand is this: if you bomb a single locomotive, that is a tactical target; if you bomb the factory that makes the locomotives, that is a strategic target. If the effect is local, this is tactical; if the effect is regarding the front, this is strategic. There is no fine dividing line between the two types of targets and indeed there is a third type of target: the operational or logistical target. This involves interdicting or attacking the enemy's supply lines, for example, or attacking transportation hubs such as railroad marshalling yards, or attacking an army group's headquarters. In this case, the effect is not just local, but may affect a large part of the front.

Since bombers could not be counted on to destroy the enemy's aircraft on the ground, it was up to fighters in the air to establish air superiority. Due to this, production emphasis was placed on fighters, at the expense of bombers and ground attack aircraft. Indeed, before the Il-2, there were no true purpose-built ground attack aircraft in the Red Air Force, as opposed to conversions of existing designs, or the Su-2, which was more of a light reconnaissance bomber than a true ground attack aircraft.

3
Single-Engined Bombers and Ground Attack Aircraft (Shturmoviks)

For the Soviets, one of the main purposes of the Red Air Force was to directly support the ground forces, and the main aircraft utilised for this was the *shturmovik*, or 'ground attack aircraft'. The Shturmovik was the Il-2, designed by Sergey Ilyushin, but it was not the only shturmovik or ground attack aircraft used by the Soviets during the Second World War.

Soviet air theorists had, by the 1920s, established the basics of ground attack and cooperation between aeroplanes and the Red Army. Tests were conducted with the R-1, the R-3, and the later R-5 aircraft (in the 1930s), but none of these aeroplanes were really suited to the ground attack role as they lacked sufficient armament and normally lacked armour protection. Some aircraft were fitted with armour, but this only detracted from what was usually a rather slow speed to begin with.

During the 1930s, the Soviet Ministry of Defence, under Defence Commissar (Minister) Marshal Kliment Yefremovich Voroshilov (1881–1969), issued various specifications for an aircraft to accomplish the task of ground support. Many different projects were proposed and many different prototypes were flown. Production aircraft were also modified for the role (such as the I-16, equipped with rockets, and the Polikarpov SSS: a modification of the R-5 light bomber and reconnaissance aircraft that saw action in this modified form during the Spanish Civil War), although as with aircraft used during the 1920s, none proved entirely satisfactory.

The *Ivanov* programme was a part of this search for an effective light bomber (*Ivanov* was how Stalin was referred to in communications). Two different prototypes were built and tested, one designed by Pavel Osipovich Sukhoi (1895–1975) and one designed by Nikolaiy Polikarpov, both of them cantilever monoplanes with a retractable landing gear. The aircraft that was eventually chosen for production was Pavel Sukhoi's entry: the Su-2. Although a good enough aircraft, it was neither particularly heavily armoured nor as well-armed as the Il-2, and it was more of a light bomber/reconnaissance aircraft in the vein of the R-5 than a dedicated ground attack aeroplane.

An interesting attempt to create a dedicated 'tank-killer' aeroplane came from the Polikarpov Design Bureau, in the form of the VIT-1 and its development, the VIT-2.

These clean, fast, and modern twin-engined monoplane aircraft featured a heavy, forward-firing armament of two 37-mm cannons, intended to knock out tanks and other ground targets. However, it was felt that with the advent of the RS-82 and RS-132 rockets, simpler aircraft could be used as anti-tank aircraft so these relatively complex aircraft did not proceed beyond the prototype stage.

The BSh-1 was a licence-built version of the Vultee V-11, itself a development of the Vultee V-1 single-engined civilian transport, which had proved useful as a light bomber for both the Nationalists and the Republicans during the Spanish Civil War. Working from this, Vultee decided to build a bomber version based on the V-1, the result being the V-11. The Soviets were impressed enough to request a licence to produce it. The BSh-1 was not heavily armoured, and the Soviets decided to use it as a transport instead of a ground attack aeroplane. This gave rise to the strange situation where a transport, the V-1, had found use as a bomber, and the bomber version, the V-11, was instead used as a transport. This still left the Soviet Union without an armoured ground attack aircraft—a lack that was not rectified until the advent of the Il-2.

Kocherigin Di-6Sh (TsKB-11)

Designed by Sergei Aleksandrovich Kocherigin (1893–1958), the Di-6 (with the internal OKB designation of 'TsKB-11') was a two-seat biplane fighter with fully retractable main landing gear that first flew on 30 September 1934. It looked rather like a two-seater version of the Polikarpov I-153 fighter, but with a conventional upper wing as opposed to the 'gull-wing' of the I-153. The crew were composed of a pilot and an observer/rear gunner.

It appears that references to the DI-6 fighting at the Battle of the Khalkhin-Gol and in the Winter War are probably not accurate. Evidently, the only combat use of the DI-6 was during the Soviet invasion of Poland during September–October 1939. The DI-6Sh, the ground attack version of this fighter, was used by the 14th ShAP to support the Horse-Mechanised Group of the Byelorussian Front.

Oddly enough, German photographs appear from early in the Great Patriotic War of DI-6s, apparently abandoned on airfields. It appears that these were ground instruction airframes that were used as decoys or dummy targets on airfields to entice the Germans to waste their bombs on these useless aircraft. Some of these DI-6s had their landing gear fixed and some were even without engines. Other than this, the DI-6 saw no use and definitely saw no action during the Great Patriotic War.

Nieman R-10

KhAI-5

The origins of what became the R-10 lay well before the Great Patriotic War. The first prototype was designed by Iosif Grigorevich Nieman (Nyeman or Neman in some sources) and built by the Kharkov Aviation Institute, or KhAI, as the KhAI-5. The origins of the KhAI-5 lay in the KhAI-1, a passenger aircraft that was a cantilever monoplane with retractable landing gear and was the first of its kind to be flown in Europe when it first flew in 1932. Forty-five were built in total and were used by Aeroflot, the Soviet civilian carrier. The KhAI-1 was also notable in being designed by students of the Kharkov Aviation Institute, under the direction of Iosif Nieman. This aircraft was developed into the KhAI-1VV (with the 'VV' for *Voenniy Variant*, or 'Combat Variant'), but did not enter production.

The KhAI-5 first flew in June 1936 and defeated a competing design, the Kocherigin R-9, which although a cantilever monoplane with an enclosed cockpit, featured a fixed, spatted main landing gear replacing its earlier, unreliable retractable gear. The KhAI-5 was a low-wing cantilever monoplane with an enclosed cockpit and fully retractable main landing gear. It was of wooden construction, with a wooden semi-monocoque fuselage.

R-10

Production of what was now designated the 'R-10' ('R' for *Razvedchik* or 'Reconnaissance') began in 1937. It was produced at both Kharkov and Saratov, with a total of 493 being produced. It was initially equipped with the M-25 engine built by the Shvetsov (Arkadiy Dmitriyevich Shvetsov (1892–1953)) OKB, the Soviet licence-built version of the Wright R-1820-F-3 Cyclone radial engine. In addition, examples were powered by the M-62, the M-63 (both developments of the M-25), and the Tumansky M-88 radial engines. The engines were equipped with a metal two-bladed variable-pitch Hamilton-Standard propeller.

The R-10 was equipped with three 7.62-mm (30-calibre) machine guns, with two mounted to fire forward in the upper decking of the forward fuselage and one mounted to be fired from a MV-3 turret (the first usage of this turret on a production aircraft). All the machine guns were rapid-fire (up to 1,800 rpm) ShKAS machine guns. The aircraft could carry up to 661 lb (300 kg) in an internal bomb bay.

The R-10 began to equip Soviet units in 1937, where they superseded the obsolescent R-5 biplanes. They apparently were not used during the Khalkhin-Gol battle in 1939, the R-5 being used instead, but they were used in the invasion of Poland in 1939 and in the Winter War of 1939–40 against the Finnish. In the Great Patriotic War, along with so many front-line aircraft, many were destroyed on the ground in the initial phases. The remaining examples were used as light bombers and reconnaissance aircraft. They also saw use as night bombers and were withdrawn from front-line service in 1943.

KhAI-5bis

This experimental version was equipped with an M-25E engine and was tested in 1938, achieving a maximum speed of 264 mph (425 kph). It did not go into production.

KhAI-52

An experiment shturmovik version of the KhAI-5, this variant was equipped with six forward-firing machine guns, with another gun for self-defence. It was capable of carrying 882 lb (400 kg) of bombs. It did not go into production.

PS-5

This version was used by Aeroflot from 1940 as mail carriers. Some sixty R-10s were converted into this configuration and could carry three passengers in addition to cargo.

Conclusion

Although an advanced aircraft when it went into service in 1937, the R-10 was obsolescent by the beginning of the Great Patriotic War. Due to its obsolescence and the relatively small production run (around 500 or so), the R-10 did not contribute greatly to the Soviet war effort.

Su-2

The result of the *Ivanov* programme, the Su-2 was in some respects a more sophisticated aircraft than the Il-2 (described further on), having a fully retractable main undercarriage, a partially retractable tailwheel, and on some versions an enclosed turret for the rear gunner. It was considerably faster than the Il-2 with a top speed of 302 mph (486 kph) in its final M-82-powered version, as compared to the 250 mph or so (403 kph) top speed of the Il-2.

Despite this, the Su-2 did not enjoy the success of the Il-2. The Su-2 lacked the heavy armour and armament of the Shturmovik (having no armour for the engine and having only four forward-firing ShKAS machine guns, as opposed to the two ShKAS machine guns and two of the powerful VYa-23 23-mm cannons carried by most Il-2s). This made it much less suitable for ground attack, and it soon became largely restricted for use as a reconnaissance aircraft, with production ending in 1942 as the Soviet Union decided to concentrate production on as few aeroplanes as possible.

Development

The *Ivanov* programme (*Ivanov* being Josef Stalin's codename in telegrams) was for a modern reconnaissance and light bomber to replace types such as the R-5, then in use with the Red Army. The programme was initiated in 1936 at the instigation of Stalin. Both Nikolaiy Polikarpov and Pavel Sukhoi built prototypes under this programme.

Pavel Sukhoi's entry in the *Ivanov* programme was a clean low-wing cantilever monoplane of mixed construction, with a wooden fuselage and an all-metal wing and horizontal tail surfaces. It was originally designated the 'ANT-51', as it was designed by the Tupolev OKB, where Sukhoi was employed at the time. The aircraft flew for the first time on 25 August 1937 powered by an M-62 radial engine of 820 hp (this engine was a developed version of the M-25, the Soviet licence-built Wright Cyclone). It had a top speed of 250 mph (403 kph) at 15,420 feet (4,700 m). This was below what was demanded by the *Ivanov* specifications, but re-engined with the 1,000-hp Tumansky M-87, the ANT-51 was capable of 291 mph (468 kph) at 18,373 feet (5,600 m). This was considered to be sufficient and the ANT-51 was ordered into production as the BB-1, with the 'BB' standing for *Blizhniy Bombardirovshchik* ('Short-range Bomber').

Su-2

The BB-1 was renamed the 'Su-2' in 1940 under the new naming convention for aircraft, where the family name of the designer was used ('Su' for 'Sukhoi'). The aircraft was initially fitted with the M-87 engine and had a gun armament of six ShKAS 7.62-mm (30-calibre) machine guns (four being mounted in the wings, one being mounted in a moveable MV-5 turret, and one firing through a hatch in the floor of the aft fuselage). The bomb load was 882 lb (400 kg), which could be accommodated in a fuselage-mounted internal bomb bay. The Su-2 could also carry ten of the RS-82 or RS-132 rockets on rails located on the underside of the wings.

The Su-2 was introduced into Soviet service in December 1939. In the early part of the war in Europe, the Soviets saw the vulnerability of single-engined bombers, as the Polish PZL P.23 Karaś and the British Fairey Battle both suffered heavy losses when attacked by modern German fighters such as the Bf 109E. The Soviets began to rethink the usefulness of such machines, which the Su-2 was similar to in general layout and purpose. This did not bode well for the future of the Su-2. One ominous sign was that the Su-2 did not participate in any of the air shows or air parades that the Soviets normally used to show off new aerial hardware. The continuing problems with the Su-2's new powerplant, the Tumansky M-88 (which replaced the lower power M-87), did not help matters. This engine continued to suffer failures during testing in 1940, such as burnt-out pistons and excessive oil consumption among other problems. These problems were solved or lessened and the Su-2 began to be produced with the improved version of the M-88: the M-88B. Earlier Su-2s with defective engines were upgraded to these engines also.

Bombs lined up before an Su-2, presumably before a mission. This Su-2 does not have the turret for the rear gunner. (*Viktor Kulikov's collection*)

An Su-2 mounted on skis. This particular Su-2 does have the MV-5 turret for the rear gunner. (*Viktor Kulikov's collection*)

This Su-2 has had a temporary winter camouflage applied to the upper surfaces in a kind of whorled pattern. The ports in the wings for the ShKAS machine guns are clearly visible as well as the opened MV-5 turret. A small bomb is mounted on a rack under the port wing. (*Viktor Kulikov's collection*)

As of the start of Operation Barbarossa, the Su-2s in the VVS numbered 213 (West Front, seventy-five; South-West Front, 114; 9th separate army (Odessa Military District), twenty-four). During the early part of the Great Patriotic War, the Su-2 saw service on all fronts and even saw service in the Battle of Stalingrad. It was found in combat that the MV-5 turret was relatively ineffective in defending the aircraft, not because of problems with the turret, but because the ShKAS machine gun fitted to it was found to be too light to cause sufficient damage to the German fighters. Although pressed into service as a ground attack aircraft during the initial phases of the war, the Su-2 was not the best aircraft for this role due to its relatively light armour and armament, problems which did not afflict the purpose-built ground attack Il-2. Nonetheless, the Su-2 was found to be a survivable aircraft because of its sturdy construction and could take a great deal of punishment and keep flying.

The Su-2 enjoyed success as a reconnaissance aircraft and continued to be used until 1944 in this role. Apparently, no Su-2s survived the war, and the 'Su-2' on display at the Great Patriotic War exhibit at Pobeda ('Victory') Park on Poklonnaya Gora (Poklonnaya Hill) in Moscow is a mock-up, although not a bad one (photographs of this mock-up appear in the colour plates section).

Su-2 M-82 (Su-4)

This final version of the Su-2 featured the new M-82 engine, a fourteen-cylinder engine developed by the Shvetsov OKB. This engine, which generated 1,540 hp, was fitted to most of the forty Su-2s that were assembled at the new *Zavod* 135 in Molotov (Perm) before production ended for the Su-2. This version is sometimes referred to as the 'Su-4'. In addition to the M-82 engine, this last Su-2 version featured enhanced armour protection for the crew.

Experimental Versions

Su-4

This designation is sometimes used for the late Su-2s equipped with the M-82 (ASh-82) engine. It appears that the true 'Su-4' also had the M-82 engine, but it was a single prototype that featured wooden wings, with the wing armament changed from four ShKAS machine guns to two UBK 12.7-mm (50-calibre) machine guns. Production was not proceeded with for this variant.

ShB

An experimental shturmovik version of the Su-2 built in 1940, this aircraft featured different landing gear from the standard Su-2, with landing gear that pivoted back 90 degrees to lie in the wings, replacing the inward retracting landing gear of the Su-2. The bomb load was increased from 882 lb (400 kg) to 1,323 lb (600 kg), which was the same as the maximum load for the Il-2. This aircraft was powered by the M-88A engine. It did not go into production because of the availability of the superior Il-2.

Conclusion

Although a sound design, the Su-2, due to various factors—such as the Soviet decision to concentrate on large-scale production of only a few combat types and to move away from lightly armoured single-engined bombers—did not have a major impact on the war. In the attack role, it was replaced by the much more heavily armed and armoured Il-2 and the larger and faster Pe-2 (which also replaced it in the reconnaissance role). In all a total of 877 (one source has 889) Su-2s were produced before production ended in March 1942. It is notable as being Pavel Sukhoi's first production design. It would not be his last, and his OKB went on to post-war fame building jet-engined fighter-bombers and fighters.

Il-2

Easily the most famous of the ground attack aircraft used by the Red Air Force during the Second World War, and one of the most (if not the most) famous Soviet Second World War aircraft, the Il-2 was by far the most heavily used VVS ground attack aircraft. It saw use from the first week of the Great Patriotic War in June 1941 until the end of the Manchurian campaign in August 1945, and over 36,000 were produced, making it the most heavily produced warplane of all time. Indeed, it is no exaggeration to say that it formed the backbone of the VVS during the Great Patriotic War. To the average Soviet citizen, it was as synonymous with the war as the Spitfire was to the British people.

Development

Il-2 Prototypes

In addition to the *Ivanov* programme, as another response to experiences gained during the Spanish Civil War, a new specification was drawn up for a dedicated armoured ground attack aeroplane; it was this specification that led directly to the Il-2.

The TsKB-55, a single-engined two-seater design with the design beginning in 1938, was chosen to meet the specification for an armoured ground attack machine. It was designed by Sergey Ilyushin at *Zavod* No. 39 in Moscow. Curiously, it still received a designation derived from the Central Design Bureau, with the Russian acronym of 'TsKB' derived from *Tsentralniy Konstruktorskoye Byuro*, which was closed by then but had been headed by Sergey Ilyushin. The TsKB later became the Ilyushin OKB and Sergey Ilyushin became its director (under which the Shturmovik would be produced as the 'Il-2'—the 'Il' referring to 'Ilyushin' as the head 'designer' or *Konstruktor* in Russian; note that the official designation of the Il-2 was simply the 'Il-2', not the 'Ilyushin Il-2', as you will sometimes see in other publications).

Initially known as the LT AM-34FRN ('LT' from *Letayushee Tank* or 'Flying Tank', S.V. Ilyushin's own term for the aeroplane, and 'AM-34FRN' referring to the intended engine), the TsKB-55 was known by the VVS as the BSh-2 AM-35 after the completion of state acceptance trials. This designation was derived from *Bronirovanniy Shturmovik*, which in Russian means 'Armoured Ground Attack Aeroplane'—a very appropriate name indeed. The BSh-1 was the Vultee V-11, an American design built under licence in the Soviet Union, where the 'B' in the name referred to *Bombardirovshchik* or 'Bomber' in Russian, while the 'Sh' referred to ground attack aeroplane, as with the BSh-2 AM-35. The AM-35 in the name referred to the engine fitted, the Mikulin AM-35, which was also used by the MiG-1 and MiG-3 fighters as well as most of the Pe-8 (TB-7) bombers.

Initially, the AM-34FRN was to have been fitted (this engine was fitted to late TB-3s), with the aircraft having the service designation of BSh AM-34FRN. With the decision to stop development of this engine, the AM-35 was chosen instead, and the aircraft became known as the BSh AM-35, before being changed to the BSh-2 AM-35. On 2 December 1940, the aeroplane's name was changed to Il-2, after the chief designer, Sergey Ilyushin (from this time on fighters had odd numbers such as LaGG-3 and MiG-3, while everything else, including bombers, had even numbers such as Tu-2 and Pe-8).

The TsKB-55 first flew on 2 October 1939, piloted by Ilyushin's chief test pilot, Vladimir Konstantinovich Kokkinaki (1904–85). The TsKB-55 was a two-seat, single-engined, armoured ground attack cantilever monoplane with a steel *Bronekorpus* or 'Armour Body' designed to protect the vital parts of the aeroplane, including the engine and the entire crew compartment. It was equipped with five ShKAS rapid-fire (1,800 rpm) 7.62-mm (30-calibre) machine guns, one for defence and four in the wings for offensive purposes. The armour shell was made from different thicknesses of steel armour plate that formed the aircraft's structure for the front half of the aeroplane; it was not just 'laid' on top of an existing structure, as an applique, as was normally done with armoured aircraft. This integral structure helped keep the weight of the aircraft down. The landing gear were of conventional tailwheel type, with the forked main landing gear retracting straight back into nacelles on the wings, the wheels being partially exposed to protect the aircraft in case of a crash landing and the tailwheel being fixed, with a streamlined metal fairing in front. All Il-2s featured a streamlined tailwheel fairing of some sort.

Although fully aware of the greater vulnerability of the liquid-cooled engine with a coolant system which was susceptible to ground fire, as opposed to an air-cooled radial engine, Ilyushin chose one of the former as the only available engine offering sufficient power. The engine he eventually chose for the prototype was the Mikulin AM-35, a V-12 liquid-cooled inline engine and development of the AM-34FRN, with 1,350 hp at take-off. The propeller was a three-bladed constant-speed VISh-22T, which continued to be used on the single-seater production examples that utilised the AM-38 engine (as opposed to the boosted AM-38F engine, which utilised the AV-5L-158 propeller).

Although the flight results were generally acceptable, the TsKB-55 was not without its issues, which would need to be corrected before the aeroplane was allowed to enter production. The aircraft did not meet the speed (225 mph—362 kph) or range (384 miles—618 km) of the specification, which called for a top speed of 240–249 mph (385–400 kph) and a range of 435–620 miles (700–1,000 km). The pilot's view was insufficient, and the take-off and landing speeds were considered too high. Moreover, manoeuvrability and stability were inadequate, and there were problems with the AM-35 caused in part by the powerful supercharger, which proved a power drain in low-level flight.

The TsKB-55 as it would have appeared for its first flight (note that the metal armour extended to cover the rear gunner's cockpit). (*G. F. Petrov photo archive*)

In addition to changes made to address some of the shortcomings listed above, the decision was made to change the first prototype to a single-seater. In this converted state, along with larger horizontal tail planes and sweepback on the wings (to correct the stability issues), it flew under the designation of TsKB-57 on 13 October 1940, with a long, streamlined fairing replacing the rear gunner's former position. The wings were given a sweepback of 5 degrees on the leading edge and the stabiliser area was increased by 3.1 per cent. Although known to the Ilyushin OKB as the TsKB-57, it was still apparently known to the VVS as the BSh-2 AM-35. At some point, the engine was changed to the AM-38, which was a low altitude version of the AM-35, delivering its maximum power at lower altitudes, with a two-speed mechanical supercharger.

Whether the decision to convert the prototype into a single-seater came from the Ministry of Defence, under People's Commissar for Defence Marshal Voroshilov, or Ilyushin himself is somewhat controversial and open to question. Traditionally, it has been claimed that the NKAP (Air Ministry) had pressured Sergey Ilyushin into making this change. However, according to Russian air historians Yefim Gordon and Sergey Komissarov, the decision was apparently made by Sergey Ilyushin himself and seems to have involved weight and production considerations, including putting the Il-2 into production as quickly as possible. At this point, the question remains unresolved and perhaps unresolvable given the passage of time.

Flight tests revealed the TsKB-57 to be a considerable improvement over the TsKB-55, with a top speed of 262 mph (422 kph) compared to the TsKB-55's 225 mph (362 kph) and improved stability, but visibility problems remained, which would be addressed in the TsKB-55P, the modified second prototype.

Development into Production Standard and First Production Examples

The TsKB-55P (the BSh-2 No. 2, the second prototype) was also converted into a single-seater with the characteristic 'hunchbacked' appearance caused by lowering the engine by 6.9 inches (175 mm) (the engine was also moved forward by 1.97 inches (50 mm)) and the pilot's position was elevated by raising his seat by 1.97 inches (50 mm) as

The TsKB-57 from the side. The stub where the radio antenna or mast should be can be seen clearly behind the pilot's canopy. Note how the propellers are natural metal, except for the top two-thirds of the back part, which are painted black to prevent the pilot from being dazzled by light reflecting off the natural metal surface. Early in the war, production Il-2s still had their propellers finished in this way. (*G. F. Petrov photo archive*)

lack of visibility was one of the complaints of the original engine and pilot installation. It also had the wing sweepback and larger horizontal stabilisers introduced on the TsKB-57. In addition, the carburettor intake was moved to the inboard portion of the starboard wing leading edge, where it would remain throughout the production run of the Il-2.

Its armament was revised to incorporate two cannons in place of two of the ShKAS machine guns, and evidently, this led to the 'P' in the name: 'P' for *Pushechniy* ('Cannon-armed'). Rocket rails were also added. This heavily modified prototype served as the prototype for the pre-production and first serial production machines; it included not only the 5-degree wing leading edge sweepback introduced on the TsKB-57 and larger stabilisers, but also the Mikulin AM-38 engine as introduced on the TsKB-57, which was fitted to all subsequent Il-2s. It was with this prototype that the Il-2 acquired the characteristic planform present on all subsequent straight-winged Shturmoviks. This aeroplane first flew on 29 December 1940.

As the AM-38 became available, which delivered its maximum power at lower altitudes, this more powerful engine (1,620 hp at take-off, or 1,600 hp according to some sources, and first used on the TsKB-57) was chosen for the production version. The offensive armament was changed from four ShKAS machine guns in the wings as on the TsKB-55/TsKB-57 to two ShKAS guns and two ShVAK 20-mm cannons in the wings. Originally, the Il-2 was designed to carry the MP-6 23-mm cannon, but this cannon proved so unsuccessful that the designers suffered unpleasant fates: Yakov Grigorevich Taubin (1900–41) was actually executed for its failure and Mikhail Nikitich Baburin (?–1944) died in a prison camp; therefore, other cannons—first the Shpitalniy-Vladimirov ShVAK 20-mm cannons then the Volkov-Yartsev VYa-23 23-mm cannons—were installed. Initially, the ShKAS guns were mounted outboard of the cannons, which was more efficient as it improved aiming and decreased the spread of the shells, but early in the production run, this arrangement was reversed and this new arrangement, with the cannons mounted outboard of the machine guns, became standard on all subsequent Il-2s. This was probably done for ease of production, or maintenance, or both.

Initially, early Il-2s had landing lights in both wings, as opposed to one only in the port wing, which configuration was used for the vast majority of Shturmoviks. These twin lights were apparently to aid in night landings. In addition, from the TsKB-55P onward, the long fairing that covered the former rear gunner position in the TsKB-57 was replaced by a much smaller and partly glazed fairing, which gave the single-seater production Il-2s their characteristic hunchbacked appearance, leading to the nickname of *Gorbatiy*—'Hunchback' or 'Humpback' in Russian.

Manufacturer's trials with the prototypes continued until 26 March 1940. The NII VVS, the testing facility for the VVS, test flew the Il-2 prototypes from 1 to 19 April 1940. The NII VVS tested the production standard Il-2 from 28 February 1941 to 20 March 1941. By the end of this testing, the first true production Il-2 had already flown, on 10 March 1941.

Il-2 Single-Seater

The single-seater Il-2 first flew in production form on 10 March 1941. This was the first Il-2 version or Shturmovik to go into production. *Shturmovik* was originally a generic term for all Soviet ground attack aeroplanes, but like the term *stuka*, which was a contraction of the generic German term for dive bomber, it became associated with a single aeroplane, in this case, the Il-2. The Shturmovik was also known by the affectionate feminine nickname of 'Ilyusha', or most commonly, simply by its designation, 'Il-2' (pronounced 'eel-dvah' in Russian). Some other Soviet nicknames were 'Flying Tank' (*Letayushee Tank*—a name proposed by Sergey Ilyushin himself) or most flatteringly 'Flying Infantryman'.

As is often related in other publications on the Il-2, the Germans were supposed to have called it *Die Schwarze Tod* ('The Black Death'); however, Soviet propaganda may have come up with this name, although that does not preclude the Germans from having used it also. Nicknames that the Germans did use were *Eiserner Gustav* ('Iron Gustav') or the *Zementbomber* or *Zementer* ('Concrete' or 'Cement Bomber'—probably because of its toughness). One source mentions the name *Betonflugzeug* or 'Concrete Aircraft' as another German nickname; another mentions *Betonvogel* or 'Concrete Bird'. These are all apparently tributes to its durability. Perhaps tellingly, the German infantry referred to the Il-2 by the grimly appropriate names of the *Fleischer* ('Butcher'), the *Fleischwolf* ('Meat Grinder'), or the *Schlachter* ('Slaughterer'). These are all tributes to its deadliness.

The names above were used with all versions of the Il-2; as mentioned previously, the single-seater Il-2 was unofficially known as the *Gorbatiy*, which means 'Hunchback' or 'Humpback' in Russian, because of the raised cockpit position used on the single-seaters from the TsKB-55P onwards, although this name was also sometimes used with the two-seaters. Straight-winged examples, both single and two-seater versions, may have been referred to by the name *Doska*, or 'Board', perhaps from the broad, flat appearance of the large wings.

There were three main versions of the single-seater Il-2, which differed not in basic shape or planform, but in construction. One of the versions was all-metal, with an all-metal construction and surface covering, except the control surfaces, which were of a metal structure with fabric covering on all Il-2 versions, and the ailerons, which were covered in metal probably for all of the metal-winged single-seater Il-2s. Note that only early single-seater Il-2s had Bf 109-type mass balances under the ailerons, and only a few had the four-stack exhausts, which version was produced for a short time by *Zavod* No. 1 in Kuibyshev along with having wooden wings, as opposed to the six-stack exhausts used by every other version of the Shturmovik, whether they had the wooden wings or not. It is not clear if the metal-fuselaged versions always had the mass balances and the ShVAK cannons (20-mm as opposed to the 23-mm cannons used on most Il-2s—the 20-mm installation on the single-seaters can usually be determined in photographs by the lack of a wing fairing), although this may indeed be the case. The 20-mm cannon can also be distinguished by its shorter barrel as opposed to the 23-mm cannon barrel.

The ShVAK 20-mm cannons were also carried on some wooden-fuselaged metal-winged single-seaters (and later, on some two-seaters whenever there was a shortage of the VYa-23 23-mm cannons). A photograph of a very early single-seater Il-2 is shown here with the small Bf 109-type balances under the ailerons, and note the original installation of the ShKAS machine guns outboard of the ShVAK cannons. In addition to the landing gear light on the port side, this aeroplane has a landing gear light on the starboard side, which only appeared on early single-seaters. Note the natural metal propellers (most probably painted black on the side facing the pilot as per pre-war custom) and the hole on the inboard starboard wing where the external carburettor filter appeared on later Il-2s.

Although not as common as the metal-winged examples, some wooden-winged single-seaters also had the early gun installation, with the ShVAK cannons mounted inboard of the ShKAS machine guns.

The second version of the single-seater, which was much more common than the versions with the metal rear fuselage, were the versions with the wooden rear fuselage, either in combination with the metal-covered outer wings, or with the wooden-covered outer wings (the third version of the single-seater Il-2). Both of the wooden rear fuselage versions were commonly used and can be told apart in photographs by the aileron balances (sometimes referred to as anti-flutter balances) near the wingtips of the metal-covered wing versions (these should not be confused with the Bf 109-type balances that were under the ailerons only on early single-seaters). These were never present on the wooden-covered wing single-seater versions (or the two-seaters with metal-covered wings, with the possible exception of converted single-seaters, which will be discussed in the section on the straight-winged two-seater).

Although hardly conclusive evidence, and even discounting photographs of Barbarossa victims, it appears from the photographic record that there were more metal-winged single-seaters constructed than wooden-winged single-seaters. All versions of the Il-2, either single-seater or two-seater, had metal-covered horizontal stabilisers with fabric-covered elevators.

Strangely, grass stalks appear to be tied around the bases of the propellers and the rudder balance of this captured or 'Barbarossa victim' Il-2, perhaps some inside Wehrmacht joke. Such 'fun' at the expense of the Il-2 disappeared as the war continued and the Shturmovik was no longer a laughing matter, or a subject for 'holiday' snapshots, but now a deadly enemy to be dreaded and hated. (*Author's collection*)

Another photograph of a Barbarossa victim Il-2, this shows the anti-flutter aileron balance towards the wingtip, the Bf 109-type aileron balance, and the simple rocket rails. This appears to have the metal rear fuselage. (*Author's collection*)

A metal-winged single-seater, armed with the early 20-mm inboard-mounted cannons, taking off. Of interest are the spots or patches on the rear fuselage, probably battle repairs. Note also the semi-circular device on the cowling; this is apparently some sort of aiming device and is occasionally seen on single-seaters. (*G. F. Petrov photo archive*)

Line up of Il-2s built at *Zavod* 1. Note the four-stack exhausts used on some of the Il-2s from this factory and the wooden wings (no wingtip aileron balances are fitted). You can clearly see the three aiming stripes on the cowling of the nearest machine. Although this first aeroplane in the line has the rectangular fairing associated with the VYa-23 23-mm cannons, the short barrels on this aircraft indicate that ShVAK 20-mm cannons have been fitted instead, at least on this aircraft. (*Viktor Kulikov's collection*)

After service introduction, the rear fuselage of the Il-2 was found to suffer from weakness in its wooden form, with some fuselages breaking apart during landing or sometimes even in flight, which was obviously catastrophic. As a field solution, this problem was solved by attaching four metal L-section reinforcing stringers or ribs to the outside of the fuselage. As a factory solution, the Shturmoviks were manufactured with more wooden structural elements added internally to the rear fuselage and a thicker wooden skin.

In an attempt to make the Il-2 better able to operate from snow-covered airfields, a fixed ski installation was tested by the Soviets. The fixed installation was not entirely satisfactory, partly because of the drag and resultant loss in speed, so a retractable installation was developed. In the winter of 1941–42, some of these Il-2s were produced with the retractable skis for use on snow-covered surfaces. Although the installation worked surprisingly well, with only a 7-mph (11-kph) speed penalty, it was soon found that wheeled Il-2s could land perfectly well on packed snow, so no further ski-equipped versions were made and the surviving ski-equipped Il-2s were presumably re-equipped with conventional landing gear. The ski-equipped version is often depicted as having a metal fuselage; however, examination of photographs has

Single-seater Il-2s on the assembly line. (*Via RART*)

led me to believe that it normally had the wooden fuselage in combination with the metal wings. It is also possible that some were produced with the wooden wings.

Another *Gorbatiy* version should be mentioned. In an attempt to provide some rear protection for Il-2s, which were suffering severe losses to the Luftwaffe, there were field modifications by the PARMs (regimental field aircraft repair workshops) to provide a simple rear gunner position. These modifications consisted of nothing more than a hole cut immediately aft of the canopy and a gun mount salvaged from some other aeroplane, such as an R-5 reconnaissance biplane or an SB fast bomber. This gun position could mount one or two ShKAS machine guns (7.62 mm or 30 calibre) or less commonly a single Berezin machine gun (12.7 mm or 50 calibre) was attached on a simple pintle mount. Over 1,000 such modifications were made in the field. In addition to the gun mounts salvaged from other aircraft, or built in the field, there was a standard factory-made add-on mount that was fitted to many of the field-modified Il-2s.

The single-seater Il-2 was never formally replaced or retired from service and continued to serve alongside the two-seater versions, until as late as 1944.

Il-2 Straight-Winged Two-Seater

As originally designed, the Il-2 was a two-seater, with a rear gunner enclosed in the armour shell that also protected the pilot and engine. Indeed, the initial prototype first flew as a two-seater (TsKB-55). This first prototype was later modified to a single-seater (TsKB-57) and the Il-2 entered production as a single-seater in 1941 (based on the TsKB-55P single-seater prototype, which was actually the second prototype). During operations in 1941 and 1942, however, it soon became apparent that the Il-2 was especially vulnerable to attacks from the rear, where German fighters could in effect sneak up on the Shturmovik unnoticed and shoot up the unarmoured and usually wooden fuselage, taking advantage of the lack of a rear gunner. Since the Il-2s often flew without effective (or even any) fighter escort during this time, this weakness was easily exploited by the Germans. Efforts to rectify this shortcoming led to field modifications, as outlined in the section above, and, soon, Sergey Ilyushin was asked to examine how to tackle this on the production line.

Pilots were vocal in the need for a rear gunner, as shown in this letter sent to Josef Stalin by Captain E. Koval of the 243rd ShAP (letter taken from *Il-2 Shturmovik Guards Units of World War 2*, by Oleg Rastrenin, p. 10):

> I consider it my duty to request that the designer and the aircraft industry improve our formidable attack aircraft. The main shortcoming of the aircraft is that it is absolutely unprotected against hostile fighters from behind. In most cases the fighter approaches from behind at 10 to 15 m (32 to 50 feet) and opens fire, trying to damage the engine or kill the pilot. Compensating for this shortcoming by providing fighter protection does not seem to be effective. Attack aircraft operate at low to extremely low altitudes, while escorting fighters have to fly at 1,000 to 1,500 m (3,300 to 5,000 feet) over the target. A rear gunner, therefore, is a necessity.

The fate of this brave pilot is not recorded (brave in not just that he was an Il-2 pilot early in the war, but also in that he sent what was essentially a letter of complaint to the *Vozhd*, or 'Boss'), but Ilyushin did work towards providing the Il-2 with rear protection and eventually re-added the rear gunner.

At first, Ilyushin tested semi-fixed installations on single-seaters, firing from behind the rear of the cockpit canopy. Test installations of two different types were constructed at the main factory, *Zavod* 18 in Kuibyshev: one with two ShKAS 7.62-mm (30-calibre) machine guns and one with a UBT 12.7-mm (50-calibre) machine gun. These aircraft were tested in February 1942. The guns had a limited traverse and were aimed using mirrors. The ShKAS installation was found to be superior, but did not go into production as the defensive value of even this installation was insufficient. What was needed was a fully moveable gun trained by a rear gunner.

Instead of the fully enclosed and armoured position of the TsKB-55 prototype, or the later experimental Il-2bis and Il-2 M-82 (or the Il-2's successor, the Il-10), and in an effort not to cause a serious disruption on the production lines, Ilyushin settled on a relatively straightforward modification of the single-seater. This consisted of the rear gunner having front and back armour (12 mm for the fuel tank armour to his back (he sat facing towards the rear) and 6 mm of steel to his front), a semi-enclosed glass covering, and a simple strap to sit on, with a single Berezin UBT 12.7-mm (50-calibre) rapid-fire heavy machine gun for defence. This arrangement remained the same for all the production two-seaters with gunners (as opposed to the two-seater trainers). The fuselage retained the same length as the later single-seaters, which had been slightly extended to improve stability.

This version passed factory and state trials and went into production in September 1942. Initially, it was produced alongside the single-seater before replacing it completely in the three factories where the Il-2 was being produced by this time (*Zavodi* 1 and 18 in Kuibyshev—today called Samara and *Zavod* 30 in Moscow, which together continued to produce the Il-2 until after the end of the Great Patriotic War). Some single-seaters were apparently modified on the production line into two-seaters, although it is not certain if metal-winged versions of such modified machines would have still had the aileron anti-flutter balances. Since some field modifications to the production standard were made, it certainly seems possible that these (perhaps as well as the factory-modified examples) would have retained the single-seater metal wings' aileron anti-flutter balances if they also retained the metal ailerons.

The straight-winged two-seater saw service trials for the first time on the *Kalininskiy* Front (Kalinin Front), with the 800th ShAP and 667th ShAP, with the first combat occurring on 30 October near Smolensk, with an attack on a German airfield. These trials continued until 25 January 1943. During these trials, there were sixty-four combat sorties and eight air engagements with the gunners shooting down seven German aircraft for the loss of three Il-2s. The straight-winged two-seater also saw heavy action during the latter stages of the Battle of Stalingrad, with some soldiering on until the end of the war (like the single-seater, it was never formally replaced or retired from service). As with the single-seater, it served in regiments alongside its replacement on the production lines, in this case, the swept-winged arrow. It continued in service until at least the Manchurian campaign in August 1945.

By the end of 1942, some 1,450 two-seaters had been produced, according to Gordon and Komissarov. As of February 1943, all factories had converted to the

This early straight-winged two-seater is photographed at a display of aeroplanes at the TSAGI (Central Aerohydrodynamic Institute) in 1943. It has the black/green scheme typical of most Il-2s before 1944. The cowling is black while the area immediately aft is green. The external VV-1 gun sight as well as the aiming lines can be seen on the upper cowling. (*G. F. Petrov photo archive*)

This view of a CMF (Black Sea Fleet) straight-winged two-seater shows the tail planes off to good advantage, with the rudder and elevator trim tab and tab actuators clearly shown. What is interesting about this Il-2 is the rather patchwork appearance of the camouflage, indicating a heavily repaired and repainted machine. For example, the rear fuselage may have been taken from another Il-2. (*G. F. Petrov photo archive*)

production of the two-seater version. One difference between the single-seater and the two-seater, besides the addition of the rear gunner, was the presence of a larger tailwheel to deal with the greater all-up weight. It is not clear if the field conversions would have had this larger tailwheel.

Fairly early during the production run of the straight-winged two-seater, the aeroplane was re-engined with the more powerful AM-38F ('F' for *Forsirovanniy*, or 'Boosted' in Russian), which raised the horsepower to 1,720 hp for take-off according to Dr Rastrenin (or 1,700, or 1,750, or 1,770 hp as sources differ on this).

Some straight-winged two-seaters were armed with two NS-37 (11P-37) 37-mm cannons (NS: Nudelman-Suranov), with one each housed in streamlined pods under each wing, with fifty rounds per gun. An important point to remember regarding two-seater Il-2s armed with the 37-mm cannons is that these were apparently only produced as straight-winged two-seaters by *Zavod* 30 in Moscow.

In any event, the vast majority of 37-mm-armed Shturmoviks were straight-winged two-seaters with wooden wings and these were phased out of production from late 1943. This happened after the introduction of the anti-tank PTAB bomblets, which were first used at Kursk in July 1943 and proved much easier for the average pilot to use. The 37-mm-armed two-seater versions retained the two ShKAS machine guns for aiming purposes, could normally only carry 220 lb (100 kg) of bombs (with an overload of 441 lb (200 kg) of bombs), and were not equipped with rocket rails, thereby limiting their ability to carry weapons other than the large cannons, another factor in the decision to discontinue production of this version. Sometimes, the 37-mm-armed example was referred to as the 'Il-2-37'.

The 37-mm-armed Il-2s were not employed operationally until August 1943 in the Kursk region, with the 2nd ShAK; they entered service the following month with the 1st ShAK. The NS-37 37-mm cannons were not nearly as successful as the PTAB, as there were problems with synchronisation and recoil that prevented these cannons from being very effective when mounted on the Il-2. Due to the recoil, the cannons needed to be re-aimed after only a few shots. Also, unlike the PTABs, the 37-mm-armed Il-2s required special training to be effective.

However, the 37-mm-armed Il-2s were not completely unsuccessful, as related by twice Hero of the Soviet Union Il-2 pilot Aleksandr Yefimov, who wrote about successfully attacking even Tigers and Panthers from the rear, where the armour was thinner. He also wrote that the cannons were able to pierce the top armour of these panzers, where the armour was also thinner than at the front and sides. In addition, the Il-2-37s were successfully used by naval units against shipping.

From photographic evidence, it is clear that some of the modifications seen on the arrow were first introduced on later straight-winged two-seaters. These included such items as a taller radio mast, a more outboard mounted pitot tube, streamlined rocket fairings, streamlined cannon fairings, and probably flush-riveting. Such modifications sometimes make it difficult to tell a late straight-winged two-seater from an arrow in photographs, as from certain angles it is difficult to detect the tell-tale swept-back leading edges and 'kinked' trailing edges of the arrow.

Two late straight-winged two-seaters flying in close formation, with a third in the background. These aircraft are finished in the three-colour scheme. (*G. F. Petrov photo archive*)

A two-seater with straight wings and the three-colour camouflage taking off from an improvised airfield, during 1944 or 1945. (*via RART*)

Il-2 from *Zavod* 1, as characterised by the longer, streamlined tail wheel fairing and the streamlined rocket fairings, but with the old-style rectangular cannon fairings. Like all Great Patriotic War arrows, this aeroplane features the three-colour camouflage scheme. The VV-1 external gun sight and aiming lines can just be made out on the upper cowling. (*Viktor Kulikov's collection*)

Il-2 Swept-Winged Two-Seater (the 'Arrow')

In 1943, Sergey Ilyushin carried out a major revision of the Il-2 to rectify its shortcomings. Although the original two-seater Il-2 was well received and the rear gunner universally appreciated by the pilots, the addition of the rear gunner changed the centre of gravity, thereby adversely affecting the originally benign handling characteristics of the Il-2. In a successful attempt to correct this, the Ilyushin Design Bureau gave the leading edge of the wing a 15-degree sweepback as opposed to the 5-degree sweepback that all earlier Il-2s had carried from the TsKB-57 onwards.

This change in the degree of sweepback restored the centre of gravity and led to the 'arrow' Il-2s having what was said to be outstanding controllability and stability. Indeed, so stable was the aircraft now that if properly trimmed it could be flown for two or three minutes without the pilot touching the control column. It was so successful that it was quickly ordered into production.

The first arrow was built by *Zavod* 18 and tested from 20 September 1943 to 9 October 1943. Following the factory and state trials, this third and final main version of the Shturmovik was put into production from late 1943, at first alongside the earlier straight-winged two-seater version, then later, as the straight-winged two-seater version was phased out on the production lines in early 1944, with the arrow becoming the sole production version.

The first swept-winged Il-2s, known as *So Strelkoi* or just as *Strielka* ('Arrow' in Russian, although confusingly *Strielka* also means 'Gunner'), apparently had

This particular Il-2 is the prototype arrow. The three-colour scheme introduced on the straight-winged two-seater is apparent on this aeroplane, piloted by chief Ilyushin test pilot V. K. Kokkinaki. Note the streamlined cannon fairings and rocket rails on this example, as well as the VV-1 gun sight and four aiming lines on the upper cowling, the streamlined cannon fairings being characteristic of *Zavod* 18, where this aeroplane was built. (*Viktor Kulikov's collection*)

the wooden covering on the outer wing panels (although the spars appear to have always been metal on all the Shturmoviks). However, it may be that *Zavod* 18 always produced their Il-2s with metal wings, including the arrow. From the middle of 1944, as the supply of aluminium increased, the wooden wing covering was supplanted on the production lines at all factories by metal-covered wings until production of the Il-2 finally ended in October 1945, after 36,163 examples of all types had been produced, with some 17,000 being of the arrow. About two-thirds of the arrows were produced with the metal-covered wings.

Besides the adoption of the swept-back wings, the arrow also used flush-riveting on the external metal components, as opposed to the round-headed rivets of earlier versions (although this feature was apparently introduced on late straight-winged two-seaters). This was done in an attempt to make the aircraft more streamlined, along with the more streamlined cannon and rocket rail fairings that appeared on many arrows. The arrow was also characterised by the long antenna mast and more outboard mounted pitot tube introduced on the later straight-winged two-seaters.

After the war, the wooden aft fuselages were often replaced with metal units, which were manufactured in 1946–47 for Soviet Il-2s, which increased the service life of the Il-2, with some serving with foreign countries until 1954. They were given the NATO codename 'Bark'; interestingly, one source mentions that the codename 'Bark' was not assigned until 1955, apparently after the Il-2 was no longer in service with any country.

Il-2 arrows in flight—the appearance of the tail wheel fairings and the streamlined 23-mm cannon fairings would indicate that these Il-2s are from *Zavod* 18 in Kuibyshev. Strangely, the rear defensive guns appear to still be covered by the canvas shroud used to protect them on the ground. Perhaps this is a propaganda photograph. (*G. F. Petrov photo archive*)

A Polish-crewed Il-2 two-seater, perhaps an arrow, although it appears to have the short antenna mast of a straight-winged two-seater, from a Polish regiment in the Red Air Force. Polish pilots and gunners flew for the Red Air Force during the closing stages of the Great Patriotic War. They helped the Red Army drive the Germans out of Poland and participated in the attack on Berlin. This Il-2 carries the three-colour scheme typical of the Shturmovik during the last two years of the war. What is interesting is the cover over the starboard wing leading-edge carburettor intake filter, which appears to be a can of some sort, probably to protect the relatively delicate mesh on both sides of the filter. The double antenna lines are an interesting variation on the normal single line. (*Author's collection*)

Specialised Variants of the Il-2

In addition to the normal ground attack variant, there were two specialised variants that were produced or converted in some numbers: the Il-2U (or UIl-2) and the Il-2KR. In this case, these were their actual Soviet Great Patriotic War designations, not post-war inventions such as 'Il-2m3' for the arrow.

Il-2U (UIl-2)

The Il-2U, sometimes written as the UIl-2 ('U' for *Uchebniy*, or 'Trainer' in Russian), was the two-seater training version of the Il-2, with two pilot positions—one for the instructor-pilot in the back and one for the trainee in the normal pilot's position. Modifications from the single-seaters had been built as early as 1942, and indeed production of this version started as early as 1942 according to Gordon and Komissarov, making it the first two-seater to go into production. Interestingly, the first thirty-four production examples had ordinary steel, not steel armour for the front fuselage structure and carried two ShKAS machine guns for gunnery training.

Not only were Il-2Us produced at the factories, but some aircraft were modified in the field. Due to this, there were different types of canopies fitted, some with the pilot's canopy still armoured, some with the armour removed. Il-2Us of all three variants were used—converted single-seaters, straight-winged two-seaters, and arrows all appeared in trainer versions. None of these variants had the gunner, as this position was taken up by the instructor's position, but some retained the wing machine guns and the ability to carry rockets for gunnery training purposes.

In addition to its training duties, the Il-2U was also used as a target towing aircraft, for anti-aircraft units to practice their shooting.

According to Dr Rastrenin, 1,211 Il-2Us were produced, although it is unclear how many field modifications were also made.

Il-2KR

In an effort to make the Il-2 more responsive to battlefield conditions, this reconnaissance, or artillery corrector version ('KR' standing for *Korrektivorshchik* or '(Artillery) Corrector' in Russian) was developed, in order to spot and photograph potential targets. It was successfully tested at the NII VVS from 27 March until 7 April 1943, by which time it had passed its state tests. It was ordered into production on 10 April 1943 by the State Defence Committee (GKO). The Il-2KR was made as both production and field-modified examples, with the production versions coming from *Zavodi* 1 and 30. It was fully armoured and carried a full fixed armament of two cannons and two machine guns in order to attack targets of opportunity while it was performing its reconnaissance missions.

This version was produced and field-modified in both straight-winged two-seater and arrow versions. Some aircraft had the rear gun replaced by a camera, the powerful AFA-35 being carried in its place. Evidently, this camera was interchangeable with the gun according to the mission. The AFA-1(M) camera could be mounted in the bottom of the fuselage, with the camera port being visible. The camera mix varied with the individual aircraft and the mission. Some field-modified Il-2KRs also carried cameras in the front of the landing gear nacelles. An easy recognition feature for the Il-2KR was the tall antenna mast, which was always mounted on the top part of the windscreen (this was likewise seen on the Il-2Us). Besides the camera(s), the Il-2KR was also equipped with a powerful RSB-3bis radio, which was fitted behind the pilot's armour plate over a lowered fuel tank, to be operated by the gunner/observer.

Combat Tactics

Initial Il-2 Tactics

According to Dr Oleg Rastrenin in *Il-2 Shturmovik Guards Units of World War 2* (p. 9), the 1940 draft of the Red Air Force Field Manual stated the intention of attack aviation:

> [To] provide air support to friendly ground forces, deliver air strikes against enemy tank formations and motorised convoys, destroy the enemy on the battlefields, in its staging areas and on the move, and attack enemy airfields. HQs, command and control posts, transport, defensive installations, bridges, crossing points and rail facilities.

As no operational manual had even been written up for the Il-2 by the beginning of the Great Patriotic War, tactics were essentially made up as they went along, and the Il-2 was used rather haphazardly, being sent in small groups of sometimes just two or four aeroplanes, often without fighter escort, against German targets. These small groups were at least partly a result of the very heavy losses the Il-2 suffered; in a sort of vicious cycle, regiments were chronically understrength as these tactics inevitably led to heavy casualties among the Il-2 units. Fighter escort, when available, was often ineffective, as the fighters flew out of range of the German flak and thereby lost sight of the low flying Il-2s they were supposed to be escorting. In addition, the inexperienced pilots flying the Il-2s would often follow the same attack pattern, not varying their altitude or line of attack, thereby allowing the Germans to position their flak more efficiently and attack the Il-2s when they were at their most vulnerable, pulling away after their attack run.

The loss rate during this initial period of use was extremely high, with Il-2s in some units averaging only five or six sorties before being lost. Some commentators have taken this loss rate as being evidence of some innate ineffectiveness on the part of the Il-2, or something fundamentally lacking in its design. I disagree; these high loss rates were a result of both the extremely heavy use of the Il-2 against very well-defended targets (even late in the war, German ground units were lavishly equipped with flak), air superiority (if not actual air dominance) by the Luftwaffe early in the Great Patriotic War, ineffective tactics by the Soviets, and a lack of training for the Il-2 pilots. As pilots, tactics, and the Il-2 itself improved, these loss rates fell dramatically, but more on that further on.

One factor that detracted from the effectiveness of the Il-2 was the absence of transmitter radios in most of the aircraft early in the Great Patriotic War. Generally, Il-2s had only receivers fitted, which affected their ability to stay in formation or relay information regarding the target, such as a change in the target. The flight leader might have a complete radio, but if he was shot down, then the formation had no means of communicating with ground forces or other pilots. The radios that were fitted were also often of poor quality and unreliable. This lack of radio contact with the ground led to friendly fire incidents, such that Il-2 pilots preferred attacking rear targets because of a fear of hitting their own troops. Obviously, this decreased the efficiency of the Il-2 on the battlefield, as it was designed to operate directly over the front lines, not to their rear. Supposedly, some Il-2s were manufactured in 1942 without any radios of any kind and did not carry any radio antennae. I have never seen a photograph of such a machine, so I suspect the number built was relatively small. In any case, it was not until 1943 that most Il-2s were fitted with both receivers and transmitters.

Another factor that detracted from the value of the Il-2 was the inaccuracy of the rockets, the RS-82 (and later the RS-132 and ROFS-132, although this last rocket was apparently more accurate than the earlier rockets). Since these rockets were so inaccurate, being unguided and with a fairly widely spread pattern, they proved most effective when fired in volleys, with several Il-2s firing at once. However, with the very small flights of Il-2s that so often characterised missions early in the war, this concentration of rocket fire was not possible, rendering the rockets rather ineffective, except with large targets such as fortifications.

In this early period of the war, it took between four and five Il-2s to knock out a light tank and twelve to fifteen to knock out a medium tank (the Germans had no heavy tanks until the Panzer Mk VI Tiger was introduced in 1942). The 100-kg (220-lb) FAB 100 bombs were judged to be the most effective anti-tank bombs at this time. The Il-2 could carry up to 216 AZh-2 bottles or ampoules of incendiary KS liquid, which proved effective against armour and artillery, such as anti-aircraft batteries (flak).

Sometimes in this initial phase of the war, the Il-2s did not take off with their full complement of weapons, from time to time even taking off without bombs, as late as the German Summer Offensive of 1942 (Case Blue—see further on). From the middle of 1942 onwards, Il-2s always carried bombs, as per orders applying to all the Il-2s in the Red Air Force.

Due to the lack of effective fighter escort, in order to avoid detection by the Luftwaffe, Il-2 pilots often flew very low to the ground to and from the target. Although this made it more difficult for the Germans to see and intercept the Il-2s, it also limited their effectiveness in two very important aspects. First, it was hard to pick out targets, and flying so close to the target made it hard to hit, as the target was upon the Il-2 and past it in no time, especially in level flight. Second, it was hard for the pilots to navigate, as landmarks were hard to see from so close to the ground. This sometimes resulted in the aircraft losing their bearings and having to call off the mission. These limitations were less important to the pilots, however, than mere survival. In the early stages of Operation Barbarossa, just surviving was a considerable achievement.

In an effort to improve the ability of the Il-2 to find its target, Pe-2 light bombers, Su-2 light bombers, SB bombers (early in the Great Patriotic War), and fighters were used as *shturmani* (plural of *Shturman*—Russian for 'Navigator'), to find their targets. Once the targets were spotted, they were marked by bombs or AZh-2 bottles.

An important point to remember about the Il-2 is that even Il-2s that were shot down or otherwise forced to crash land could often be repaired and returned to combat. The Il-2 was a very tough and strongly built aeroplane that could absorb a considerable amount of damage and still be repairable. Many shot-down Il-2s were therefore not irreparable or irrecoverable losses, although the Germans would have counted them among their victims or 'kills', and these same 'shot down' Il-2s would then return to service to continue the war against the Axis. According to Gordon and Komissarov, 90 per cent of the damaged Il-2s that were recovered were repaired at local units and PARMs and presumably sent back to combat units. This may seem like a high percentage of aircraft repaired, but remember that only those Il-2s that seemed repairable would have been likely to be recovered in the first place. The remaining 10 per cent recovered were sent to repair factories or were written off as irreparable.

Change in Tactics

As with many other warplanes, so much of the Il-2's success (or lack of it) stemmed from the tactics its pilots were instructed to adopt. As outlined above, early in the war, the tactics consisted of sending a handful of Il-2s, often unescorted, against heavily defended German positions. Not surprisingly, the Il-2s suffered heavy losses, both from enemy fighters and from enemy flak. From the spring of 1942 onwards, after the initial operations of 1941 had been analysed, there were attempts to change these obviously flawed tactics. These initial operations showed that a well-trained pilot could destroy two German tanks from a distance of 1,000–1,300 feet (305–396 m), while an average pilot could destroy one tank. In both instances, this was if the pilot had been accurately guided to the enemy.

One of the biggest problems facing the Il-2 early in the war was the lack of effective (or sometimes any) fighter escort. Even if able to engage the German fighters, Soviet fighters early in the war were no match for the German pilots, who were generally much better trained, experienced, and equipped. Without effective fighter escort, the Il-2 endured severe losses, which were only partly alleviated with the addition of the rear gunner.

Even before the tactics were decisively changed in 1942, successful attempts to change the tactics occurred as early as September 1941. These tactics involved Il-2s diving on their targets from around 2,000 to 3,000 feet (610 to 914 m), which increased accuracy but also resulted in greater losses to flak and enemy fighters. These first attempts were stopped as they required Il-2s to fly at higher altitudes which put them at a greater risk to flak and Axis fighters. Indeed, Colonel Shcheglikov, CO of the 66th ShAP of the Reserve Front Air Force, who had put into effect these tactical changes was officially reprimanded by his superior officer, General Nikalayenko, CO of the Reserve Front Air Force, in a directive dated 14 August 1941. General Nikalayenko went so far as to prohibit Il-2s from flying at medium altitudes. Small comfort, perhaps, but the reprimanded officer was later proven correct in his tactics as they were adopted (or 're-invented') for the Red Air Force Il-2s as a whole starting in the spring of 1942.

The new tactics additionally included having the Il-2s flying in larger groups of from eight to twelve aircraft. This gave the Germans more targets to contend with and also enabled the Il-2s to protect each other better, especially while flying in a defensive circle (sometimes called the 'circle' or 'wheel of death'), where each aeroplane was able to protect the Il-2 in front of it (or in back when equipped with a rear gunner). As the rockets, although powerful, were so inaccurate, using Il-2s in greater numbers also increased the likelihood of the rockets finding a target, especially if they were fired in salvos from each Il-2. Another change in tactics was to have one or two Il-2s tasked with suppressing the German flak. Once the flak had been taken care of, the Il-2s could make repeated passes at their targets, until all their munitions had been exhausted. A manoeuvre that decreased the chance of being hit by flak was the zigzag, while flying in a scissors pattern also enabled the Il-2s to attack a target from both sides.

Against so-called 'soft' targets such as enemy personnel and trucks (lorries), the Il-2s would fly at very low altitudes of 16 to 32 feet (5 to 10 m) or dive at a shallow angle of 10 to 15 degrees from a height of around 300 to 650 feet (91 to 198 m). Against 'hard' targets such as bunkers, the Il-2s would execute a shallow dive of around 30 degrees, which reduced their signature as a target for flak and improved their accuracy. From the summer of 1942 onwards, diving attacks were used against armoured vehicles.

Some of these enhanced tactics, which doubled the efficiency of Il-2 strikes, were developed by the NIPAV (*Naoochno-Ispyatelniy Aviatsionnogo Vooruzheniya*: 'Aviation Armament Scientific Testing Range') in June and July 1942. In addition to some of the changes mentioned above, it was found that three runs at the target were needed to inflict significant damage, and that the different armament (rockets, bombs, and guns) should be used separately on each run, with the sequence commonly being first the rockets, then the bombs, and finally the guns.

Dr Oleg Rastrenin believes that the changes to tactics made in 1942 increased the combat efficiency of the Il-2 from two to two-and-a-half times what it had been in 1941. By mid-1944, the efficiency had increased by six to eight times what it had been early in the war.

One of the disadvantages of flying at higher altitudes, which had landed the unfortunate Colonel Shcheglikov in hot water with his CO, was that not only did it more greatly expose the Il-2 to flak, but also to enemy fighters. During 1941 and 1942, attacks by Axis fighters accounted for 60 per cent of all Il-2 losses.

It was found that the best way to counteract these attacks, in the face of the all too often ineffective fighter cover, was to use the Il-2 itself to fight against its attackers. Although slower in a full turn than German fighters, the Il-2 was able to out-turn the fighters in a half-turn, so they could double back on their pursuers and become the attackers. Another tactic involved having the Il-2 decelerate sharply, whereby the faster German fighter would often fly past the Shturmovik, putting it within range of the Il-2's powerful forward-firing armament. More than a few German fighters were thus surprised to find themselves suddenly in front of the business end of the Il-2, where the heavy cannons and machine guns could then make quick work of the fighter.

Yet another useful tactic was to sideslip the Il-2 in a 20-degree bank, which caused aiming problems for the Germans. Of course, these tactics needed training on the part of the Il-2 pilots, which in the early part of the Great Patriotic War was frequently lacking. However, well-trained pilots with some combat flying training could and did use the Il-2 successfully against their pursuers. At the beginning of 1943, the pilots of the 11th GvShAD actually underwent aerial combat training.

An example demonstrating the Il-2's aerial combat ability occurred on 5 February 1943 near Livna, when Lieutenant Galchik from the 299th ShAD was able to shoot down a Bf 109 by throttling back sharply and banking to starboard, causing the fighter to overshoot, enabling Lieutenant Galchik to fire his cannon, which caused the Bf 109 to burst into flames and crash.

Definitive Tactics

By late 1943, the Il-2's tactics had matured to the point where the Shturmovik had become an extremely effective weapon over the battlefield—one much feared by the Axis. One of the changes involved the addition of full radios (receivers and transmitters were now installed on all Il-2s), which allowed for much better command and control both from the air and the ground. From the middle of 1943 onwards, all Il-2s were so equipped. This allowed for changes in tactics and for targets to be immediately transmitted to the Il-2s in flight, either from forward observers on the ground or from the flight commander, or others in the air.

When Axis armour was deployed in an offensive formation, the Il-2s used a long circular pattern, called the 'Circle (or Wheel) of Death' (not to be confused with the wheel-like defensive formation of the same name Il-2s often adopted when attacked by Axis fighters, described previously). In this pattern, the Il-2s would circle around their targets, using their armament in a shallow diving attack, then circle around for additional passes until all their ordnance had been used. This was similar to the *Vertushka* used by the Pe-2. This attack pattern enabled them to loiter over the battlefield, while mobile flak panzers were attacked by Il-2s especially tasked with their destruction; they could continue loitering until the entire unit had used all their firepower against the German formation, often with devastating results.

These attacks could involve from two to four groups of Il-2s, with each group composed of twenty to thirty aircraft, which would reach the target in a column of four to six Il-2s. The leading group would attack the target first, then circle around while the other groups attacked. These attacks could last up to ninety minutes. As Il-2 formations grew in size as the war progressed, these 'circles' became long, extended ovals. However, with the near disappearance of the Luftwaffe from the skies, these elongated, drawn-out formations were no longer vulnerable to air attack. With full radio sets in each aeroplane, commanders were also now able to keep these longer formations in good order, something that would have been difficult or impossible earlier in the war. In addition, aircraft were now often painted in quick recognition markings, making it easier to keep track of different aircraft formations while in the air.

Another type of attack was the simultaneous attack which involved six to eight Il-2s attacking in a column, with the total number of Il-2s involved being from sixty to 100 aircraft. In this type of attack, the Il-2s only spent a short amount of time over the battlefield, which meant that they could not use all of their ammunition. It was moreover difficult to reform the columns after the attack. However, such simultaneous attacks also lowered losses to enemy fighters and flak.

Changes in tactics were made not only in the air, but also on the ground, where forward observers (or forward air controllers) were attached to field units to direct the Il-2s to their targets. These 'direction centres' were headed up by experienced commanders who directed the Il-2s to their targets and kept them apprised of local conditions and reconnaissance and intelligence reports. This close cooperation between the Il-2s and the ground forces also helped to reduce friendly fire incidents, always a problem on chaotic battlefields, as the Il-2s were made aware of any changes in the position of Soviet troops, even while the Il-2s were in the air. Friendly fire incidents continued to happen, but at a much lower rate than had been the case earlier in the war, when ground communication with the Il-2s was much less efficient.

One change that helped the Il-2 specifically, and the Red Army generally, was the gradual disappearance of the Luftwaffe from the Eastern Front, especially from the middle of 1943 onwards. This disappearance was partly due to the high losses incurred in the fighting on the Eastern Front, but also due in part to large numbers of the German fighters being withdrawn to the German homeland and occupied Europe to defend against the Anglo-American strategic bombing campaign (the 'Combined Bomber Offensive'), which had greatly increased in intensity from 1943 onwards.

Without fighters to contend with, the Il-2s had an easier time of it against German positions, although they still had to contend with heavy German flak. One result of this was that the percentage of Il-2s lost to fighter action fell, while the percentage that fell to flak increased. A good illustration of this can be seen from the summer of 1943, during the Battle of Kursk, where the percentage of Il-2s lost to flak was 49 per cent, while the number lost to fighters was 37 per cent, with the remaining 14 per cent being attributed to missing in action and other causes. Compare this to the initial period of the war, 1941–42, when according to Dr Rastrenin the losses to fighters was about 60 per cent. Some units reported losses of up to 65 per cent from flak.

In reaction to the increase in flak, the Il-2s were operated in much greater densities than they had been earlier in the war, with the number being increased on each front by six to seven times what it had been in the initial phases of the Great Patriotic War. At times, the density was eighty Il-2s per kilometre of front line, which translates to one Il-2 per 41 feet (12.6 m) of frontage. The large numbers of aircraft employed helped to overwhelm the German defences.

One of the factors that led to the effectiveness of the Il-2 in their operations in Ukraine in 1944 was the large numbers that they were now deployed in. For the main line of advance for the 27th Army, which was part of the 1st Ukrainian Front under General Vatutin, the density of Il-2s was thirty-two per kilometre of front line. This allowed the 2nd ShAK, which provided the Il-2s supporting the 27th Army, to ensure a continuous presence over the battlefield in support of the 27th Army. Later in the war, the Il-2s would be operated in ever-greater densities, as in the Battle of Berlin.

Experimental Versions

There were continuing attempts to improve the Il-2, often involving the armament. One of the main shortcomings of the single-seater version was the total lack of any defensive armament to protect the rear of the aircraft. This lack enabled German fighters to attack the vulnerable wooden rear fuselage section with relative impunity; great numbers of Shturmoviks were lost this way. Not waiting for Ilyushin to come up with a solution, some regiments took matters into their own hands by modifying single-seaters into *ad hoc* two-seaters in the field.

IL-2 with ShFK-37 Cannons

With the inaccuracy of aerial rockets and the inability of most bombs to destroy a tank without a direct hit, the Red Air Force looked for a more efficient way to destroy tanks. In an attempt to increase the tank-killing capability of the Il-2, some single-seaters were fitted with ShFK-37 37-mm cannons (designed by Boris Gavriilovich Shpitalniy (1902–72), one of the inventors of the ShKAS 7.62-mm machine gun and the ShVAK 20-mm cannon) in underwing pods. These did see some trial combat use, in November and December 1941; according to Gordon and Komissarov, nine were also used at Stalingrad. The type never went into large-scale production because of problems with synchronising the firing of the cannons, which caused aiming problems due to the asymmetrical recoil (a problem which arose again in the later two-seaters with 37-mm cannons). The cannon pods were different from those used on the 37-mm-armed two-seaters.

IL-2 M-82

Aware of the possibility of a decrease in the supply of the AM-38 engine, Sergey Ilyushin decided to re-engine two metal-winged single-seater IL-2s with the Shvetsov M-82 radial engine (later known as the ASh-82 after its designer Arkadiy Shvetsov). Sporting an unarmoured cowling and with a fully enclosed gunner installation similar to that used on the Il-2bis (and the TskB-55), the first IL-2 M-82 initially flew on 8 September 1941, with Ilyushin's chief test pilot, Vladimir Kokkinaki, at the controls.

Another IL-2 M-82, this time fitted with the boosted M-82IR engine, also flew, with a similar configuration to the first Il-2 M-82 prototype and again without armour protection for the engine. This boosted engine also had radial shutters which adjusted the flow of air to the engine, as on the La-5 fighter, which was also equipped with the M-82. Although the installation was successful, the Il-2 M-82 suffered from the same problem as the Il-2bis (see further on), in that its production would have necessitated too many changes to the basic airframe. At one time, Ilyushin had proposed that a small production batch be produced, but this suggestion was not acted upon. This version was sometimes referred to as the 'Il-4', not to be confused with the twin-engined medium bomber of the same designation.

At least one source mentions that a handful were actually produced, although it seems that if they were produced, they did not see any combat. Gordon and Komissarov mention that a single-seater example, using the M-82IR, was produced. This

The initial Il-2 M-82 seen from the side. (*Viktor Kulikov's collection*)

'production' variant featured armour plating on the underside of the cowling. Apparently, at least one was produced and test flown, although it is unclear if it ever saw any actual combat.

IL-2BIS

Perhaps the best attempt to provide the Il-2 with a good defensive capability was the Il-2bis. The Il-2bis differed from the production two-seaters in having a fully armoured and completely enclosed rear gunner installation, similar to that fitted originally to the Il-2 prototype and the Il-2 M-82 (and the later Il-10). The gunner fired his machine gun through a blister, which was itself protected by a round plate of armoured glass. In addition to the UBT Berezin 12.7-mm (50-calibre) heavy machine gun mounted in the Berezin-designed blister, the Il-2bis carried two ShVAK 20-mm cannons (in the outer position in VYa-23-type fairings), two ShKAS machine guns, and eight rocket rails (like the single-seaters). It had the smaller-type tailwheel typical of the single-seaters. Dr Rastrenin states two Il-2bis were produced by *Zavod* 1, but the record is unclear as to what happened to the second prototype, or if it was ever tested in combat.

The first Il-2bis was tested in actual combat and successfully completed nine sorties, although unfortunately, it was downed on its tenth sortie by ground fire. Despite this loss, the Il-2bis was extremely well received, particularly by the gunners, who found the gunner installation to be well protected and roomy. It was felt that this sense of protection and relatively commodious accommodation contributed to the gunner's efficiency. However, the gunner installation necessitated the deletion of the aft fuel tank; to make up for this, two of the four wing root bomb bays were now occupied by fuel tanks. This limited the bomb-carrying capability of the Il-2bis, and it was this shortcoming, as much as anything else, which led to the decision not to proceed with serial production of this modified Il-2, as the production aircraft had a fairly small bomb load as it was.

IL-2 WITH MV-3 TURRET

In yet another attempt to improve the defensive capabilities of the Shturmovik, one example was fitted with a MV-3 turret ('MV', from Mozharovskiy-Venevidov, the two designers), as fitted to some Soviet bombers, such as some of the Tupolev SBs and the Il-4. Although it protected the gunner better than the semi-enclosed position of the normal two-seater, the large turret was heavy and caused considerable drag and this version was not put into production. Gordon and Komissarov mention that this aircraft was a modified two-seater, and the date they give for its conversion (May 1943) would seem to confirm this, but photographs appear to show a modified metal-fuselaged single-seater.

Although this was a one-off example, there are photographs of Il-2s that show what appear to be single-seaters fitted with a UTK-1 turret, which was similar to the MV-3 (but in the Il-2 installation it does not have the glass enclosure) with the characteristic ammunition holder attached to the UBT machine gun. These were field-modifications, with the turrets probably taken from wrecked or unserviceable Il-4s.

Besides improving the armament, another recurring (and related) theme was improving protection for the rear gunner. The casualty rate for the gunners may have been seven times that of the pilot (although a mortality rate of six or seven times that of the pilot appears to be an oft-repeated exaggeration—Gordon and Komissarov mention that the casualty rate was 50 per cent more than that of the pilot). Nonetheless, the gunner was poorly protected in comparison with the pilot (although I wonder in comparison how well-protected the gunners were on other two-seat aircraft used during the war by other countries).

The Il-2 M-82 and Il-2bis attempted to address this problem, but there were other attempts. In 1945, some kits were made by Ilyushin for installing extended armour in the field (internally in the gunner's cockpit) to protect the rear gunner. These were sent to combat units, but it is unclear how many were installed during the Great Patriotic War. The additional armour only added an extra 90 lb (41 kg) to the aircraft. It does appear that some were fitted before the end of the Great Patriotic War. In addition, some late production machines may have had this armour factory-installed, but it appears that these were not delivered until after the end of the Great Patriotic War. According to Gordon and Komissarov, some 593 examples with the extended armour had been produced by *Zavodi* 1 and 30 by the end of 1945.

Il-2 in Detail

GENERAL DESCRIPTION

The Il-2 was a single-engined, armoured ground attack cantilever monoplane with a steel armour shell designed to protect the vital parts of the aeroplane, including the engine and the pilot's enclosed cockpit. It was normally equipped with two machine guns and two cannons in the wing for offensive purposes. In addition, disposable armament in the form of rockets under the wings and bombs under the wings and in wing root bomb bays were usually carried. The single-seaters carried only the pilot, while the two-seaters carried a rear gunner in addition to the pilot, the rear gunner manning a moveable machine gun for rear defence. The Il-2 had retractable main landing gear and a fixed tailwheel.

Major Subassemblies

The Il-2 was composed of subassemblies that were attached together at the factory to complete the aeroplane. These main subassemblies consisted of the front fuselage (with the wing centre section), the outer wings, the rear fuselage, and the horizontal tail planes. Interestingly, sometimes, the subassemblies were painted before the aircraft had been completed; for example, I have seen painted outer wings being attached to unpainted fuselages and painted outer wings being attached to already painted fuselages. For transport purposes, the Il-2 could be broken down even further than the main subassemblies, with the engine detached from the front fuselage.

Armour

The armoured shell was made from different thicknesses of steel armour plating that formed the aircraft's structure for the front half of the fuselage, and it was not just 'laid' on top of an existing structure as applique armour, as was often the case with other armoured aircraft. This method of using the armour as part of the structure of the aircraft harkened back to the Junkers J.I of the First World War, although it is unclear if Sergey Ilyushin was aware of or influenced by this aeroplane. The Il-2's integral armour structure helped keep the weight of the aircraft down. The armour plate itself varied in thickness from 4 mm (0.16 inches) to 12 mm (0.47 inches for the plate behind the pilot) and was joined with rivets and bolts. The single-seaters carried a total of 1,716 lb (778 kg) of armour. The two-seaters carried a total of some 2,100 lb (953 kg) of armour.

For early single-seaters, the pilot was protected in the back by a panel of 64 mm armoured glass (or 'transparent armour' as the Soviets referred to it). This was soon replaced by a plate of 12-mm (0.47-inches) KhD carburised steel armour, with two small cut-outs on either side containing armoured glass that enabled the pilot to retain a small amount of rearward vision.

Initially, the armour was made of AB-1 tempered steel armour, but this was changed in early 1942 to AB-2 armour, which used less nickel and molybdenum, but was still as resistant as the earlier armour.

In addition to the steel armour, the Il-2 also carried an armoured windscreen, armoured on all three sides. The armoured glass, called K-4 glass, was 2.52 inches in thickness (64 mm) and was mounted on a layer of plexiglass, to which it was attached by a viscous adhesive. This applied to the arrows, at least, although all Il-2s carried an armoured windscreen of some type. The panels themselves were segmented, with the front of the windscreen consisting of five pieces, for example. The idea was that if one piece was hit, the cracking or other damage would be limited to that one piece and not the entire windscreen panel.

In practice, the steel armour proved effective in stopping shells up to 50 calibre (12.7 mm) in size and could stop even larger shells if they struck the armour at less than a

90-degree angle. Although it came at a price in terms of weight, the armour no doubt made the Il-2 more survivable against enemy fire and many a pilot and gunner owed their lives to it. The heavy losses of the Il-2 would have been even heavier without it.

The armoured fuselage section was not actually made at the Il-2's main factories, but at separate factories. These armoured shells or bodies (*Bronekorpus* in Russian, which means 'Armour Body') were then sent to the main factories, where they were incorporated with the wings, rear fuselage, and tail planes to complete the aircraft. The rear fuselage was bolted to the rear part of the armour body, and the wing centre section was attached to the bottom and sides of the armour body.

Fuselage

The front portion of the fuselage on all Il-2s consisted of steel armour plates of varying thickness, as described above. The rear fuselages on some early Il-2s were metal (aluminium alloy), but most Il-2s had wooden rear fuselages. As noted in the section on the single-seater, initially, there were problems with weakness in the wooden rear fuselage; at first, this was dealt with by bolting on four L-section external metal stringers. Eventually, the problem was solved by adding more wooden structural elements and a thicker skin to the wooden rear fuselage. Some Il-2 arrows after the war had their wooden rear fuselages replaced by newly produced metal rear fuselages to increase their service life. Yugoslavia, for example, replaced the wooden rear fuselages with metal rear fuselages of local manufacture.

For most Il-2s, the fuselage was 38.06 feet in length (11.6 m), whereas with the earlier versions of the single-seaters it was 37.57 feet (11.45 m) long. The fuselage was made longer to improve the Il-2's stability.

The wooden rear fuselage was of an oval section covered by formed birch plywood that was glued together with casein glue and consisted of layers that were positioned at 90-degree angles to each other for strength (this plywood was called *shpon* in Russian). These *shpon* layers were made of 0.5-mm-thick sheets that were glued together in sheets of four to ten layers—2–5 mm (0.08–0.2 inches) thick—and affixed to wooden frames, stringers, and longerons with glue and nails.

The metal rear fuselage was likewise of an oval section and consisted of *kolchug* (the Soviet version of the aluminium alloy 'duralumin') sheets riveted to *kolchug* frames and stringers, with the sheets having a width of 0.8–1 mm (0.03–0.04 inches).

Wings

The cantilever monoplane wings came in several different versions, varying by wing covering, wing structure, and basic planform. There were two basic planforms—the 'straight wing' version and the 'arrow wing' version. Used on both the straight-winged versions and the arrow-winged versions, the so-called 'wooden wings' were never built entirely of wood, but consisted of outer wings with either a plywood covering over an all-metal structure, or a plywood covering over a wooden structure with metal spars. All the Il-2s had metal wing spars, with chromansil (a steel/chromium alloy) caps and aluminium webs. The inner wing sections were always all-metal (aluminium alloy) on all the Il-2s. The wings utilised the Clark YH aerofoil and were 47.9 feet in width (14.6 m). It appears that this was the width for both the straight wing and the arrow wing.

The arrow wing differed from the earlier straight wing in having a leading-edge sweepback of 15 degrees, as opposed to 5 degrees with the straight wing (this 5-degree sweepback had been introduced on the TsKB-57 prototype). This increased sweepback carried on over to the trailing edge, which had a distinctive 'kink' as opposed to the straight edge of the straight-winged variants. As mentioned above, this sweepback was done to restore the centre of gravity, which had been adversely affected with the addition of the rear gunner. On both types of wing planforms, whatever the covering, the aileron trim tabs extended beyond the aileron trailing edge (some plastic kits miss this feature).

It seems that the balances towards the wing tips (anti-flutter balances) only appeared on those single-seaters with metal wings and metal-covered ailerons. After the single-seaters, all Il-2s, even those with metal wings, appear to have had fabric-covered ailerons, without the anti-flutter balances. Later Il-2s, beginning with later straight-winged two-seaters, had the pitot tube moved from its original more inboard location in the starboard wing to an outboard location closer to the wingtip.

This straight-winged two-seater shows the black banding on the wings typical of the black/green scheme common with this variant, and the general planform. Of interest is the worn port wing root, where the paint has been worn down to the bare aluminium. This was common on all Il-2 variants, which despite their often short lives, were heavily used. The missing wing panels on the starboard wing were not the result of battle damage, but tests on this Il-2 to determine the reasons for and rectify the problem of fabric and wood separation on the wooden outer wings. This problem was eventually solved by applying better bonding agents for the fabric and sometimes also attaching strengthening strips that held the fabric and wood to the metal outer spars. (*Via RART*)

Tail Planes

The cantilever horizontal tail planes consisted of aluminium alloy stabilisers and fabric-covered metal structured elevators. These remained the same for all versions of the Il-2. The rudder was also fabric covered and metal structured, but the fixed fin was either wooden or metal according to the construction of the rest of the rear fuselage as it was integral with the fuselage. A large streamlined steel balance was attached to the top of the rudder on all Il-2s. Although the bane of all Il-2 plastic modellers (they are almost unfailingly broken off during kit assembly), this balance is actually quite substantial in reality. It is made out of steel, attached to a steel rod that then has steel flanges riveted to the aluminium rudder structure (I possess the top of a preserved Il-2 rudder, and even after more than seventy years, the balance is still solidly attached to the rudder). The rudder trim tab was flush with the rudder's trailing edge. The tail planes were 16.08 feet width (4.9 m) from the TsKB-57 on. This does not appear to have ever changed for any production versions of the Il-2.

Control Surfaces

The ailerons, which were of Frise type, were mechanically controlled by push-pull rods linked to a gear that was connected to the control column. A Frise-type aileron was an aileron having a nose portion projecting ahead of the hinge axis and a lower surface in line with the lower surface of the wing. Although split in two, with the geared trim tab attached to the inner part, each aileron acted as a single unit. Both ailerons had mechanically controlled metal trim tabs that extended beyond the aileron trailing edge. The ailerons were always of metal structure, metal-covered on the metal-winged single-seaters, and fabric covered on all other Il-2s. The earliest single-seaters had a small Bf 109-type aileron mass balance under the aileron, while all the metal-winged single-seaters had a long anti-flutter balance that was attached to the aileron and extended to the wing's leading edge, where it was attached to a mass balance, very similar in size and shape to the rudder balance.

Wires connected to the two rudder pedals in the cockpit controlled the rudder. The rudder had a trim tab that was controlled by wires linked to a small wheel on the port side of the cockpit. The trim tab did not extend beyond the rudder's trailing edge. The trim tab was of all-metal structure, while the rudder was of aluminium alloy structure with fabric covering on all Il-2s.

A long push-pull rod (similar to those used with the ailerons) that ran along the starboard side of the fuselage interior and was connected to the control column assembly mechanically controlled the elevators. When the control column was moved fore and aft, the rod (and the elevators) moved accordingly. The elevators themselves were of the usual aluminium alloy structure with fabric covering. The trim tabs, one per each elevator, were metal. Although the restored Il-2 in the Prague Aviation Museum in Kbely, in the Czech Republic, has trim tabs that extend beyond the trailing edge of the elevators, this does not appear to be normal for the Il-2. It is not clear if this is peculiar to some arrows, to the Czechoslovakian machines, or to this particular aeroplane, which has undergone at least two restorations. It is interesting to note that the flyable Il-2 of the Flying Heritage Collection has flush trim tabs.

The flaps were pneumatically operated, using a control stick mounted on the port console, with the flaps being moved by push-pull rods. The flaps had settings of 17 and 45 degrees. The take-off setting for the two-seaters was 17 degrees, which the flaps could be locked at. There was a small external indicator on the port wing root, which indicated the degrees that the flaps were set at. The flaps were all-metal and were split into two pieces on both sides, with one piece retracting into the centre section, and the outer piece retracting into the detachable outer portions of the wings.

Landing Gear

The landing gear were of a conventional tailwheel type, with the forked main landing gear retracting straight back into nacelles on the wings, the wheels being partially exposed even with the doors closed, which gave some protection to the aircraft in case of a crash landing and the tailwheel being fixed, with a streamlined metal fairing in front. Interestingly, for the arrow (and some late straight-winged two-seaters) the tailwheel fairing seemed to vary by factory. The main landing gear were retracted and lowered pneumatically, with a wire-operated retraction system activated by a hand crank in the cockpit as an emergency backup system. Apparently, the main landing gear nacelles came in two different versions, differing slightly by planform, but when or at which factory this change occurred is unclear from the record. On all Il-2s there were small rods on both wings that indicated whether the undercarriage was down or up: if the rods were up, the undercarriage was down; if the rods were down, the undercarriage was up.

The folding drag or breaker struts for the main undercarriage at first consisted of riveted square section steel members, but these proved too weak and led to bad landings and even crashes. These were replaced by welded round section members, which proved much stronger. This change was made during the production run of the single-seater in 1942, according to Dr Rastrenin. The entire main landing gear structure was made out of steel.

The main tyres were 800 × 260 mm in diameter. Some tyres were slightly larger at 860 × 260-mm, although it is unclear from the documentation when this change was made and how many Il-2s used these larger main tyres. These larger wheels were probably introduced during the production of the two-seater versions to deal with the greater all-up weight.

The tailwheel was fixed, with a metal fairing in front. Although the tailwheel was not steerable, it was moveable and could be locked in place with a lever in the cockpit. The leg and struts were steel. Early in the war, the tailwheel opening was often covered in a leather or bezant boot.

At least one factory (*Zavod* 30 in Moscow, which sent many of its Il-2s to the Northern Front) continued to use a leather or bezant boot around the tailwheel strut to protect the tailwheel opening from exposure to mud, snow, and water, which could rot the wooden rear fuselage structure. The tailwheel changed in size from the single-seaters to the two-seaters: the single-seaters had a 300 × 120-mm tyre, while the two-seaters had a 400 × 150-mm tyre. This larger tyre was used to deal with the greater all-up weight of the two-seaters. To accommodate this larger tyre, a larger recess was provided under the rearmost part of the fuselage.

Pneumatic System

The pneumatic system consisted of two compressed air bottles in the rear fuselage, which could be filled from a hatch in the port side of the fuselage. The pneumatic system powered the landing gear, the flaps, and the engine starter motor, as well as firing and recharging the fixed guns.

Engine

All production Il-2s carried some form of the Mikulin AM-38 V-12 liquid-cooled inline engine. The engine was 46.7 litres (10.27 gallons) in displacement, with a weight of 1,940 lb (880 kg) in its AM-38F version. There were two basic variants of this engine: the AM-38, carried by most of the single-seaters, and the AM-38F ('F' for *Forsirovanniy*: 'Boosted'), which most of the two-seaters carried. This engine was basically a low altitude development of the AM-35, which was an engine optimised for high-altitude usage and was utilised by the MiG-1 and MiG-3 fighters as well as some of the TB-7/Pe-8 heavy bombers. The AM-35 engine had itself been developed from the AM-34. In addition, the AM-38 was developed into the more powerful AM-42, which was carried by the Il-2's successor, the Il-10.

The unboosted AM-38 was initially rated at 1,600 or 1,620 hp for take-off—sources differ on this. The AM-38F was rated at from 1,700 to 1,770 hp for take-off—sources also differ with this version of the engine (Dr Rastrenin states that it was 1,720 hp for take-off). Whether boosted or not, all AM-38 engines had a single-stage mechanical supercharger mounted at the rear of the engine.

Fuel System

From August 1943 onwards, the original metal fuel tanks were replaced with fibreglass tanks. These were superior as parts of the metal on the metal tanks would push outward where a bullet exited, preventing the rubber covering the tanks from properly sealing the hole. When bullets penetrated and exited the fibreglass tanks, they left a clean-edged hole that was much easier for the rubber covering to seal. In addition to this, the Il-2s also fed CO_2 from the engine exhaust gases to fill the tanks as they were emptied. This greatly reduced the risk of ignition if the tanks were hit by enemy gunfire.

Coolant System

The coolant radiator was placed in the middle of the S-shaped duct that travelled from above the engine to an under-fuselage housing (which contained the oil radiator). A large wheel located on the outside of the port cockpit console facing the pilot controlled the coolant radiator shutters.

Oil System

The Il-2's oil system consisted of three tanks: two tanks on either side of the engine under the cylinder heads and a small triangular section reservoir tank on top of the engine intake trunk. On single-seaters, it appears that most were lacking the starboard tank; it may be that the starboard tank was added with the addition of the AM-38F engine, but the documentation that I have read is silent on this. The oil radiator was housed in an armoured under-fuselage mounting, where it was protected by armoured doors or shutters that could be rotated to protect the under-fuselage radiator both fore and aft. A small lever mounted on the starboard side of the cockpit controlled these shutters.

Engine Starting System

This consisted of two different systems. The first was a small pneumatic motor under the front of the engine, and the second involved the Hucks starter system, whereby a shaft fitted to the small 'dog' on the front of the spinner was turned around by a motor mounted on a lorry (truck).

Throttle System

The engine throttle system consisted of a small lever mounted underneath the sill of the armoured windscreen. When it was moved forward, the engine throttled up; when it was moved back, the engine throttled down.

Propellers

The Il-2 normally carried either of two different propellers, depending on which version of the AM-38 was used. Both propellers were aluminium three-bladed constant-speed propellers and were left-handed in rotation. The AM-38 used the smaller VISh-22T propeller, 11.17 feet in diameter (3.4 m). The AV-5L-158 propeller used with the AM-38F engine was 11.81 feet in diameter (3.6 m). According to Gordon and Komissarov, sometimes the AV-5L-124 propeller, which was 11.79 feet in diameter (3.59 m), was substituted for the VISh-22T propeller. The Il-2 was tested with a four-bladed propeller, but this was not adopted as it offered no real advantage over the three-bladed propeller.

Electronic Equipment

The radio normally fitted to the Il-2 was the RSI-4 radio. Originally, only a few aircraft were equipped with both receivers and transmitters. From 1943, all Il-2s were equipped with two-way radios. The Il-2KR carried the more powerful and larger RSB-3bis radio set. Radios (and electronics in general) were never a strength of Soviet engineering, so the radios were not comparable in quality to German or American radios, for example, and at certain engine rpms, the radios could be overcome by static. Early two-seaters carried a short radio mast, but this was changed in later two-seaters and the arrows to a longer radio mast, presumably to improve transmission and reception. The single-seaters carried a relatively long radio mast.

Weapons Control

The guns in an Il-2 were fired from the control column by pressing one or both of two small paddle levers, with one controlling the machine guns and the other controlling the cannons. The number of bombs and rockets that were released when the appropriate buttons on the control column were pushed were set using two boxes on the starboard side of the cockpit, one box for the bombs, and the other for the rockets. Early Il-2s had only one such weapons release box. There was a large stick on the starboard side of the pilot, the master weapons release, which could release all the bombs and rockets at once, if needed.

Gun Sight/Aiming

Initially, the Il-2 was fitted with the PBP-1B reflector-type gun sight. However, not only was this gun sight of limited use for rocket aiming and bombing, but its position in the cockpit often injured Il-2 pilots upon a crash landing. Due to this, the gun sight was removed from later single-seaters and replaced by a simple post sight, called the VV-1 gun sight, which consisted of a post on the upper cowling and concentric rings on the windscreen. Although not very accurate, it was simple and immune to breaking down; it was therefore considered adequate and utilised by most Il-2s. It was fitted to Il-2s from the beginning of 1942, probably after the aiming lines on the cowlings were added.

White lines painted on the cowling were used as an aid in aiming weapons; they were introduced probably in late 1941 or early 1942 on the single-seaters. Most Il-2s carried three of these, although some had four.

Gun Armament

The Il-2 was normally equipped with two Shpitalniy-Komaritskiy ShKAS rapid-fire (1,800 rpm) 7.62-mm (30-calibre) machine guns and two Volkov-Yartsev VYa-23 23-mm cannons in the wing for offensive purposes. The machine guns carried 750 rounds apiece, while the 23-mm cannons carried 150 rounds apiece. The Il-2 was originally intended to carry the MP-6 23-mm cannon, but this cannon proved unsuccessful. Some aircraft, especially earlier versions, possessed two Shpitalniy-Vladimirov ShVAK 20-mm cannons which carried 250 rounds apiece and which were characterised by smaller and shorter barrels than the 23-mm cannons. At times, even into the production of the straight-winged two-seaters, the 20-mm cannons were installed in place of the 23-mm cannons due to shortages of the latter. By the time of the production of the arrow, all Il-2s were produced with 23-mm cannons installed.

With the ShKAS 7.62-mm (30-calibre) machine guns, the spent shell casings were collected in the area between the front wing spar and the wing's leading edge. In some Il-2s, they apparently ejected out of the wing through a small tube exiting out of the bottom of the leading edge of the wing. It is not clear when the change in shell ejection was made, but the two-seaters did not have this tube. It may be that only wooden-winged single-seater Il-2s had this ejection tube, and this may have been done to keep the spent shell casings from damaging the wooden leading edge.

The VYa-23 23-mm cannon was covered by a rectangular fairing where it exited the wing leading edge. It appears that this fairing covered the recharging tube mounted on top of the cannon barrel. Some arrows (and perhaps some late straight-winged two-seaters) had a more streamlined fairing, such as those manufactured by *Zavod* 18 in Kuibyshev.

Overall, the Il-2 pilots considered the VYa-23 23-mm cannons to be their most effective weapons, as they were much more accurate than their bombs and rockets and were still powerful enough to wreak havoc on unarmoured and lightly armoured vehicles, artillery, and troop concentrations.

In addition to the fixed armament, two-seaters featured a Berezin UBT 12.7-mm (50-calibre) heavy machine gun for defence on a VUB-3 semi-circular mount, manned by a rear gunner. The UBT was equipped with 150 rounds of ammunition and was aimed with a K8-T reflector gun sight, with the spent shell casings being collected in a bag attached to the machine gun. The rear gunner also often carried a submachine gun (most likely the ubiquitous Shpagin PPSh-41 submachine gun) for additional protection and use against ground targets. In addition, the pilot would sometimes direct the gunner to use his UBT against ground targets.

Zavod 30 produced about 1,200 of the straight-winged two-seaters with two of the powerful Nudelman-Suranov NS-37 37-mm cannons mounted in underwing pods equipped with fifty rounds per gun. These cannons replaced the 20-mm and 23-mm cannons normally carried by the Il-2, although the ShKAS machine guns were retained for aiming purposes. Although very powerful, these cannons were not a great success, as they had a strong recoil and were not properly synchronised, causing the aircraft to yaw to one side or the other upon firing. This ruined the aiming, making this essentially a one-pass, one-shot weapon. In the hands of a well-trained pilot, they proved deadly to German tanks, but the PTAB bomblets could be used by any pilot, so production of the 37-mm-armed example was ended in late 1942 or early 1943 after some 1,200 or so had been built.

A view of the gunner's position from the side on a straight-winged two-seater. The gunner's canopy can be seen in the open position, and you can see the wire that keeps it from opening further. The line leading into the fuselage is probably compressed air being fed into the air bottles that ran the pneumatic system on the Il-2. (*G. F. Petrov photo archive*)

Rear gunner's position. The gunner is *Starshina* (Sergeant Major) Gennadiy Mamyrin of the 6th GvShAP, 1st Baltic Front, March 1945. Notice the small inset window in the gunner's canopy; this was present on some arrows and even some straight-winged two-seaters, being a characteristic of Il-2s produced by *Zavod* 1 and *Zavod* 18. The handle above the gun is for manually recharging it, although some late-war UBT machine guns were fitted with an additional tube above the gun barrel, which automatically recharged the gun. (*Viktor Kulikov's collection*)

Disposable Armament (Bombs and Rockets)

The single-seaters were at first limited to 882 lb (400 kg) of bombs; later, the maximum bomb load was increased to 1,323 lb (600 kg). At first, the two-seaters were limited to 661 lb (300 kg) but this was also later increased to a normal load of 882 lb (400 kg), with a maximum bomb load of 1,323 lb (600 kg). Gordon and Komissarov state that the first two-seaters were limited to 661 lb (300 kg) of bombs because of concerns regarding stress on the wooden wings. Whether this bomb restriction also applied to the early metal-winged two-seaters is not clear.

The Il-2 could carry bombs in internal bomb bays located two per wing near the wing roots and in underwing mounts (using DER-40 bomb racks) under the bomb bay doors. The wing root bomb bays could each carry bombs of up to 220 lb (100 kg) in size. The underwing bombs could be mounted even on aircraft that were carrying bombs in the wing root bomb bays. On rare occasions, the Il-2 carried more than 1,323 lb; for example, late in the war, Shturmoviks were flown without rear gunners on some missions to enable them to carry more bombs, but the size of the bomb load was evidently not recorded. The largest bomb load carried by an Il-2 was 1,960 lb (889 kg) in a test, although I am not aware of this amount ever being carried into combat. One pilot carried some 1,600 lb (726 kg) of bombs into combat, but this was due to an error on the part of his loading crew. Not surprisingly, the pilot noticed that his Il-2 was behaving rather sluggishly.

With the early Il-2s, bombs were winched up into the bomb bays through small panels in the upper wing. Later, larger panels, apparently first introduced in late 1941 or early 1942, allowed bombs to be loaded directly on to the top of the closed bomb bay doors. Bombs up to 33 lb (15 kg) could be loaded in this way, although larger bombs were still winched up into the bomb bays.

In addition to large bombs, the Il-2 often carried PTAB, anti-tank shape-charged bomblets of around 5.5 lb (2.5 kg) apiece. The Il-2 carried 192 of them in its internal wing root bomb bays according to one source, although Dr Rastrenin states that up to 280 of these bomblets could be carried. These bomblets proved particularly effective against armour, even against heavily armoured tanks such as the Panther (Panzer Mk V) and the Tiger (Panzer Mk VI) tanks, as the tops of these tanks were not as heavily armoured as the front and sides. Their very first combat use was on the opening day of Operation Citadel, 5 July 1943.

AZh-2 ampoules, with KS inflammable liquid, could be loaded into the bomb bays, with up to 216 being carried. These flammable ampoules proved to be effective even against tanks, with the flaming liquid covering vision ports and observation devices and the fire could not be suppressed. However, the effectiveness of this weapon depended on flammable objects near the target and the weather.

All Il-2s, save some trainers and the 37-mm-armed two-seaters, carried rockets under the wings. The single-seaters normally carried eight rockets, four per side, whereas the two-seaters normally carried four rockets, two per side. Initially, the Il-2 was only equipped with the RS-82 rockets, the 82 referring to the diameter in millimetres. The rockets were carried on unstreamlined RO-82 rocket rails. Later, the larger RS-132s, of 132 mm diameter, were also carried. It does not appear that mixed loads were carried, with both RS-82s and RS-132s on the same aircraft, probably due to the different ballistic trajectories of the rockets. The RS-82 and RS-132 rockets were armour-piercing projectiles, although they were supplemented from spring 1942 by the more effective armour-piercing RB-82 and RB-132 rockets. The ROFS-132 were also fitted, which were very powerful fragmentation-type rockets, and were longer than the RS-132s, although of the same diameter. From later in 1942, M-8 (82-mm) and M-13 (132-mm) rockets were also fitted, which were developments of the RS-82 and RS-132 rockets respectively. As part of general efforts to better streamline the Il-2, some later straight-winged two-seaters and most arrows carried streamlined rocket rails.

One of the most unusual items that the Il-2 carried was aerial grenades, fitted to the DAG-10 launcher, which fired AG-2 timed grenades that could be released to explode behind the aircraft, thereby destroying an enemy aircraft or persuading the pilot to maintain a more respectful distance. These grenades had small parachutes that deployed when they were used. The Soviets claimed some success with these unconventional defensive weapons, and they were also fitted to some Il-10s and Pe-2s.

In August 1941, some Il-2s were equipped with two rearward firing rockets for protection from the rear, but this did not prove to be a success and was not used on a large scale.

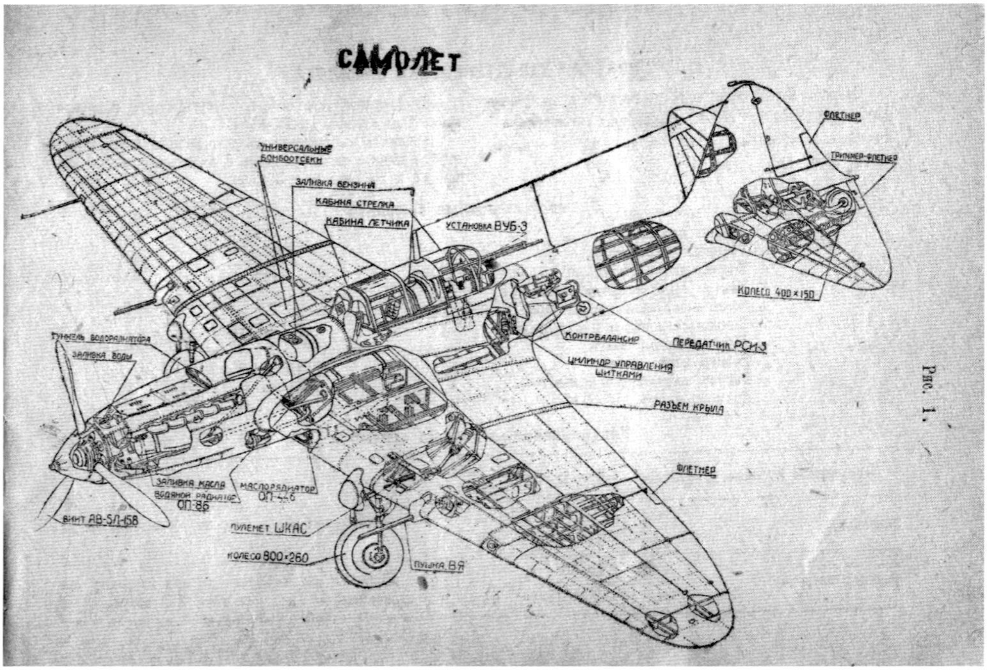

Cutaway of the Il-2. This is of a straight-winged two-seater with metal wings. Notice that it has the outboard mounted pitot tube of later straight-winged two-seaters, but still retains the shorter antenna mast. This drawing shows the AV-5L-158 propeller, so the engine represented is the AM-38F engine used by most two-seaters. (*From the 1944 Il-2 Parts Guide*)

Conclusion

The Il-2 was undoubtedly the single most important warplane used by the Soviet Union during the Second World War. Not only was it the single most-produced aeroplane, but its effect upon the war was the greatest. The Great Patriotic War was first and foremost a ground war, and the contributions of the dedicated ground-attack Il-2 are hard to calculate.

I will leave the final appraisal of the Il-2's efforts during the Great Patriotic War to the expert on the Il-2, Dr Rastrenin, from his book *Il-2 Shturmovik Guards Units of World War 2* (p. 84):

> From their poorly-organised attempt to stem German advances into the Soviet Union in 1941, Il-2 units had been transformed into a highly effective airborne artillery capable of operating with pinpoint accuracy against enemy strong points ahead of advancing forces. Through hard-won combat experience in the dark days of 1941–42, the Shturmovik had evolved into the scourge of the Wehrmacht's once vaunted panzer units.

General notes regarding specification tables: N/A means not applicable to this aircraft, a '?' indicates there is a question regarding the available information (the information may be conflicting or unclear, for example), and a blank space means no information is available for that particular characteristic. The imperial measurement is first, followed by the metric measurement in parentheses.

Il-2 Specification Table

Designation	TsKB-55	TsKB-57	Il-2 AM-38	Il-2 AM-38	Il-2 AM-38F	Il-2-37	Il-2KR	Il-2 AM-38F	Il-2 M-82 (experimental)	Il-2bis (experimental)
Year	1939	1940	1941	1942	1943	1943	1943	1944	1942	1942
Maximum Speed: mph (kph)	261 (420)	272 (437)	263 (423)	249 (400)	261 (420)	240 (387)	239 (385)	252 (405)	280 (450)	246 (396)
Range: miles (km)	384 (618)	528 (850)					378 (609)	450 (724)	316 (508)	402 (647)
Service Ceiling: feet (m)								18,045 (5,500)		
Armament (Cannons)	N/A	N/A	2 × ShVAK 20-mm cannons	2 × VYa-23 23-mm cannons or 2 × ShVAK 20-mm cannons	2 × VYa-23 23-mm cannons (occasionally 2 × ShVAK 20-mm cannons)	2 × NS-37 37-mm cancan	2 × VYa-23 23-mm cannons	2 × VYa-23 23-mm cannons	2 × ShVAK 20-mm cannons	2 × ShVAK 20-mm cannons
Armament (Machine guns)	4 × ShKAS 30-calibre (7.62 mm) machine guns	4 × ShKAS 30-calibre (7.62 mm) machine guns	2 × ShKAS 30-calibre (7.62 mm) machine guns	2 × ShKAS 30-calibre (7.62 mm) machine guns	2 × ShKAS 30-calibre (7.62 mm) machine guns	2 × ShKAS 30-calibre (7.62 mm) machine guns	2 × ShKAS 30-calibre (7.62 mm) machine guns	2 × ShKAS 30-calibre (7.62 mm) machine guns	2 × ShKAS 30-calibre (7.62 mm) machine guns	2 × ShKAS 30-calibre (7.62 mm) machine guns
Armament (Moveable)	1 × ShKAS 30-calibre (7.62 mm) machine gun	N/A	N/A	None (normally)	1 × Berezin UBT 50-calibre (12.7 mm) machine gun	1 × Berezin UBT 50-calibre machine gun (12.7 mm) machine gun	1 × Berezin UBT 50-calibre machine gun (12.7 mm) machine gun	1 × Berezin UBT 50-calibre (12.7 mm) machine gun	1 × Berezin UBT 50-calibre (12.7 mm) machine gun	1 × Berezin UBT 50-calibre (12.7 mm) machine gun

Maximum Bomb Load: lb (kg)	551-661 (250-300)	882 (400)	1,333 (600)	1,333 (600)	1,333 (600)	441 (200)	882 (400)	1,333 (600)	1,333 (600)	1,333 (600)
Rockets	N/A	N/A	8 (normally)	8 (normally)	4	N/A	4	4	6	8
Empty Weight: lb (kg)		7,971 (3,616)	8,988 (4,077)	9,168 (4,159)	9,893 (4,487)	10,313 (4,678)	9,788 (4,440)	10,086 (4,575)	8,800 (3,992)	8,677 (3,936)
All-up Weight: lb (kg)		10,419 (4,726)	11,898 (5,397)	12,500 (5,670)	13,450 (6,101)	13,838 (6,277)	13,548 (6,145)	13,759 (6,241)	11,710 (5,312)	12,617 (5,723)
Maximum Weight: lb (kg)			12,147 (5,510)	13,201 (5,988)	14,021 (6,360)			14,201 (6,360)	12,907 (5,855)	
Engines/ take-off hp per	1 × AM-35 1,350	1 × AM-38 1,600	1 × AM-38 1,600	1 × AM-38 1,600	1 × AM-38F 1,720	1 × AM-38F 1,720	1 × AM-38F 1,720	1 × AM-38F 1,720	1 × M-82 1,700	1 × AM-38 1,600
Crew	2	1	1	1 (normally)	2	2	2	2	2	2
Length – feet (m)	37.68 (11.48)		37.57 (11.45)	38.06 (11.6)	38.06 (11.6)	38.06 (11.6)	38.06 (11.6)	38.06 (11.6)	38.06 (11.6)	38.06 (11.6)
Wingspan – feet (m)	45.6 (13.9)	47.9 (14.6)	47.9 (14.6)	47.9 (14.6)	47.9 (14.6)	47.9 (14.6)	47.9 (14.6)	47.9 (14.6)	47.9 (14.6)	47.9 (14.6)

Il-10

Although the Il-2 was an indispensable part of the Soviet Union's military during the Second World War, it was inevitable that the time would come for a replacement. What the VVS wanted was an aircraft that retained the Il-2's good qualities, such as its armour and armament, but in a smaller, faster, and more manoeuvrable airframe. The result was the Il-10, also from the Ilyushin OKB.

Unlike the Il-2, the Il-10's development was a bit more convoluted and involved several designs, which are described below. Although the Il-8 was not the first in terms of its designation (that distinction belongs to the Il-1), since it was directly evolved from the Il-2, at least in its first incarnation, I have included it first.

Il-10 undergoing heavy maintenance. Note that it has the same wing armament as the Il-2, with two 23-mm cannons and two 7.62-mm machine guns. Note also that the UBT gun (for the rear gunner) has been covered with a protective canvas. (*Viktor Kulikov's collection*)

Il-8

Sergey Ilyushin, mindful that a successor would be needed for the Il-2, began creating its replacement during the war. The first design, the Il-8, was essentially a scaled-up Il-2 with a more powerful AM-42 engine. Initially known as the Il-2M, its name was changed to the Il-AM-42, then the Il-8 AM-42. Please note that the original name, Il-2M, had nothing to do with the spurious post-war designation now often and erroneously used for the straight-winged two-seater. Originally, it even featured the Il-2's wooden rear fuselage. Although much faster than the Il-2, with a top speed approaching 300 mph (483 kph), it did not offer enough of an advance to proceed within this form. A more thorough redesign was called for. The redesigned Il-8 was almost a new aeroplane, featuring a new, more streamlined fuselage and landing gear that turned nearly 90 degrees to lie flat in the wing, as opposed to the underwing fairings the Il-2 and original Il-8 had used to house the main undercarriage. Another difference from the first Il-8 and the subsequent Il-10 was the usage of a four-bladed propeller on the redesigned Il-8.

This 'new' Il-8 started its official factory testing on 6 March 1945 and continued until 14 May 1945, when the Il-8 was submitted for state acceptance trials, which started on 27 May 1945 and went to 7 July 1945. Generally, the aircraft received good marks, but its top speed of 316 mph (509 kph) at 9,200 feet (2,800 m) was inferior to that of the Il-10, which had by this time already entered service. Due to this, development was not proceeded with. Instead, the successor of the Il-2 (the Il-10) would come from a different source.

Il-1

Although the Il-2I fighter development had not proved a success, the Ilyushin bureau created one more armoured fighter: the Il-1. This was a heavily armoured single-seater, with a smaller, more streamlined shape than the Il-2, without the rear gunner. It was constructed completely of metal, and, like the Il-8, it featured landing gear that retracted directly into the wings, rather than the underwing nacelles of the Il-2. In appearance, it resembled a smaller version of the second variant of the Il-8. Even though the Il-1 was much faster than the Il-2I, having a top speed of around 380 mph (612 kph), it was still considered to be too slow to engage in air-to-air combat with the new German types. It did provide a basis for the Il-2's replacement, and with a rear gunner added to the basic design, it appeared as the Il-10 shturmovik, which at first was simply known as the two-seat Il-1 attack aircraft.

As compared to its single-seat fighter precursor, the two-seater featured a redesigned wing and a rear gunner who was surrounded by armour, unlike the Il-2, where the gunner sat outside the main armour. This two-seat Il-1 may have first flown on 18 April 1944, although this is not certain.

Il-10

This aircraft was the true successor to the Il-2 in Soviet service. Although sometimes lumped in together with the Il-2 under the rubric of 'Shturmovik', the Il-10 was a completely new aeroplane, incorporating lessons learned during the Il-2's service. It was constructed completely of metal, and except for steel armour and the fabric-covered control surfaces, it was covered by a stressed-skin aluminium alloy. It was a smaller and better-streamlined aeroplane than the Il-2, incorporating fully retractable main landing gear that rotated through 86 degrees to retract into the wings and a partially retractable tailwheel, as with the larger second version of the Il-8. It carried the more powerful AM-42 engine, a development of the Il-2's AM-38, capable of generating 2,000 hp at take-off. These changes made the Il-10 some 85 to 90 mph (137 to 145 kph) faster than the Il-2, with a top speed of around 340 mph (547 kph). In addition, its smaller size gave it a manoeuvrability approaching that of single-seat fighters, especially in the horizontal plane.

During the Second World War, the Il-10 carried the same fixed armament as the Il-2, comprised of two ShKAS 7.62-mm (30-calibre) machine guns and two VYa-23 23-mm cannons. For defence, it retained the UBT 12.7-mm (50-calibre) machine gun, although with the Il-10, the gunner was in a completely enclosed position and was protected by the front fuselage's armour shell on the sides, back, and bottom of the aircraft. The bomb load of 1,323 lb (600 kg) remained the same as the Il-2. It could also carry four rockets under the wing, as with the two-seater Il-2s, although it was not normally so equipped.

Some commentators on the Il-2 have noted the relatively light ordnance load and short range of the Il-2 as being drawbacks to its design. It is interesting that not only did the wartime Il-10s have the exact same gun fit (two ShKAS and two VYa-23s in the wing, as well as a UBT for defence), but they also had the exact same disposable ordnance load of 1,323 lb (600 kg). Obviously, this armament, including the disposable ordnance load, was considered sufficient by the VVS. In addition, the range of the Il-10 was not much more

Il-10 on an improvised airfield. (*Viktor Kulikov's collection*)

than the Il-2—around 500 miles (805 km) as opposed to around 450 miles (724 km) for the Il-2. If the ordnance load and range had been considered major drawbacks, these would have been changed in the Il-10, which was a completely different design from the Il-2.

The Il-10 continued to be produced long after the war. From 1947 onwards, heavier armament (in the form of four NS-23 23-mm cannons) was fitted, and the rear gunner was provided with a B-20 20-mm cannon. The last Il-10 was the Il-10M, a heavily modified version that was constructed in small numbers in the Soviet Union from 1952 to 1954. The Il-10M featured a longer fuselage and a completely redesigned, more angular wing. In addition to the Soviet Union, Czechoslovakia produced and exported its own version, under the designation of B-33, which featured the heavier post-war armament, using the shorter fuselage and the wing of the Great Patriotic War Il-10.

As with the Il-2, some Il-10s were produced as trainer versions, with the instructor sitting in the aft position, the same as the Il-2Us. These training versions were known collectively as the UIl-10 (or CB-33 if they were of Czech manufacture). Some of these trainers were provided to the foreign air forces which used the Il-10 after the war.

The Il-10 saw service during the last month of the Great Patriotic War, alongside the Il-2, and during the Manchurian campaign. It was also used during the Korean War by the North Koreans and by the Chinese against the Taiwanese during the 1950s and against the Tibetans during the early 1960s. It continued in service with the Chinese until the early 1970s.

Il-16

There is another variant in this line of shturmoviks that should be mentioned: the Il-16. This was similar to the Il-8 and the Il-10, but with smaller dimensions than the Il-10, including a shortened rear fuselage and a fully retractable tailwheel with doors. It retained the four-bladed propeller of the second Il-8. The Il-16 was designed to be a lighter and more manoeuvrable aircraft than the Il-10; it also had less armour. This was balanced by a higher top speed, with the Il-16 topping out at 388 mph (624 kph) at 11,150 feet (3,400 m). Part of the increase in top speed was due to the new engine, the experimental Mikulin AM-43NV, which was more powerful than the AM-42 used on the Il-10, developing 2,300 hp compared to the latter's 2,000 hp.

Vladimir Kokkinaki, Ilyushin's chief test pilot, flew the first Il-16 prototype on 10 June 1945. From the start, there were problems associated with the AM-43NV engine, most notably violent vibrations. There were also stability problems, in part due to the short fuselage of the Il-16 combined with the torque of the powerful engine. The second prototype featured a less rigid engine bearer to deal with the vibration problems and a longer rear fuselage and larger vertical tail to deal with stability issues. These changes did work to a degree, with less vibration and more stability than the initial prototype.

A production machine was completed on 1 October 1945 and was turned over to the production plant's testing facility. The record is silent on what the results of the testing were, but further events made it a moot point. Even more examples were under assembly. However, as the problems with the AM-43NV engine could not be solved, the engine was never to enter mass production; as a result, the Il-16's development was stopped in the summer of 1946.

Service Use

The Il-10 first entered service trials for the Soviet Union in October 1944 on the Eastern Front. Like most new aircraft, it suffered its fair share of teething problems, and its service entrance was not without problems; for example, the AM-42 engine had a tendency to catch fire—a rather considerable problem that was eventually solved. There were also problems with the landing gear, as the tyres were suited more for unprepared fields than concrete runways and had a limited life. The landing gear were also less rugged than the Il-2's.

Its first combat action during the Great Patriotic War took place during 15 April 1945. Only three Il-10 regiments took part in the Great Patriotic War: the 571st ShAP, the 108th GvShAP, and the 118th GvShAP. It was the 571st ShAP that saw the most action, and it was the first Il-10 unit to see action. Il-10s saw heavy action during the short, but sharp Manchurian campaign.

The Il-10 began to replace the Il-2 in shturmovik regiments during the Second World War, with some twelve regiments converting, but total replacement took some time and was not completed until after the war in the late 1940s.

As of 1 January 1955, there were attack air regiments with a total of over 1,800 aircraft. Of these, some 1,700 were Il-10s and the much-revised Il-10M, with 130 MiG-15bis fighter-bombers. The Il-10s were withdrawn from service by the Soviet Union in 1956, with their place being taken by jet-powered fighter-bombers, such as the MiG-15bis.

Conclusion

The Il-10, although it became an excellent ground-attack aircraft, did not have the same impact on the war as its older stablemate, the Il-2. This is easy to understand, as the Il-10 was produced in nowhere near the same numbers and was not introduced into service until late 1944, when the outcome of the war was no longer in doubt. Nevertheless, the Il-10 saw action in the closing days of the Great Patriotic War and saw heavy action during the Manchurian campaign in August 1945. It also enjoyed a long post-war career, seeing action during the Korean War and being produced until 1954; it also saw service with the Chinese until the 1970s. In this respect, it was more analogous to the post-war American Douglas A-1 (AD) Skyraider than the Il-2.

Il-10 female rear gunner next to her gun position. Unlike most wartime countries, Soviet women served in combat. (*Viktor Kulikov's collection*)

Line-up of Il-10s. (*Viktor Kulikov's collection*)

Il-10 rear gunner climbing into his position. His gun is the UBT 12.7-mm (50-calibre) machine gun. In contrast to the Il-2, his position is completely enclosed by glass, and by armour on all other sides. Note the open access door on the rear fuselage in the lower part of the photograph. (*Viktor Kulikov's collection*)

Il-10 Specification Table

Type	Il-8: first version	Il-8: second version	Il-16	Il-10 Prototype	Il-10: GPW	UIL-10	Il-10: Post-War	Il-10M
Year	1943	1945	1945	1944	1945	1945	1947	1952
Maximum Speed: mph (kph)	293 (472)	316 (509)	357 (575)	342 (551)	337 (543)	348 (560)		318 (512)
Range: miles (km)	378 (609)	441 (709)	270 (435)	497 (800)	497 (800)			500 (805)
Service Ceiling: feet (m)								22,966 (7,000)
Offensive Armament	2 × VYa-23 23-mm cannons, 2 × ShKAS 30-calibre (7.62 mm) machine guns	2 × VYa-23 23-mm cannons, 2 × ShKAS 30-calibre (7.62 mm) machine guns	2 × VYa-23 23-mm cannons, 2 × ShKAS 30-calibre (7.62 mm) machine guns	2 × VYa-23 23-mm cannons, 2 × ShKAS 30-calibre (7.62 mm) machine guns	2 × VYa-23 23-mm cannons, 2 × ShKAS 30-calibre (7.62 mm) machine guns	2 × VYa-23 23-mm cannons, 2 × ShKAS 30-calibre (7.62 mm) machine guns	4 × NS-23 23-mm cannons	4 × NR-23 23-mm cannons
Defensive Armament	1 × Berezin UBT 50-calibre (12.7 mm) machine gun	1 × Berezin BT-20 20-mm cannon	1 × Berezin BT-20 20-mm cannon	1 × Sh-20 20-mm cannon	1 × Berezin UBT 50-calibre (12.7 mm) machine gun	N/A	1 × Berezin B-20 20-mm cannon	1 × Berezin B-20EN 20-mm cannon
Rocket Armament				4 × RS-82 or RS-132	4 × RS-82 or RS-132	4 × RS-82 or RS-132	4 × RS-82 or RS-132	4 × RS-132
Maximum Bomb Load: lb (kg)	2,205 (1,000)	2,205 (1,000)	1,102 (500)	1,323 (600)	1,323 (600)	441 (200)	1,323 (600)	1,323 (600)
Empty Weight: lb (kg)	11,607 (5,265)	11,266 (5,110)	9,513 (4,315)	11,133 (5,050)	10,412 (4,723)	10,077 (4,571)		11,801 (5,353)
All-up Weight: lb (kg)	16,006 (7,260)	16,777 (7,610)	13,184 (5,980)	13,966 (6,335)	14,077 (6,385)	12,522 (5,680)		15,653 (7,100)
Maximum Weight: lb (kg)					14,330 (6500)			16,138 (7,320)
Engines/ Take-off hp per	1 × AM-42 2,000	1 × AM-42 2,000	1 × AM-43NV 2,300	1 × AM-42 2,000	1 × AM-42 2,000	1 × AM-42 2,000	1 × AM-42 2,000	1 × AM-42 2,000
Crew	2	2	2	2	2	2	2	2
Length: feet (m)	42.36 (12.91)	42.42 (12.93)	35.07 (10.69)	36.48 (11.12)	36.48 (11.12)	36.48 (11.12)	36.48 (11.12)	38.94 (11.87)
Wingspan: feet (m)	47.9 (14.6)	47.9 (14.6)	41.01 (12.5)	43.96 (13.4)	43.96 (13.4)	43.96 (13.4)	43.96 (13.4)	45.93 (14)

4
Short-Range Twin-Engined Bombers

Aleksandr Yakovlev's first venture into combat aircraft was not in the realm of fighters, with which his name is forever linked in terms of the Second World War, but with a fast, small, twin-engined two-seater light bomber and reconnaissance aircraft. This aircraft, the BB-22, gave rise to two designs, the Yak-2 and the Yak-4, neither of which, for various reasons, proved to be great successes. In all, only 201 of these aircraft were produced, and most were destroyed during the first six months of the Great Patriotic War. They did not have any great impact upon the war, but are interesting nonetheless as being the first of Yakovlev's purpose-built warplanes.

Yak-2

The first of the Yakovlev OKB's combat aircraft, the Yak-2 was developed from the experimental Ya-22 fast, twin-engined aircraft. Only a relatively small number of Yak-2s were produced, and they were used only in the first six months or so of the Great Patriotic War as light bombers and reconnaissance aircraft. None survived until the end of the war.

Development

Ya-22

For his first combat aircraft, Yakovlev wanted to develop the fastest twin-engined aircraft he could, an aircraft that might be suitable as a bomber, a reconnaissance aircraft, or even a fighter. To that end, he created a small, streamlined monoplane aircraft with two inline engines. This aircraft was labelled the 'Ya-22' by the Yakovlev OKB. Its construction was typical of Yakovlev in being of mixed construction. The wings were of wooden construction, with two spars and a wooden covering. The ailerons were of aluminium structure with a fabric covering, while the underwing flaps were all-metal. The fuselage was more complex, with a nose and rear fuselage of welded steel-tube construction, the nose having an aluminium covering while the rear fuselage was fabric-covered, with the top of the fuselage being plywood-covered. The centre section was of

Ya-22 undergoing tests in January and February 1939. The aircraft is mainly finished in red, which was typical for Yakovlev prototype aircraft. Note the high gloss finish. (*Viktor Kulikov's collection*)

wooden construction and was integral with the wooden wing. The landing gear were hydraulically retractable and closed by doors, with the main landing gear wheels being slightly exposed even when retracted to give the aircraft some protection in the case of a forced landing. The engines were two M-103 engines of Klimov design with a maximum power of 960 hp driving a VISh-22 propeller. The pilot was accommodated in the nose, while the navigator/gunner was in a separate compartment situated behind the wing.

The Ya-22 first flew on 22 February 1939. The aircraft was found to handle well. The aircraft was also able to achieve the impressive top speed of 352 mph (567 kph). Stalin was said to have been so impressed by this performance that he ordered the aircraft to be put into production immediately, in an order dated 15 March 1939. The aircraft was to have the designation 'BB-22', with the 'BB' standing for *Blizhniy Bombardirovshchik*, or 'Short-Range Bomber'. This was before the NII VVS had even had a chance to evaluate the aircraft.

BB-22 (Izdeliye 70)

Before entering production, however, NII VVS testing uncovered many changes that needed to be made to the Ya-22 to turn it into even a marginally effective warplane. Tests revealed that these changes involved being able to carry a bomb load of 882–1,543 lb (400–700 kg) and to accommodate a rear gun for defence, with the navigator/gunner being moved forward to sit behind the pilot in the same cockpit. The cooling system for the engine was found to be wanting. Although the climb to 22,966 feet (7,000 m) was supposed to take 8.7 minutes, in reality, it took thirty-three minutes, which was unacceptable from an operational standpoint. This slow climb was due to having to regularly level out in flight to give the engines and coolant a chance to cool down.

A BB-22 jacked up for repairs after a crash-landing. (*Viktor Kulikov's collection*)

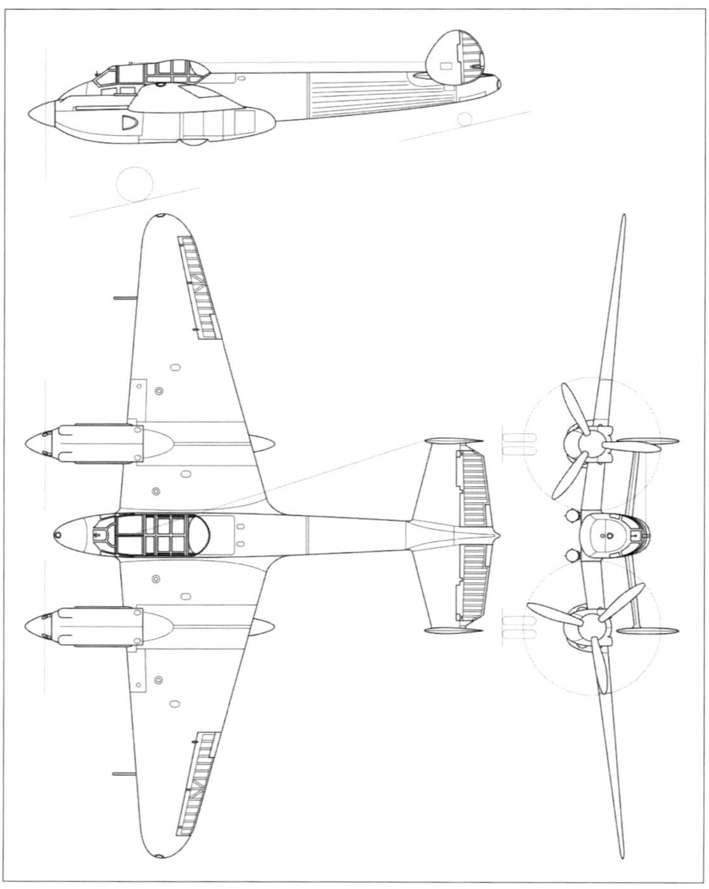

Three-view drawing of a Yak-2. (*By Kaboldy. Wikimedia*)

In addition to the provision of the rear gun (a ShKAS 7.62-mm machine gun), a similar weapon was fixed in the nose to be used by the pilot. The nose gun had 450 rounds and the rear gun had 1,000 rounds.

The first production aircraft (or pre-production aircraft; sources differ) flew on 20 February 1940, although it had first rolled out on 31 December 1939. In January 1940, even before the first flight of the initial production aircraft, an order for 580 BB-22s to be produced in 1940 was placed, of which 300 were to be produced at Z.81 at Moscow-Tushino. In service, the designation was changed from 'BB-22' to 'Yak-2', as the new Soviet designation system now honoured the chief designers in the names of their aircraft.

In service, the Yak-2 showed itself to be an immature aircraft, with numerous defects. Nonetheless, some 111 were produced. On 21 June 1941, seventy-three Yak-2s were apparently still in service at Kiev and the Western District. In the first days of Barbarossa, many of these Yak-2s were destroyed on the ground, but a few survived to be used operationally as light bombers and reconnaissance aircraft. It is not clear when the last Yak-2 was used up (they do not appear to have been withdrawn, but used until there were no more), but it is doubtful that any survived 1942.

A Yak-2 in flight over the Soviet countryside. (*Viktor Kulikov's collection*)

Yak-4

This aircraft, a development of the Yak-2, although meant as an improved version, suffered much the same fate as that aeroplane as most of the aircraft were destroyed in the first months of the Great Patriotic War. Remarkably, one Yak-4 continued in use with the Northern Fleet as a reconnaissance aircraft into 1944. One source states it was used until the end of the war (1945).

Development

BB-22bis (Izdeliye 70bis)

In an effort to eliminate at least some of the deficiencies of the Yak-2, the BB-22bis was developed. One of the most important differences between the BB-22bis and the Yak-2 was the use of more powerful engines, the 1,100-hp M-105s replacing the 960-hp M-103s of the Yak-2. The troublesome engine cooling system of the Yak-2 was redesigned, with one change being the relocation of the oil coolers from the sides of the engine nacelles to underneath the engines in a 'chin' installation. It is possible that the first Yak-4s (as the BB-22bis was soon redesignated) did not feature this chin installation.

Yak-4

The BB-22bis, or Yak-4, replaced the Yak-2 on the production lines at Z.81 in November 1940. Another change from the Yak-2, apart from the more powerful M-105 engines, was more fuel in the form of two additional tanks in the outer wings. The construction of the aircraft was the same as that of the Yak-2. Despite the more powerful engines, the Yak-4 still had defects, one of the most serious being centre of gravity problems with the full bomb load of 882 lb (400 kg); this problem had also afflicted the Yak-2. The aircraft had poor engine performance and the cockpit, which housed both the pilot and the navigator/gunner, was considered to be cramped, not surprising considering the small cross-section of the fuselage. The total production was just ninety aircraft, even less than that of the Yak-2. The final twenty-one were not delivered until April 1941, just before the beginning of Barbarossa, which gave the crews little time to become familiarised with their aircraft.

In combat, the Yak-4 was found to be a fast aircraft that did not burn easily, but the small bombload and weak armament of two rifle-calibre guns did not make the Yak-4 a particularly impressive warplane. As with the Yak-2, most Yak-4s were gone by the end of 1941, although as mentioned previously, one Yak-4 served with the 118th Reconnaissance Polk of the Northern Fleet until at least as late as 1944, as well as possibly into 1945.

Conclusion

Neither the Yak-2 nor the Yak-4 had any great impact on the war due to the small numbers used. They are notable mainly for being Aleksandr Yakovlev's first purpose-built warplanes.

A Barbarossa victim Yak-4 in 1941. Note that the star on the fabric-covered rear fuselage has been cut away by a souvenir hunter. (*Viktor Kulikov's collection*)

This crash-landed Yak-4 has been painted in the Great Patriotic War camouflage of black/green, so this is probably from the second half of 1941. (*Viktor Kulikov's collection*)

5
Light Nuisance Bombers

One of the interesting features of the Eastern Front was the extensive use of obsolete or training aircraft by both sides for what was called 'nuisance bombing'. This was normally conducted at night, when it was also called 'night harassment', and although the small bombs usually carried by these aircraft caused relatively little damage, the commotion they created kept the enemy soldiers on edge and robbed them of a good night's sleep, a precious commodity in any war. The Soviets were the first to utilise this tactic on a large scale, almost from the start of the Great Patriotic War, using especially the U-2 light utility aircraft (usually referred to as the 'Po-2' in the West; this was its Soviet designation from 1944 on). These aircraft were suitably equipped with bomb racks under the wings and often equipped with a DA or ShKAS machine gun for the observer. The R-5, described previously, was also used as a nuisance bomber.

The tactic was successful enough for the Germans to copy the technique, first with the *Storkampfstaffeln* in 1942, then with the larger *Nachtschlachtgruppen,* being equipped with trainers and obsolete warplanes such as the Ar 66 trainer biplane and the He-46 parasol monoplane battlefield reconnaissance aircraft. Nuisance bombers were used by both sides until the end of the Great Patriotic War.

U-2/Po-2

This aircraft, designed by Nikolaiy Polikarpov, first flown in 1927, was in the general class of the British Tiger Moth biplane. Like the Tiger Moth, it was a small, all-wooden two-seater aircraft, with tractable flying characteristics that lent itself to use not only as a trainer, but also for use as an agricultural aircraft (as a crop-duster, for example). Thousands of Soviet pilots got their first taste of flying on the *Kukuruznik* (the 'Corn-cutter', so named for its low flights over fields), and the aircraft was produced in the tens of thousands before, during, and after the war. By the beginning of the Great Patriotic War in 1941, 13,000 U-2s had already been produced. Indeed, it was one of the most produced aircraft of all times, and more may have been produced than even the Il-2 (figures vary, but as many as 40,000 U-2/Po-2s may have been produced, although one source has 33,000 being produced, and around 30,000 may be closer to the actual number built).

Among its many uses was perhaps surprisingly that of a light bomber, hence its inclusion in this work. With its mid-1920s design, all-wooden construction, and rather stately performance, it seemed an unlikely combat aircraft. Nonetheless, it proved to be so successful in the role of a light bomber that it was produced especially for this role, in which it saw use throughout the war (and even after; the North Koreans used it as a nuisance bomber during the Korean War (1950–53), where it gained fame as 'Bed Check Charlie'). Post-war, it was known by NATO as the 'Mule', a rather suitable nickname given its sturdiness and usefulness.

The U-2 (or Po-2 as it was designated from 1944 after the death of Nikolaiy Polikarpov on 30 July 1944) was produced in the Soviet Union from 1928–52, one of the longest production runs of any aircraft ever, and it was produced in Poland until at least 1955 (as the CSS-13). Some aircraft were still being built from knock-down components by aircraft repair and maintenance shops and aero clubs until as late as 1959. Although no longer in service anywhere, even today a few Po-2s are still flying on the warbird circuit, with at least one flying in the United Kingdom and two flying in the United States (one with the Flying Heritage Museum collection, which also has a flyable Il-2).

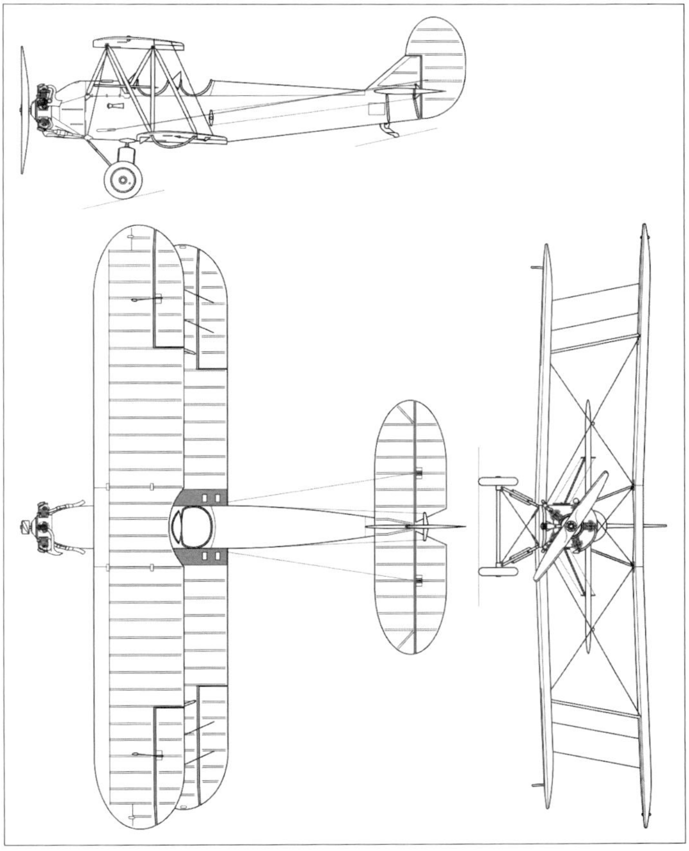

Three-view drawing of a U-2. (*By Kaboldy. Wikimedia*)

Development

First Prototype

This aircraft, which first flew in early 1927, was designed to be as simple as possible, with many interchangeable parts, including the wings, which were square-tipped, and the tail planes. Even the control surfaces were designed to be interchangeable. The unfortunate result was a clunky, overweight, and un-aerodynamic aircraft with a top speed of only 75 mph (120 kph). Its handling was also subpar; clearly, a major redesign was in order, so a second prototype was built.

Second Prototype

This aircraft was in effect the 'true' prototype of the U-2 series, as it was so extensively redesigned as to be almost a new aircraft when compared to the first prototype. It dispensed with that design's obsession with 'simplicity' and interchangeability of parts. It was first flown on 7 January 1928 by the famed test pilot Mikhail Mikhailovich Gromov (1899–1985). By not trying to be as simple as possible, the result was an aircraft with good flying qualities, good enough that the U-2 remained essentially unchanged from this prototype until the last example was built in the 1950s. One immediately recognisable difference between this redesigned prototype and the first prototype was the rounded wingtips, which were kept to the end of the U-2's production, and a larger tail, which gave it better stability.

U-2 (UT)

Designed as a basic trainer, this aircraft was well-suited for the role with its combination of manoeuvrability and stability (it was almost impossible to initiate a spin because of its longitudinal stability). The initial name of 'UT' stood for *Uchebno-trenirovochniy*, or basically, 'Trainer'. The aircraft could be fitted with a retractable hood over the rear cockpit for blind (instrument) flying. Thousands of the basic trainer version were produced, and thousands of Soviet pilots first flew on the U-2. It was still used extensively as a trainer during and even after the Great Patriotic War.

U-2S-1

Due to its ability to land and take off from remote unprepared locations, the U-2 proved suitable for adaptation as a medical evacuation aircraft, for both civilian and military uses. This version could accommodate one patient in a stretcher and a sitting attendant or patient under a hinged cover on the fuselage. The fuselage as a result had a larger rear section than the standard U-2. The pilot still sat in an open cockpit. The 'S' in the designation stood for *Sanitarniy* or 'Ambulance'.

U-2S-2

This improved aerial ambulance version of the U-2, which replaced the S-1 from 1940, featured a larger covered compartment for the evacuees, with more room to accommodate the stretcher patient and the sitting attendant (or patient).

U-2S-3

Modified by regimental workshops, this version of the U-2 ambulance allowed for two stretchers to be carried side-by-side in the fuselage. The ambulance versions of the U-2 saw extensive use in the Great Patriotic War.

U-2VVS

Although it is commonly thought that the development of the armed version of the U-2 occurred during the Great Patriotic War, the first armed versions were developed before the Second World War, as early as 1931. In this case, the aircraft was seen not as a night-time nuisance bomber, but as an army co-operation aircraft, of the type then much in vogue with the RAF, for example. In this capacity, it would follow the army and act as both a reconnaissance aircraft and a light bomber, attacking targets of opportunity. The Soviets referred to such an aircraft as an 'escort' aircraft, as it escorted the ground troops and provided them with support. It was the head of the Red Air Force at the time, Yakov Ivanovich Alksnis (1897–1938, a Latvian), who had insisted that it be armed, to increase its usefulness as an army co-operation aircraft.

The aircraft passed its state tests in 1933 and was given the service designation of 'U-2VVS', where the 'VVS' stood for *Voyenno-vozdushniye siliy*: the 'Military Air Forces' (Red Air Force). Some 468 were built in 1935 and 1936.

Although it was armed and intended as a combat aircraft, the U-2VVS saw use before the war as a bomber trainer. It is not known how many survived until the Great Patriotic War, to perhaps be used in their original role as a light reconnaissance bomber.

U-2VOM

This version of the U-2 was an M-11D-powered example that was equipped to carry liquid-filled incendiary charges. These incendiary devices consisted of bags filled with a napalm-like substance. The bags were carried in two containers, one being under the fuselage, the other being in the fuselage behind the observer, the containers also being able to carry other devices such as fragmentation bombs or hand grenades. There was also a ShKAS machine gun mounted on top of the lower port wing.

Five examples of this 'flamethrower' version of the U-2 were built and were used in combat in 1942, but the type did not enter large-scale production.

U-2LNB/Po-2LNB (U-2VS (Mod. 1943))

The definitive standardised production version of the U-2 nuisance bomber was the U-2LNB (Po-2LNB from 1944), where the 'LNB' stood for *Lyoghkiy Nochnoiy Bombardirovshchik* or 'Light Night Bomber' in Russian, or the U-2VS (Mod. 1943). The 'VS' in U-2VS stood for *Voskovaya Seriya*, or 'Military Series'. It was this version, along with the field-modified bomber conversions, that earned fame for the U-2 in the Great Patriotic War as a bomber. It was known by the Germans as the *Nahmaschine*, or 'Sewing Machine' due to the distinctive sound of its M-11 engine. One name the Finnish gave it was the *Hermosaha* ('Nerve Saw') for much the same reason.

Equipped with skis for winter usage, this U-2LNB is fully armed, with bombs under the wings and fuselage, and a machine gun for the rear gunner in its stowed position. (*Viktor Kulikov's collection*)

Members of the famous *Nachthexen* in front of one of their U-2 aeroplanes. (*Viktor Kulikov's collection*)

This U-2 in flight has the wartime black/green camouflage and although it has the mount for the rear gun, none has been fitted. (*Viktor Kulikov's collection*)

Painted in winter camouflage, this U-2, with its bombs and rear gun, appears ready for take-off on a combat mission. (*Viktor Kulikov's collection*)

It was this aircraft that was the mount of the famous 588th Night Bomber Regiment (588th NBAP), whose flight crew were composed entirely of women. It was these women who were known to the Germans as the *Nachthexen* ('Night Witches'), in honour of the nocturnal visits they paid to German positions. This unit proved to be very successful and by the end of the war had been awarded twenty-three Hero of the Soviet Union titles. Due to its success, this unit was awarded Guards' status as the 46th Tamansky GvNBAP (the 46th Tamansky Guards Night Bomber Regiment). They were just one of the more than sixty regiments and squadrons which used the U-2 on combat missions during the Great Patriotic War.

In addition to having a mount for the ShKAS machine gun and underwing bomb racks for up to 661 lb (300 kg) in small bombs, the U-2LNB was also characterised by having exhaust mufflers, which hid the exhaust flames and made the aircraft quieter.

U-2P (U-2M)

A floatplane, this version of the U-2 was produced in small numbers. The aircraft was equipped with a single main float under the fuselage and small stabilising floats under the wings. The 'P' stood for *Poplavkoviy* or 'Float-equipped'. The 'M' in the designation stood for *Morskoiy* or 'Marine/Naval'.

U-2NAK

This version of the basic U-2 was an artillery spotter aircraft, with the 'NAK' standing for *Nochnoiy Artilleriyskiy Korrektivorshchik* or 'Night Artillery Spotter'. The most important difference between this version and the standard U-2 was the provision of an RSI-4 radio, which the observer used. The aircraft was also equipped with an exhaust flame/noise suppressor as with the U-2LNB.

Five prototypes were built and tested in combat between 10 and 28 July 1944 by the 2nd Air Army of the 1st Ukrainian Front, 62 miles (100 km) east of Lvov. Although all these aircraft were eventually lost, the type was proven successful enough that series production was undertaken and the aircraft was used late in the war. The missions were flown at night at an altitude between 1,969 feet (600 m) and 3,281 feet (1,000 m), with the U-2NAK gliding silently above the target.

Combat Tactics

The U-2's apparent drawbacks and anachronisms, such as an all-wooden construction and slow speed (it topped out at about 93 mph (150 kph)), actually proved to be advantageous in its role as a light, night-time intruder. Its wooden construction made it nearly invisible to German early-warning radar in a sort of early form of stealth, and its slow speed, where its maximum speed was less than the stalling speed of modern German monoplane fighters, made it quite difficult to intercept, especially as it flew at extremely low altitudes near the target. The U-2s flew at dusk at low altitudes from their front-line airfields to the jumping-off airstrips, called *Aerodomy Podskoka*. It was from these airstrips that the U-2s flew their nocturnal missions.

One U-2 tactic involved turning the engine off near the target and gliding in, which made it nearly silent as it made its attack run. Evidently, the engine was easy to restart, or the result would have been an unexpectedly short mission. Another, perhaps safer, tactic involved throttling the engine back to reduce its noise. A first U-2 would execute this nearly silent attack and would quickly leave after dropping its bombs, before the Axis flak could respond. A second aircraft would approach from a different direction, attacking the now aflame target. Having the aircraft attack from different directions made it more difficult for the flak to respond. The Germans found out to their consternation that the flak was largely ineffective against the U-2s and merely served to give their positions away.

A particularly dangerous tactic involved having one U-2 fly into the German defences, to draw flak and searchlights, which positions were then attacked by the other U-2s. This tactic was used by the famous all-female U-2 unit, the 588th NBAP.

The effect on the morale of the German soldiers was considerable. A Wehrmacht soldier wrote as quoted in the book, *Polikarpov U-2/Po-2* by Martin Velek (p. 21):

> These aircraft do not allow us to live—we can neither light a fire in a stove, nor a small campfire outside, the U-2 crews spot them and drop bombs on them; they find us every time—therefore we have to sit the whole night in trenches to avoid mass casualties[.]

Conclusion

The contribution of the liaison/light transport, training, and ambulance versions of the U-2/Po-2 to the Soviet war effort was considerable. This much is certain. The combat contribution of the U-2LNB/U-2VS is a little harder to determine. Although the actual material effect of the bombing attacks on the Axis may have been relatively minor, certainly when compared to the enormous losses inflicted on men and materiel by the Il-2 and the Pe-2, the psychological effect was not so minor, as can be seen from the quote cited above. Although the Germans were able to defend themselves to an extent against the Il-2 and Pe-2, inflicting heavy losses on these aircraft, they were never able to come up with a suitable deterrent to the small, slow, and low-flying U-2. This inability to defend against the U-2 and the constant raids on the Germans were a major irritant, and, over time, no doubt adversely affected the morale of the German and other Axis soldiers. Perhaps the most telling testament to its effectiveness is seen in the wholesale effort by the Axis from 1942 to copy the tactics of the U-2 light nuisance bombers. As has been said, imitation is the sincerest form of flattery.

U-2/Po-2 Specification Table

Type	First Prototype	U-2 Trainer	U-2LNB (Po-2LNB, U-2VS Mod. 1943)
Year	1927	1933	1943
Maximum Speed: mph (kph)	88 (142)	93 (150)	81 (131) with maximum bomb load
Range: miles (km)		249 (400)	280 (450)
Service Ceiling: feet (m)		12,533 (3,820)	5,085 (1,550) with maximum bomb load
Defensive Armament	N/A	N/A	1 × ShKAS 7.62-mm machine gun
Maximum Bomb Load: lb (kg)	N/A	N/A	661 (300)
Empty Weight: lb (kg)	1,671 (758)	1,400 (635)	1,704 (773)
All-up Weight: lb (kg)	2,233 (1,013)	1,962 (890)	2,231 (1,012)
Maximum Weight: lb (kg)			3,086 (1,400)
Engines/ take-off hp per	1 × M-11 ?	1 × M-11G 110	1 × M-11D 125
Crew	2	2	2
Length: feet (m)	26.57 (8.1)	26.8 (8.17)	26.8 (8.17)
Wingspan: feet (m)	36.09 (11)	37.4 (11.4)	37.4 (11.4)

UT-1 (AIR-14)

The U-2 biplane was not the only training aircraft adapted for an offensive role during the early stages of the Great Patriotic War. The UT-1 aircraft, developed as a trainer in the pre-Second World War era by the Yakovlev OKB, was also converted for use as a light ground attack/bomber aircraft, seeing action in the first half of the war.

Development

The UT-1 was a simple, cantilever monoplane with fixed undercarriage. Unlike the similar two-seater UT-2, the UT-1 was designed as a single-seater aircraft, to be used for aerobatic training. Construction was mixed, with wooden wings covered in plywood and fabric and a fuselage constructed of a steel tube structure, which was covered in fabric. The prototype, powered by a 100-hp M-11 five-cylinder radial engine, first flew in May 1936. The VVS expressed interest in the AIR-14, as it was then designated, and it went into production in 1937 as the UT-1, with the 'UT' standing for *Uchebno-trenirovochniy* or 'Trainer' (more literally, 'Educational Trainer'). The aircraft was quite manoeuvrable and had a top speed of 160 mph (257 kph). Some 1,241 were built in total, and it was widely used as an intermediate-level aerobatic trainer.

Combat Use

Due to heavy losses by military units in the summer of 1941, it was decided to impress quasi-civilian aircraft such as the UT-1 and UT-2 into use as communications/liaison aircraft by the AVMF and the VVS. It was soon decided that these types could also serve in the light bomber role, especially at night. Over a hundred UT-1s were therefore modified for use as a light ground attack aircraft. The aircraft usually had the spatted undercarriage fairings removed, to enable them to operate better from rough forward airfields. The combat modifications involved fitting four RS-82 rockets under the wings, in many cases also fitting two ShKAS machine guns on the wings. The guns were apparently fitted in two ways: one involved a very simple installation with the guns being installed exposed on top of the wings, without any type of fairing, and the second involved fitting the guns under the wings in fairings. These armed UT-1s were mainly used in the Caucasus region in the nocturnal attack role, by the 46th Air Regiment of the Black Sea Fleet, for example. They were used at Stalingrad into 1943, but soon after were replaced by Il-2s. The UT-1 continued to be used as a trainer until at least 1946.

UT-2 (Ya-20)

The UT-2 was a trainer designed in the mid-1930s to provide intermediate or transition training for military pilots, that is, training between that provided by the U-2 primary trainer and front-line aircraft. Besides being built and used in the thousands for this role, up to 2,000 were used during the Great Patriotic War as light night harassment bombers. In all, some 7,243 UT-2s were built and it served with Eastern Bloc aero clubs into the late 1950s. It received the NATO nickname of 'Mink'.

Development

Design of what was then known as the Ya-20 was made in the winter of 1936–37. It was a development of the earlier AIR-10 aircraft. The Ya-20 was similar in basic design to the UT-1, although it featured two cockpits, the front position being occupied by the trainee-pilot, with the rear cockpit being occupied by the instructor-pilot. Like the UT-1, it had a cantilever monoplane wing, with strut-braced tail planes and spatted main undercarriage. Although the tail planes were of a metal structure, with a fabric covering, the aircraft was mainly of wooden construction, with plywood and fabric covering. The engine on the first prototype was an inline Renault Bengali 4 engine of 140 hp.

The prototypes were tested in the summer of 1937, showing a top speed of 149 mph (240 kph). It was decided in September 1937 to put the type into production as a transition trainer occupying an intermediate position between the U-2 primary trainer and front-line aircraft. The aircraft received the service designation of 'UT-2', and the production aircraft were powered by the M-11, the same engine that powered both the UT-1 and the U-2 trainers.

It was found with the first production version of the aircraft that it was easy to put into a spin, so the aircraft was redesigned. The redesigned aircraft was produced from 1939. In 1940, it was decided to use the aircraft as an *ab initio*, or primary trainer. The first version had a top speed of 149 mph (240 kph), while the redesigned second version had a top speed of 127 mph (205 kph).

Combat Use

As with the UT-1, it was decided that the UT-2 would be useful as a light night bomber. Up to 2,000 were used in this role during the Great Patriotic War, with the needed modifications being made in the field as opposed to the factory. These modifications involved turning the aircraft into single-seaters (keeping the instructor's cockpit), often with ShKAS guns mounted on top of the wings, one per wing, to fire outside of the propeller arc. In addition, light droppable ordnance could be carried under the fuselage, including PTAB anti-tank bomblets, fragmentation bombs, and up to three FAB-100 bombs for a bomb load of 661 lb (300 kg). Four RS-82 rockets could also be carried under the wings.

Like the UT-1, the UT-2s were used by AVMF units of the Black Sea Fleet and VVS units in the Caucasus and at Stalingrad, often in the same units with the UT-1. After late 1943, the UT-2s were used to support partisans.

Yak-6

Although developed as a light, twin-engined transport, some Yak-6s were used in the light night bomber harassment role. In addition, following from the success of the *ad hoc* Yak-6 bombers, a purpose-built bomber variant, the Yak-6 NBB, was developed and flew, at least in prototype form.

Development

The Yak-6 was designed as a light utility aircraft by the Yakovlev OKB, but one that was more advanced and capable than the single-engined biplane U-2 and R-5, as the war had shown the need for a more capable aircraft. Development started in April 1942 and the aircraft that resulted was a small, twin-engined monoplane aircraft, with a mainly wooden structure, cantilever wings, and braced tail planes. The aircraft was covered in plywood and fabric. The prototype of the Yak-6 first flew in June 1942, which was a remarkably short period of time, since development had only started in April of that year. It was powered by two of the M-11 radial engines, the same engine that powered the U-2. The prototype passed its state trials in September 1942, with the first production examples appearing in November 1942. The aircraft proved popular in service, but suffered from some handling problems such as a propensity for spinning under certain circumstances. It was because of these handling problems that a decision was made on 25 September 1943 to end production.

Although used mainly as a light transport, the Yak-6 was also used in the night harassment role carrying small bombs. It is unclear from the record if some of these

Yak-6 bombers also carried the defensive gun carried by the Yak-6 NBB (see below). The Yak-6 had a top speed of 116 mph (187 kph). Some aircraft had retractable main landing gear, while others had fixed gear. In all, 381 Yak-6s were produced.

Experimental Version

Yak-6 NBB

Although developed as a light, twin-engined transport, an experimental Yak-6 was built specifically for use in the light night bomber harassment role under the designation of 'Yak-6 NBB', where the 'NBB' stood for *Nochnoiy Blizhniy Bombardirovshchik* or 'Short-Range Night Bomber'. This aircraft included a rear-facing ShKAS machine gun fired from a circular opening in the top of the aircraft; it was equipped to carry up to five 220-lb (100-kg) light bombs under the centre section of the wing for a total bomb load of 1,102 lb (500 kg). It featured retractable landing gear.

Apparently, two aircraft were built to this standard and tested, although it is unclear how many additional aircraft were built, if any, or if the aircraft saw any service. The sources seem to be quite confused about this aircraft, and in the records, the standard Yak-6 transports that were used for night bombing may have been confused with these purpose-built bomber prototypes. It is even possible that some of the Yak-6 night bombers were converted to the NBB standard, complete with the rear-firing machine gun position. It is also possible that some Yak-6s late in the war were equipped to carry up to ten RS-82 rockets under the wings; at least one aircraft was tested with this armament.

The Yak-6NBB experimental night bomber at the NII VVS airfield at Kratovo (note the characteristic hexagonal pavement). (*Viktor Kulikov's collection*)

6
Dive Bombers

The success of the German Ju 87 Stuka dive bomber in the early stages of the Second World War did not go unnoticed by the Soviets, and they set about creating a dive bomber for the Red Air Force. In addition, their examination of the Ju 88 also led the Soviets to believe they should create a twin-engined dive bomber.

Ar-2

Aleksandr Alexandrovich Arkhangelsky (1892–1978), a close associate of Andrey Tupolev and one of the main designers of the SB, created a dive bomber development of the Tupolev SB, the Ar-2. The Ar-2 was designed with much smaller wings, including dive brakes, and was faster than the SB, having a top speed of nearly 300 mph (298 mph (480 kph)) in its production version. Although a reasonably good aeroplane, its career was cut short by the Great Patriotic War, in which many were destroyed in the first few months, and by the appearance of the superior Pe-2 dive bomber, which led to the cancellation of its production and its replacement by the Pe-2. The Ar-2 disappeared from front-line units in 1943.

As an interesting side note, even though the Ar-2 was a development of a Tupolev design, and Arkhangelsky had been a member of the Tupolev OKB, the aircraft was named after Arkhangelsky himself ('Ar'-2) instead of Tupolev because Andrey Tupolev was technically an enemy of the state while the Ar-2 was being designed and flown. Otherwise, it might have been designated as the 'Tu-2'.

Development

SB-RK

This aircraft was developed in parallel to the SB-MMN level bomber, but was equipped as a dive bomber. In general, it was similar to the SB-MMN, with a smaller tail and wings as compared to the standard SB. Like the SB-MMN, it was equipped with twin M-105 engines, but these were in new, more streamlined nacelles. The

An Ar-2 Barbarossa victim (note the triumphantly smiling German serviceman in the pilot's cockpit) probably in the summer of 1941. The aircraft appears to have been captured intact. (*Viktor Kulikov's collection*)

streamlined nacelles were possible because the radiators were now located in the wing, and the common name for this variant, SB-RK, reflected this, with the 'RK' standing for *Radiatory-Krilyo* or 'Radiator-Wing' in Russian. Gordon and Komissarov state that it was originally intended to be a level bomber as with the SB and the SB-MMN, but the decision was taken to develop it as a dive bomber instead as it was considered obsolescent as a level bomber.

The SB-RK was first flown in late April 1940 by factory test pilot M. Lipkin. During the factory tests, the aircraft showed a top speed of 314 mph (505 kph); Maslov has a top speed of 306 mph (492 kph) at an altitude of 15,420 feet (4,700 m). The aircraft was tested at the NII VVS from 11 to 16 May 1940. During the NII VVS tests, the aircraft showed a top speed of 298 mph (480 kph). The aircraft was fitted with dive brakes and was tested with these between 27 July and 11 August 1940.

One of the enhancements recommended as result of testing was the replacement of the standard SB-type nose, with twin ShKAS guns, with a longer and more streamlined 'F-1' nose equipped with one ShKAS gun, somewhat similar to that used on the SB-MMN. As with the SB-MMN, the navigator was given dual controls so he could control the aircraft, if needed. During testing, it was determined that the aircraft suffered from engine cooling problems, and the wings needed to be finished to a higher standard to improve streamlining. Despite this and other defects, the aircraft was recommended for production. Three SB-RKs modified with the new nose were built and tested. The wings on these new aircraft were also equipped with dive brakes, and the fuel capacity was increased by the installation of two additional fuel tanks. These aircraft were the true production pattern aircraft for what became the Ar-2, and they were completed in the second half of 1940.

Ar-2

Production of the modified SB-RK began in October 1940 at Z.22 in Moscow. The SB-RK was redesignated as the 'Ar-2' in December 1940 under the new Soviet aircraft naming convention. By March 1941, 198 Ar-2s had been built, when production was stopped so resources could be allocated to the Pe-2 dive bomber.

The defensive armament of the Ar-2 consisted of a ShKAS machine gun on a ball mounting in the extreme nose, which gave it a 50-degree range of movement, a ShKAS mounted on a TUR-9 semi-circular mounting in the top of the aft fuselage, and a ShKAS attached to a retractable MV-2 mount on the aft fuselage underside.

In service, the Ar-2 was considered to be an improvement over the SB, with superior performance and handling, better vision for the pilot and navigator, and its dive-bombing capabilities were considered good. Like other Soviet bombers of the early 1940s, such as the SB and the Il-4 (DB-3), it suffered from a weak defensive armament (although it was considered to be more effective than that for most SBs). It also suffered from engine cooling problems—another common complaint with various Soviet aircraft. Many Ar-2s were destroyed in the opening stages of the Great Patriotic War, as it was assigned to front-line units, alongside the SB, which units bore the brunt of the initial German assault. It continued to be used in diminishing numbers until as late as 1943, when it disappeared from service. As it served in units alongside the much more famous SB, its wartime exploits are not well-recorded. Apparently, none survived until the end of the Second World War.

Conclusion

As few were produced (under 200), with many of these destroyed in the initial phases of the conflict, the Ar-2 had no great effect upon the Great Patriotic War, although it was used in ever-diminishing numbers until 1943.

Pe-2

This twin-engined aircraft, designed by Vladimir Petlyakov, was originally a high-altitude fighter project, designated as the '100' and designed, like Andrey Tupolev's Tu-2 ('103' or 'ANT-58', described further on), while Petlyakov was still under NKVD detention. As the VI-100, it first flew on 22 December 1939. However, what the VVS desired and needed at the time was a modern dive bomber (the VVS had seen the success of the German Ju 87 dive bomber in Western Europe), not a high-altitude fighter. The VVS already had the MiG-1 high-altitude fighter being developed, which would be able to handle any high-flying attackers. In addition, the Soviets had purchased and examined the twin-engined Ju 88 in 1940, which was capable of dive-bombing and were impressed enough to want a twin-engined dive bomber of their own. Therefore, the Pe-2, as it was named from 1942, was redesigned from a fighter into a dive bomber.

First entering service in 1940, the Pe-2 was used throughout the Great Patriotic War as a dive bomber, level bomber, reconnaissance aircraft, and ground-attack aircraft. It

Crew in front of their Ar-2 in the winter of 1941–42. (*Viktor Kulikov's collection*)

Close-up of the nose section of an Ar-2. Compared to the SB, which the Ar-2 was developed from, the nose is much more streamlined and mounts only a single machine gun on a gimballed mount. Note the quilted cover over the starboard engine to provide it with some protection from the winter cold (the port engine would have been similarly adorned). (*Viktor Kulikov's collection*)

generally replaced Tupolev SBs in front-line service. Even after the entry into service of the Tu-2 twin-engined tactical bomber, it continued to be used as a dive bomber as it was found to be more suitable for that role than the Tu-2, which had originally been designed and built with that capability (having also been influenced by the Ju 88). A dedicated fighter version, the Pe-3, was also built, although only in small numbers. In service, the Pe-2 was sometimes known as the *Peshka* or 'Pawn'.

The Pe-2 was notable for being the aircraft of a mainly female-equipped bomber regiment, the 587th BAP. This polk later became the 125th Guards Dive Bomber Regiment in September 1943. Five members of the polk were awarded the title of the Hero of the Soviet Union, including Mariya Dolina, who graces the cover of this book. During the war, the polk flew 1,134 missions and dropped over 980 tons of bombs.

With the death of Vladimir Petlyakov in a crash in a Pe-2 on 12 January 1942, Aleksandr M. Izakson became head of the OKB. Izakson was then replaced by Aleksandr I. Putilov in the spring of 1942, who was, in turn, replaced by Vladimir M. Myasishchev in the middle of 1943. Myasishchev continued to develop the Pe-2 as head of the OKB until the end of the war (the Petlyakov OKB was dissolved in 1946). Myasishchev was given his own OKB in 1951 (OKB-23 was his second OKB; his first OKB, OKB-482, had been dissolved in 1946), which went on to develop a jet-powered strategic bomber that became the M-4/3M Bison.

The Pe-2 continued to be used post-war in the Soviet Union and other countries, when it was given the NATO nickname of 'Buck'. The Pe-2 was provided by the Soviet Union post-war to Soviet Bloc or Communist countries, such as Poland, Bulgaria, Hungary, and Yugoslavia. The Pe-2 was the most heavily produced twin-engined bomber in Soviet history, with over 11,000 being produced (sources differ on the exact number built, with two sources having 11,247 produced, another having 11,427, and one purporting to be from official sources 11,070; perhaps it depends on if the Pe-3 fighter is included). Whatever the exact number, it was four times the number of Tu-2s that were produced—nearly twice the number of either SBs or Il-4s.

Development

Although Vladimir Petlyakov had been arrested by the NKVD, this did not mean that the NKVD excused him from his aeronautical work. Indeed, Petlyakov was a part of the same *sharashka* (special prison) where Tupolev designed the aircraft that became the Tu-2.

VI-100

In response to a requirement for a high-altitude fighter, Petlyakov designed the VI-100 (the 'VI' stood for *Vysotniy Istrebitel* or 'High-altitude Fighter'). The aircraft that emerged was a very clean monoplane fighter, with fully retractable main landing gear and a fully retractable tailwheel, all landing gear being completely enclosed by doors. In keeping with the generally sleek appearance of the VI-100, it was equipped with inline M-105R engines mounted in streamlined cowlings. As befitted its high-altitude role, the VI-100 had two pressurised cabins for the two crew members (the pilot and the observer/rear-gunner), who were housed in a single long fairing, and the M-105R engines were equipped with TK-2 turbo-superchargers. The turbo-superchargers fed compressed air to the pressurised cabins. The aircraft was armed with two ShVAK 20-mm cannons and two ShKAS 7.62-mm machine guns fixed in the solid nose cone, as well as a single ShKAS fixed in the tail cone firing aft for defensive purposes. The ability to load bombs under the wings was looked at, so the aircraft could be used as a fighter-bomber (there was no internal bomb bay). It was unusual for a Soviet aircraft for the number of systems that were electrically operated by small servo-motors; this resulted from the pressurisation of the aircraft as it was easier to seal electrical cable openings than openings for conventional linkage cables.

The VI-100 was first flown on 22 December 1939 by test pilot Pyotr M. Stefanovskiy. The aircraft achieved a top speed of 334 mph (538 kph) at an altitude of 13,123 feet (4,000 m).

Since it was believed that high-altitude bombers would not be a major problem for the Soviet Union in any conflict with Germany (and that indeed proved to be the case), it was decided to modify the VI-100 into a dive bomber, which it was felt was needed. The Soviets were duly impressed by the success of the Ju 87 dive bomber in

The VI-100 prototype, the predecessor to the Pe-2. (*Viktor Kulikov's collection*)

A side-view of the VI-100. (*Viktor Kulikov's collection*)

the German conquests of Poland and Western Europe; they were also impressed by the dive-bombing capabilities of the twin-engined Ju 88, which they had examined in great detail. This was clearly a case of 'we want one of those, too'.

PB-100

With the decision to stop the development of the VI-100 as a high-altitude fighter and to develop it into a dive bomber, Petlyakov was given all of a month and a half to effect this complete change in mission. Things moved quickly in Josef Stalin's Soviet Union, especially when the *Vozhd* wanted it so. Accordingly, the Petlyakov OKB dutifully set about to modify the VI-100 into the 'PB-100' ('PB' standing for *Pikiruyushchiy Bombardirovshchik* or 'Dive Bomber'). The TK-2 superchargers and pressurised cabins of the VI-100 were removed as unnecessary for the PB-100 in its new role, where it would be operated from medium and low altitudes. The other modifications that turned the PB-100 into the production Pe-2 are described further on.

Pe-2 Production Series

Below I shall describe some of the most important or interesting series of the Pe-2. The Pe-2 was normally known just as the 'Pe-2', without any other designation or suffix, so the series number was important to know in order to understand the equipment standard for each particular aircraft. Of course, retrofits and modifications in the field rather muddied the picture, but the series number still gives a good general idea of the fit (and performance) of each Pe-2.

Pe-2 Series 1

The first production series of the Pe-2, as the PB-100 had been renamed in 1940, differed in many respects from the original VI-100 fighter and the modified PB-100. Its fuselage was significantly different, with a cockpit cabin replacing the two cabins of the VI-100/PB-100 that had been connected by a long dorsal fairing. The pilot and the navigator were housed in this new cabin, which featured a single canopy affording all-around vision. The vertical tails were redesigned and made larger; the portion of the horizontal tail planes that had extended beyond the vertical tail planes was deleted. The solid nose was replaced by an extensively glazed nose, which enabled the pilot to see the target while dive-bombing.

The armament fit now comprised a single moveable ShKAS machine gun for the navigator, firing from the aft portion of the canopy, with a 'turtle deck' that retracted into the fuselage to enable him to fire his gun. This turtle deck was raised when the weapon was not in use in order to streamline the aircraft. Another ShKAS was placed in a ventral position on the aft fuselage, to be fired by the radio operator, who now became the third crew member (the VI-100 had only two crewmen). The nose armament consisted of two more ShKAS machine guns fixed in the nose and operated by the pilot, the ShVAK cannons of the VI-100 being deleted. The engines remained the M-105R, but these were now without the redundant TK-2 turbo-superchargers of the VI-100.

This earliest Pe-2 series compared favourably with the German Bf 109E fighter in terms of speed. At an altitude of 16,404 feet (5,000 m), its top speed was 335.5 mph

Above: An early Pe-2; note the natural metal propeller blades and the rear gunner's streamlined 'turtle deck'. (*Viktor Kulikov's collection*)

Right: A crew in front of their early Pe-2. Note the natural metal propellers, the clear nose cone, and the extensive under nose glazing, which was reduced over the Pe-2's production run. (*Viktor Kulikov's collection*)

A Pe-2 in white winter camouflage in flight. In this instance, the rear gunner's turtle deck has been retracted. (*Viktor Kulikov's collection*)

Only partially winter-camouflaged, this Pe-2 also features the retracted turtle deck. (*Viktor Kulikov's collection*)

One of the Pe-2s captured by the Finnish, this aircraft has been repainted in Finnish markings. Note that the small windshield for the radio operator has been deployed on the middle fuselage. (*Viktor Kulikov's collection*)

(540 kph), while the Bf 109E-3 had a top speed of 336 mph (540.7 kph) at 19,685 feet (6,000 m). This parity would change as the war went on, and the Germans upgraded their equipment with the Bf 109F and G fighters, as well as the Fw 190 fighter. On the other hand, with more equipment, heavier armament, and heavier armour, the speed of the Pe-2 dropped in the series succeeding the Series 1. This was not helped by the often poor fit and finish of the rapidly produced Pe-2s. With more powerful engines and better streamlining, later series of the Pe-2 would regain much of this lost speed, but they never again would achieve parity with the German fighters in terms of horizontal speed.

Pe-2 Series 13

Some of the complaints regarding the Pe-2 centred on its armament. In this series, one of the two ShKAS guns in the nose, the starboard one, was replaced by a more powerful UBK 12.7-mm (50-calibre) machine gun. The ventral ShKAS, which had suffered from stoppage problems, was replaced by a UBT.

Pe-2 Series 22

In this series of the Pe-2, the engine was upgraded from the M-105R to the M-105RA, equipped with a VISh-61B propeller, which was optimised for this engine.

Pe-2 Series 83 (Pe-2FT)

One of the shortcomings of the Pe-2 that became apparent with combat experience was the lack of enough defensive firepower. The 7.62-mm (30-calibre) ShKAS machine gun that the navigator/gunner used was found to be relatively ineffective against the sturdy aircraft of the Luftwaffe. To alleviate this deficiency, a 12.7-mm (50-calibre) UBT machine gun was mounted in the navigator/gunner's gun position in the rear of the cockpit cabin. The gun was not mounted in a turret, but in an open position mounted on tubes that extended from the crash pylon into the fuselage, which allowed the gunner a wide field of fire. The field of fire was 45 degrees to either side, and the gun could be elevated from 45 degrees upward to -6 degrees downward. The retractable turtle deck fairing was dispensed with.

The 'FT' in the informal designation 'Pe-2FT' apparently stood for *Frontovoiy Trebovaniye* ('Frontal Request'), as it was the result of requests from frontal units for a Pe-2 with a more effective defensive armament. Although the position was open to the environment, which must have been none too comfortable for the gunner especially in winter, the extra defensive power of the heavy UBT machine gun was undeniable and appreciated. As a result, besides being introduced on the production line, aircraft in the field were modified with this new gun position, which took two specialists from four to six hours to fit. The designation 'Pe-2FT' is sometimes used in literature for those series of the Pe-2 equipped with the VUB-1 turret, but this is incorrect.

Pe-2 Series 105

In this series, the RPK-2 radio-compass/direction finder was replaced by the more modern and longer-ranged RPK-10 radio-compass/direction finder. The RPK-10 was mounted as an external loop antenna under the nose, replacing the streamlined under nose fairing of the RPK-2.

Pe-2 Series 110

A major upgrade to the defensive armament was made with the provision of a true, rotating turret mounting for the UBT with this series. Although the FT mounting had improved the defensive firepower of the Pe-2, it was open at the back and was uncomfortable for the navigator/gunner, especially in winter. This was solved with the fully enclosed turret of this series, the VUB-1 turret, which had been specifically created for the Pe-2 by Petlyakov designer I. I. Toropov. This turret had a theoretical traverse of 110 degrees to port, 88 degrees to starboard, and 55 degrees upward. However, in practice, the movement was initially limited to 45–50 degrees to either side due to the slipstream hitting the gun. This problem was solved by fitting two small vanes or 'ears' that counterbalanced the airflow; this was later reduced to one vane. All Pe-2 series from this series on carried the VUB-1 turret.

A ShKAS machine gun was provided for the radio operator/gunner to operate from round windows in the sides of the fuselage, the weapon being moveable from one side to the other. Extra armour protection was provided for the crew.

The series 110 first left the production line in June 1942 and went into service, seeing heavy combat use at Stalingrad.

Photographed during take-off in the winter of 1943, this Pe-2 shows the FT gun installation, with the UBT machine gun. (*Viktor Kulikov's collection*)

This rear view of a Pe-2 shows an example fitted with the FT gun mounting. It appears to also have the *Gneis* radar, as evidenced by the multiple aerials. (*Viktor Kulikov's collection*)

Turret-armed Pe-2s in flight. (*Viktor Kulikov's collection*)

Pe-2 Series 179

This version featured the more powerful M-105PF engines (with 1,260 hp at take-off) replacing the M-105RA engines. This engine was also used with the Yak-1, the Yak-7, and the LaGG-3 fighters. The M-105PF was maximised for use at low and medium altitudes. The maximum speed of the Pe-2, which had degraded with the addition of more armour and armament, was now increased by 15.5 mph (25 kph). Some of the older versions of the Pe-2 with the M-105RA engines were re-engined with the M-105PF. Due to the different mounting of the M-105PF (the propeller shaft was mounted 2.36 inches (60 mm) higher than that of the M-105RA), the cowlings had to be modified to take the new engines, with the resultant gaps covered with riveted inserts. Despite the new engines, the propellers used with the M-105RA continued to be utilised, the VISh-61B, which were not optimised for the new engines.

Pe-2 Series 205

This series featured various modifications to enhance the streamlining and aerodynamics of the Pe-2. One of these modifications involved improved sealing of the joints of the often-ill-fitting parts. The VUB-1 turret was also modified to have one vane (or 'ear') instead of the two vanes that had characterised the earlier versions of the turret. The engine cowlings were better streamlined by the deletion of two small inlets on both sides. Fairings were placed in front of the dive brakes. The combination antenna mast and pitot tube were also moved forward.

One of the members of the all-woman Pe-2 regiment (the 125th GvBAP), Mariya Dolina, who became a Hero of the Soviet Union, is seen standing in front of one of the regiment's Pe-2s. Note the exhaust stubs instead of the collector tubes on the engine. These were first introduced on the series 205. (*Public Domain*)

Another member of the 125th GvBAP, Ekaterina Fedotova, is seen in the cockpit of her swallow-adorned Pe-2. (*Viktor Kulikov's collection*)

During the run of the series 205, ejector tube exhausts were introduced on about 100 aircraft, replacing the collector tubes used previously on the Pe-2. This modification gave a small amount of increased thrust from the exhaust. The Pe-2 series 205 had a top speed of 323.7 mph (521 kph) at 12,139 feet (3,700 m) as compared to the top speed of 303.2 mph (488 kph) of the Pe-2 Series 95.

The first of the series 205 production aircraft left the Z.22 line in June 1943, just in time for Operation Citadel, the battle for the Kursk salient. By the time of the Kursk battle in July 1943, the Pe-2 had become the most numerous multi-engined bomber in Soviet service.

Pe-2 Series 211

On this series, the exterior bomb fittings were placed in the wing instead of in teardrop-shaped fairings, no doubt to reduce drag (as had been done on the experimental Pe-2A). The propellers were changed to the VISh-61P, which now took full advantage of the additional power provided by the M-105PF engine. Despite the heavier weight of these Pe-2s as compared to earlier versions, the top speed was increased from 3–19 mph (5–30 kph) over the 1943 production aircraft, depending on the altitude.

Pe-2 Series 275

The defensive armament of the Pe-2 received a very interesting upgrade with this series; ten aerial grenades (AG-2) dispensed from a DAG-10 installation in the tail (one source has these installed from the Series 179). These grenades were equipped with parachutes and were supposed to explode in the path of any pursuing fighters. Even if the fighter was not destroyed, the grenade explosion would no doubt come as a great surprise and cause a certain amount of concern to the fighter pilot, even causing him to cease his pursuit. Evidently, not all aircraft of this series were so equipped.

Pe-2 Series 301

With this series, the upper hatch for the radio operator/gunner was changed (one source states that this change was introduced on the Series 310). The hatch was redesigned so that the retractable windscreen was now located in front of the hatch instead of being an integral part of it. The hatch had been designed in the first place to enable the radio operator/gunner to look out the back of the aircraft, thus allowing him to search for any pursuing fighters, if the navigator was disabled and unable to do so.

Pe-2 Series 354

With this series, the individual engine ejector tube exhausts that had been fitted to some series 205 aircraft were made standard, the collector tubes now being discarded.

Pe-2 Series 359

Besides featuring the revised radio operator's hatch, this series also featured improved sights, radio equipment, and oxygen equipment. All the aircraft of this series featured the individual exhaust stubs, which had been made standard with the Series 354 aircraft.

Pe-2 Series 382

This series was equipped with a self-starting system for winter operations.

Pe-2 M-82 (Pe-4)

Due to concerns about the continuing availability of the M-105 engine, which was also used for the Yakovlev and LaGG-3 fighters, the possibility of re-engining the Pe-2 was explored. It was decided to fit the powerful new Shvetsov M-82 radial engines to the Pe-2 airframe; this was done experimentally with other aircraft at this time such as the Il-2 and the Il-4. It was also hoped that this engine change would enhance the performance of the Pe-2. As the Pe-2 was twin-engined, most of the modifications were limited to the engine nacelles, which, of course, had to be redesigned to accommodate the larger diameter radial engines. The nacelles were made not just wider, but longer, and the rear bomb bays were removed. The now unnecessary cooling intakes on the wing leading edge were removed, and the landing gear were lengthened, which resulted in the main wheels being situated 2.36 inches (60 mm) forward as compared to M-105-powered Pe-2s.

The first Pe-2 M-82 flew for the initial time in June 1942 near Z.22 (which was located in Kazan'). Unfortunately, the M-82 was still an underdeveloped engine at this time and the aircraft suffered because of its unreliability. One big problem was the tendency for the engines to catch fire on start-up, never a good thing. Despite these problems, on one test flight, the aircraft displayed a top speed of 339 mph (545 kph) at 19,357 feet (5,900 m), which was some 31–34 mph (50–55 kph) higher than the Pe-2s being manufactured during the winter of 1942–43. This improved performance persuaded the OKB to continue testing this variant, despite its problems. In January, state tests started at the NII VVS at Kratovo. Around fifty test flights were conducted between January and March 1943.

The production Pe-2 M-82s were able to match this top speed of 339 mph (545 kph) at 20,341 feet (6,200 m). The Pe-2 M-82s were equipped with the AV-5L-118 propeller, which had a larger spinner than that fitted to the propeller for the M-105 engine. Thirty-two production aircraft were produced at Z.22 in 1943, with the first leaving the plant in August 1943.

Thirty-two aircraft was not a large production run and two factors kept this number down. The first was that the M-82FN (ASh-82FN) engines used by the Pe-2 M-82 were needed for the La-5 fighters, and there were persistent problems with the oil coolant system for the M-82s on the Pe-2 M-82. Of the thirty-two production aircraft, only twenty-four were actually accepted by the VVS. These served mainly with RAPs (*Razvedivatel'niy Aviatsionniy Polk:* 'Reconnaissance Air Regiment'), with aircraft assigned to the 48th GvDRAP (*Gvardiya Dalniy Razvedivatel'niy Aviatsionniy Polk*: 'Guards Long-Range Reconnaissance Air Regiment'), the 57th GvDRAP, and the 99th GvDRAP. Some also served with the 11th ODAP (Independent Reconnaissance Aviation Regiment) and the 39th ODAP. For reconnaissance purposes, the aircraft were equipped with the AFA-B camera and the dive brakes were removed.

The VVS had decreed that from 21 June 1943, the Pe-2 M-82 was to be known as the 'Pe-4' but evidently, this designation was not commonly used. It is not clear from

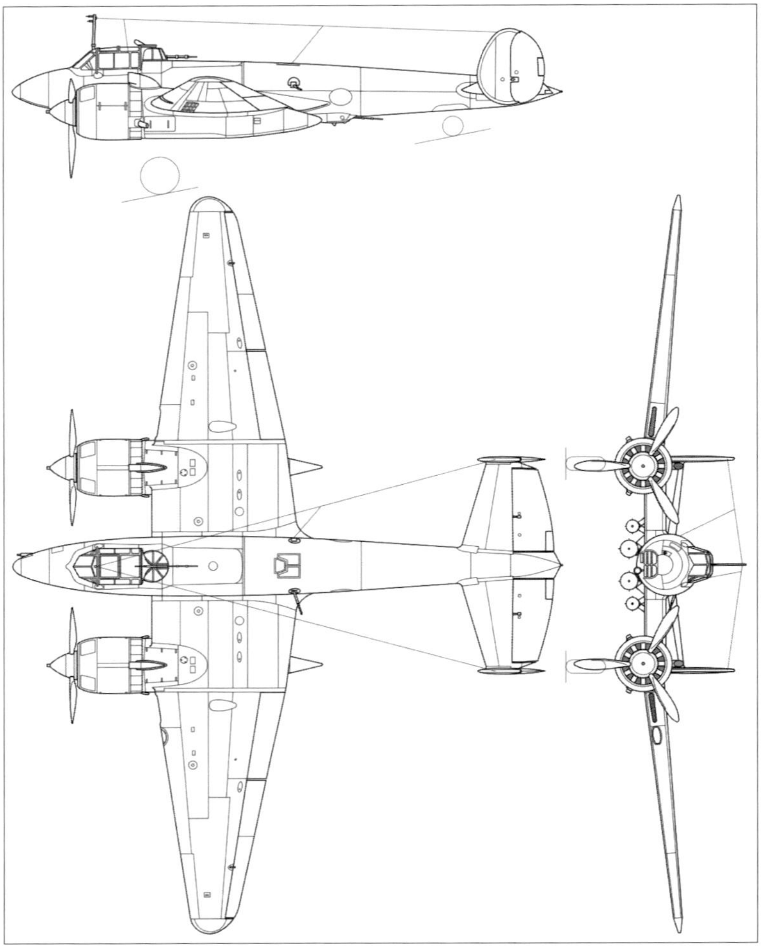

Three-view drawing of a Pe-2 M-82. (*By Kaboldy. Wikimedia*)

Side view of the Pe-2 M-82 (Pe-4). (*Viktor Kulikov's collection*)

Three-quarters rear view of the Pe-2 M-82. The wooden 'beaver tail' shows up to good advantage here. (*Viktor Kulikov's collection*)

the record how long the Pe-2 M-82s remained in service, but they may have served until the end of the Great Patriotic War. Since the M-82 was in large-scale service from 1943, procuring replacement parts and engines would not have been a problem with the Pe-2 M-82.

Pe-2R

With good range, good speed, and an adequate payload the Pe-2 was a natural for a long-range reconnaissance aircraft. Pe-2s built or modified for this role were designated 'Pe-2R' where the 'R' stood for *Razvedchik* or 'Reconnaissance' in Russian. Both production Pe-2Rs and those modified in the field had the redundant dive brakes removed and cameras added. Extra fuel was added in the form of two 76.6-gal (290-l) drop tanks, which added 311 miles (500 km) to the Pe-2R's range. Some 700 to 800 Pe-2Rs may have been produced as such, and they would have had the same modifications as the Pe-2 bombers that were being produced at the same time.

Pe-3

Given that the Pe-2 design had started out as a fighter, it was perhaps inevitable that it would also be built in that role, and it was indeed produced as a fighter, as the Pe-3 (odd numbers being used for fighters). Although built as a fighter, this version of the Pe-2 is included here as it still retained some of the bombing capability of the Pe-2 and was often used as a bomber, despite its reduced bomb load. It was also used as a reconnaissance aircraft alongside the Pe-2.

The circumstances of the Pe-3's genesis were rather remarkable. The Soviets felt that they needed a twin-engined fighter, something along the lines of the German Bf 110. They also felt that due to the need to get this aircraft into production as quickly as possible (a war was on), it needed to be based upon an existing design. The obvious

With the propeller blades now painted black, this Pe-2 shows to good advantage the circular antenna of the direction finder. This aircraft may be a reconnaissance version as it appears to have some apparatus protruding from the bomb bay, perhaps cameras, and it carries two drop tanks to increase its range. (*Viktor Kulikov's collection*)

choice was the Pe-2, which had originally been designed as a fighter (the VI-100). The GKO issued a decree on 2 August 1941 for Petlyakov to create this new fighter, with the prototype ready for delivery by 6 August 1941. Amazingly, Petlyakov was able to suitably modify a Pe-2 into the Pe-3 in this timeframe, and this aircraft was flown for the first time on 7 August 1941, by Maj. Fyodorov. On 8 August 1941, NII VVS test pilot Col. Vasiliy A. Stepanchonok completed the manufacturer's tests and the Pe-3 was submitted for state testing. This must have set some sort of record for accelerated development and testing of an aircraft, even in the wartime Soviet Union.

Among the changes made to the Pe-3 as compared to the Pe-2 was the deletion of the radio operator/gunner, leaving a two-member crew. As a result, the ventral gondola and the rear-firing gun were deleted, although a small ventral fairing was still present.

Pe-3bis

This variant of the Pe-3 was an effort to upgrade this aircraft, especially in regards to its gun armament. One of the main complaints of the Pe-3 was the relatively light forward-firing armament in the nose. It had only one ShVAK 20-mm cannon and one ShKAS 7.62-mm machine gun, compared to the powerful armament of two 20-mm cannons and four 7.92-mm machine guns of the equivalent Bf 110.

Interestingly, part of the impetus for the changes that resulted in the Pe-3bis resulted from a letter from a squadron commanded named Captain Zhatkov to Secretary of the Council of People's Commissars Georgiy Maksimilianovich Malenkov (1902–88). In this remarkable letter, Captain Zhatkov complained about the armament, stating the need for ShVAK cannons in the nose, and the replacement of the defensive ShKAS of the navigator with a UBT machine gun. Captain Zhatkov's criticisms, and those of other pilots, were taken to heart and the Petlyakov OKB made changes in September 1941 to a Pe-3 to modify it into what became the Pe-3bis. The modified aircraft was tested in September and October 1941.

One of the main changes between the Pe-3bis and the earlier Pe-3s was the provision of the VUB-1 turret, which greatly improved the defensive armament. The nose was equipped with two UBK machine guns and one ShVAK 20-mm cannon. The wings were now equipped with leading edge slats to improve take-off and landing characteristics, never the Pe-2/Pe-3's strength. The production Pe-3bis served with the Pe-3 in four VVS regiments from 1942.

Pe-2UT (UPe-2)

Given the much less than perfect landing characteristics of the Pe-2 (it had a high landing speed, was prone to stall, and had an incipient bounce upon landing), it was decided that a trainer version was needed. In this variant, the normal cockpit was kept, but a new cockpit, complete with a sliding canopy and duplicate controls was situated immediately aft. The instructor-pilot sat in this cockpit, with the trainee in the front cockpit. The turret had to be deleted to accommodate the instructor's cockpit, but the Pe-2UT ('UT' for *Uchebno-Trenirovochniy*: 'Primary Trainer') retained machine guns in the nose and in the ventral position, and could carry bombs for bombing practice. The instructor-pilot had a relatively poor view forward, but it was still considered sufficient. The instructor and the trainee were able to communicate through a SPU-3 intercom system. The trainee's controls were automatically disconnected when the instructor took control. Sometimes, the Pe-2UT was known as the 'UPe-2', the 'U' standing for *Uchebniy* or 'Trainer'.

Despite this need for a trainer version, the first Pe-2UT was not test flown at the NII VVS until September 1943. Production of the Pe-2UT proceeded at Z.22, where all of them were built. The Pe-2UT was modified in line with the bomber version, incorporating the various improvements introduced to the bomber. In all 671 Pe-2UTs were built new.

After the war, Pe-2UTs were delivered to Bulgaria, Czechoslovakia, and Poland. The Czechoslovakian versions were designated as the CB-32. The Polish received eleven Pe-2UTs in total.

Combat Tactics

In order for an aeroplane to be properly utilised, the correct tactics need to be devised for it. The single man most responsible for developing the proper combat tactics for the Pe-2 as a dive bomber was twice Hero of the Soviet Union Ivan Semyonovich Polbin (1905–45).

At the beginning of the Great Patriotic War, the Pe-2 was used as a level bomber because the pilots and crew had not had time to be properly trained to use it in its intended role as a dive bomber. Due to this, accuracy suffered and the aircraft was made more vulnerable to fighters and flak, as it had to fly straight and level before releasing its bombs.

Although shown standing in front of an SB, twice Hero of the Soviet Union Ivan Semyonovich Polbin was the most important Pe-2 tactician, who perfected the Pe-2's combat tactics. (*Viktor Kulikov's collection*)

In an effort to utilise the Pe-2 in its intended role as a dive bomber, Lt Col. (at the time) Polbin in early 1942 instituted a formation for use by his unit's Pe-2s called the *Vertushka* or 'Merry-go-round'. This involved having the Pe-2s form up in a circle at 1,640–1,969 feet (500–600 m) intervals, diving at 70 degrees on the target. As one of the Pe-2s was pulling up out of its dive, another was already diving; this kept the target under constant attack, putting tremendous pressure on the Axis defences. These tactics were similar to those being tried out on the Il-2, except that the diving angle was much greater. Col. Polbin also sought to improve the escort fighter coverage of the Pe-2. To this end, the fighters were divided into a group which provided high cover for the Pe-2s, and a lower group of two or three fighters that would even follow the Pe-2s into the dive to provide close cover. These tactics improved the bombing accuracy and reduced losses from flak and enemy fighters.

Col. Polbin was not the only Soviet airman working on improving the Pe-2's tactics, as in August 1942, Col. A. G. Fedorov was directed to begin working on a paper incorporating combat experiences and recommendations for the Pe-2. This paper included the ideas of Col. Polbin. In addition to the combat tactics of Col. Polbin, the paper also explained better ways to take off and land in the somewhat tricky Pe-2. The Pe-2 could take off more easily when power was applied to the port engine, which counteracted the tendency of the aircraft to veer to the right. He also worked to improve the landing of the Pe-2, so the tendency of the aircraft to bounce could be lessened. Together, these improvements in the usage of the Pe-2 greatly boosted its ability as a combat aircraft. Improvements in the armour, armament, and engine power over time only enhanced this ability.

Col. Polbin's contributions to the Pe-2's combat effectiveness did not go unnoticed and he was eventually promoted to the rank of Major-General. Unfortunately, on 11 February 1945, his fortieth birthday, General Polbin was killed in action. By this time, the aircraft he had done so much to improve had greatly helped to ensure the impending defeat of the Third Reich.

Experimental Versions

Pe-2A

In an attempt to improve the Pe-2's performance, the Petlyakov OKB, with the TsAGI's assistance, created the Pe-2A in 1943. Since the first Pe-2 series, the performance, especially the top speed, had been steadily decreasing, due to the weight of increased armour and armament and the poor fit and finish of the heavily and quickly produced Pe-2s. By 1943, some Pe-2s were struggling to reach 300 mph (483 kph). The Pe-2A was an attempt to find ways to reverse this unfortunate trend.

To improve the streamlining, the RPK-10 DF loop was relocated to inside the wooden nose cone. The water radiators were enlarged and the shape of the intakes was improved, and the external bomb racks were relocated into the wings. Some of these changes made their way into the production Pe-2s; for example, the internally mounted bomb racks were introduced from the series 211 Pe-2s on.

Pe-2B

The Pe-2A was not the only major effort to increase the performance of the Pe-2, and the Pe-2B was built to explore further means of improvement. This aircraft was built in 1944. The Pe-2B was characterised by the improved 'FZ' gun mount and new wooden outer wings with a new aerofoil (NACA 230) and an increase in wing area which improved the landing characteristics. These wings were later replaced by metal outer wings with the NACA 230 aerofoil limited to the leading edge back to the front spar.

Pe-2D

This was a bomber variant fitted with the VK-107A engines in September 1944. Little else is recorded of this experimental Pe-2 version.

Pe-2F

The low-mounted wing of the Pe-2, which had been inherited from its fighter predecessor, the VI-100, was not optimal for accommodating an internal bomb bay and limited the size of the bombs that could be carried internally. The Pe-2F attempted to rectify this by moving the bottom of the middle fuselage down by nearly 1 foot, 11.8 inches (300 mm) relative to the wings. The larger main wheels that were also fitted necessitated the deletion of the nacelle bomb bays, so the maximum internal bomb load remained the same at 1,323 lb (600 kg), although larger bombs could now be fitted internally. In addition, the maximum bomb load overall was increased to 3,307 lb (1,500 kg) as compared to the standard Pe-2's normal maximum load of 2,205 lb (1,000 kg).

In addition to the change in the wing/fuselage junction, the tankage was changed from eleven to twelve tanks, and the water radiator intake for the engine was made larger and adjustable. After initial flight testing in 1942, the Pe-2F was re-equipped with the Klimov M-107 engines, which were more powerful than the original M-105 engines. The aircraft was first tested with the new M-107 engines on 30 September 1942. However, at this time, the very underdeveloped M-107 was clearly unsuitable for flight operations and nearly every flight ended in a forced landing because of engine problems. Due to this, production Pe-2s were not equipped with the M-107.

Pe-2 FZ

Both the FT installation and the VUB-1 turret were not without flaws, so an attempt to create a better installation for the navigator/gunner resulted in the Pe-2FZ in 1943. The 'FZ' turret was fitted with two UBT machine guns, as opposed to the one UBT of the VUB-1 turret and the FT installation. At the same time, the canopy was raised for the pilot and navigator which gave them more room in the cockpit, which improved their comfort and efficiency. However, even though tests conducted in 1943 were successful and this modified aircraft was recommended for production, none were produced, probably because of concerns that it would affect the production rate of the Pe-2. One factor that may have also contributed to the decision not to proceed with the production plans of the Pe-2 FZ was the efforts to develop the Pe-2I, described below, which promised much higher performance for the Pe-2.

Pe-2I

This was an attempt to create a Soviet analogue to the British Mosquito, which the Pe-2 had already been compared to. Instead of adding more armour and armament, which had been the trend in Pe-2 production, the Pe-2I reduced the defensive armament, the crew was reduced to two, and the bomb load was limited to the internal carriage. In addition, more powerful VK-107A engines were fitted (these engines had a maximum horsepower of 1,650 compared to the 1,260 of the M-105PF). This was done in an effort to make the Pe-2 faster, so it could rely more upon speed as opposed to defensive firepower to protect itself from enemy fighters. The 'I' in the name may have been for *Istrebitel'* or 'Fighter', although with only one gun in the nose it is hard to see how this aircraft would have made much of a fighter. It is possible that a fighter role may have also been envisaged for this aircraft, with a stronger forward-firing armament. It was also possible that it the 'I' was an internal OKB designation that had nothing to do with it being a fighter (or used as a fighter).

Two guns were to be fitted: one of the new Berezin B-20 20-mm cannon under the nose (although a Berezin 12.7-mm machine gun was fitted to the prototypes and production aircraft instead) and a remote-controlled UB 12.7-mm machine gun in a tail barbette, which had limited traverse and was operated by the navigator.

The aircraft first flew on 6 April 1944, flown by Captain A. G. Vasilchenko. Despite problems with the temperamental VK-107A engines, the aircraft achieved very good performance, showing a speed of 345 mph (556 kph) at sea level (faster than any production Pe-2's top speed at any altitude) and a maximum overall speed of 408 mph (656 kph). In addition, Vasilchenko found the Pe-2I to be easier to handle than the standard Pe-2. The aircraft had a service ceiling of 36,809 feet (11,000 m). In tests with a captured Bf 109G-4, the German aircraft was unable to catch the Pe-2I at any altitude up to 22,966 feet (7,000 m). It should be remembered that captured aircraft were not always in optimum condition due to them having sometimes been well-used even before their capture and possible repair. However, even taking this into account, the Pe-2I showed impressive capabilities when flown against this captured fighter aircraft.

There were problems such as the long take-off run and the problematic engines; nonetheless, by the end of May 1944, it was decided to build a small batch of production Pe-2Is at Z.22. However, by October 1944, these aircraft had still not been built due to the desire not to disturb the production of the standard Pe-2s and the difficulty in solving the issues with the VK-107A engine. There were also delivery problems with the remote-controlled tail barbette.

By November 1944, the second prototype of the Pe-2I had passed its state tests. However, production of the first aircraft of the small series of Pe-2Is was not completed until February 1945. It does not appear that any of these five production Pe-2Is were ever issued to service units and the type was never produced in quantity due to reliability problems that were never solved.

Pe-2M

Providing more powerful offensive and defensive armament to the Pe-2 had been a constant theme during the production of this aircraft, and the Pe-2M, based upon the Series 359 airframe, represented a last effort to do so, in addition to improving the general performance at the same time. The 'M' in the name apparently stood for *Modifitsirovanniy* or 'Modified'. The new Berezin B-20 20-mm cannons were installed in a fixed position in the nose, in the navigator's turret, and in the ventral position for the radio operator. Like the Pe-2I, the Pe-2M used the VK-107A engines, which provided much more power than the standard M-105PFs of the production Pe-2s. The Pe-2M left the plant in September 1944.

The Pe-2M displayed impressive performance with a top speed of 391 mph (630 kph) at 16,404 feet (5,000 m). A widened fuselage allowed the internal carriage of 4,409 lb (2,000 kg) of bombs compared to the 1,323-lb (600-kg) internal bomb load of the production Pe-2. However, many defects were also noted, many of them involving the VK-107A engines. In any event, as of June 1945, all development on the Pe-2 was ordered to stop, in part because of the presence of the generally superior Tu-2, whose production and development was continued post-war. As a consequence, only four Pe-2Ms were constructed, with none going to the VVS.

Pe-2 M-1

In the OKB's continuing effort to improve the performance of the Pe-2, the experimental Klimov M-1s were installed on this example. The M-1 was developed from the M-105 and was generally the same size and shape, but the cylinders were increased in bore. The engine had 1,350 hp at sea level. A distinctive feature of the new engine installation was the fitting of three sets of exhausts per engine, with one set on each side of the engine as per usual practice, but with another set of exhausts on the top of the engine nacelle.

With these engines installed, the Pe-2 M-1 exhibited a top speed of 357 mph (575 kph) at 20,341 feet (6,200 m). Despite the increase in top speed, the Pe-2 M-1 was not proceeded with as the Klimov OKB decided not to put the M-1 engine into production.

The Pe-2 in Detail

Since the Pe-2 was in large-scale production throughout the war and underwent many design changes, there is no such thing as a 'typical' Pe-2. However, below I will describe the Pe-2 series 205 as a sort of 'typical' mid-to-late Pe-2, armed with the VUB-1 dorsal turret. In some instances, I will note differences between earlier and later series Pe-2s.

General Description

The Pe-2 was a mainly metal, low-winged, twin-engined cantilever monoplane with a fully retractable main landing gear and a fully retractable tailwheel. The pilot and navigator sat in a fully enclosed cockpit, with a radio operator/gunner in an enclosed position in the mid-fuselage. The tail unit was composed of twin vertical tails mounted on the ends of the cantilever horizontal tail planes.

Fuselage

The circular-section fuselage was usually made out of a metal semi-monocoque construction, although some Pe-2s had a wooden rear fuselage in an effort to save on scarce aluminium supplies. The wooden rear fuselages were constructed of wooden frames with plywood skinning. The wooden tail cones were more common than the full-wooden rear fuselages. The wooden tail cone was wider than the metal cone and was sometimes referred to as the 'beaver tail'. The fuselage was constructed in three sections, bolted together, with closely spaced frames and no stringers. The skin was built from DI-6T aluminium alloy that varied from 0.06 inches to 0.08 inches (1.5 to 2 mm) in thickness.

The pilot was seated to port, while the navigator, who sat behind him, was to starboard on a fold-away seat. This offset position improved the navigator's view forward. The radio operator/gunner was positioned aft of the wings in a separate cabin from the pilot and the navigator, there being no access between the two cabins as the bomb bay and the centre wing structure were located between the cabins.

Armour Protection

The pilot sat in an armoured seat, while the navigator/gunner sat on an armoured seat and was protected on three sides by armour plating. The radio operator/gunner also had armour, including armour plating on the underside of the fuselage to protect him when he was in a prone position firing the ventral gun.

This frontal view of a Pe-2 shows the extensive nose glazing typical of early versions. Note that this aircraft also has the natural metal propellers and appears to be painted in green overall topside, indicating that it is an early (or even prior to) Great Patriotic War example. Notice how the under-nose DF loop at the rear of the nose glazing is enclosed in a streamlined fairing. Also note the crew access ladder just aft of this fairing. (*Viktor Kulikov's collection*)

Compared to a photograph of the nose of an earlier Pe-2, the reduction in the amount of the nose glazing can be seen in this later Pe-2. Note the polar bear with the bomb figure painted on the nose. At the left upper part of the picture, the ShKAS nose gun can just be made out. (*Viktor Kulikov's collection*)

In what is likely a posed photograph, the crew of this turret-armed Pe-2 go over their notes placed on the horizontal stabiliser. Note what appears to be a patch on the fuselage star, probably covering some battle damage. This aircraft appears to have the wooden rear fuselage. (*Viktor Kulikov's collection*)

Wings

The wings were cantilever, low-mounted, and were of two-spar all-metal construction, with electro-hydraulically operated split Schrenk flaps. A Schrenk-type flap was a flap that was lowered from the bottom only, with the top being a fixed integral part of the wing. The wing was divided into three sections, with a centre section and two outer sections. The dihedral on the centre section was 0 degrees, while the dihedral on the outer sections was 7 degrees. The spars were T-beams constructed of steel, while the walls and ribs of the wing were made of D-16 duralumin with lightening holes. The skin was thin, from 0.02 to 0.03 inches (0.6 to 0.8 mm) in thickness. Unlike the fuselage, which featured no stringers, the wings were stiffened by thick triangular stringers. The wings were mounted at an incidence of 2 degrees to the fuselage centre line.

The welded steel tube structure lattice dive brakes were mounted under the wings and were electrically operated and used for dives of between 50 and 70 degrees. On the series 205, small fairings were fitted in front of the dive brake operating arms to better streamline them. The brakes were operated automatically by two AP-1 systems, one that extended them for the dive and one that retracted the brakes upon recovery from the dive. Outlet louvres for the radiators were mounted on either side of the engines, venting through the wing upper surfaces.

Pe-2 with retractable skis and the turret fitted. Note the dive brake under the wing. (*Viktor Kulikov's collection*)

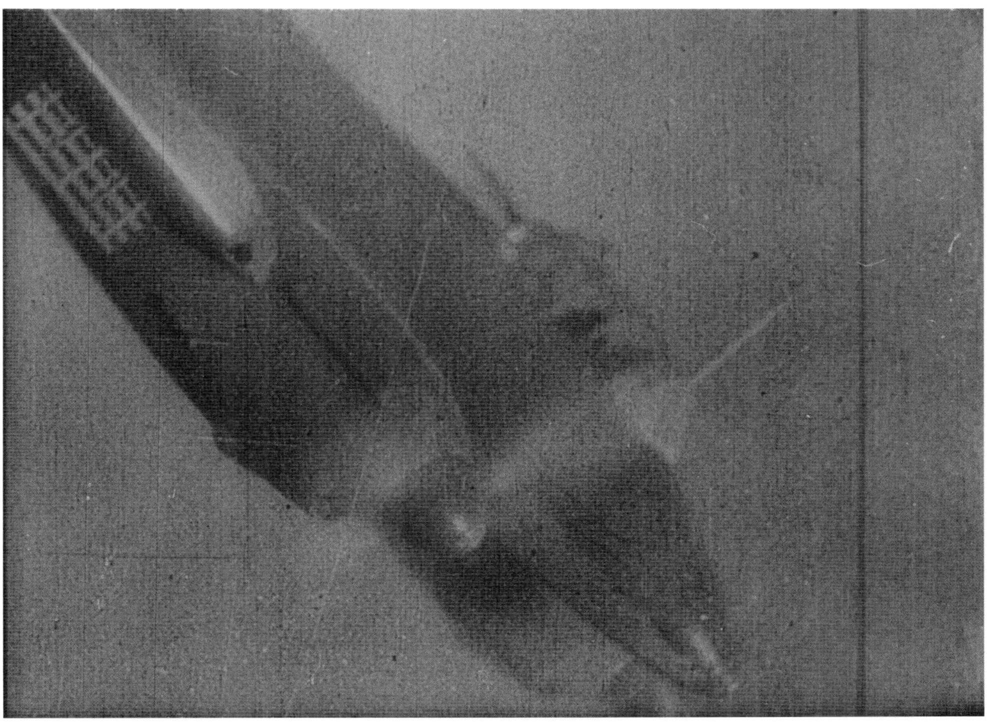

Although not of the best quality, this still from a film shows the dive brakes deployed. (*Viktor Kulikov's collection*)

Although the Pe-2 was not noted for its fine fit and finish, a victim of the need for quick production, this example appears to be reasonably well-finished, with nothing too out of place. Of note are the vents on both sides of the wing behind the starboard engine. These vents let out the warm air generated by the engine. (*Viktor Kulikov's collection*)

Tail planes

The tail planes consisted of two fins and rudders, attached to the ends of the cantilever horizontal stabilisers, with the vertical tail planes being perpendicular to the ground and parallel to each other. The horizontal tail planes had a dihedral of 8 degrees to the horizontal and an incidence of 1 degree 15 minutes to the fuselage centre line; they were adjustable to 3 degrees 45 minutes. The tail planes' construction was of metal, with the stabilisers having two metal spars, with a metal covering except for the rudders and elevators, which were of a metal structure with fabric covering. On those Pe-2s fitted with the wooden rear fuselages, the fixed horizontal tail planes were also of wood, although the vertical tail surfaces remained of metal structure.

Control Surfaces

The ailerons, twin rudders, and elevators were all made of a dural (aluminium alloy) structure, covered by fabric. The flaps were all-metal, of the Schrenk type, which were split to allow clearance for the engine nacelles, and electro-hydraulically operated. They could be lowered to 45 degrees. All the control surfaces had trim tabs, except for the port aileron. These trim tabs were most likely dural-covered (one source has them as being fabric-covered, but this seems unlikely as it goes against Soviet practice where even wooden-structure trim tabs were sometimes covered in dural).

The elevators were metal structured with fabric-covering, could be moved upward 31 degrees, and moved downward 18 degrees. The rudders, which were also fabric-covered metal structures, could move 25 degrees to either side. All these control surfaces were fitted with trim tabs.

Engine

The engine for nearly all service variants of the Pe-2 bombers was the Klimov M-105 twelve-cylinder twin-row vee-type liquid-cooled inline engine, also known as the VK-105 from 1944 on, after its designer, Vladimir Yakovlevich Klimov (1892–1962). This engine also powered a few SBs, the Ar-2, most of the Yakovlev fighters, as well as the LaGG-3 fighter. In the series 205, the engine was the M-105PF, with 1,260 hp for take-off. This replaced the M-105R of earlier versions, which had 1,100 hp at take-off.

The only Pe-2 service variant which did not feature the M-105 was the Pe-2 M-82, which was built in small numbers. It was fitted with the Shvetsov M-82FN (ASh-82FN) fourteen-cylinder twin-row radial engine. This was the same engine that powered the Tu-2 bomber and the La-5 and La-7 fighters.

During cold weather, the engines would be protected with quilted covers that helped to keep the engine warm during the often-frigid Soviet weather.

Landing Gear

Both the main landing gear and the tailwheel were retractable, retracting aft, and completely enclosed by doors when retracted. The main landing gear consisted of two

Shown from the front, this Pe-2 is being warmed up on a cold day, as shown by the tubes leading to the covered engines. The tubes lead down to a heating device that is creating warm air. Note that the nose has also been covered. (*Viktor Kulikov's collection*)

oleo struts on either side of the main wheels, while the retractable tailwheel was held in a forked strut. The main wheels were 900 × 300-mm in size.

Electrical System

The Pe-2 was unusual for a Soviet aircraft in the large number of systems that were operated by small electrical motors ('servo-motors'). In the first Pe-2s, there were as many as fifty electrical motors, but later this number was reduced to as few as eighteen. Nonetheless, many systems that on other Soviet aircraft were completely mechanically, hydraulically, or pneumatically operated were at least partly electrically operated on the Pe-2.

Fuel System

The fuel system on the Pe-2 consisted of nine fuel tanks that were self-sealing with a rubberised covering and were protected from ignition by the typical Soviet CO_2 neutral gas protection system. The Pe-2 had originally carried eleven fuel tanks, but this was changed to nine from the Series 64 aircraft on.

Electronic Equipment

The series 205 was equipped with the RSB-3 radio. From the series 265 on, this was replaced by the RSB-3bis, which had a greater range.

On the series 205, the combination radio antenna/pitot tube was moved forward and was mounted on the port side of the windscreen.

Fixed Armament

The fixed armament consisted of different combinations of ShKAS and UB machine guns, depending on the series. On the series 205, the fit was one UB machine gun to starboard and one ShKAS machine gun to port mounted in the nose cone. The pilot operated these guns, using a PBP-1 gunsight. These guns could either be used for forward defence or for strafing ground targets.

Moveable Armament

As with the fixed armament, the moveable armament for the Pe-2 consisted of differing combinations of ShKAS and UBT machine guns depending on the series. On the series 205, the moveable armament consisted of two UBT machine guns and a ShKAS machine gun. The UBT machine guns were fitted to the rotating VUB-1 turret for the navigator/gunner and in a ventral position for the radio operator/gunner in an LU (*Lyukovaya Ustanovka*: 'Hatch Installation'). The ShKAS was fired through round windows on both sides of the fuselage and could be moved from one side to the other, operated by the radio operator/gunner.

On the early series Pe-2s, the moveable armament for the navigator/gunner consisted of a single ShKAS mounted on a pillar, the TSS-1 mount. This was then changed to a UBT machine gun in an open position (the FT mount), the installation being braced by tubes to the fuselage. Finally, this position was equipped with the fully enclosed VUB-1 turret mounting the UBT machine gun. A different turret, the FZ, was tested, but was never used on production Pe-2s.

The radio operator was responsible not just for the ventral gun, but for the operation of a ShKAS machine gun, which could be moved from side to side and fired through the round window shown in this photograph, taken in January 1942. This window was present on both sides of the mid-fuselage. The rather serious looking radio operator is Sergeant Olzon Taphanaev, a Buryat (a Mongol-speaking people). (*Viktor Kulikov's collection*)

This close-up of the VUB-1 turret shows well the twin vanes fitted to early examples of this turret, as well as the UBT heavy machine gun that was fitted to all examples of this turret. Note the aft position of the radio antenna mast. (*Viktor Kulikov's collection*)

Disposable Armament

The bombs were carried in a mid-fuselage internal bomb bay, in small bomb bays in the rear of the engine nacelles, and on wing racks mounted under the inboard sections of the wings. A maximum bomb load of 2,205 lb (1,000 kg) could be carried. The wing racks could carry either four 551-lb (250-kg) bombs or two 1,102-lb (500-kg) bombs for this maximum load of 2,205 lb (1,000 kg). If these large bombs were not carried under the wings, the internal bomb bays could be used, accommodating smaller bombs than those used on the underwing racks. The fuselage bomb bay could accommodate four FAB-100 220-lb (100-kg) bombs, while the nacelle bomb bays could carry a FAB-100 each for a total of 1,323 lb (600 kg) carried internally. This was the same load that the Il-2 carried, but then the Il-2 was only single-engined and was carrying around 2,000 lb (907 kg) of steel armour.

As the Pe-2 was developed from a low-winged fighter, the VI-100, the bomb bay was not as capacious as it might have otherwise been because of the presence of the central wing structure. An effort had been made to correct this with the mid-winged Pe-2F, but this version never entered service.

Conclusion

The Pe-2 was the most heavily produced twin-engined bomber of the Soviet Union, ever, with some 11,247 being produced. It was not without its faults, such as poor one engine out performance and difficulties in landing that were never completely corrected, but it was successful enough, especially as a dive bomber, that it continued to be used even after the introduction of the in some ways superior Tu-2. Its aerial contribution to the Soviet Union's war against the Germans was probably second only to that of the Il-2, and it served from the first day of the Great Patriotic War to the last.

Pe-2 Specification Table

Type	VI-100	PB-100	Pe-2 series 1	Pe-2 series 87	Pe-2 series 110	Pe-2 series 205	Pe-2 series 354	Pe-2 M-82	Pe-3bis	Pe-2I
Year	1939	1940	1940	1942	1942	1943	1945	1943	1942	1945
Maximum Speed: mph (kph)	334 (538)	332 (535)	335.5 (540)	303 (488)	314 (506)	324 (521)		339 (545)	329 (530)	408 (656)
Range: miles (km)	870 (1,400)	1,056 (1,700)	746 (1,200)	771 (1,240)	777 (1,250)	870 (1,400)			1,243 (2,000)	1,150 (1,850)
Service Ceiling: feet (m)		39,370 (12,000)	28,871 (8,800)	29,199 (8,900)	26,247 (8,000)	26,247 (8,000)			27,231 (8,300)	36,089 (11,000)
Offensive Armament	2 × ShKAS 7.62-mm machine guns, 2 × ShVAK 20-mm cannons	3 × ShKAS 7.62-mm machine guns	2 × ShKAS 7.62-mm machine guns	1 × ShKAS 7-62-mm machine gun, 1 × UBK 12.7-mm machine gun	1 × ShKAS 7-62-mm machine gun, 1 × UBK 12.7-mm machine gun	1 × ShKAS 7-62-mm machine gun, 1 × UBK 12.7-mm machine gun	1 × ShKAS 7-62-mm machine gun, 1 × UBK 12.7-mm machine gun	1 × UBK 12.7-mm machine gun	2 × UBK 12.7-mm machine guns, 1 × ShVAK 20-mm cannon	1 × UBK 12.7-mm machine gun
Defensive Armament		1 × ShKAS 7.62-mm machine gun	2 × ShKAS 7.62-mm machine guns	1 × ShKAS 7.62-mm machine gun, 2 × UBT 12.7-mm machine guns	1 × ShKAS 7.62-mm machine gun, 2 × UBT 12.7-mm machine guns	1 × ShKAS 7.62-mm machine gun, 2 × UBT 12.7-mm machine guns	1 × ShKAS 7.62-mm machine gun, 2 × UBT 12.7-mm machine guns	1 × ShKAS 7.62-mm machine gun, 2 × UBT 12.7-mm machine guns	1 × ShKAS 7.62-mm machine gun, 1 × UBT 12.7-mm machine gun	1 × UBT 12.7-mm machine gun
Rocket Armament	N/A	N/A	10 RS-82						N/A	
Maximum Bomb Load: lb (kg)		2,205 (1,000)	2,205 (1,000)	2,205 (1,000)	2,205 (1,000)	2,205 (1,000)	2,205 (1,000)	2,205 (1,000)?	1,543 (700)?	4,409 (2,000)

Empty Weight: lb (kg)	12,979 (5,887)		12,926 (5,863)	12,214 (5,540)	12,390 (5,620)	13,669 (6,200)	14,290 (6,482)			15,609 (7,080)
All-up Weight: lb (kg)	15,873 (7,200)	15,873 (7,200)	16,614 (7,536)	16,786 (7,614)	17,130 (7,770)			17,637 (8,000)	17,350 (7,870)	
Maximum Weight: lb (kg)						18,783 (8,520)			18,298 (8,300)	19,969 (9,058)
Engines/ take-off hp per	2 × M-105 1,100 (or M-105R 1,100)	2 × M-105 1,100 (or M-105R 1,100)	2 × M-105RA 1,100	2 × M-105RA 1,100	2 × M-105PF 1,260	2 × M-105PF 1,260	2 × M-105PF 1,260	2 × M-82A 1,700	2 × M-105RA 1,100	2 × VK-107A 1,650
Crew	2	3	3	3	3	3	3	3	2	2
Length: feet (m)	41.63 (12.69)	41.93 (12.78)	41.93 (12.78)	41.93 (12.78)	41.93 (12.78)	41.93 (12.78)	41.93 (12.78)	41.93 (12.78)	41.54 (12.66)	43.96 (13.4)
Wingspan: feet (m)	56.27 (17.15)	56.27 (17.15)	56.27 (17.15)	56.27 (17.15)	56.14 (17.11)	56.14 (17.11)	56.14 (17.11)	56.14 (17.11)	56.2 (17.13)	56.36 (17.18)

7
Medium Bombers

The Soviets recognised the need for bomber types somewhere in between the large four-engined types (such as the TB-3 and Pe-8) and small single-engined and twin-engined light bombers (such as the Il-2 and the Pe-2). This is where twin-engined aircraft such as the Tupolev SB and the Tupolev Tu-2 came into play. These were aircraft that were easier to produce than the large four-engined strategic bombers, but had greater range and load-carrying capabilities than the light bombers.

SB

When first designed in early 1934, the Tupolev SB was one of the most advanced bombers in the world, featuring an all-metal flush-riveted stressed skin construction, with retractable main landing gear and enclosed positions for the crew. It first flew in 1934 and went into service in 1936. It was the main twin-engined bomber at the start of Operation Barbarossa, at which time hundreds were lost. After seeing heavy usage in the first two years of the war, the SB continued to be used in second-line duties such as a trainer and glider tower until the end of the war. Some twenty-seven were apparently still in service with the Pacific Fleet in the Far East at the time of the Manchurian campaign, but it is not clear if these saw any use. In all, some 6,547 SBs were produced (one source has 6,366 being produced, another 6,656; as often happens with Soviet aircraft, production figures from different sources do not agree entirely, although they are usually fairly close, as in this case).

Please note that there is some disagreement about the exact designations of the SB variants; in particular, the prominent Soviet Aviation historian Mikhail Maslov has taken issue with some of the designations commonly used in Western publications. According to Mr Maslov, the commonly seen designations such as 'SB 2M-103' were not adopted by the VVS until shortly before the Great Patriotic War. I have nonetheless used these designations, as they were used during the war. In some instances, alternate designations will be shown in parentheses after the more common (or correct) form.

Development

ANT-40RTS (ANT-40-1)

The ANT-40, the prototype of the SB series, was built in two versions. The first version—the first to fly on 7 October 1934—was the ANT-40RTs, the 'RTs' standing for *Rayt-Tsiklon* (it was also known as the ANT-40-1), equipped with two Wright Cyclone radial engines of 730 hp. 'ANT-40' was the internal design bureau designation. The Wright Cyclones were American-supplied engines, though the Soviet licence-built version, the M-25, was constructed by the Shvetsov OKB.

ANT-40IS (ANT-40-2)

The second prototype of the SB was the ANT-40IS, the 'IS' standing for the Russian for 'Hispano-Suiza', the engines that were used to power this aircraft. These were not Soviet-built copies of the Hispano-Suiza, but the actual French-supplied engines. Later, the Soviets would licence-build these engines as the M-100.

SB 2M-100

This, the first production version of the SB, was equipped with two Klimov M-100 engines of 750 hp each. These engines were copies of the Hispano-Suiza 12 Ybrs engines that had powered the ANT-40 IS prototype (ANT-40-2). As with the prototype, the engine was mounted with an oval housing in front for the forward-facing radiator. The propeller was a two-bladed metal propeller. These aircraft were produced in 1936. It appears that because of production difficulties with producing flush-riveted aircraft, the aircraft changed to round-headed rivets during production. All subsequent production SBs featured round-headed rivets. The prototypes had featured flush-riveting.

SB 2M-100A

Very similar to the SB 2M-100, this version differed mainly in having the more powerful M-100A engines, which was signified in the change in designation. These engines developed 860 hp as compared to the 750 hp of the M-100 engines, giving the SB 2M-100A a top speed of 263 mph (423 kph) at 13,123 feet (4,000 m). These aircraft were equipped with VISh-2 three-bladed variable-pitch propellers to take advantage of the added power and were produced during 1937.

SB 2M-103

The SB was once again re-engined in an effort to squeeze more performance out of it. This time, the new engine was the Klimov M-103, with 960 hp. In addition, with the exception of the examples built through the first half of 1939 (which could be easily mistaken for later SB 2M-100As), the SB 2M-103 featured new, streamlined nacelles (first tested on the SB-bis-3, described further on). The new nacelles discarded the front-mounted radiators that had characterised all previous inline-engined SBs, in favour of radiators mounted under the engines, and a cowling that smoothly faired into the propeller spinner. These new nacelles were used on the SB 2M-103s built from the second half of 1939. This greater power and streamlining gave the SB 2M-103 a top speed of 280 mph (450 kph) at 13,451 feet (4,100 m) as compared to

Above: The ANT-40RTS (ANT-40-1), the prototype of the SB, 1934. (*Viktor Kulikov's collection*)

Right: The ventral gun position, with the gun being a ShKAS machine gun. Note the corrugated inner skin of this part of the fuselage. This is from the ANT-40IS (ANT-40-2, the second prototype); most SBs had a similar installation, 1934 or 1935. (*Viktor Kulikov's collection*)

The ANT-40IS (ANT-40-2), the second prototype of the SB, under construction, 1934 or 1935. (*Viktor Kulikov's collection*)

ANT-40IS cockpit. Production aircraft had a similar cockpit, 1934 or 1935. (*Viktor Kulikov's collection*)

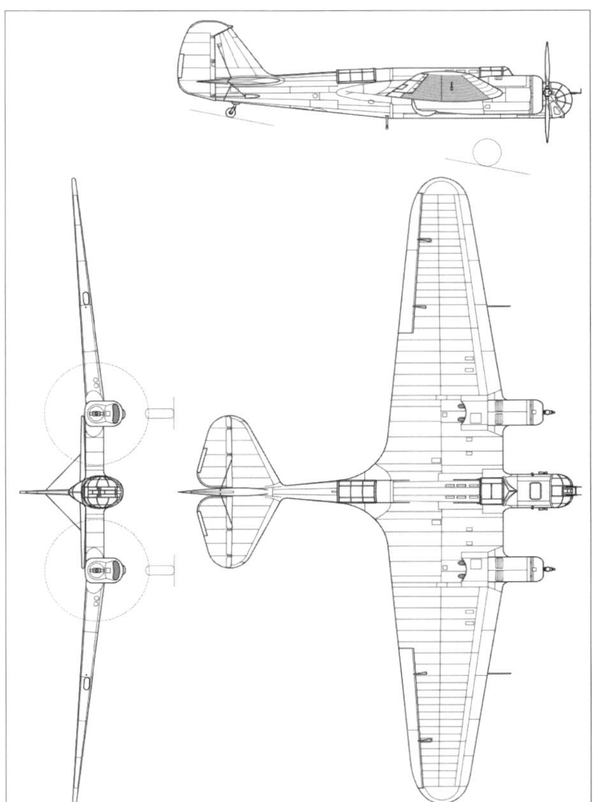

Above: ANT-40IS cockpit, 1934 or 1935. (*Viktor Kulikov's collection*)

Right: Three-view drawing of a SB 2M-100A. (*By Kaboldy. Wikimedia*)

Pre-war SB 2M-100As in overall natural metal. Notice the round-headed rivets (the prototypes had flush-riveting). Note also how the top half of the back portion of the propeller is painted black. This was typical of pre-war Soviet aircraft. (*Viktor Kulikov's collection*)

Barbarossa victim SB from 1941. This photograph shows the nose and the forward-mounted engine radiators to good advantage. (*Viktor Kulikov's collection*)

A Great Patriotic War SB 2M-103A in flight. The aircraft appears to be painted in the black/ green camouflage. (*Viktor Kulikov's collection*)

A Soviet airman poses in front of an SB 2M-103A with its engines running. The aircraft appears to be freshly painted. (*Viktor Kulikov's collection*)

the top speed of 263 mph (423 kph) for the SB 2M-100A. All SB 2M-103s featured external bomb racks, and some featured a rear-view mirror on top of the pilot's windscreen.

As mentioned previously, the first SB 2M-103s featured the oval, frontal radiators of previous SBs. These aircraft were produced in 1938-39. At first, these were replaced by adjustable under engine air intakes, with a retractable door that could completely close off the intake. This intake door feature was taken from the SB-bis-3 experimental variant. The SB 2M-103s built in the second half of 1939 featured these variable intake doors. The 1940 version of the SB 2M-103 featured fixed intakes, with the lips moved forward on the nacelles. The aircraft built in the second half of 1940 featured a landing light.

Some SB 2M-103s, besides featuring the new engines in the new streamlined nacelles, also featured improved defensive armament positions. Although the nose position remained the same, with two ShKAS guns moving up and down with limited traverse, the aft positions were different. Utilising the installations first tested on the SB 2M-100A (Modified), a MV-3 turret, with 360 degrees of traverse was fitted in the dorsal (mid-upper) position, replacing the TUR-9 installation, while a MV-2 gun position was fitted to the underside on a few SB 2M-103s, the MV-2 featuring better traverse than the original ventral gun position. Some aircraft were built at the factories with the MV-3 turrets in 1940, while others had them fitted in the field.

ShKAS machine gun in a Tur-9 mount for the dorsal gunner. The canopy slides forward to give the gunner the ability to use his gun. (*Viktor Kulikov's collection*)

Right: Another view of the dorsal mount, this time with the gunner manning the position. (*Viktor Kulikov's collection*)

Below: Nose section of a late SB, as shown by the closed off slots for the twin ShKAS machine guns. Earlier SBs had these slots partially open. (*Viktor Kulikov's collection*)

Finnish SB 2M-103A. This aircraft is fitted with the MV-3 turret. (*Viktor Kulikov's collection*)

A crew talks over their mission in front of their SB 2M-103A. The twin ShKAS machine guns in the rather bulbous nose are shown well here. (*Viktor Kulikov's collection*)

Line-up of SB 2M-103As in 1944. Due to the late date, these are most likely training aircraft. Note the lack of spinners. (*Viktor Kulikov's collection*)

SB 2M-104

These aircraft, equipped with the Klimov M-104 engine, were produced in early 1940 and did not differ in external appearance from the SB 2M-103s produced at this time.

SB 2M-105

The SB 2M-105 was equipped with the Klimov M-105 engine (later used by the Ar-2) and was produced in late 1940 and early 1941. At least some of the SB 2M-105s had the Ar-2/Il-4 type MV-2 mount. These were the last SBs in production.

SB Dive Bomber

This version of the SB was a dive bomber that was produced at Z.22 before it switched to producing the Ar-2 dive bomber. It was produced after the SB was tested during the Winter War as a dive bomber. Unlike the Ar-2, it was equipped with a MV-3 turret like some of the SB 2M-103s. These aircraft were produced from the second quarter of 1940 and were distinguished by the installation of the PAN-23 sight and PB-3 bomb racks for dive bombing.

USB (Trainer)

The USB (*Uchebno Skorostnoiy Bombardirovshchik*: Trainer Fast Bomber) was a trainer version of the SB, where the instructor-pilot sat in an open cockpit in the nose directly in front of the cockpit, where the trainee-pilot sat. When the instructor took the controls, the trainee's controls were automatically disconnected. The prototype underwent state tests from 11 to 16 March 1938. Z.22 built a few new USBs, but most were field conversions.

Nose of an SB trainer with the open instructor's cockpit in front of the enclosed cockpit which now housed the trainee-pilot. The dark object below the instructor's cockpit is a venturi tube. (*Viktor Kulikov's collection*)

Experimental Versions

SB-bis

In an effort to improve the performance of the SB, the M-103 engine, of 960 hp, was installed on the SB-bis. It was modified by Z.22 and was test flown from 15 to 21 September 1937. In addition to the new engines, it featured a larger tailwheel, an improved electrical system, and flight controls for the navigator. The M-103 engines were fitted with VISh-2 three-bladed propellers with variable-pitch. Even with the more powerful engines and the more efficient propellers, the SB-bis showed no performance improvement over the production SB, probably due to its increased weight (2,112 lb (958 kg)), so work continued with efforts to improve the performance.

SB-bis-2 (S-bis2)

The SB-bis-2 differed from the SB-bis in having a polished wing. It was tested through March 1938, but again showed no improvement over the production SB in terms of performance so work continued on improving the SB's performance.

SB-bis-3 (S-bis3)

The frontal radiators that the SBs had featured from the second prototype limited the pilot's view to either side. In order to improve his view, more streamlined nacelles with under engine mounted radiators were tested on this aircraft. The radiators featured variable position doors, which could be opened, or could completely close off the radiator openings. In addition, there were two oil-coolant radiators in each wing. This aircraft was tested from

The adjustable engine radiator intake doors on the SB-bis-3 (SB-bis3). These doors were used initially on the SB 2M-103A. (*Viktor Kulikov's collection*)

1 November 1937 to 17 February 1938. Although the intent may have been to improve the pilot's view, which the new nacelles did, there was also an improvement in streamlining that enabled the SB-bis-3 to achieve a top speed of 277 mph (445 kph) at 14,764 feet (4,500 m). The M-103s with the new nacelles were intended to be introduced into production in the second half of 1938, although these were not actually introduced until the second half of 1939, the first SBs with the M-103 engines retaining the original front-mounted radiators.

SB 2M-100A (Modified)

The revised armament system carried by some of the SB 2M-103s, with the MV-3 turret and the MV-2 under fuselage gun position, were first tested on this modified SB 2M-100A. This enhanced defensive gun protection was influenced by experiences in the Spanish Civil War, which had shown the defensive armament to have a limited field of fire. These installations proved successful enough on this experimental version that they were introduced in the production of the SB 2M-103 and were retrofitted to some SB 2M-100As and SB 2M-103s replacing the original gun installations.

SB 'Pterodactyl'

Perhaps the most striking-looking member of the SB family was this unusual aircraft, which was used to test tricycle landing gear. A SB 2M-103 with the variable radiator intake was modified with a lengthened nose and a fixed tricycle landing gear. This aircraft was intended to provide information about tricycle landing geared aircraft that could be used in the development of future Soviet aircraft.

The experimental SB 'Pterodactyl' was used to test the tricycle landing gear configuration before the Great Patriotic War. (*Viktor Kulikov's collection*)

The stalky nose landing gear were attached to the lengthened, solid (unglazed) nose by a main strut with two bracing struts on the side. The normal retractable main landing gear were replaced by fixed units mounted rearward of the position of the normal gear on the nacelles. These units were braced to the fuselage, with the nacelles being heavily braced to the fuselage, no doubt to give the whole installation added strength.

The aircraft was assigned by the TsAGI to the NII VVS at Kratovo for testing. Test pilot Mark L. Gallai tested the aircraft and found it easier to take off and land than conventional tailwheel equipped 'tail-dragger' aircraft. Testing continued from late 1940 until the outbreak of the Great Patriotic War, when testing was ended. Although no production Soviet bombers featured tricycle landing gear during the war, Lend-Lease aircraft (such as the A-20 and B-25 bombers and the Bell P-39 Airacobra fighter) did, which all saw heavy use with the VVS. It was only after the war ended did Soviet bombers with tricycle landing gear enter service, such as the Tu-4.

SB-MMN (MMN-2 M105)

With various refinements, such as a smaller, redesigned wing and more powerful M-105 engines of 1,100 hp, this was an effort to modernise the basic SB design. The wings were shorter in span and featured redesigned outer panels, with the spars being replaced by walls, and the wing area was decreased by 86 sq. feet (8 sq. m). A redesigned tail, like that used in the Ar-2, was fitted. In addition to the more powerful engines and redesigned wings, it also featured a more streamlined nose, with only one ShKAS mounted in the clear nose cone to be operated by the navigator. The navigator was equipped with controls to fly the aircraft in an emergency (this feature was present in the Ar-2 dive bomber). A MV-3 dorsal turret was also fitted.

Only one example was built as it was only 5 mph (8 kph) faster than the SB 2M-103 at 285 mph (459 kph) (Gordon and Komissarov give a figure of 284 mph

(458 kph)), which was considered an insufficient increase in performance over the standard SB and because of its smaller wing, which gave it a higher landing speed. This sole prototype was passed on to Aeroflot after testing had ended, in which service it was nicknamed the *Shchuka* ('Pike'), probably due to its long, streamlined fuselage.

SB-RK

This aircraft was developed in parallel to the SB-MMN level bomber, sharing some common features, such as the M-105 engines and the smaller wing (compared to the standard SB), but it was developed into a dive bomber. It became the Ar-2. For a full description of this aeroplane, see the previous section on the Ar-2.

B-1 (SBB-1)

Neither the SB-MMN nor the SB-RK (Ar-2) were the most modified developments of the SB design. Another effort was made to keep the line going in the form of the 'B' or 'B-1'. It was also known as the SBB-1, with the 'SBB' standing for *Skorostnoiy Blizhniy Bombardirovshchik* or 'Fast Short-range Bomber'. This aircraft differed substantially from the basic SB design, featuring for the first time twin fins and rudders mounted at the end of cantilever horizontal stabilisers (all the previous versions of the SB had featured wire-braced horizontal stabilisers). It had a smaller wing similar to that characteristic of the SB-MMN and the SB-RK (Ar-2). Development of this aircraft started in 1939, at least partly in competition to Polikarpov's new design, the SPB (see the section of experimental bombers further on). It was intended that it would replace the SB in service.

Besides the change in the tail design, the B-1 also differed from the basic SB in the use of simpler construction, using extrusions and U-shaped parts to replace the harder to produce and repair tubular elements of the SB. The smaller wing also differed from the SB's wing in having a wooden leading edge and a smooth upper plywood skin attached to the metal framework. This was done to reduce drag and improve performance. One notable feature of the B-1 was the fitting of a sliding canopy or cupola for the radio operator/gunner. This was later used on the Ar-2, and modified versions of it were used on the Pe-2 and the Tu-2.

In addition to the B-1, which was designed to be a high-speed bomber (like the original SB), another variant, the B-2, was designed as a dive bomber. In the event, this variant was apparently not built, and the B-1 was flown for the first time on 6 November 1940 at Moscow's Central Airfield. The aircraft suffered a landing mishap on 22 November 1940 when the port landing gear strut broke while taxiing. The damage was not too extensive, and the aircraft was repaired and testing was continued, with a top speed of 354 mph (570 kph) being recorded in January 1941. Although this was greater than the Pe-2's top speed, the Pe-2 was already in production at this point so the decision was made not to produce the B-1. Despite this, testing and improvement continued until mid-1941. On 15 December 1941, the aircraft was sent to the rear, where its final fate was not recorded.

The B-1 after its landing mishap on 22 November 1940. The aircraft was repaired and flown again after this accident. (*Viktor Kulikov's collection*)

Conclusion

Although advanced at the time of its introduction into service in 1936, the SB, although by far still the most numerous bomber in VVS service in June 1941, was obsolete by the time of the German invasion. Advancements to its airframe, mainly in the form of more powerful engines, were not enough to keep the production versions up-to-date. Like many Soviet bombers, it suffered from insufficient defensive firepower and needed to be used with extensive fighter escort or at night. Nonetheless, during the darkest days of the war, it was of necessity used heavily, and if nothing else, its sacrifices in the first six months of the war assisted in slowing down the German advance, helping to give the Soviet Union enough time to regroup and stop the Germans before Moscow. It was also the first of the modern Tupolev bombers to go into service, and the Tupolev name would become synonymous with bombers after the war.

SB Specification Table

Type	ANT-40RTs	ANT-40IS	SB 2M-100	SB 2M-100A	SB 2M-103A	SB MMN	SB-RK (Ar-2 Prototype)	B-1 (SBB-1)
Year	1934	1935	1936	1937	1939	1939	1939	1940
Maximum Speed: mph (kph)	202 (325)	249 (400)	244 (393)	263 (423)	280 (450)	285 (458)	298 (480)	354 (570)
Range: miles (km)	870 (1,400)	870 (1,400)	1,359 (2,187)		1,181 (1,900)	472 (760)	932 (1,500)	547 (880)
Service Ceiling: feet (m)	22,310 (6,800)	30,840 (9,400)	29,528 (9,000)	31,365 (9,560)	30,512 (9,300)	29,528 (9,000)	33,136 (10,100)	46,250 (14,100)

Defensive Armament	4 × ShKAS 7.62-mm machine guns	4 × ShKAS 7.62-mm machine guns	4 × ShKAS 7.62-mm machine guns	4 × ShKAS 7.62-mm machine guns	4 × ShKAS 7.62-mm machine guns	1 × ShKAS 7.62-mm machine gun 1 × Ultra-ShKAS 7.62-mm machine gun	4 × ShKAS 7.62-mm machine guns	4 × ShKAS 7.62-mm machine guns
Rocket Armament	N/A	N/A	RS-82	RS-82				
Maximum Bomb Load: lb (kg)	1,102 (500)	1,102 (500)	1,102 (500)	1,323 (600)	3,307 (1,500)	2,205 (1,000)	3,527 (1,600)	2,205 (1,000)
Empty Weight: lb (kg)	6,905 (3,132)				10,066 (4,566)	10,626 (4,820)	9,766 (4,430)	9,733 (4,415)
All-up Weight: lb (kg)	10,399 (4,717)	10,692 (4,850)	12,408 (5,628)	12,672 (5,748)	14,065 (6,380)	14,154 (6,420)	13,889 (6,300)	13,142 (5,961)
Engines/ take-off hp per	2 x Wright Cyclone 730	2 x Hispano-Suiza 750	2 x M-100 750	2 x M-100A 850	2 x M-103A 960	2 x M-105 1,100	2 x M-105 1,100	2 x M-105R 1,100
Crew	3	3	3	3	3	3	3	3
Length: feet (m)	40.35 (12.3)	40.08 (12.217)	40.27 (12.273)	40.27 (12.273)	40.27 (12.273)	41.93 (12.78)	40.26 (12.27)	40.26 (12.27)
Wingspan: feet (m)	62.34 (19)	66.6 (20.3)	66.6 (20.3)	66.7 (20.33)	66.7 (20.33)	59.06 (18)	59.06 (18)	52.49 (16.0)

Tu-2

The Tu-2 is interesting in being one of the few aircraft to have been designed in a prison (along with the Pe-2, described previously). Andrey Tupolev had been designated as an 'Enemy of the State' in 1937 and arrested, despite being the most important aircraft designer in the Soviet Union. The charge was, of course, absurd, but Tupolev was placed with other arrested aircraft designers and engineers under the ever-watchful supervision of the NKVD, where the designers continued to work upon aeroplane designs.

The Tu-2 was normally used in the tactical role, to bomb targets in support of ground units. However, although technically a tactical medium bomber, the Tu-2s large bombload (nearly 7,000 lb (3,175 kg)) enabled it to also be used in a strategic role, attacking strategically important targets in Berlin, for example, as part of the 18th Air Army, the successor to the ADD. It continued in production and use long after the war, not finally being retired by the Chinese until perhaps as late as the early 1980s.

Development

First of the Breed: the '103'

The decision to build a twin-engined dive bomber led to the design of the 'ANT-58', as the design was initially called. After approval of the mock-up, the aircraft was given the designation of '103'. Three '103's were to be built: one with Mikulin AM-37 liquid-cooled inline engines and two with Klimov M-120 'Y'-type air-cooled inline engines with TK-2 turbo-superchargers.

A Very Special Workplace

It might be a good idea here to give some background on the very interesting circumstances under which what would become the Tu-2 was designed. Before the Great Patriotic War, Andrey Tupolev had been head of the TsAGI, the Central Aerodynamic and Hydrodynamic Institute, the Soviet equivalent of the American NACA (the predecessor of NASA). While still head of the TsAGI, Andrey Tupolev was arrested by the NKVD, the State Security Police, on 21 October 1937 on trumped-up and frankly ridiculous charges of being part of a Russian Fascist party, during Josef Stalin's purges of the mid to late 1930s ('The Great Terror'). This arrest came despite the fact that he was the most renowned and most accomplished aircraft designer in the Soviet Union at the time and was known worldwide.

The OTB NKVD ('Technical Office of the NKVD') was also apparently referred to as the TsKB-29, or 'Central Design Bureau 29'. The designers were moved from the 'Bolshevo' camp to this installation on 23 February 1940. The OTB NKVD was housed in a building that had been built for Tupolev for his OKB at the beginning of the 1930s, when he was still in the good graces of Stalin; it overlooked the Yauza River in Moscow. The special NKVD prison was called a *sharashka*. This installation was officially called *Zavod* 156, or Z.156 (also known as the 'TsKB-29') and was surrounded by barbed wire, leaving no doubt that however relatively comfortable the working conditions might have been, at the time the NKVD still considered this to be a prison and its workers, their prisoners.

Tupolev was not the only aviation designer housed here in this *sharashka*. As mentioned previously, Z.156 also housed Vladimir Petlyakov, who at one time had worked under Tupolev under happier circumstances. Z.156 was divided into four specialised technical departments, or 'stations'. The abbreviation for these departments was 'STO', which then became '100' (*Sto* being Russian for '100'). Since Petlyakov's group was the first, his department was assigned the number '100', which then became the number of his project (the VI-100, described previously). Vladimir Myasischev's group was second and was assigned the number '102' (one wonders what happened to number '101', however). This became the number of his project, the DVB-102, an advanced high-altitude long-range bomber which first flew in 1942, but did not enter production (this experimental aircraft is described further on).

Andrey Tupolev's department was the third department and was assigned the number '103', which became the number for his project. For some reason, the designer Dmitriy Lyudvigovich Tomashevich's (1899–1974) group, which was formed last, was given the number '110', although it was not the eleventh group. This number became the number of his project, a one-engined high-altitude fighter, which first flew in late 1942, although it was not produced. The stations each functioned as a separate design bureau to work on their separate projects. Generally, the NKVD was responsible for providing the stations with what they needed for their work, but did not intervene in the design process itself. The NKVD did sign off on the technical documents prepared by the stations, however. The designers were still their prisoners, after all.

From Prison to First Flight

The design work started in the fall of 1939, at the Bolshevo camp, even before the move to Z.156. However, most of the design work for the 'FB', as the '103' was initially called, took place at Z.156. The 'FB' designation was from *Frontovoiy Bombardirovshchik* or 'Frontal Bomber' in Russian. Lavrentiy Pavlovich Beria (1899–1953), the feared head of the NKVD, had promised Andrey Tupolev that if his aircraft flew, he would be released from prison. If it did not fly, one can well imagine Tupolev's fate. For Andrey Tupolev, therefore, the success of the '103' was not just a matter of professional pride, but of life (and freedom) or death. There can be little doubt that Tupolev threw himself into the new project with all of his considerable energy and designing ability. No doubt, the designers helping him, such as Dmitriy Tomashevich, were in much the same situation. That the eventual design was an outstanding one could be ascribed to being one-part inspiration and one-part desperation.

Two innovations were necessary to make the '103' a viable design. The first concerned the internal bomb bay, which needed to be able not just to drop bombs in horizontal flight, but from a dive. This design was accomplished by the engineer A. I. Nekrasoviy, another NKVD prisoner. The second involved the development of a bombsight that would enable the aircraft to accurately dive bomb. This sight, called the OTB, was designed by the mathematician, navigator, and engineer G. S. Frenkel, also an NKVD prisoner.

By March 1940, the VVS had given the project the green light, and the aircraft was renamed from the 'FB' to the '103' (or 'ANT-58' under what was effectively the Tupolev Bureau, or OKB) after the mock-up was approved on 21 April 1940. Work on Tupolev's earlier 'PB' project had apparently already ended by this time (perhaps in September 1939). In order to assist in the design of the '103', Andrey Tupolev was asked to present a list of engineers he wanted; the NKVD obligingly scoured its prisons and camps to secure these engineers for Tupolev.

As finalised in February 1940, the specifications called for an aircraft 42.42 feet long (12.93 m), with a wingspan of 59.06 feet (18 m), a maximum bomb load of 4,409 lb (2,000 kg), a maximum level speed of 435 to 460 mph (700 to 740 kph, which were unrealistically high figures). The service ceiling was to be 42,651 to 45,932 feet (13,000 to 14,000 m—also very ambitious numbers), and the maximum range was to be 1,243 to 1,553 miles (2,000 to 2,500 km), with six ShKAS 7.62-mm (30-calibre) machine guns and a crew of three. The dive speed was to be the same as that stipulated for the 'PB': 559 mph (900 kph).

THE '103' (ANT-58)

The first of the Tu-2 series to fly, this aircraft was equipped with two Mikulin AM-37 V-configured twelve-cylinder liquid-cooled inline engines of 1,380 hp at take-off. The propellers fitted were VISh-61T three-bladed units with a diameter of 11.15 feet (3.4 m). Construction of the first prototype of the '103' was begun in May 1940 and was completed on 8 January 1941. After completion of the prototype, it was transported to Shchelkovo airfield. The first flight took place on 29 January 1941, flown by test pilot M. A. Nyukhtikov. Andrey Tupolev actually watched the first flight of his creation from the roof of Z.156, which was still effectively his prison. The OKB tests ran from January to May 1941 and the state tests went from June to July 1941. The state tests were not completed because of the outbreak of war. During the tests, the maximum speed recorded at sea level was 300 mph (482 kph), and the overall top speed was 395 mph (635 kph) at 25,591 feet (7,800 m), impressive figures indeed. The normal bomb load was to be 2,205 lb (1,000 kg), with a maximum bomb load of 4,409 lb (2,000 kg).

The main landing gear were of a single oleo type, with a forked attachment to trap the main wheels (a similar arrangement was used for the retractable tailwheel, which had its own doors). The main landing gear, like the tailwheel, retracted to the rear and was completely enclosed by doors. The main wheels were 1,142 × 432 mm in size, while the tailwheel had a 470 × 210-mm tyre. The main landing gear doors were slightly bulged to accommodate the main wheels.

The aircraft, as befitted its high top speed (faster than that of operational fighters at the time), was very streamlined, with a low cockpit canopy flush with the top of the fuselage and a mid-upper gunner's canopy that was raised only slightly. Although not affording good vision for the crew, the canopy arrangement did contribute to the overall excellent streamlining and speed of the aircraft. A single pilot sat in the cockpit, with the navigator housed in the nose. The ventral gun position was flush with the underside of the fuselage, the radio operator/gunner operating this gun in addition to the mid-upper (or dorsal) gun. The total number of the crew was three, comprising a pilot, navigator, and radio operator/gunner. The two inline engines were housed in well-streamlined cowlings. Even after the conclusion of regular flight testing, the '103' continued to be used for other tests. In 1943, it was returned to Moscow; a year later, it was converted into the 'SDB-1' fast day bomber (see the section on experimental variants further on for information about this version).

THE '103U' ('59')

During the brief period of the Soviet-German 'thaw', after the signing of the Molotov-Ribbentrop brokered Non-Aggression Pact on 23 August 1939, a Soviet delegation of aviation specialists visited Germany in 1940 to examine some of the latest Luftwaffe aircraft, including the Ju 88 bomber (which was bought and taken back to the Soviet Union), which like the '103', could be used as a dive bomber. This aircraft impressed these aviation experts, who were particularly interested in the way that the crew were concentrated in the front fuselage. The Germans believed that this crew configuration improved communication and morale during combat, and the Soviets were impressed enough to install these changes into the '103' design. The number of the crew was now increased from three to four on the '103'.

The 103U (Tupolev ANT-59) at the NII VVS during tests in June 1941. (*Viktor Kulikov's collection*)

This redesigned '103' was christened the '103U' (OKB designation 'ANT-59', the 'U' apparently standing for *Uluchshenniy*: 'Improved' in Russian). Instead of having the navigator in the nose as in the original '103' design, the navigator was now seated behind the pilot, from which position he could move around to also operate a defensive gun directed aft. Both the pilot and the navigator sat under a raised canopy, quite different from the low, streamlined canopy of the first '103'. The navigator was also equipped with a fold-away control column from which in his new position behind the pilot, in an emergency he could control the aircraft.

Work on the '103U' began in July 1940. The nose was lengthened by around 300 mm or about 1 foot. The dorsal gunner's position was now flush with the fuselage between the cockpit canopy and the dorsal gunner's canopy, with the fuselage aft of the gunner's canopy being slimmer than on the original '103' design to give the ventral gunner better vision (overall the fuselage was slimmer in side profile). The ventral gunner was still equipped with a small circular window above his position to give him some light. Eventually, a slightly larger vertical tail was also installed to improve stability and compensate for the greater length of the '103U' as compared to the original '103' design.

As an interesting side note, one might well ask why Germany would be showing (and even selling) some of their latest (and best) front-line aeroplanes to a country that they fully intended to invade, and soon. The answer is rooted in the Nazis' contempt for what they saw as the Jewish-controlled Slavic/Asiatic 'subhumans' that they supposed the Soviets to be. They did not believe that either the Soviets would be able to understand the advanced features of these Luftwaffe aircraft, or if they did, the Germans believed that they would not have time to make any changes to their aircraft incorporating these features before the Soviet Union were overrun and defeated by

German forces. Unfortunately, for the Germans, they were wrong on both counts. This would not be the last time that the Germans underestimated Soviet capabilities.

This aircraft still featured the inline AM-37 engines (now of 1,400 hp at take-off), but the new cockpit configuration was the one that was to be featured on all production Tu-2s until the end of production in 1951 (or 1952). The redesigned aircraft was completed on 9 April 1941. The propellers used were VISh-61P three-bladed units, with a diameter of 12.47 feet (3.8 m). An interesting feature of the propellers was that the spinners featured a hole of 5.9 inches (150 mm) which allowed air to flow into the cowling for cooling purposes. The first flight was made on 18 May 1941 by pilot M. A. Nyukhtikov and engineer V. A. Miruts. On 27 May 1941, the results of the testing were reported to Beria, Zhigarev, and Shakhurin (the heads of the NKVD, VVS, and the aircraft industry, or NKAP, respectively). The '103' was obviously considered an important aeroplane. State testing of the '103U' was done at basically the same time as the '103', from May to July 1941.

Due to its greater weight and wider cockpit, the '103U' was somewhat slower than the '103'. The drag of the wider front fuselage was actually lower than it might have been because Tupolev had inadvertently created an 'area rule effect', whereby the widening of the fuselage in front of the wing roots actually lessened what the drag would normally be expected to be. It had a maximum speed at sea level of 291 mph (469 kph) and 379 mph (610 kph) at 25,600 feet (4,800 m). Its service ceiling was 34,500 feet (10,500 m) and the '103U' had a range of 1,180 miles (1,900 km). Although slower than the '103', the performance was considered sufficient enough for the GKO to issue an order on 27 June (or July according to one source) 1941 to begin production (Operation Barbarossa had started on 22 June 1941). The '103U' crashed on 6 July 1941 (see below), but this did not affect the decision to produce the aircraft. Also despite this eventual crash, Beria kept his word and duly freed Andrey Tupolev, who was finally released from NKVD detention on 21 July 1941. However, Tupolev had been convicted in 1940 and given a ten-year sentence, and he was not finally exonerated and officially rehabilitated until 1955, some two years after Josef Stalin's death.

The tests revealed that there were problems with the propellers and instability. The instability was dealt with by increasing the area of the vertical stabilisers. A much more serious problem showed itself on 6 July 1941 when the right engine caught fire and the fire could not be extinguished. The pilot Mikhail A. Nyukhtikov survived, but the navigator and an engineer named A. Akopyan were killed. This happened during weapons testing. An investigation revealed no defects in the design, and as noted above, the order to begin production was proceeded with. Yet first, one more major change to the basic design had to be made: the choice of engines.

The '103V' ('60')

Both the GKO and NKAP orders had specified that the third '103' prototype be equipped with the experimental air-cooled M-120TKs. However, the unavailability of these engines led to the decision to re-engine the third '103' prototype aircraft with Shvetsov M-82 radial engines, which were for reasons explained below, available in abundance. The lack of development on the experimental AM-37 engines, and the need for the plant manufacturing the AM-37 to build AM-38 engines for the desperately needed Il-2 Shturmovik ground attack aircraft, also led to the decision to use the M-82 engines instead. The M-82s, on the other hand, were available in abundance as the aircraft that they were designed for, the Su-2 light bomber, was slated to have its production ended in 1942, leaving the Shvetsov OKB, which produced the engines at Z.19 in Molotov (now Perm), with hundreds of surplus M-82s stored in warehouses. This re-engining led to the '103V', the true prototype of the first production Tu-2s.

The '103V' aircraft was completed at the new Z.166 in Omsk Siberia in mid-November 1941, which had been rapidly constructed for the production of the '103'. Known as the '103V 2M-82A ('60')', it first flew on 15 December 1941 with test pilot M. P. Vasyakin at the controls (Vasyakin would later fly the Tu-2 in combat). Due to the 'V' in the designation, the aircraft acquired the nickname of 'Vera'.

Joint OKB and state tests ran from 15 December 1941 to 22 August 1942 (one source states 1 August 1942), by which time other examples of the aircraft were nearly ready for combat trials, such was the length of these tests. Part of the problem with the tests was that the aircraft originally tested was so unsatisfactory due to the poor reliability of its engines that it was replaced by a production '103V' (actually Tu-2 No. 308) so the tests could be completed. During the tests on the original '103V', the engines had to be changed no less than eight times.

The tests showed the maximum speed to be 323 mph (521 kph) at a height of 10,500 feet (3,200 m). This top speed was well below that of the '103' and '103U' and was at least partially due to the greater drag of the radial M-82 engines. The service ceiling was also less at 29,500 feet (9,000 m) and the range was 1,255 miles (2,020 km). The armament consisted of two ShVAK 20-mm cannons in the wing roots, two ShKAS 7.62-mm (30-calibre) machine guns for operation by the pilot, and one ShKAS machine gun and two UBT 12.7-mm (50-calibre) machine guns for defence, to be operated by the navigator, the radio operator, and the ventral gunner. Ten RS-132

The first production '103V' at Omsk, Siberia at Z.166 in spring 1942. (*Viktor Kulikov's collection*)

132-mm rockets could also be mounted under the wings. It is not clear from the record how much the rockets were used in combat (or even if they were used at all, even by the early versions of the Tu-2). The normal bomb load was 2,205 lb (1,000 kg), with a maximum overload of 6,614 lb (3,000 kg) for short-range missions.

Other than the reliability of the engines, other problems were noted such as the equipment layout not being optimal, and the hydraulic system needing to be simplified. However, the one engine only performance was noted to be good; with one engine, the aircraft could even climb at the normal weight of 23,149 lb (10,500 kg). The diving characteristics were found to be good. The aircraft was cleared for production at Z.18 by NKAP order No. 533 dated 17 June 1941, which was just five days before the opening of Operation Barbarossa and the start of the Great Patriotic War.

The Early Tu-2 Series ('Tu-2VS')

At first, the Tu-2, sometimes known as the 'Tu-2VS' (although it is unclear if this name was ever used during the Great Patriotic War), was to be produced at Z.18, at Voronezh on the Don. Then the Germans invaded, and Z.18 was evacuated to Kuibyshev (now Samara), on the Volga River. Here it became the main factory for the production of the Il-2. As it was, it never produced a single Tu-2.

With the evacuation of Z.18, the initial series of Tu-2s were now to be produced at Z.166 in Omsk, by NKAP Order No. 163, dated 29 July 1941. This was a bit of a problem, as no such plant existed at this time. Hastily, a production plant was built, as mentioned above in the section on the '103V'. The first factory equipment from Z.156 in Moscow arrived at Omsk on 12 July 1941; the last arrived by the end of that August. By September 1941, Tupolev had completed the transfer of drawings to Z.166 from Z.156. The plant manager of Z.166 was director L. P. Sokolov.

The plan was for forty-five aircraft to be produced by the end of 1941, with 600 during 1942, but the plan was much too optimistic and only 10 had actually been produced by early 1942. Tupolev had been appointed the head of Z.166 by the NKAP on 7 October 1941 and by the end of 1941, his entire Tu-2 design staff were in place. The head of the design team was Dmitriy. S. Markov and the head engineer in charge of flight testing was E. K. Stoman, who had been with Tupolev in NKVD detention at Z.156. As it was, the testing of the '103V' was not completed until 22 August 1942 for the reasons given previously, by which time the aircraft was already in production. By NKAP Order No. 234, issued on 28 March 1942, the aircraft's name was changed from the '103' to the 'Tu-2', the 'Tu' reflecting Andrey Tupolev's family name.

All the production documentation had been completed by January 1942. The first production Tu-2 was produced by February 1942 (one source says March 1942), and five were produced by April 1942, with an additional series produced by 5 April 1942. Most of the initial series of Tu-2s, eighty in all, were produced as dive bombers although a few were produced as reconnaissance aircraft.

From 17 May 1942 until 29 July 1942, three serial production Tu-2s were used for tests at the NII VVS to determine their suitability for military trials. They did not have an auspicious start. On 23 May, aircraft c/n 100102 crashed during landing. A second aircraft crashed on 26 May. The remaining Tu-2 continued with the NII VVS tests.

The first production '103V', view from the front, at Omsk, Siberia at Z.166 in spring 1942. It appears that construction work is still being done on the factory. (*Viktor Kulikov's collection*)

Early series Tu-2 number '717' re-engined with M-82FN (ASh-82FN), during tests with the new engines. The aircraft is still in the black/green scheme. Note the plain stars. (*Viktor Kulikov's collection*)

Despite the crashes, an NII VVS report issued on 22 August 1942 stated that the Tu-2 was suitable for use in the horizontal bombing role limited to 16,404 feet (5,000 m) in altitude. It was noted that the wheel braking system needed to be improved because of problems while landing (the aircraft would veer unexpectedly on landing, sometimes causing it to crash) and that the defensive armament needed to be strengthened. In addition, there were problems with the rudders' sensitivity. The radio operator, in the dorsal position, had his ShKAS 7.62-mm (30-calibre) machine gun replaced by a Berezin UBT 12.7-mm (50-calibre) heavy machine gun in the spring of 1942, and the navigator had his ShKAS replaced by the heavier UBT in the fall of 1942. The ventral gun may have continued to be a ShKAS machine gun on these early Tu-2s; the record is unclear on this.

Another problem that was noted for the Tu-2 was the complexity of the systems, especially the hydraulic system, and there were also problems with the constant-speed propellers. A special commission set up by the NKAP with the famous fighter designer Nikolaiy Polikarpov as its chairman specifically noted the complexity of the Tu-2 and that it cost more to produce than other aircraft. On the other hand, the commission did note some positive aspects of the Tu-2, such as it was stable around all three axes, was easy to pilot and could fly easily on one engine. The hydraulic system was picked out for special note as being complex to produce and operate, lowering the combat survivability of the Tu-2. The report also noted that with its two forward-firing ShVAK cannons, two forward-firing ShKAS machine guns, and ten RS-132 rockets, the Tu-2 could be used as a ground attack aircraft, if frontal armour were provided for the pilot and the navigator.

One of the recommendations of the commission was that the wheel brakes for the Tu-2 be replaced with 'Douglas' brakes, presumably those used on the Li-2, the Soviet licence-built version of the Douglas DC-3 (C-47). It was hoped that this would ameliorate some of the landing problems with the Tu-2, where it could turn unexpectedly upon landing, due in part to the inadequate brakes, with their lack of synchronisation, and difficulty in use. Evidently, the lack of an ability to lock the tailwheel also contributed to these landing difficulties, although it is unclear when the tailwheel was made lockable.

From 13 September 1942 to 28 October 1942, when the aircraft crashed, a production Tu-2 (c/n 100308, the eighteenth production Tu-2) was tested at the NII VVS, flying forty-four flights to determine the flight characteristics of the production Tu-2. This aircraft did not have the dive brakes fitted, perhaps so rockets could be fitted under the wings. The maximum speed at sea level was 276 mph (444 kph), the top speed at 10,499 feet (3,200 m) was 324 mph (521 kph), the service ceiling was 29,528 feet (9,000 m), and the range was 1,255 miles (2,020 km). For this particular aeroplane, the armament was three ShKAS (with two mounted in the nose and with one of the three being for defensive purposes), two UBT machine guns for defence, and two ShVAK cannons in the wings. Ten RS-132 rockets could be carried under the wings (these do not appear to have been carried very often by the Tu-2). The production Tu-2 was fitted with three-bladed AV-5V-167A propellers, with a diameter of 12.47 feet (3.8 m). Although both the speed and ceiling were less than what had originally been contracted for, the top speed by a considerable 41 mph (66 kph) and the ceiling being less by over 2,625 feet (800 metres), the climbing and landing data were in line with the contract.

Although it appeared almost identical to the '103U' except for the replacement of the AM-37 inline engines with the radial M-82 engines, there were quite a few detail differences between the production Tu-2 and the '103U'. There was more armour protection for the crew. The second wing spar, in the centre section, was strengthened. The control of the flying surfaces was made easier. Since no water radiators were needed for water-cooled engines, this space in the centre section was now occupied by two additional fuel tanks with a capacity of 137.37 gal (520 l). The radio compass was changed from the RPK-22M to the RPK-7. The wing leading edges were now free of air intakes, as the radiators had been removed from the wings.

Due to the shortage of aluminium during the Great Patriotic War, the wingtips, forward fuselage, and the tail cone were made of wood on production Tu-2s to conserve aluminium.

The Tu-2 Redesigned (The 'Tu-2S')

Convinced that the Tu-2 was a good design, Tupolev sought to improve it, even after production had apparently been ended for good in 1942. Tupolev believed that a 'standard' bomber could be created from the Tu-2 that could be used, with modifications, for a variety of tasks: a dive bomber, a reconnaissance aircraft, a long-range bomber, and a trainer. The bomber needed to be simple and easy to produce. Three of the early Tu-2s, produced in October 1942, were used to test structural improvements, including simplification of its various systems. These improvements included removal of the dive brakes and their attendant dive recovery system, the control system was simplified, the two ShKAS machine guns in the nose were removed per VVS recommendation, and the fuel system was simplified. The hydraulic system was simplified by going to a high-pressure system. The most fully modified of these three machines was Tu-2 serial no. 100716, also known simply as '716'. With these modifications, '716' became the *Etalon* (or 'Standard') for what became the Tu-2S. We shall meet this particular aircraft again.

When production resumed on the Tu-2, the exact same bomber was not produced, as some improvements had been made to the design, some of these changes being detailed above, these improvements taking into consideration suggestions and complaints regarding the original version. These changes also reflected Andrey Tupolev's desire to simplify the design and make it easier and cheaper to produce.

One of the main complaints regarded the engines, as there had been considerable problems with the M-82As fitted to the original version, such as with the magnetos and carburettors, and these engines were replaced by the boosted and fuel-injected ASh-82FNs (M-82FNs, originally 'M-82FNV') on the Tu-2S. At 1,850 hp at take-off, these engines were more powerful than the earlier engines, which only produced 1,700 hp at take-off. The installation of these fuel-injected engines removed the problems that had been occurring with the carburettors on the earlier M-82s, as the ASh-82FNs did not have carburettors, featuring direct fuel injection instead. High-altitude

Tu-2S on the ground. (*G. F. Petrov photo archive*)

performance was also improved. These engines were first tested on the '103V', now designated the '103V' 2M-82FNV. The tests were conducted at the beginning of July 1943 and were successful enough that the NKAP Order No. 430 dated 20 July 1943 prescribed these engines for the production Tu-2s. These new ASh-82FN engines were identical to those fitted to the La-5FN and were fitted to all subsequent mass-produced Tu-2s.

There were changes made to simplify this 'new' Tu-2, with an eye towards streamlining production, lowering costs, reducing weight, and improving survivability. One change involved fixing in place the previously moveable stabiliser at an angle of 1 degree 10 minutes as measured from the fuselage centreline. Some of the other changes made were reducing the number of hydraulic instruments and controls from ninety-three to thirty-eight, reducing by half the weight of the wiring, and making the hydraulic system simpler in part by reducing to a fourth the original length of the hydraulic piping (from 1,467 feet (447 m) to 367 feet (112 m)). The hydraulic tank was moved to the front of the aircraft. These simplification measures decreased the weight of the structure of the production Tu-2S by 882 lb (400 kg). Some of the weight reduction was from the following systems: 331 lb (150 kg) from the hydraulic system, 243 lb (110 kg) from the fuel system, 187 lb (85 kg) from the electrical system, and 55 lb (25 kg) from the navigation system.

The electrical system was considerably simplified, with fewer fuses and less wiring. Similar efforts were made to simplify the fuel system. The number of valves was reduced from 100 to thirty-eight valves, and the flexible connections were reduced from 258 to 126 connections. Fuel tanks eight, nine, and ten were removed and the wing tankage was able to be increased due to the removal of the dive brakes and their related equipment (one source states that the number of fuel tanks was reduced from twenty to fourteen tanks). There were other changes, such as adding armour plating to the starboard side of the navigator's position, the electrical system was now powered by one generator instead of two, the dive brakes were no longer fitted (as noted above), the AFA-B camera was replaced by the AFA-BI camera, the hydro-magnetic compass GMK-2 was fitted, etc. The above is only a very partial list of the myriad design changes made to the structure and systems of the early version of the Tu-2 to transform it into the Tu-2S. Despite the very close external similarity of the two versions and similar performance, and having the same basic structure, internally, they were quite different aeroplanes, with the Tu-2S being much simplified.

As noted above, all these changes made the Tu-2S lighter by 882 lb (400 kg) and easier to produce and maintain than the initial Tu-2 series. These changes also made the Tu-2S tougher and more survivable as there were fewer lines, pipes, and equipment to be knocked out of action. Supposedly these changes made to the Tu-2 reduced the manufacturing complexity by 15 to 20 per cent, which made the Tu-2S easier, cheaper, and faster to produce. With these changes, the Tu-2S now took at least 3,000 fewer hours to produce than the early version of the Tu-2.

This improved version of the Tu-2 was given the service designation of 'Tu-2S' ('S' for *Standart* or 'Standard' in Russian), while the Tupolev OKB designation was '61'. In addition to the improved engines, the defensive armament was standardised on three aft-firing 12.7-mm (50-calibre) UBT machine guns, with one being fired by the navigator in a gun position at the back of the cockpit canopy, and one being fired by the radio operator in the mid-upper position. The ventral gunner fired the third gun through the ventral canopy. The two ShKAS guns in the nose were deleted as the VVS felt that these were unnecessary, while the 20-mm ShVAK cannons in the wing roots were retained for use by the pilot. In addition to bombs in the bomb bay, the Tu-2 could now carry torpedoes on underwing racks, in addition to bombs of up to 2,205 lb (1,000 kg) on these same wing racks.

Aircraft '716' had these modifications applied to it at Z.156 in July through August 1943. No. '716' was also fitted with the new M-82FNV (ASh-82FN) engines. With these modifications, it first flew on 26 August 1943 with the OKB, before being handed over to the NII VVS in September 1943 for state tests, the state tests ending on 16 December 1943. The GKO Order No. 3754, dated 17 July 1943 had required that the aircraft have a maximum speed of 342 mph (550 kph), a ceiling of 29,528 feet (9,000 m), and a range of 1,243 miles (2,000 km). It was this order that also re-instated the Tu-2 into production, to now be built at Z.23 in Moscow.

During the tests, '716' showed an improvement over the earlier Tu-2 with a top speed of 315 mph (509 kph) at sea level compared to 276 mph (444 kph) for the earlier version of the Tu-2. The top speed overall increased to 340 mph (547 kph) at 17,717 feet (5,400 m) as compared to 324 mph (521 kph) at 10,449 feet (3,200 m) for the earlier machine. The service ceiling was 31,168 feet (9,500 m) compared to the early Tu-2's 29,528 feet (9,000 m) and the range was also increased by 75 miles (120 km) compared to the earlier Tu-2. These numbers were close to or exceeded the numbers specified by the GKO order. Nonetheless, some problems still remained, such as directional instability, which had been apparent in the earlier version of the Tu-2, and the view of the navigator was still considered lacking. However, despite these shortcomings, it was decided to put this improved version of the Tu-2 into full-scale production as it was felt that the Tu-2 had better performance than other Soviet and foreign bombers in the same class.

By the time of these tests, Tupolev and his OKB staff had already moved from Omsk (Z.166) back to Moscow, to Z.23 (at Fili). In accordance with GKO Order No.

3754, this factory was now tasked with the production of the Tu-2S, which aircraft incorporated the changes made to '716' as fitted with the ASh-82FN engines. This factory would produce all the Tu-2S used during the Second World War.

During the state tests, the Tu-2S was tested against a captured Fw 190A-4 fighter. The results were interesting. At low levels, for example at an altitude of only 3,281 feet (1,000 m) the Fw 190 had difficulty catching up to the Tu-2S because of the small difference in speed between the two aircraft at this altitude. At higher altitudes, it was easier for the German fighter to overtake the Tu-2S as the difference in speed increased. Nonetheless, it was difficult for the Fw 190A-4 to attack the Tu-2S from the front, due to the relatively high speed of the Tu-2S, and it was normally relegated to attacking the tail. While attacking from above, the Fw 190 was always within the zone of fire from the defensive guns of the Tu-2S.

Combat Tactics

As with any aeroplane, so much of its success is dependent on using the proper tactics. For the Tu-2S, this consisted of carrying the correct bombs for the mission involved and flying in proper formations. The bombs that were used could be high-explosive FAB-100, FAB-500, or FAB-1000, depending on the size and toughness of the target. The large FAB-1000 (2,205-lb/1,000-kg) bombs were useful against enemy fortifications, for example. Armour-piercing PTAB and BRAB bombs could also be carried, the PTABs being especially useful against tanks. Even with the maximum bomb load of 6,614 lb (3,000 kg), the aircraft was still found to be easy to handle. Earlier in its usage, there was a shortage of the large calibre bombs, and the Tu-2s were forced to carry smaller bombs, and therefore a smaller bomb load.

For the most part, the defensive armament provided good protection for the aircraft, especially in the case of attacks from the rear. The pilot's two 20-mm cannons would have proved to be a deterrent to frontal attacks. It was also found that flying in formations of three aircraft, or nine aircraft provided a density of fire that helped repel attacks by German fighters.

The optimum altitude for bombing depended on the target. For larger targets, the bombing altitudes were mostly from 3,281 to 9,843 feet (1,000 to 3,000 m), but bombing from an altitude of up to 13,123 feet (4,000 m) did occur. For smaller targets such as bridges and fortified strong points, the altitudes used were 984 to 1,640 feet (300 to 500 m) or 1,640 to 3,281 feet (500 to 1,000 m).

Although the earlier version of the Tu-2 was equipped for dive bombing, including dive brakes, the Tu-2s were used mainly for level day bombing against large targets, as it was found that the Pe-2 was more than adequate for the dive-bombing role. At first, the Tu-2s were limited to only a 2,646-lb (1,200-kg) bomb load. By September 1944, this was increased to 2,976 lb (1,350 kg). Eventually, the full load of 6,614 lb (3,000 kg) was allowed and was used for short-range missions.

Above: Tu-2S in flight.
(*G. F. Petrov photo archive*)

Right: Tu-2S in flight over
Moscow in 1945.
(*Viktor Kulikov's collection*)

Experimental Variants

From the inception of the '103', Tupolev had planned for the aircraft to fulfil different roles, not just that of a dive bomber. Among the other roles considered were that of a reconnaissance aircraft, a long-range bomber, a torpedo bomber, a fighter, and a high-speed day time bomber. Development of these different aircraft was limited during the Great Patriotic War because of the need to concentrate on producing the standard tactical bomber version.

Below are descriptions of some of the experimental versions that were developed during the Second World War. Wholly post-war developments, such as the Tu-8 long-range bomber will not be described. These Tu-2 variants are listed alphanumerically by their military designation, such as 'Tu-2D', or the OKB design number (*Izdeliye* or 'Object' number), such as '63' if there is no service designation, and not necessarily by when they were built chronologically.

Tu-2D Long-Range Bomber ('62')

As early as the initial design phase of the '103', a long-range version had been projected, with longer wings housing two additional fuel tanks on each side, the '103D' (with the 'D' most likely standing for *Dalniy* or *Dalnaya*, 'Long-Range' in Russian, although one source states that the term '103D' was not actually used at the time). This aircraft was never built, due to the need during the war for Tupolev to concentrate on the standard tactical bomber version of the Tu-2. With the Great Patriotic War's successful conclusion no longer really in doubt, in late 1943 or early 1944 Tupolev had time to again begin looking at a long-range version of the Tu-2. In addition, during the later phases of the war, beginning in 1943 there was a need for a longer-ranged aircraft to keep up with the fast-moving offensive operations of the Red Army.

This long-range development of the Tu-2 featured longer wings with an additional fuel tank in each wing. The first version still featured the standard production nose configuration, with the navigator seated behind the pilot, and still featured the ASh-82FN engines. It first flew on 17 June 1944 (or 12 July; sources differ) and underwent OKB tests from 3 July 1944 to 23 September 1944. The state tests went from 20 November 1944 to 23 April 1945. The tests revealed a range of 1,758 miles (2,830 km). This range was greater than that for the production Tu-2S, but this first version of the Tu-2D was not recommended for production because of the large number of defects encountered. This aircraft was used for experimental work until 1947 when it was retired.

The second version had the navigator now placed in front of the pilot in a lengthened and widened nose section and had larger vertical tails. The factory tests went from 20 October 1944 to 1 March 1945, and it was tested by the state between 18 July 1945 (one source mentions 18 June) to 31 October 1945 at the NII VVS. The main defect noted was the lack of range; tests revealed that the aircraft fell short of the specified range at high speed by 249 miles (400 km), and the maximum range was shorter by 124 miles (200 km). The speed and ceiling were noted as being inferior to the first '62'. At one point, a passenger version of the '62' was proposed, with a much-modified fuselage accommodating passengers, but there was to be no production ensuing for either version of the '62', although the second '62' would be further modified into other post-war Tu-2 variants.

'63' (SDB)

This was a high-speed bomber development of the Tu-2 ('SDB'—*Skorostnoiy Dnevnoiy Bombardirovshchik*—'Speedy Day Bomber' in Russian). It was meant to be the Soviet equivalent to the British Mosquito as a day bomber that could escape interception because of its speed, the Mosquito having suitably impressed the Soviets with its abilities. Indeed, the Soviets actually tested a Mosquito B.IV version, provided to them by the British. The GKO issued an order on 22 May 1944 for two SDBs to be built by Z.156. These aircraft were assigned the OKB designation of '63'. They were developed from the original '103', with the first prototype SDB being fitted with more powerful AM-39s, which at 1,870 hp were significantly more powerful than the AM-37s originally fitted to the '103' (rated at 1,380 hp). The new engines drove AV-5LV-221 three-bladed propellers with a diameter of 11.81 feet (3.6 m). The dive brakes were removed and the crew were reduced to two, presumably the pilot and the navigator/bombardier, who also functioned as the defensive gunner. This first version of the SDB retained the low cockpit canopy and unbroken top fuselage line of the original '103'. The armament was comprised of two ShVAK 20-mm cannons in the wings and a single UBT 12.7-mm (50-calibre) machine gun for defensive purposes.

The aircraft first flew on 21 May 1944 and the OKB tests continued until 31 May 1944. The state tests began on 5 June 1944 and ended 6 July 1944. The top speed at sea level was 327 mph (527 kph), and the maximum speed was an impressive 401 mph (645 kph) at 21,800 feet (6,650 m). The range was 1,137 miles (1,830 km).

The second aircraft was modified compared to the first one and incorporated some of the features of the Tu-2S, with different canopies for the cockpit and the dorsal gunner, although these canopies were still different from those used on the production Tu-2S. The main landing gear were also changed; instead of being forked, there was an axle on the outside of the single oleo leg of the landing gear that the wheel was now attached to. Although the main wheels remained the same, the tailwheel was increased in size. The vertical tails were increased in size. This second aircraft, the SDB-2, was completed in October 1944.

Compared to the original SDB, it had AM-39Fs instead of the AM-39s, the 'F' (for *Forsirovanniy* or 'Boosted' in Russian) indicating that these engines were boosted, but still using the same propellers as the original SDB. An additional UBT machine gun was also added, this belonging to the new ventral gun position that had now been included. The maximum bomb load was 8,818 lb (4,000 kg). The SDB-2 first flew on 14 October 1944. The NII VVS testing took place from 29 November 1944 to 4 April 1945. The state tests went from 5 April 1945 to 16 May 1945. The maximum speed was slightly lower than that for the first prototypes, being a still impressive 398 mph (640 kph) at 22,500 feet (6,850 m). However, the speed at sea level was increased from 327 mph (527 kph) to 339 mph (547 kph). One problem that was noted was the poor view of the navigator.

Despite the excellent overall performance, especially the speed of the SDBs, this version of the Tu-2 did not go into production as Tupolev had decided on using an enhancement of the Tu-2S, the Tu-10 ('68'), which was a mostly post-war development for the fast bomber role.

Tu-2S 2ASh-83

On 20 July 1944, the NKAP through Order No. 444 directed the Tupolev OKB to test the experimental high-altitude ASh-83 engines fitted to a Tu-2. The Tu-2 chosen for this was the first Tu-2S (our old friend aircraft 'No. 716'), which was fitted in 1945 with this engine of 1,900 hp driving a four-bladed propeller. Although the engine installation was very similar to that used with the ASh-82FN, it differed in having a long air intake over the cowling (similar to that used on the La-5FN fighter). The installation also featured seven individual exhausts per side, like the La-7 fighter, and not the single exhausts per side, as featured on the production Tu-2s.

The aircraft first flew on 18 May 1945 with A. D. Perelyot as the pilot. The aircraft was tested from August 1945 until May 1946, when the engines were worked on. The aircraft was tested again by the NII VVS from 22 August to 21 November 1946. The range was a disappointing 1,030 miles (1,660 km), but the maximum speed was an impressive 395 mph (635 kph) at 23,294 feet (7,100 m). Despite the excellent speed, development was not proceeded with as the ASh-83 remained an experimental engine and never went into large scale production. This aircraft is sometimes referred to as the 'Tu-2M', which is an apparently erroneous designation not used by the Soviets at the time.

Tu-2Sh Ground Attack Bomber

Several different variants of a *shturmovik* or ground attack version of the Tu-2 were built, differing mainly in their fixed armament.

The first version was equipped with no fewer than eighty-eight (eleven rows of eight guns) Shpagin PPSh-41 submachine guns fitted into the bomb bay, to fire downwards and forwards at an angle of 30 degrees depression. Each gun carried seventy-one rounds. The decision to test this system on two Tu-2S was made on 10 October 1944 at a meeting with head of the Red Air Force Marshal A. A. Novikov. This system was called the 'Battery PPSh'. It was intended to be used against enemy infantry. Although the firepower was devastating, it would have been of short duration, and it would have been difficult (or impossible) to rearm the guns in flight, so the idea was abandoned. The effectiveness of more conventional anti-personnel weapons such as fragmentation bombs also made this version redundant.

Other *shturmovik* versions resorted to more conventional type armament, with large cannons in the nose (such as the post-war Tu-2RShR-57). A version tested in 1944 had a 75-mm cannon that was loaded by the navigator and fired through the nose. This version was intended to be a train-buster. It was tested at a shooting range (it apparently was not test fired in the air), but this version was unsuccessful because of the undue stress put on the airframe by the firing of this large and powerful cannon.

Although all were powerfully armed, none of the ground attack variants of the Tu-2 went into production, as the Soviet Air Force continued to rely upon single-engined *shturmoviks* (Il-2 and Il-10) for its ground support.

The Tu-2 in Detail

The below description is for a Tu-2S from Z.23 in Moscow. Where changes were made during the production run, these will be noted by the series number, where available. The description covers both aircraft produced during the Second World War and those produced post-war, when the majority of Tu-2s were actually produced.

General Description

The Tu-2 was a mainly metal, shoulder-winged, twin-engined cantilever monoplane with a fully retractable main landing gear and a fully retractable tailwheel. The pilot and navigator sat in a fully enclosed cockpit, and the two gunners in the rear fuselage were also protected by canopies. The tail unit was composed of twin vertical tails mounted on the ends of the horizontal tail planes.

Fuselage

The oval-section fuselage was made out of a mostly metal (or was all-metal for post-war Tu-2s) semi-monocoque construction, although most Great Patriotic War Tu-2s had a wooden nose and tail cone in an effort to save on scarce aluminium supplies. This wooden nose was replaced by a metal nose on Tu-2s from the series 20 on according to one source. The wooden nose was covered in .24 inches (6-mm) plywood. It appears that the post-war Tu-2s were equipped with the metal nose. The early Tu-2s had a clear conical cover at the very tip of the wooden nose, probably made out of plexiglass. The Tu-2S had a semi-conical clear tip to its nose, with the top half of the tip being either wooden or metal according to the construction of the rest of the nose. The tail cone was also wooden on the Great Patriotic War Tu-2s. The tail cone was apparently made out of metal from the series 44 on.

The fuselage was constructed out of three main sections: the nose (wooden during most of the Great Patriotic War), the centre section (which housed the bomb bay and the wing attachments), and the tail section (which the horizontal tail planes were attached to and included the wooden tail cone during the Great Patriotic War).

The upper part of the nose section, before the series 20 Tu-2s, was made of plywood to the third frame, and the lower part was made of plexiglass panels 0.24 inches (6-mm) thick. This enabled the pilot to observe the ground while bombing and would enable him to spot any fighters coming from below and to the front of the aircraft. From the series 57 on (another source states from the series 48 on), the area of the plexiglass was extended by 20 inches (.5 m) to the rear on the starboard side back to the bomb bay, as the pilot's lower view, especially during dive bombing, was considered inadequate. This improved view also helped the pilot to see landmarks and targets on the ground while in level flight.

The pilot sat under the slightly bulged cockpit canopy 4.72 inches (120 mm) to the left of the centre line of the fuselage. The pilot's seat, made out of stamped steel armour plate, was adjustable, being able to move vertically up or down 3.15 inches (80 mm) and horizontally 9.84 inches (250 mm, from the series 50 on). The navigator sat behind the pilot on a folding seat and could turn around to operate a rearward-facing UBT 12.7-mm machine gun for defence. The windscreen was made out of armoured glass. The canopy frames were made out of welded steel tubing. The top of the cockpit canopy, consisting of three panels, opened to the port where it was held open by a strut, while the starboard side of the canopy, consisting of five panels, swung down, to allow access to the cockpit for the pilot and the navigator. A radio mast, which also incorporated a pitot tube, was mounted offset to the port side above the armoured windscreen. From the series 48 on, the top of the cockpit canopy was made flat. It was perhaps at this time that the pitot tube was moved to just underneath the top of the antenna mast; it had been mounted lower down in previous versions of the Tu-2.

The central part of the fuselage housed the bomb bay, which started at frame ten and ended with frame twenty-two. The centre section itself started at frame ten and ended at frame twenty-three so it can be seen that the rather capacious bomb bay occupied almost the entire centre section. The frames ten, twelve, thirteen, fifteen, seventeen, and nineteen were reinforced to handle the weight of the bombs hanging in the bomb bay. The rear of the bomb bay had two small windows, which enabled the radio operator to inspect the status of the bomb bay while in flight. There were two bulkheads composed of sealed metal and impregnated fabric that kept exhaust gases from entering the cockpit, improved the aerodynamic qualities of the aircraft, and helped to prevent the spread of fire.

The aft fuselage was located from frame twenty-three to forty. A camera was located between frames twenty-four and twenty-six, and it consisted either of an AFA-IM or of a NAFA-19 camera for photographing at night. The radio operator/

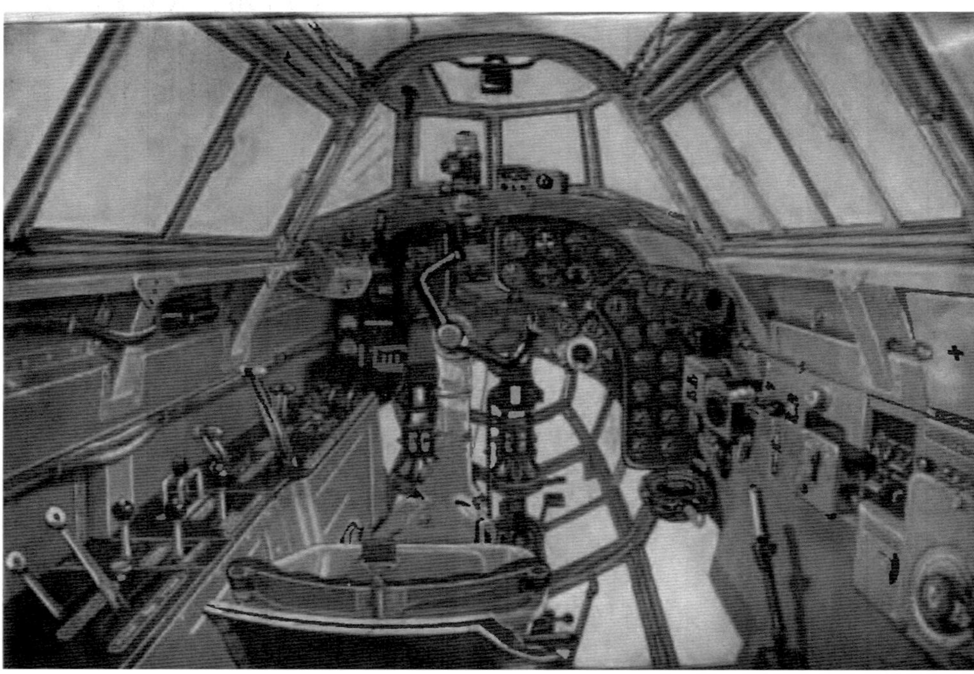

Tu-2 cockpit. (*Drawing from the 1945 Tu-2 Flight Manual*)

gunner was located between frames twenty-four and twenty-nine. The ventral gunner from the series 20 to the series 43 was equipped with three enlarged windows (larger than the earlier windows), to give better lighting for his position. The windows were located at frames thirty-three to thirty-five, and the glass was 0.12 inches (3 mm) thick. From the series 44 on, the three windows were replaced by one large window on each side. Between frames thirty and thirty-three, there was a ventral hatch for the evacuation of the radio operator and the ventral gunner. The ventral gun position was located between frames thirty-three and thirty-six, the ventral gunner laying down to operate his UBT machine gun. He was protected from below and the back by armour.

The wooden tail cone, as used in the Great Patriotic War Tu-2s, consisted of a structure of three wooden frames with stringers, covered by a wooden, probably plywood veneer. From the series 44 or 45 on, it was replaced by a metal cone.

Armour Protection

One change that was made to the Tu-2S over the early version of the Tu-2 was the provision of more armour for the crew. The total weight of the armour on the Tu-2S was 538 lb (244.2 kg). The pilot had a seat made out of armour 0.59 inches (15 mm) thick and he was protected on the port side by a sheet of armour 0.59 inches (15 mm) thick. The navigator was protected on the underside by a sheet of armour 0.31 inches (8 mm) thick, on the starboard side by 0.24 inches (6 mm) thick armour, and from the back by armour 0.59 inches (15 mm) thick. The radio operator/gunner was protected by a plate of armour 0.24 inches (6 mm) thick on the underside and had a plate of armour 0.47 inches (12 mm) protecting him on the back. The ventral gunner was protected by a sheet of armour that was composed of two layers: one 0.79 inches (20 mm) thick and another layer 0.06 inches (1.5 mm) thick to protect the gunner from shrapnel.

Wings

The wings were cantilever, shoulder-mounted, and were of two-spar all-metal construction, except for the wingtips, which were of wooden construction on the Great Patriotic War Tu-2s. Metal units from the series 52 on replaced the wooden wingtips. The engines and the main landing gear were attached to the front spar. In combination with corrugated skin panels (covered by smooth dural panels), the two wing spars formed a torsion box for the wing centre section, which was very strong and could bear up to 95 per cent of the torsional loads. This centre section also featured ten ribs. In addition to the two main spars, the flaps were attached to a rear auxiliary spar. From the series 59 on, the leading edges were fitted with de-icing boots, which worked by pulsating the rubber edges. The starboard wing had a landing light that could extend from under the outer part of the wing, and it could retract back in. The wings were initially covered with a dural skin of 0.03 inches (0.8 mm) and 0.05 inches (1.2 mm), which was later changed to a thicker skinning of 0.04 inches (1.5 mm) and 0.08 inches (2 mm). The leading edges of the wing were smooth, with no air inlets, as there were no radiators to cool, the engines on the Tu-2S being air-cooled radials.

Tail planes

The tail planes consisted of two fins and rudders, attached to the ends of the cantilever horizontal stabilisers (which were themselves attached to the fuselage by four bolts), with the vertical tail planes being perpendicular to the ground and parallel to each other. The tail planes' construction was of metal, with the stabilisers having two metal spars, with a metal covering except for the rudders and elevators, which were of a metal structure with fabric covering. Originally, the skin of the stabilisers was 0.03 inches (0.8 mm) thick, but this was changed to 0.04 inches (1.5 mm) later. The starboard rudder and both elevators had electrically controlled trim tabs. The fins (vertical stabilisers) consisted of two spars with eight ribs and were of all-metal construction. The elevator construction consisted of one spar and thirteen ribs with a fabric covering.

The horizontal stabilisers were mounted with a dihedral of 6 degrees 52 minutes and were of a 433 Gottingen profile (these profiles were developed by Gottingen University in Germany). On the early version of the Tu-2, the incidence of the horizontal stabilisers could be adjusted, but with the Tu-2S the stabilisers were fixed, as part of the simplification and lightening programme that characterised the Tu-2S. From the series 59 on, the leading edges were fitted with de-icing boots, as with the wings and the vertical tail planes.

Control Surfaces

The ailerons, twin rudders, and elevators were all made of a dural structure, covered by fabric. The Schrenk-type flaps were all-metal, split to allow clearance for the engine nacelles, and hydraulically operated. These were capable of opening up to 45 degrees for landing (one source states that they could open up to 55 degrees) and were set to 15 degrees for take-off. The flaps were attached to a rear auxiliary wing spar. The Frise-type ailerons were split into three sections, with the inner section of the starboard aileron having a trim tab that could be moved up or down 15 degrees, and the two outboard sections for both ailerons had fixed metal trim tabs that could be bent up or down on the ground.

The ailerons themselves could be moved up 25 degrees and down 15 degrees. The moveable aileron trim tab was electrically operated. This moveable trim tab was on the starboard wing only; the port wing only featured the two ground-adjustable tabs.

The rudder trim tab, present only on the starboard rudder, could be moved 15 degrees in either direction. The elevators could be moved up 35 degrees and down 20 degrees. The elevator trim tabs could be moved 6 degrees up only. The trim tabs were all electrically operated (except, of course, for the ground-adjustable tabs on both of the ailerons).

Engine

The basic engine for all production variants of the Tu-2 bombers was the M-82 fourteen-cylinder twin-row air-cooled four-stroke radial engine with a two-speed supercharger, also known as the ASh-82 from 1 April 1944 on, after its designer, Arkadiy Shvetsov. One of the features of this engine was that it had a short stroke, which decreased the diameter of the engine from what it would have been. This, in turn, allowed the engine to be housed in a smaller diameter cowling, which decreased drag. In fact, the Tu-2 had a well-designed, close-fitting cowling, which combined with the large propeller spinner, gave it good streamlining for a radial-engined aircraft. This engine had been developed from the M-62 single-row engine, itself a development of the M-25, a licence-built version of the famous American R-1820 Wright Cyclone nine-cylinder single-row radial engine, which powered the B-17 Flying Fortress and the first Douglas DC-3s, among other famous aeroplanes.

The Tu-2s carried two of the ASh-82 engines. The engines could be started mechanically by Hucks starter dogs on the front of the spinners fitted by shafts to starter trucks but were normally started pneumatically from compressed air from the AK-50M compressor, which was mounted on the right engine's gearbox. An oil tank of 13.21 gal (50 l) was located behind the engine's firewall. From the series 15 on, there was a system for warming the engines—a very useful feature indeed in a central Russian winter.

An interesting feature of the engines was that the engine assemblies were interchangeable between the port and starboard sides, with an easily removed front assembly, or 'power-egg'. This made the replacement of engines relatively easy from a maintenance standpoint and added to the general ease of maintaining the Tu-2. Some twin-engined aircraft were 'handed', with engines that swung propellers in opposite directions, such as the American Lockheed P-38 Lightning fighter. This eliminated torque, but the engines were slightly different, which made maintenance more difficult, and made using the engines for either side impossible. In contrast, the Tu-2 was built for easy maintenance.

ASh-82FN engine. (*Viktor Kulikov's collection*)

Although the eighty early version Tu-2s built in 1942 had the unboosted M-82A engine, the variant fitted to the vast majority of the Tu-2s was the ASh-82FN (M-82FN), with boosting and direct fuel injection. This was the same engine fitted to the La-5FN and La-7 fighters. In the ASh-82FN version, the engine was capable of 1,850 hp at take-off. As with the La-5FN and La-7, there were louvres fitted to the front of the engine that could be opened and closed to control the flow of air over the engine cylinders. The louvres were different from those used on the Lavochkin fighters in that they were iris-like instead of being two sets of discs with fixed blades and could be controlled either automatically or manually controlled by the pilot.

A small air inlet over the engine fed the supercharger (as with the La-5 fighter) and there was a broad and shallow intake under the engine for the oil cooler. The inlets over the engine were enlarged and equipped with dust filters from the series 61 on. The exhaust was collected from the fourteen cylinders on each engine to exit via one exhaust on each side of the engine, with seven of the cylinders feeding into the one exhaust, protruding through the cowling. At some point during production, apparently post-war, the external exhaust pipe was shortened. The engine installations were attached to the front wing spar via welded steel trusses.

The engine drove a constant speed three-bladed AV-5V-167A metal propeller with rounded tips for the Tu-2S, but post-war this was changed from the series 59 on to a constant speed AV-9VF-21K four-bladed propeller with blunt tips. The three-bladed propeller had a diameter of 12.47 feet (3.8 m) while the four-bladed unit had a diameter of 11.81 feet (3.6 m). The three-bladed unit had a R-7E speed regulator, while the four-bladed unit had a R-9SMI speed regulator. A large conical spinner usually covered the propeller.

The engines were installed in close-fitting cowlings which resembled those fitted to the radial-engined Lavochkin fighters (the La-5 and La-7), which also utilised the ASh-82 engine. From the series 20 on, the cowlings were made even more close-fitting, which required small fairings being fitted to cover the rocker heads on the engine cylinders. Single panels on either side of the engine opened up to allow easy access for maintenance. Three latches on the bottom kept the cowling panels locked together.

Landing Gear

Both the main landing gear and the tailwheel were retractable, retracting aft, and were completely enclosed by doors when retracted. The main landing gear consisted of a single large oleo strut which was symmetrically forked to attach to the wheel on either side. The tailwheel was similarly forked. The main wheels were equipped with hydraulic drum brakes and had oleo-pneumatic shock absorbers. All the units were hydraulically operated, with a compressed air backup system. The main wheel tyre size was 1,100 × 425 mm (two sources state 400 mm; this may have been for the earlier Tu-2 variant), and from the series 51 on was 1,100 × 395 mm and used a higher air pressure. The tailwheel tyre size was 470 × 210 mm, which from the series 51 on was increased to 530 × 230 mm, probably to deal with the greater all-up weight. The tailwheel strut could be locked in place, which assisted in take-offs and landings. The freely moving, unlockable tailwheel of the early version of the Tu-2 had caused slewing, which led to some accidents.

Electrical System

The electrical system powered the cockpit lights, the radio equipment, and the heating. The cockpit used ultraviolet lighting for night flying. The electrical power was supplied by a GS-1000V generator, with a GSK-1500V from the series 52 on. The Tu-2s built at Z.166 after the war featured a GSN-3000V generator.

Fuel System

The fuel system on the Tu-2S consisted of nine fuel tanks. The main fuel tank was housed in the fuselage above the bomb bay, between the two wing spars. The wing tanks consisted of two inner and two outer fuel tanks in each wing, housed between the two spars. The total capacity was 740 gal (2,800 l—one source says 2,880 l (761 gal), and another says 3,000 l (793 gal), though the fuel capacity may well have varied from series to series). The tanks were of welded steel sheet construction of 1–1.2-mm thickness, with self-sealing rubber seals, and featured the normal Soviet fire-suppression system of neutral gases being pumped into the fuel tanks as they were emptied so that an explosive fuel vapour–air mix would not build up, the gas displacing this dangerous mixture. The neutral gases were supplied to the fuel tanks from the exhaust of the starboard engine, after cooling and being passed through a filter.

Hydraulic System

The hydraulic system was used to power the landing gear, the wheel brakes, the landing flaps, radiator flaps, and the bomb bay doors. The total volume was 8.72 gal (33 l).

Oil System

The oil system contained 72.91 gal (276 l) of oil, housed in two tanks, the pumps, oil lines, and the radiators.

Oxygen/Pneumatic System

The Tu-2 was equipped with eight 1.06-gal (4-l) oxygen canisters which were mounted on brackets in the aft fuselage and provided oxygen to the crew. The ShVAK 20-mm cannons in the wing roots were reloaded pneumatically.

Electronic Equipment

The Tu-2S was initially fitted with the RSB-3bis radio. This was replaced by the RSI-6 from the series 51 on. An SPU-4 intercom was used for onboard communication between the crew. At least some of the Tu-2s used an RPK-7 radio compass, while others used the RPKO-10M radio compass. Later still an RPK-2B radio compass was used, from the series 50 until the series 63 aircraft. From the series 63 aircraft on, blind flying equipment in the form of an RV-2 radio altimeter, an ARK-5 radio compass, and an MRP-48 bearing receiver was fitted. From the series 35 onwards, an 'identification friend or foe' (IFF) SCh-3 UHF system was fitted. The electronic equipment was continuously changed and upgraded on the Tu-2S during production, so there was no standard set of equipment, except for a specific series.

Fixed Armament

The fixed armament consisted of two Shpitalniy-Vladimirov ShVAK 20-mm cannons in the wing roots on all production Tu-2s, which could be used for ground attack strafing, or to discourage head-on attacks from enemy fighters. These were located between the first and third wing ribs. The pilot aimed these cannons using a fighter-type reflector gun sight, the PBP-1, which could also be used for dive bombing. Each cannon was equipped with 150 rounds and was cooled by air. The guns were fired electrically and the reloading was done using compressed air. The spent cartridges and links were ejected from chutes under the wings. The firing button was located on the pilot's steering wheel. These two cannons gave the Tu-2S the very same forward-firing armament as the La-5 and La-7 fighters. The early version of the Tu-2 also featured two ShKAS machine guns mounted on either side of the nose that were fired by the pilot. These were deleted from the Tu-2S as being unnecessary.

Moveable Armament

The moveable armament consisted for the Tu-2S of three Berezin UBT 12.7-mm (50-calibre) heavy machine guns on flexible mounts (the earlier version had the smaller ShKAS 7.62-mm (30-calibre) machine guns on at least some of the mounts). K-8T reflector gun sights were used to aim the guns. The rear portion of the radio operator's canopy could be slid forward (to the front of the aeroplane) over the radio operator's head to allow the use of his machine gun. When not in use, this portion of the canopy slid back, to fully enclose the radio operator's cabin, with a small slot in the bottom of the canopy to clear the machine gun when it was stowed.

With the continuing development of the Tu-2, the gun mounts were changed. With the series 48 Tu-2S, the navigator received a new gun position, the VUS-1, which replaced the BUSh-1 blister-type installation, and the gun now had 170 rounds (the gun on the BUSh-1 had 190 rounds) and a K-8T gun sight with an OMP-6 stabiliser. It appears that from the series 44 on the radio operator/dorsal gunner's mount was changed from the VUB-2B to the VUB-68 mount, with 250 rounds, with the K-8T or K-20T gun sight with the OMP-6 or OMP-7 stabiliser. From the series 50 on, the radio operator had a fixed canopy over his gun mount, replacing the moveable canopy. From the series 46 on, the ventral gunner was equipped with the LU-68 gun mount, with 350 rounds (or 300 rounds according to one source), replacing the earlier LU/Pe-2 mount with its 300 rounds (it was called the LU/Pe-2 because it was based on the Pe-2's ventral gun installation). The guns were equipped with bags that caught the spent shell cartridges and links. On some late Tu-2s, the UBT for the dorsal gunner was replaced by a Berezin B-20E 20-mm cannon, perhaps from the series 50, when the fixed gunner's canopy was apparently introduced. There are photographs, which show what looks to be a 20-mm cannon in the mid-upper position, under the fixed canopy.

The field of the fire for the navigator's gun was 45 degrees to the right and left, 90 degrees up, and 10 degrees down. For the radio operator's gun, the field of fire was 110 degrees to the right and 105 degrees to the left, 65 to 70 degrees upwards, and 15 degrees downwards. The ventral gunner had a field of fire of only 23 degrees to

Radio operator's gun position with UBT. (*Viktor Kulikov's collection*)

Navigator's gun position with UBT. (*Viktor Kulikov's collection*)

the right and left, 45 degrees down, and 1 degree up. This field of fire for the three defensive machine guns gave good protection from most angles, especially to the rear.

From the series 52 on, the moveable guns had a PAU-22 gun camera to record the shooting results, and from the series 57 on, the pilot also had a gun camera.

Disposable Armament

One of the most important features of the Tu-2 was its capacious bomb bay and excellent bomb load, up to 8,818 lb (4,000 kg) in some post-war versions. With this weight of bombs, some of the bombs had to be mounted on the underwing bomb racks, located near the wing roots, with one on each side. The bomb bay itself was large and could accommodate a single 4,409-lb (2,000-kg) bomb, one of the biggest bombs in the Soviet wartime inventory. This ability for a medium bomber to carry such a large bomb was considered a definite plus for the Tu-2. A more normal bomb load would have consisted of smaller bombs in the bomb bay.

Normally, the bomb load did not exceed 6,614 lb (3,000 kg), consisting of three 2,205-lb (1,000-kg) bombs, with one in the bomb bay and two under the wings; however, this heavy load was used only on short-range missions, with a more normal bomb load being 2,205 lb (1,000 kg) or 4,409 lb (2,000 kg). As an alternative to the 1,000-kg bombs, four FAB-250 (551-lb (250-kg)) bombs could be carried, with two in the bomb bay and two under the wings on the wing root bomb racks, for a total of 2,205 lb (1,000 kg). If the smaller FAB-100 (220-lb (100-kg)) bombs were carried,

Open bomb bay. (*Viktor Kulikov's collection*)

up to nine could be accommodated internally in the bomb bay for a total of 1,984 lb (900 kg) if no other bombs were carried. Besides carrying the FAB high explosive type bombs, the Tu-2 could also carry the BRAB armour piercing bombs, PTAB anti-tank bomblets, and fragmentation bombs.

The bombs were aimed by the navigator for level bombing, using the OPB-1R sight (or OPB-1D from the series 24). For dive bombing, the PBP-1 sight could be used.

Conclusion

Although hobbled at the time of its introduction in 1942 by an immature engine, the M-82, if not for a poor decision by Stalin to halt production, with the continued improvement of the M-82, the Tu-2 would have made a much more important contribution to the war. As it was, it was heavily used in the final year of the war, where its speed, good offensive and defensive gun armament, and excellent bomb load enabled it to become one of the finest medium bombers of the war. Its continued development and production after the war also showed what a fundamentally sound design Andrey Tupolev had first conceived of in his NKVD prison. Post-war, the Tu-2 replaced both light and medium bombers such as the Il-4, the Pe-2, the B-25, and the A-20. Without the success of the Tu-2, Andrey Tupolev would not have lived to contribute so greatly to Soviet aviation in the post-war period with his bombers and airliners. If for that reason alone, the Tu-2 must count as one of the most important Soviet designs of all time.

Tu-2 Specification Table

Type	'103'	'103U'	'103V' (Tu-2 Prototype)	Tu-2 (Z.166)	No. 716 (Tu-2S Prototype)	Tu-2S (Z.23)
Year	1941	1941	1941	1942	1943	1944
Maximum Speed: mph (kph)	395 (635)	379 (610)	323 (521) or 328 (528)	324 (521)	340 (547)	340 (547)
Range: miles (km)	1,180 (1,900)	1,180 (1,900)	1,242 (2,000)	1,255 (2,020)	1,305 (2,100)	1,305 (2,100)
Service Ceiling: feet (m)	34,780 (10,600)	34,449 (10,500)	29,528 (9,000)	29,528 (9,000)	31,168 (9,500)	31,168 (9,500)
Offensive Armament	2 × ShVAK 20-mm cannons, 2 × ShKAS 7.62-mm machine guns	2 × ShVAK 20-mm cannons, 2 × ShKAS 7.62-mm machine guns	2 × ShVAK 20-mm cannons, 2 × ShKAS 7.62-mm machine guns	2 × ShVAK 20-mm cannons, 2 × ShKAS 7.62-mm machine guns	2 × ShVAK 20-mm cannons	2 × ShVAK 20-mm cannons

Defensive Armament	2 × ShKAS 7.62-mm machine guns	3 × ShKAS 7.62-mm machine guns	2 × Berezin UBT 12.7-mm machine guns, 1 × ShKAS 7.62-mm machine gun	2 × Berezin UBT 12.7-mm machine guns, 1 × ShKAS 7.62-mm machine gun	3 × Berezin UBT 12.7-mm machine guns	3 × Berezin UBT 12.7-mm machine guns
Rocket Armament	N/A	10 RS-132 132-mm rockets?	10 RS-132 132-mm rockets	10 RS-132 132-mm rockets	N/A	N/A
Maximum Bomb Load: lb (kg)	4,409 (2,000)	4,409 (2,000)	6,614 (3,000)	6,614 (3,000)	6,614 (3,000)	6,614 (3,000)
Empty Weight: lb (kg)	16,812 (7,626)	17,246 (7,823)	16,171 (7,335)	16,757 (7,601) or 16,347 (7,415)	16,477 (7,474)	16,477 (7,474)
All-up Weight: lb (kg)	21,936 (9,950)	23,005 (10,435)	22,802 (10,343)	23,232 (10,538)	22,839 (10,360)	22,839 (10,360)
Maximum Weight: lb (kg)	24,233 (10,992)	25,302 (11,477)	25,955 (11,773)	25,942 (11,767)	25,944 (11,768)	25,044 (11,360)
Engines/ take-off hp per	2 × Mikulin AM-37 1,380	2 × Mikulin AM-37 1,400	2 × Shvetsov M-82A 1,700	2 × Shvetsov M-82A 1,700	2 × Shvetsov ASh-82FN (M-82FN) 1,850	2 × Shvetsov ASh-82FN (M-82FN) 1,850
Crew	3	4	4	4	4	4
Length: feet (m)	43.31 (13.2)	45.28 (13.8)	45.28 (13.8) or 44.98 (13.71)	45.28 (13.8)	45.28 (13.8)	45.28 (13.8)
Wingspan: feet (m)	61.88 (18.86)	61.88 (18.86)	61.88 (18.86)	61.88 (18.86)	61.88 (18.86)	61.88 (18.86)

8
Long-Range Bombers

Perhaps because of the immense size of their country, the Soviets had fairly early on developed a fascination for long-range aircraft that found expression in civilian aircraft such as the record-setting ANT-25 of the 1930s. This interest was not limited to civilian spheres, however, and the Soviet military was also interested in the combat capabilities of long-range aircraft, especially bombers. From the 1920s, large twin- and four-engined aircraft were built and put into service to explore and exploit these capabilities. Some of these aircraft saw use in the Second World War and will be the subject of the following discussion.

TB-3 (ANT-6)

This very large four-engined aircraft, designed by Andrey Tupolev, was one of the first large multi-engined all-metal cantilever monoplane bombers to go into service anywhere in the world when it entered Soviet service in 1932. It was, in some ways, a four-engined development of the earlier twin-engined TB-1. Constructed of an all-metal structure with a corrugated metal covering so typical of the German-designed Junkers aircraft (whose aircraft influenced Tupolev), it featured a fixed landing gear and was thoroughly obsolete by the beginning of the Great Patriotic War. It saw service at Lake Khasan in 1938, Khalkhin-Gol (as a bomber and transport), the 1939 invasion of Poland (as a transport), and the Winter War. It was also used by the Chinese Air Force against the Japanese in the Sino-Japanese War (1936–45). In these conflicts, it was usually used in its primary role as a bomber. Unlike several Soviet aircraft, such as the Tupolev SB bomber, it did not see service in the Spanish Civil War.

By the time of the beginning of Operation Barbarossa (22 June 1941), the TB-3 had been officially retired from front-line service (in 1939). As obsolete aircraft, the 541 TB-3s still in Soviet service (516 with the VVS and twenty-five with the AVMF) were no longer front-line aircraft so they were based to the rear, where they luckily survived the initial aerial onslaughts of Operation Barbarossa by the Luftwaffe. This luck was not to last very long, however.

TB-3 4M-17F in flight. (*Viktor Kulikov's collection*)

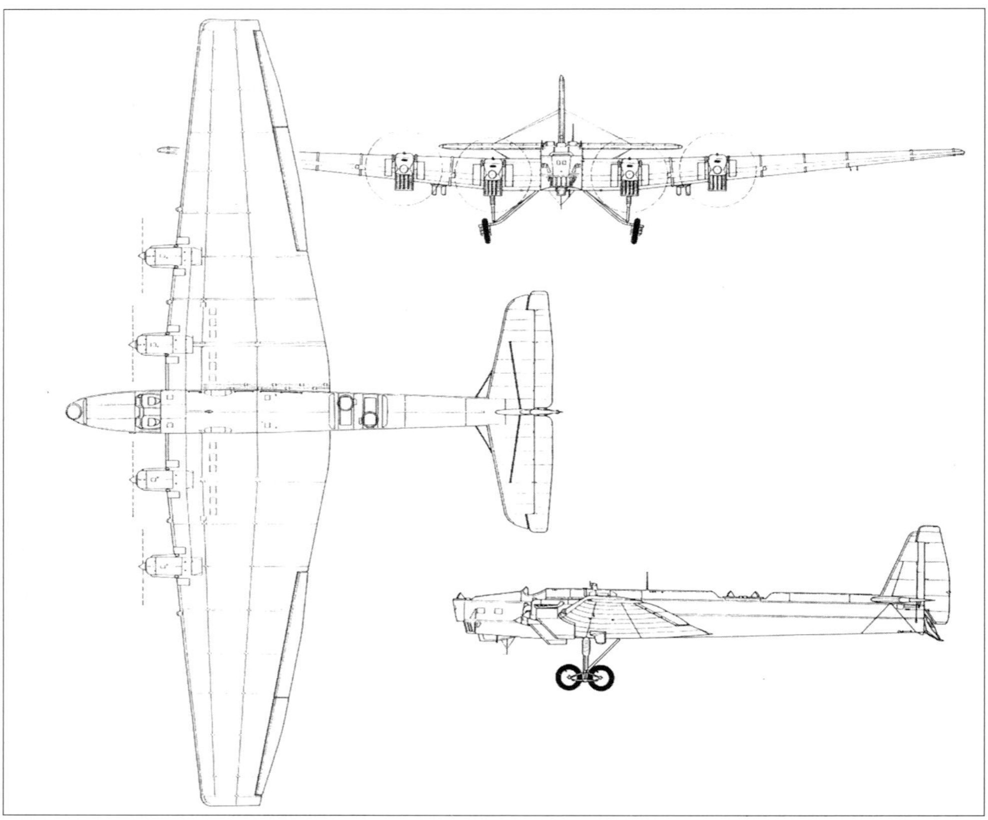

Three-view drawing of TB-3 4M-17F. (*By Kaboldy. Wikimedia*)

Since it had escaped destruction (for the moment), out of necessity, the TB-3 saw action in the opening days of the war as an unescorted day bomber in what were little more than suicide missions in the Soviets' mostly vain attempt to halt or even slow down the seemingly inexorable German advance. Due to its heavy losses during day operations, the TB-3 was quickly moved completely to night operations, seeing action as early as 23 June 1941 as a night bomber. In 1942, with the establishment of the ADD, most TB-3s were assigned to it. As a night bomber, it was still being used against the Wehrmacht as late as the Battle of Kursk in the summer of 1943 and continued in service until the end of the war in non-combat roles; it was even being used as late as 1949 in the Arctic as a civilian transport.

The TB-3 was utilised heavily during the war as a transport, for carrying cargo and for carrying paratroopers, and was involved in a massive paratrooper operation around Vyazma in January 1942. Some of the wartime bomber versions were equipped with two MV-3 enclosed turrets amidships, possibly taken from other bombers, such as the Il-4. It was superseded as a long-range bomber by the much more modern TB-7 (Pe-8: see further on), but on 1 July 1945, twenty (one source has twenty-five, another has ten) TB-3s were still listed as a part of the 18th Air Army (the former ADD), although these were transports.

As a kind of precursor to the stand-off missile-carrying bombers of the post-war era, some TB-3s were used as part of the *Zveno* ('Flight' in Russian) programme, in which they carried 'parasite' fighters above and/or below their wings. The TB-3s served as the 'Mother Ship', or *Aviamatka*. These installations had been designed by the engineer Vladimir Sergeyevich Vakhmistrov (1897–1972) in combination with Andrey Tupolev. The fighters can be thought of as being a kind of piloted cruise missile. This programme was developed before the war, testing with the TB-3 starting in 1934 (the earlier TB-1 had also been tested with this system). This system was used for a short time during the early stages of the Great Patriotic War, and it is described in the combat usage section.

Development

The TB-3, or 'ANT-6' as it was initially designated, can be seen as a logical extension of the TB-1 twin-engined design, only with four engines to give it greater range and load-carrying capability. The TB-3 design grew out of a specification issued by the Special Technical Bureau to Andrey Tupolev (with the participation of the Red Air Force) in 1925 for a long-range four-engined aircraft. This aeroplane was to have a top cruising speed of 93 mph (150 kph), a range of 186–217 miles (300–350 km), and be capable of carrying 3,748 lb (1,700 kg) of payload, with 2,205 lb (1,000 kg) of this being bombs. These were not particularly stringent requirements, but they would be increased in the following years. In March 1927, the Red Air Force expanded the role of the aircraft to include that of a night bomber with a combined engine power of 2,400 hp. Due to the complexity of the design, even though it was based upon an existing design (the TB-1), Tupolev successfully lobbied the *Aviatrest* (the State Aviation Industry Trust, the predecessor of the NKAP) to have the first flight of the aircraft delayed until 1930. The design of the aircraft was also prolonged by the Red Air Force not finalising its specifications until 1929.

Like the TB-1, the TB-3 was of all-metal, mainly aluminium alloy construction, with a tubular framework covered by corrugated metal panels (as with Junkers' designs of the 1920s and 1930s). The cantilever wing was supported by four tubular wing spars. Even the control surfaces were covered in metal skinning.

The mock-up for the design was approved on 21 March 1930 and the prototype was completed on 31 October 1930. The prototype ANT-6, powered by American Curtiss V-1570 Conqueror V-12 liquid-cooled inline engines of 600 hp, flew for the first time on 22 December 1930 at Monino, piloted by Mikhail M. Gromov. As no indigenous Soviet engines were powerful enough, it was necessary to fit the ANT-6 with these imported engines. The aircraft was re-engined with German BMW VI engines with wooden propellers replacing the metal propellers, the original TB-1-type single main wheels replaced by tandem wheels, and armament fitted. Thus modified, the aircraft was tested from 10 January 1932 to 21 February 1932.

The armament consisted of ring-mounted twin Degtyaryov DA 7.62-mm (30-calibre) machine guns in the nose, and in two positions amidships. There were also two retractable 'dustbin' turrets mounted under the wings. The dustbin turrets mounted only one gun apiece giving a total of up to eight defensive machine guns, which was quite heavy for the time. The middle gun positions, mounted one in front of the other, could slide from side to side. The standard bomb load was to be 4,009 lb (2,000 kg), with the bombs loaded on under the fuselage and underwing racks, in addition to an internal bomb bay.

The landing gear on a TB-3 4M-17F. This two-wheel tandem arrangement was introduced on the first TB-3 prototype and was used by all the TB-3 4M-17Fs. One of the wheels has a hub covering the spokes, while another does not. (*Viktor Kulikov's collection*)

Dorsal gun positions on a TB-3. This consisted of two gun positions, each mounting twin machine guns. These are Degtyaryov guns as shown by the drum magazines. (*Viktor Kulikov's collection*)

The underwing 'dustbin' turrets fitted to some TB-3s. There were two of these, mounting a single gun, and located under each wing. They were retractable. Note the under fuselage bomb racks. (*Viktor Kulikov's collection*)

Bombs being loaded on to the under fuselage racks on a TB-3. (*Viktor Kulikov's collection*)

Production of the aircraft with Mikulin M-17 engines (Soviet licence-built copies of the German BMW VI engines) was approved on 20 February 1931, with the aircraft now given the service designation of 'TB-3'. The 'TB' in the name stood for *Tyazhyoliy Bombardirovshchik* ('Heavy Bomber'). The first pre-production aircraft flew on 4 January 1932. The first production aircraft flew on 27 February 1932.

TB-3 4M-17F

This first production version of the TB-3 featured four of the M-17F engines. Production took place at two factories: *Zavod* 18 in Voronezh and *Zavod* 39 in Moscow. One problem that appeared was that the production aircraft were considerably heavier than the original prototypes. This resulted from the somewhat haphazard construction of the production aircraft, as compared to the carefully constructed prototypes. As a result of this haphazard construction, the prescribed thicknesses of the metal parts were not always adhered to, and there were variances from aircraft to aircraft, with the thicker than need be parts adding to the weight of the aircraft. The armament was the same as with the prototype with the BMW VI engines.

Around half of all TB-3s produced (411) were of the TB-3 4M-17F version, and some of these aircraft served into the Great Patriotic War as both bombers and transports (military and civilian). Some were converted into G-2 civilian transports.

TB-3 4M-17F on the ground. Note the *boroda* ('beard') under the nose. (*Viktor Kulikov's collection*)

TB-3 4M-17F on the ground. This example is missing the *boroda* and appears to be painted in overall green topside, probably with a blue underside. (*Viktor Kulikov's collection*)

TB-3 4M-17F Barbarossa victim in 1941. Note how panels from the wing leading edge fold down; these created platforms for crew servicing the engines. (*Author's collection*)

TB-3 4M-17F preparing for take-off, sometime during 1941. This aircraft has had black bands applied over the green topside, and appears to have plain red stars. (*Viktor Kulikov's collection*)

A TB-3 crew stands with their winter-camouflage TB-3 in the background. The MV-3 turrets that were fitted to some Great Patriotic War TB-3s can be seen. (*Viktor Kulikov's collection*)

A close-up of the MV-3 turrets on a Great Patriotic War TB-3. Each turret mounts a single ShKAS machine gun. Note the corrugated skinning of the aircraft. (*Viktor Kulikov's collection*)

TB-3 4M-34

With the M-17F engines, the performance of the TB-3 could charitably be described as stately, with a top speed of around 130 mph (209 kph), at best. In an effort to correct this and give the TB-3 better performance all around, the new more powerful Mikulin M-34 engines were substituted for the M-17Fs. The first TB-3 equipped with these new engines flew on 8 March 1933. The armament for most of these aircraft remained the same as with the TB-3 4M-17F. The retractable dustbin turrets were apparently no longer fitted to the last bombers of this version, which instead featured a gun firing through a ventral hatch. Some 111 TB-3 4M-34s were produced.

TB-3 4M-34R

This version of the TB-3 was equipped with the geared M-34R engines. In addition to the M-34R engines, this version featured a tail gunner position, which necessitated a small cut-out at the bottom of the rudder. Some 150 TB-3 4M-34Rs were produced.

TB-3 4M-34RN

The M-34RN engine had a greater compression ratio than the M-34R and a supercharger, and it was capable of producing 970 hp, compared to the 830 hp of the M-34. This TB-3 differed considerably from earlier versions, having an enclosed nose gun position (introduced from 1936 on), large 6.56 feet (2 m) single wheels for the main landing gear replacing the tandem two-wheel bogies, and a tailwheel replacing the tail skid (one source has the tailwheel fitted to the TB-3 4M-34R; it may have been fitted at some point to the TB-3 4M-34Rs). The DA guns were replaced by the new rapid-fire ShKAS 7.62-mm (30-calibre) machine guns. The tail gunner now had a transparent 'lobster-back' windscreen to provide some protection from the slipstream. At least some of the TB-3 4M-34RNs were fitted with a large glazed dorsal enclosure equipped with a ShKAS machine gun on a TUR-8 mount. A ventral position, mounting a single ShKAS gun, was fitted to provide protection for the rear and below.

At some point during the production run, the aircraft had the engines equipped with four-bladed fixed-pitch wooden propellers. These propellers were fitted after tests with a production TB-3 from late 1935 to early 1936, although originally this aircraft had the four-bladed units fitted only to the inner engines, before having them fitted to the outer engines as well. The production TB-3s were apparently also initially fitted with the four-bladed units confined to the inner engines, before all engines were so fitted.

The first TB-3 4M-34RN flew for the initial time in March 1934, but this TB-3 version was not ready for its official tests until 17 August 1935. This aircraft then became the standard for 1936 production TB-3s. Some 124 TB-3 4M-34RNs were built according to NKAP records, although this number may have also included the externally very similar TB-3 4AM-34FRN and TB-3 4AM-34FRNN.

TB-3 4M-34 on the ground. This aircraft appears to be painted in a light colour, probably light grey. Note the deeper and further aft-mounted radiators of the M-34 engine as compared to the M-17. (*Viktor Kulikov's collection*)

AM-34 engine on a TB-3. Of note are the upturned exhaust tubes and the four-bladed propeller. (*Viktor Kulikov's collection*)

The tail gun position introduced on the TB-3 4M-34R. The rudder's base had to have a cut-out to accommodate this position. This is an early installation without the protective 'lobster-back' windshield. (*Viktor Kulikov's collection*)

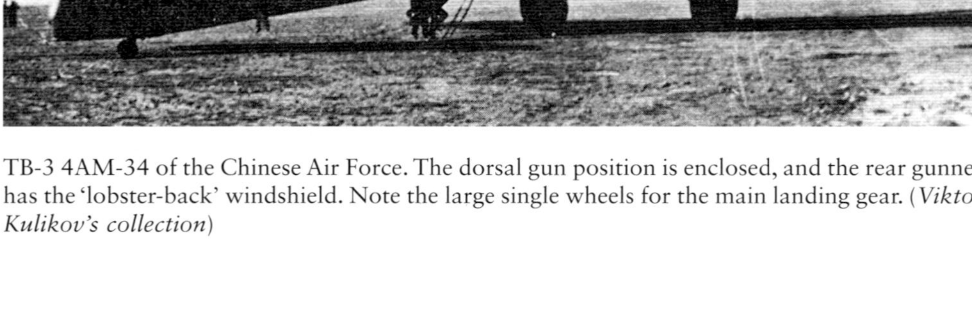

TB-3 4AM-34 of the Chinese Air Force. The dorsal gun position is enclosed, and the rear gunner has the 'lobster-back' windshield. Note the large single wheels for the main landing gear. (*Viktor Kulikov's collection*)

Single turret installation on a TB-3. (*Viktor Kulikov's collection*)

Soviet TB-3 4AM-34 in flight. This is a pre-war aircraft, with the green topside and the black-outlined red stars. (*Viktor Kulikov's collection*)

TB-3 4AM-34 preparing for take-off. This aircraft has the black over green camouflage that was applied with the start of the Great Patriotic War. Note the four-bladed wooden propellers on the engines and the enclosed nose gun position. (*Viktor Kulikov's collection*)

TB-3 4AM-34FRN

The TB-3 was equipped from 1936 with the improved AM-34FRN engines (with the 'AM' for Aleksandr Mikulin, the chief designer). These TB-3s, along with those equipped with the AM-34FRNN engines, were the last TB-3s to be produced, with production ending in 1937 (or 1938, sources differ; according to the NKAP, one TB-3 was produced in 1938). This engine, with the 'F' standing for *Forsirovanniy* ('Boosted'), produced 1,200 hp on take-off.

TB-3 4AM-34FRNN

This last production version of the TB-3 featured AM-34FRNN (or AM-34FRNV) engines, which were very similar to the AM-34FRN engines fitted previously but were now equipped with direct fuel injection, although the power remained the same (1,200 hp). These aircraft were produced from 1936–37 (or possibly into 1938, again, sources differ).

G-2

TB-3s used by Aeroflot were designated as the 'G-2'. These appear to have all been aircraft modified from military TB-3s, so the configurations would have differed, depending on which military variant they were modified from. In addition to the gun positions being closed over, at least some (perhaps all) of the G-2s had enclosed cockpits, and some could be equipped with skis for winter operation. In 1935–38, around fifty TB-3s with either M-17F or M-34 engines were assigned to Aeroflot. The aircraft could carry either passengers (up to forty) or cargo (up to four tons). By the beginning of the Great Patriotic War, thirty-five G-2s were still in service, and they were used throughout the war and after, until 1947. The special arctic civilian variant is described below.

ANT-6A 'Aviaarktika'

Z.22 in 1936 produced several aircraft (one source has five aircraft, another has four) that were intended for use in the Soviet Arctic. Unlike the G-2s, which were modified for civilian use from ex-military aircraft, these 'Aviaarktika' aircraft were built especially for their civilian role, from airframes that were removed from the production line. The aircraft had an enclosed cockpit, all the gun openings were removed and covered, single large wheels instead of tandem bogies were fitted, and metal three-bladed variable-pitch propellers were used in place of the fixed-pitched wooden propellers used by most TB-3s. The aircraft could be fitted with skis in place of the wheels, with the wheels being carried under the fuselage (or the skis were carried under the fuselage, if the wheels were fitted). The aircraft were very colourful, with an orange paint scheme with blue accents. Some aircraft were equipped with the AM-34FRNV engines in 1937, which replaced the original M-34R engines.

Despite its civilian role, the ANT-6As were modified for use as bombers. One was used in the Winter War as a night bomber. During the Great Patriotic War, from October 1941, all the ANT-6As were modified as bombers with the TB-3's standard gun armament and bombing equipment. They served in the Northern Soviet Union under the AVMF of the Baltic Fleet. One aircraft was lost in 1941, but three others continued to be used until 1944 as bombers, after which they were seemingly converted back into a civilian configuration. These served into the late 1940s, perhaps as late as 1949, in the Arctic in their original civilian role. These were apparently the last TB-3/ANT-6s of any type to be in use.

Conclusion

At the time of its introduction in 1933, the TB-3 was something of a trendsetter, being the first all-metal four-engined cantilever monoplane strategic bomber to enter service anywhere in the world. In that sense, it was a kind of harbinger for all the four-engined monoplane bombers of the Second World War. During the 1930s, it gave good service in a variety of roles. Altogether, 819 aircraft were produced from 1932 to 1938. Although by the Second World War, and particularly by the start of the Great Patriotic War, the TB-3 was completely obsolete, it still saw heavy usage first as a bomber (mainly as a night bomber, until 1943) and transport, then only as a transport and continued to be used after the war as a transport. No examples survive intact today, although a wreck was found in 1992 and may eventually be restored.

TB-3 Specification Table

Model	ANT-6	TB-3 4M-17F	TB-3 4M-34	TB-3 4M-34R	TB-3 4M-34RN	TB-3 4AM-34 FRN	TB-3 4AM-34 FRNN	ANT-6A 'Aviaarktika'
Year	1930	1932	1933	1933	1934	1936	1936	1936
Maximum Speed: mph (kph)	144 (232)	122 (197)	129 (207)	150 (242)	179 (288)	186 (300)		171 (275)
Range: miles (km)		838 (1,350)		1,292 (2,080)				1,553 (2,500)
Service Ceiling: feet (m)	15,420 (4,700)	12,500 (3,800)	12,795 (3,900)	16,732 (5,100)	22,310 (6,800)	26,247 (8,000)		
Defensive Armament	N/A	5 to 8 × DA 7.62-mm machine guns	5 to 8 × DA 7.62-mm machine guns	5 to 8 × DA 7.62-mm machine guns?	4 × ShKAS 7.62-mm machine guns?	4 × ShKAS 7.62-mm machine guns?	4 × ShKAS 7.62-mm machine guns?	None (normally)
Maximum Bomb Load: lb (kg)	N/A	4,409 (2,000)	4,409 (2,000)?	4,409 (2,000)?	4,409 (2,000)?	4,409 (2,000)?	4,409 (2,000)?	None (normally)
Empty Weight: lb (kg)	20,668 (9,735)	24,178 (10,967)	26,235 (11,900)	26,544 (12,040)	27,745 (12,585)			27,558 (12,500)
All-up Weight: lb (kg)	35,367 (16,042)	37,920 (17,200)	39,904 (18,100)	38,912 (17,650)	39,882 (18,090)			53,021 (24,050)
Engines/ take-off hp per	4 × Curtiss Conqueror 600	4 × Mikulin M-17F 715	4 × Mikulin M-34 830	4 × Mikulin M-34R 830	4 × Mikulin M-34RN 970	4 × Mikulin AM-34FRN 1,200	4 × Mikulin AM-34FRNN 1,200	4 × Mikulin M-34R 830
Crew		11	11?	8?	8	8?	8?	
Length: feet (m)	79.4 (24.2)	80.05 (24.4)	79.4 (24.2)	82.35 (25.1)	82.61 (25.18)	82.61 (25.18)	82.61 (25.18)	82.61 (25.18)
Wingspan: feet (m)	132.87 (40.5)	129.6 (39.5)	132.87 (40.5)	130.45 (39.76)	137.30 (41.85)	137.30 (41.85)	137.30 (41.85)	137.30 (41.85)

Pe-8 (TB-7, ANT-42)

Except for the obsolete TB-3, which by 1941 could no longer be considered even a marginally modern warplane, the only four-engined strategic bomber the Soviet Union possessed by the start of the Second World War was this massive aircraft, designed by Vladimir Petlyakov, who had worked on the TB-3 under the leadership of Andrey Tupolev.

Initially known as the 'ANT-42', after the head of the design bureau Andrey Tupolev ('ANT' for 'Andrey N. Tupolev'), the aircraft first flew on 27 December 1936. By the time it entered service in 1939, the designation had been changed to 'TB-7'. Since Andrey Tupolev had by this time been imprisoned, the 'ANT' designation was no longer used (it was considered in bad taste to use the initials of an 'Enemy of the State'). From 1942, after the death of Vladimir Petlyakov in a crash, it was known by the designation of 'Pe-8' (the even numbering of non-fighters, including bombers, by this time was established).

The Pe-8 remained in use throughout the war, mostly under the ADD or its successor, the 18th Air Army of the VVS. Pe-8s bombed Berlin in 1941 and saw combat during the Battle of Stalingrad, where they were used for bombing tactical targets. In the bombing of the East Prussian fortress city of Königsberg on 5 April 1943 a radial-engined Pe-8 (Pe-8 M-82) dropped the enormous 11,023-lb FAB-5000 bomb (or 5,000-kg bomb—the heaviest bomb carried by a Soviet bomber during the war) on that city's heavy fortifications.

Though few in numbers, the Pe-8 saw heavy usage. For example, during the Battle of Kursk in 1943, radial-engined Pe-8 M-82 versions dropped FAB-5000 bombs on Wehrmacht tanks and other armour. Other German or German-allied cities to be bombed by the Pe-8 included Berlin and Bucharest, the capital of Romania.

Although considerably larger in size, in terms of performance and configuration the Pe-8 can be considered the Soviet equivalent of the British Avro Lancaster and the American Boeing B-17 Flying Fortress heavy bombers. However, unlike these aircraft, the Pe-8 was not produced in large numbers and was not a major factor in the war. For most of the Great Patriotic War, it was not a part of the Red Air Force, but was a part of the independent ADD (*Aviatsiya Dal'nevo Deystviya*) or 'Long-range Aviation' (from 1942 to late 1944), which was an independent military arm under the direct control of the *Stavka*, the Soviet High Command. The ADD was dissolved in late 1944 and its aircraft were incorporated into the Red Air Force as the 18th Air Army (18th VA), although the Pe-8 may have flown its last bombing mission in August 1944. After the war, the Pe-8 saw service as a transport in the Soviet Arctic into the 1950s, the Arctic seeming to be the last stop for several large Soviet bombers, including the earlier TB-1 and TB-3. The Pe-8 continued in this role until the mid-1950s, although unfortunately, no Pe-8s have been preserved. Perhaps this is not so surprising since in total only ninety-three (or ninety-six) TB-7/Pe-8s were produced.

Production TB-7 (Pe-8) with the AM-35A engines. (*Viktor Kulikov's collection*)

Development

ANT-42

As early as 1931, the NII VVS had issued specifications to the TsAGI for a modern replacement for the TB-3. Design of what became the Pe-8 actually started in 1934, when specifications for a replacement for the TB-3 were issued by the Red Air Force. The specifications called for an aircraft capable of a top speed of 273 mph (440 kph) at an altitude of 32,808 feet (10,000 m), and carrying 4,409 lb (2,000 kg) of bombs. These were ambitious figures for 1934 and were more than twice the performance figures of the TB-3. On 27 June 1934, Andrey Tupolev directed his bureau to begin the design of the 'TB-7' (its VVS designation, the 'TB' standing for *Tyazhyoliy Bombardirovshchik* or 'Heavy Bomber'). Although the Tupolev bureau designed the aircraft, the actual design was undertaken by Vladimir Petlyakov under the direction of Andrey Tupolev, and the aircraft received the internal design bureau designation of 'ANT-42', indicating that it was the forty-second design of Andrey Tupolev.

The preliminary design was submitted to the VVS in December 1935, at the same time that the mock-up was being reviewed. Both the design and the mock-up were approved and work began on the first prototype, the ANT-42.

The design that emerged was a modern monoplane bomber, with all-metal construction and metal covering except for the control surfaces. The large cantilever wings were of two-spar construction, and the top of the pinched-in pear-shaped central fuselage was relatively narrow, necessitating the co-pilot to sit behind the pilot, both being seated offset to the port side in a raised fairing that extended back to the dorsal turret. The inboard engine nacelles, which housed the retractable main landing gear along with the inner engines, also housed gunners located at the rear of the very deep nacelles, operating a single gun on a semi-circular mount. In addition to these gun positions, there were nose, dorsal, and tail turrets, as well as a ventral gun position. A partially glazed gondola was located under the nose, as a sort of 'Beard' (*Boroda* in Russian) that could accommodate the navigator for bomb-aiming.

This was similar to the installation that had been fitted to many early TB-3s, which Petlyakov was heavily involved in the design of.

To give the new bomber the necessary high-altitude performance demanded by the specifications, supercharged engines were needed. Here an interesting solution was devised; a separate engine, a Klimov M-100, was used to drive the supercharger that then supplied compressed air via ducts to the Mikulin AM-34FRNs that powered the aircraft. The M-100 engine was housed in the central part of the fuselage, above the wing centre section structure, the fairing housing the pilots also accommodating part of the engine. This arrangement was given the designation of 'ATsN', from *Agregat Tsentral'novo Nadduva* ('Centralised Supercharging Unit').

The ANT-42 flew for the first time on 27 December 1936, piloted by Mikhail M. Gromov. The ATsN installation, although already fitted to the ANT-42, was not used for the initial time until 11 August 1937. The testing showed that the aircraft had a top speed of 250 mph (403 kph) at 26,247 feet (8,000 m), with a range of 1,864 miles (3,000 km). Testing also revealed defects, mainly concerning the underdeveloped AM-34FRNs. As it turned out, the AM-34FRNs never entered into large-scale production, although a relatively small number were produced and used on some TB-3s.

ANT-42bis

Development of the second prototype, the ANT-42bis, took some of the issues encountered in testing the first prototype into account. The fuselage was widened by 3.94 inches (100 mm) and the tail bracing struts were deleted, the horizontal tail planes becoming cantilever structures. Joint manufacturer and state testing started on 11 August 1938. Armour and armament were also fitted. The engines and the ATsN

The flaps on the ANT-42bis (TB-7). The large under nose bomb aimer's position can just be seen at the right of the photograph. The semi-retractable dorsal turret, mounting a 20-mm cannon, can also be seen. (*Viktor Kulikov's collection*)

installation were the same as that used on the ANT-42 (by now also referred to by its VVS designation of 'TB-7'). It was intended that the ANT-42bis was to become the standard, or *etalon* for the production TB-7s to be built at Z.124 in Kazan'. The ANT-42bis first flew on 26 July 1938. While the ANT-42 was still being tested, the NII VVS had recommended it for production.

TB-7/Pe-8

The production TB-7s were to be equipped with the AM-34FRN engines with the M-100 in the ATsN installation. Four of the ATsN installations were supplied by TsIAM before they refused to deliver any more, and only the first two TB-7s had these installed. There were also problems with the supply of the AM-34FRN engines, as large-scale production was not undertaken with these engines. Because of these issues, the NKAP stopped production of the TB-7 in early 1940. One main external difference between the ANT-42 prototypes and the production TB-7 was the deletion of the *boroda*, the under nose gondola for the bombardier/navigator.

Pe-8 AM-35A

Despite halting production of the TB-7 in early 1940 with full cancellation even being considered, the NKAP still realised that a long-range bomber was needed, so a replacement engine was required for production to restart on the TB-7. The unavailability of the AM-34FRN had made it necessary for replacement engines to be mounted on the production TB-7s (or 'Pe-8'; after the death of chief designer Vladimir Petlyakov in 1942, the TB-7 was renamed the Pe-8, the 'Pe' in the designation referring to his family name).

It was decided to install the Mikulin AM-35A on the TB-7 as replacements for the AM-34FRNs. The AM-35A engines, which also powered the high-altitude MiG-3 fighter, had a take-off hp of 1,350. It was also decided that the M-30 and M-40 aero-diesels of the Charomskiy OKB might be used. Both engines were tested on the TB-7.

By the end of 1940, Z.124 had delivered eighteen TB-7s to the VVS, most of them equipped with the AM-35A engines. These engines had the advantage of being more reliable than the M-30 and M-40 aero-diesels.

Pe-8 M-30

As mentioned above, the Charomskiy M-30 aero-diesel was considered as a replacement engine for the AM-34FRN on the TB-7 (Pe-8). These diesel engines gave the promise of long-range for the bomber. The M-30 featured a centrifugal supercharger and was found to be more reliable than the similar M-40 engine, which was tested on a TB-7 (see below). It is unclear how many TB-7s/Pe-8s were fitted with the M-30, which was less reliable than the AM-35A, and some of these aircraft were refitted with AM-35As, but as late as 1944, some Pe-8s were produced with the ACh-30B, which was a development of the M-30.

Pe-8 M-40

In the spring of 1941, a TB-7 was equipped with the Charomskiy M-40 aero-diesel engines. This engine had a take-off rating of 1,500 hp. Compared to the M-30, this

A Pe-8 in 1943. It appears to be equipped with the AM-35A engines. (*Viktor Kulikov's collection*)

A posed photograph of a crew walking away from their Pe-8 AM-35A, apparently after a mission. That this was not actually after a mission can be surmised by the presence of covers over the nose machine guns. (*Viktor Kulikov's collection*)

The Pe-8 AM-35A that carried Soviet Foreign Minister Molotov to Washington D.C., USA, in 1942, photographed in Washington with interested American officers examining what to them was an exotic aeroplane. (*Viktor Kulikov's collection*)

A Pe-8 AM-35A in flight. (*Viktor Kulikov's collection*)

Close-up of the dorsal turret. The gun is the ShVAK 20-mm cannon. (*Viktor Kulikov's collection*)

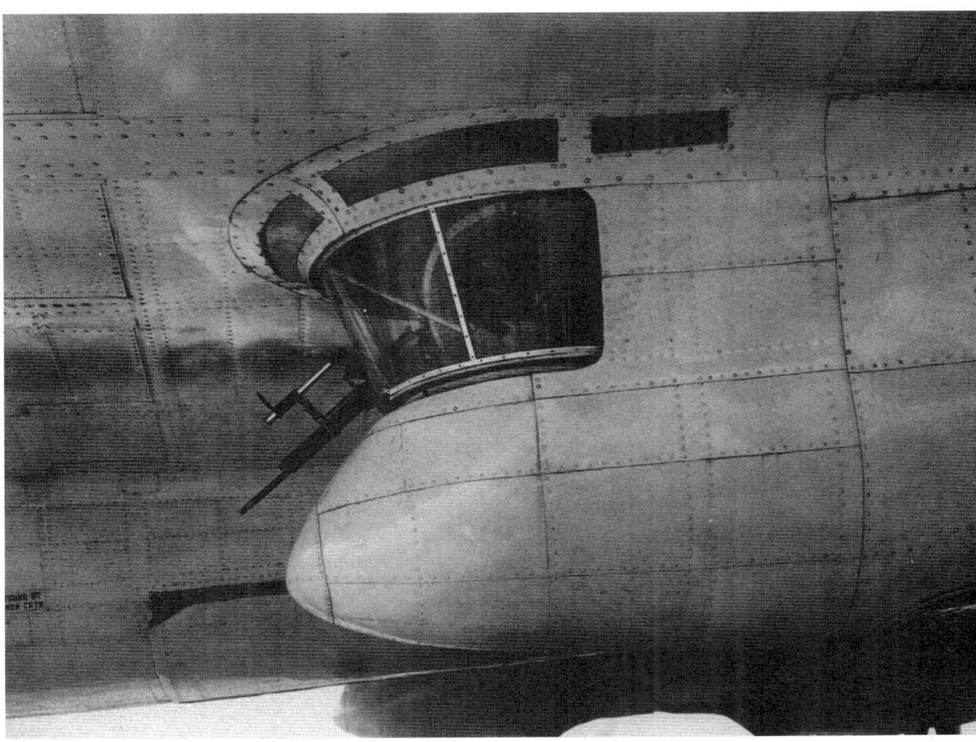

Close-up of the MV-10 turret mounted in the inboard nacelles of this Pe-8 AM-35A. This turret mounted a single machine gun. (*Viktor Kulikov's collection*)

A Pe-8 M-30 in flight. Note the 20-mm cannon fitted to the tail turret; the nose turret mounts twin ShKAS machine guns. (*Viktor Kulikov's collection*)

engine was less reliable and suffered from problems with its manually controlled fuel feed that could cause the engines to stall at high altitudes. Due to this problem, the M-40 was not fitted to production TB-7s/Pe-8s.

Pe-8 M-82

Since production of the Mikulin AM-35A engine had ended in 1942 so the Mikulin AM-38 engine for the Il-2 could be produced in its place, the supply of the AM-35As stopped and a new engine was needed, once again, for production to continue on the Pe-8. The M-30s had proven to be less than ideal, so the Shvetsov M-82 radial engine (ASh-82), which powered the Tu-2 and the La-5, was considered for installation on the Pe-8.

Pe-8s with the M-82/ASh-82 were produced at Z.124 in 1943 and 1944. At first, there were problems with the turbo-supercharger installation, but this was solved. The Pe-8 M-82 had a range of 2,610 miles (4,200 km) with a bomb load of 4,409 lb (2,000 kg), while the Pe-8 AM-35A had a range of 2,299 miles (3,700 km) with the same load, and the Pe-8 M-30 had a range of 3,393 miles (5,460) with the same load. Despite the greater power of the M-82s, which was appreciated, the AM-35A was more reliable. The M-82 also put out a larger, more visible exhaust flame, which enabled German night fighters to locate the Pe-8 M-82s easier. As time went on, and German night defences improved, the loss rate for the Pe-8 edged up. In 1942, the loss rate was one per 106 flights, but by 1944, it was one per forty-six flights. This was a

A Pe-8 M-82 with its crew. This aircraft appears to have the later three-colour camouflage over a black underside. (*Viktor Kulikov's collection*)

Single gun nose mount in a Pe-8 M-82. (*Viktor Kulikov's collection*)

different situation from that with the Il-2, whose loss rate gradually decreased as the conflict wore on. By 1944, fifty-two Pe-8s had been lost, fourteen to the Axis.

Some Pe-8s had an Il-4-type single ShKAS gun installation in the nose, which replaced the nose turret with its twin ShKAS guns. This gave the nose a more streamlined shape. This installation was fitted to later Pe-8s but it is not clear from the record when this was done, or how many Pe-8s were built with or modified with this nose.

Conclusion

Despite being comparable to the British four-engined bombers (such as the Lancaster and Halifax) and the American four-engined bombers (such as the B-17 and B-24), the Pe-8 was produced in very small numbers. As such, it did not have the impact of the British and American 'heavies', which were produced in the thousands. The Soviets decided that it was more important to have many more twin-engined bombers such as the Il-4 and the Pe-2, than to divert production to such a large and complex aircraft. In this respect, the Soviet doctrine was similar to the Germans', who had concentrated on twin-engined bomber designs at the expense of four-engined bombers.

In addition, in place of pre-war doctrine which placed some emphasis on strategic bombing, the Soviets concentrated on tactical and logistical or operational targets during the Second World War, instead of strategic targets, such as factories and cities. Due to its small production run, the Pe-8 had little impact on the war as a whole, where twin-engined bombers such as the aforementioned Il-4 and Pe-2, and the single-engined Il-2 took centre stage in the struggle against Nazi Germany. In a sense, the Pe-8 was the victim of a numbers game, of a system that valued quantity over everything else, especially if it met the tactical needs of the Red Army.

Pe-8/TB-7 Specification Table

Model	TB-7 (ANT-42) Prototype	TB-7 (ANT-42bis)	TB-7 AM-34FRN	Pe-8 AM-35A	Pe-8 M-40	Pe-8 M-82
Year	1936	1937	1938	1941	1941	1943
Maximum Speed: mph (kph)	250 (403)	267 (430)	267 (430)	275 (443)	244 (393)	261 (420)
Range: miles (km)	1,864 (3,000)	2,175 (3,500)	2,175 (3,500)	2,299 (3,700)	3,790 (6,100)	2,610 (4,200)
Service Ceiling: feet (m)	35,433 (10,800)	36,909 (11,250)	36,909 (11,250)	30,500 (9,300)	30,184 (9,200)	26,247 (8,000)

Defensive Armament	6 × DA 7.62-mm machine guns	6 × DA 7.62-mm machine guns	1 × ShKAS 7.62-mm machine gun, 6 × ShVAK 20-mm cannons	6 × ShKAS 7.62-mm machine guns	6 × ShKAS 7.62-mm machine guns	2 × ShVAK 20-mm cannons, 3 × UBT 12.7-mm machine guns
Maximum Bomb Load: lb (kg)			8,818 (4,000)	8,818 (4,000)	8,818 (4,000)	13,228 (6,000)
Empty Weight: lb (kg)	39,430 (17,885)	39,683 (18,000)	40,830 (18,520)	40,941 (18,571)	43,453 (19,710)	41,425 (18,790)
All-up Weight: lb (kg)	52,602 (23,860)	52,911 (24,000)	54,220 (24,594)	59,525 (27,000)	57,320 (26,000)	59,966 (27,200)
Maximum Weight: lb (kg)	66,139 (30,000)	70,548 (32,000)	70,548 (32,000)	73,853 (33,500)	73,853 (33,500)	79,366 (36,000)
Engines/ take-off hp per	4 × Mikulin M-34FRN 1,200 1 × Klimov M-100A in fuselage to drive the supercharger for the main engines	4 × Mikulin M-34FRN 1,200 1 × Klimov M-100A 1,000 in fuselage to drive the supercharger for the main engines	4 × Mikulin AM-34FRNV 1,200 (first two fitted with the Klimov M-100 in the fuselage)	4 × Mikulin AM-35A 1,350	4 × Charomskiy M-40 1,500	4 × Shvetsov M-82 1,400
Crew			9	10	10	11
Length: feet (m)	76.77 (23.4)	80.06 (24.4)	74.74 (22.78)	76.12 (23.2)	76.12 (23.2)	76.12 (23.2)
Wingspan: feet (m)	127.99 (39.01)	129.59 feet (39.5)	127.95 (39)	128.38 (39.13)	128.38 (39.13)	128.38 (39.13)

Il-4 (DB-3)

First flying in 1935 (as the TsKB-26), the DB-3 was designed by Sergey Ilyushin of Il-2 fame (the designation was changed to 'Il-4' in March 1942, with the 'Il' standing for 'Ilyushin', the family name of the designer). In its most developed production form, the IL-4 (DB-3F), it was a little larger than the slightly earlier Tupolev SB (a twin-engined 'fast' bomber) and longer-ranged than the SB. Most importantly, it had nearly twice the bomb load. In many ways, it was the Soviet equivalent of the German Heinkel He 111, both being twin-engined medium bombers designed in the mid-1930s that continued to serve until the end of the Second World War, the Il-4 as the Soviet Union's standard long-range bomber, despite its obsolescence.

It was also used as a long-range reconnaissance aircraft, a torpedo bomber, and a transport. Indeed, as a torpedo bomber the Il-4 continued in service for some time after the war, in a role that it had fulfilled with some success during the Great Patriotic War, and it was replaced by the piston-engined Tu-2T and the jet-engined Il-28T 'Beagle' in this role post-war, the Il-4T finally being retired in 1952. After the war, the Il-4 was given the NATO (or ASCC: 'Allied Self-Coordinating Committee') reporting name or nickname of 'Bob', although this apparently happened in 1954, two years after the Il-4 (as the Il-4T) had been retired from service with the Soviet Union. The ASCC can never be accused of not being thorough. In all, some 6,784 Il-4/DB-3s were constructed from 1936 to 1946.

Development

Before working for his own design bureau (OKB), Ilyushin had been the deputy head of the TsAGI. On 13 January 1933, a design bureau (the 'TsKB', *Tsentralniy Konstruktorskoye Byuro*, or 'Central Design Bureau') was established at Z.39 by order of P. I. Baranov, the People's Commissar of Heavy Industry and the head of the main department of aviation industry. It was here that Sergey Ilyushin as deputy director and head of the experimental design bureau began work on what became the DB-3.

At the same time that Sergey Ilyushin was designing the BB-2 ('BB' standing for *Blizhniy Bombardirovshchik* or 'Light Bomber'), Andrey Tupolev was designing what became the SB fast bomber to meet the same requirements. Design of the BB-2 (which had the internal Ilyushin designation of 'TsKB-26') started in early 1933; outside of gliders, it was Ilyushin's first aeroplane, and a rather ambitious one at that, as it was designed to be a fully modern bomber. The SB design won out over the BB-2 and was produced in large numbers as has been described previously.

However, in the early 1930s, the VVS was also looking for a more modern replacement for the TB-3 long-range bomber, which was just entering service. This new replacement was needed for the second half of the 1930s. The requirement called for an aircraft capable of a top speed of no less than 217 mph (350 kph), and a range of 1,864 miles (3,000 km) while carrying a bomb load of 2,205 lb (1,000 kg). It was out of this requirement that Ilyushin, as part of the TsKB design bureau, developed the re-engined TsKB-26 as a private venture (something of a rarity under the Soviet system) from the BB-2, this re-engined TsKB-26 to be capable of long-range flight.

TsKB-26 (BB-2 2M-85, BB-2 K-14)

In order to provide a truly up-to-date replacement for the TB-3, Ilyushin intended for the production versions of his bomber to be all-metal, smooth-skinned cantilever monoplanes with retractable landing gear. First, however, he needed adequate engines to get the long-range he wanted, which was a bit of a problem as aero-engine development in the Soviet Union lagged behind that of the major aircraft-producing nations of the West. A solution to this was found in the licence-production of the French Gnome-Rhone 14 Kdrs Mistral Major twin-row fourteen-cylinder radial engine (this engine eventually led to a whole line of Soviet engines by the Tumansky

OKB). The aircraft with these engines were known as the BB-2 K-14 ('K-14' being the designation for the Gnome-Rhone 14 Kdrs in the Soviet Union), with Ilyushin's in-house designation being 'TsKB-26'.

The OKB of Sergei Konstantinovich Tumansky (1901–73) was given the task of licence-building this engine, which was known to the Soviets as the 'M-85', with A. Nazarov being responsible for its development. The M-85 engine entered production in 1934 and had a take-off power of 765 hp. It was this engine that was actually used on the TsKB-26, not the original imported French engines.

Work on what became the TsKB-26 started in June 1934 at Z.39 at Moscow-Khodynka. The TsKB-26 mock-up (as the BB-2) was officially approved on 29 December 1934 and the completed TsKB-26 was rolled out on 1 June 1935, a year after work had started on the design. It looked as if the aircraft might not be built, as the SB had been selected for production in place of the BB-2/TsKB-26. However, Ilyushin was able to successfully argue that the BB-2/TsKB-26 met the requirement for a replacement for the TB-3 as a long-range bomber. In this case, it was now competing against Tupolev's DB-2 (ANT-37) design. As the BB-2/TsKB-26 had incorporated features from the beginning that were designed for long-range bombing, it was easily 'convertible' to its new role as a long-range bomber prototype.

The TsKB's chief test pilot (later the Ilyushin OKB's chief test pilot), Vladimir K. Kokkinaki, flew the TsKB-26 on its first flight in June 1935. Factory tests showed that the aircraft handled well and had good single-engined performance. It achieved a maximum speed of 205 mph (330 kph) at sea level, and 242 mph (390 kph) at 10,663 feet (3,250 m). It was more manoeuvrable than expected by the Red Air Force. The TsKB-26 was the first twin-engined aircraft to be looped in the Soviet Union. Indeed, at one demonstration before Soviet dignitaries in the summer of 1935, namely Kliment Voroshilov, People's Commissar of Defence, and Sergo Ordzhonikidze, People's Commissar of Heavy Industry, Vladimir Kokkinaki put the TsKB-26 through its aerobatic paces. It was recorded that the dignitaries were duly impressed. In fact, the Soviet dignitaries were so impressed that they asked Ilyushin to prepare the TsKB-30 (the all-metal production version of the TsKB-26) for state tests as quickly as possible, as the basic TsKB-26 design appeared to meet the requirements for a new long-range bomber.

This aircraft was what today would be called a 'technology demonstrator' or 'proof-of-concept' aircraft as it was used to demonstrate the potential of the DB-3 design, but was not intended to be a pattern for the production aircraft. As such, it differed from the TsKB-30 and production DB-3s in featuring a wooden fuselage covered by plywood veneer, adopted to allow the aircraft to be built quickly. It did, however, have metal wings and horizontal tail planes. While testing on the TsKB-26 continued, work on the all-metal TsKB-30 had already started.

The load-carrying ability shown by the TsKB-26 made it a natural aircraft for gaining aerial records. The Soviet Union had joined the FAI (*Federation Aeronautique Internationale*) and was eager to prove its technological prowess to the world. The first aerial world record ever garnered by the Soviet Union was achieved on 17 June 1936 when V. K. Kokkinaki carried a 1,102-lb (500-kg) payload to a height of 37,054 feet (11,294 m) in the TsKB-26.

TsKB-30

As what might be termed the first 'true' prototype of the DB-3, the TsKB-30 differed from the earlier TsKB-26 in several ways, the most important in that it was of all-metal construction as opposed to the mixed construction of the TsKB-26. Unlike the TsKB-26, the TsKB-30 was built specifically with the requirements of the long-range bomber replacement for the TB-3 in mind. It was equipped to carry both defensive and offensive armaments in the form of manned gun stations and an internal bomb bay, and it even had provisions for carrying large-size bombs externally. The gun stations, of which there were three, were equipped with single ShKAS 7.62-mm (30-calibre) rapid-fire machine guns. The stations were distributed in the form of an enclosed nose position with a TUR-8 mount, a low-profile dorsal or mid-upper turret, and a ventral position. The horizontal tail planes were enlarged because of a lack of longitudinal stability in the TsKB-26, a tailwheel replaced the TsKB-26's tail skid, and the nose was slightly longer. The engine cowlings were improved in shape.

I am not so certain about one change that is usually noted: a change from an open cockpit on the TsKB-26 to an enclosed cockpit on the TsKB-30. For a windscreen, the glazing in front of the pilot on the TsKB-26 was unusually elongated. It appears to me more like a sliding cockpit canopy that was slid to the front and was perhaps normally if not always left or locked in the slid-forward position, as was the case with some I-16 *tip* 5 fighters. It is possible that it was kept in this forward position to allow the pilot easy egress out of the cockpit in the event of an emergency. The TsKB-26 was an experimental aircraft after all. Soviet aviation historians Yefim Gordon, Sergey Komissarov, and Dmitry Komissarov seem to share this conclusion and refer to the

The Ilyushin OKB's chief test pilot, Vladimir K. Kokkinaki, standing in front of the TsKB-30, the prototype of the DB-3. (*Viktor Kulikov's collection*)

TsKB-26's canopy as a single-piece forward sliding canopy in their book on the Ilyushin OKB. In any event, the cockpit canopy on the TsKB-30 consisted of a fixed windscreen and an aft sliding canopy portion and was indeed enclosed.

The TsKB-30 was taken aloft for the first time by Vladimir K. Kokkinaki, on 31 March 1936. State tests of the TsKB-30 started in the summer of 1936. These tests showed that at 6,393 lb (2,900 kg), the bombload of the TsKB-30 was nearly five times that of the Tupolev SB, which had a bombload of 1,323 lb (600 kg). It was slower, with a top speed of 249 mph (400 kph), which was 15 mph (24 kph) slower than the SB. The aircraft was found to have good take-off and landing characteristics, good flight handling, and good single-engined performance. Although generally pleased with the test results, the Red Air Force wanted the aircraft to incorporate self-sealing fuel tanks and a crew intercom, both requests following from experience with their bombers during the Spanish Civil War (1936–39). With these changes in mind, the TsKB-30 was ordered into production as the 'DB-3'.

When compared to the German He 111B medium bomber, the DB-3 had a longer range and a higher top speed than the German bomber. A pre-production DB-3 was tested from May to October 1937 and exhibited a top speed of 242 mph (390 kph) at 16,404 feet (5,000 m). The He 111B was some 6.21–12.43 mph (10–20 kph) slower at all altitudes and had a service ceiling that was 4,593 feet (1,400 m) lower than the DB-3. For the period of 1937–38, it was considered that the DB-3 had a superior performance to comparable aircraft in France, Germany, the United Kingdom, and the United States.

A note about the 'DB-3A' and 'DB-3B' designations should be made. These were informal designations; although widely used, they did not appear in official documents, where the aircraft was simply referred to as the 'DB-3'.

DB-3 (DB-3 2M-85, DB-3S)

This was the first production variant of the DB-3/Il-4 line. Mass production of this first variant of the DB-3 was ordered in August 1936, before the state tests had even concluded. This initial version was sometimes called the 'DB-3S', with the 'DB' standing for *Dalniy Bombardirovshchik* or 'Long-Range Bomber'. The '3' signified that this was the third long-range bomber design for the VVS, the DB-3 winning out over the Tupolev DB-2 or ANT-37 (the DB-1 or ANT-36 was a bomber developed from Tupolev's long-range aircraft, the ANT-25, and of which some ten or twenty were built). The 'S' stood for *Seriyniy* ('Series-built'). The first eight examples of the DB-3 (or DB-3S) were delivered to the VVS in late 1936, less than a year after the TsKB-30 had first flown.

The DB-3 utilised the then state-of-the-art construction in the Soviet Union, the so-called 'cut-and-fit' method (this was also used with the contemporaneous Tupolev SB). The wings were quite complex, consisting of chrome-molybdenum steel tubes, with the spar sections being riveted together to create a complete spar. Although this method was time-consuming, it did result in a light and strong wing structure. The fuselage construction was comprised of frames, and much welding was needed in its construction.

As with the TsKB-30, the DB-3 had a top speed of 249 mph (400 kph). The crew consisted of a pilot, a navigator/bombardier/gunner, and a radio operator/gunner. *Zavod* 18 at Voronezh and *Zavod* 39 at Moscow-Khodynka were tasked with the

Above: A pre-war DB-3 in flight, in what appears to be an overall natural metal finish. (*Viktor Kulikov's collection*)

Left: A pre-war DB-3 during the winter, with its properly attired crew. This aircraft appears to be finished in a light grey scheme. What appears to be another DB-3 in the background is equipped with skis. (*Viktor Kulikov's collection*)

production of the DB-3. Unfortunately, the complex construction of the DB-3 slowed down production such that in 1937 Z.18 built only twelve aircraft, and Z.39 fared little better, building thirty-three aircraft, for a total of only forty-five aircraft built in 1937.

The DB-3 featured three ShKAS machine guns for defence. They were disposed of with one gun on the TUR-8 nose mounting, with 500 rounds, one gun in an SU low-profile rotating turret with 1,000 rounds, and one ventral gun on a LU mounting with 500 rounds per gun. The radio operator/gunner was responsible for both the turret and the ventral gun. The internal bomb bay could carry ten 220-lb (100-kg) bombs and external bomb racks could accommodate bombs up to 2,205 lb (1,000 kg), for an overload bomb load of 5,512 lb (2,500 kg), which was a record for a twin-engined bomber at that time. An OP-2 optical bombsight was used for aiming the bombs.

First entering service in 1937, the DB-3 starting replacing the TB-3 in front-line long-range bomber units. Given the slow initial production rate of the DB-3, this replacement did not happen as quickly as the Red Air Force would have hoped.

DB-3A (DB-3 2M-86)

There were to be three stages to be implemented in improving the DB-3; the first was the 'A' stage, then the 'B' stage, then the 'V' stage (the 'V' stage was not implemented because of the more thorough redesign that resulted in the DB-3F). The major improvement of the 'A' stage, the DB-3A, over the DB-3 (DB-3S) was the replacement of the M-85 engine with the M-86 engine. The M-86 was a development of the M-85 that had 950 hp at take-off, whereas the M-85 was some 185-hp weaker, with only 765 hp available for take-off. As fitted to the DB-3A, the M-86 featured a fixed-pitch three-bladed metal V-85 propeller with a diameter of 11.48 feet (3.4 m). The DB-3A had the same defensive armament and positions of the initial DB-3.

DB-3B (DB-3 2M-87A)

The fitting of the improved M-87A engine to the DB-3 airframe in 1938 resulted in the DB-3B (the 'B' stage). The M-87A had the same horsepower rating of the M-86 at take-off but had better performance at altitude. The M-87A installation was characterised by cowlings with tapered lips and with blisters over the valve reduction gear of the engines. The fixed-pitch V-85 propeller was replaced on the DB-3B with a VISh-3 two-pitch three-bladed metal propeller with a diameter of 10.66 feet (3.25 m). At some point in the production of the DB-3, the raised pilot canopy of the *Moskva* long-distance record-setting aircraft was introduced, and it appears that at least some of the DB-3Bs had this raised hood; perhaps all of them did.

The DB-3B differed from the DB-3A not only in the engine used, but the landing gear were strengthened, armour protection for the crew was introduced, and the fuel tanks were provided with the neutral gas system for protection.

In terms of defensive armament, the DB-3B was equipped the same as the DB-3 and DB-3A. The bomb load consisted of bombs from 17.6 lb (8 kg) up to 2,205 lb (1,000 kg), and, as with the DB-3 and DB-3A, they were aimed using an OP-2 bombsight.

In addition to *Zavodi* 18 and 39, a new production line was established for the DB-3s at Z.126 at Komsomolsk-na-Amure (Komsomolsk-on-Amur) in Siberia in

Two views of a DB-3 in the black/green Great Patriotic War scheme.

1938. This *zavod* had completed thirty DB-3s by the end of 1938, for a total of 400 DB-3s built in 1938 (one source has 399), which was quite an improvement over the forty-five that had been built in 1937.

DB-3T (TsKB-53)

Built pursuant to a requirement from the Soviet Navy for a torpedo bomber, this version was modified from the bomber version to be able to carry air-dropped torpedoes and mines. The 'T' in the designation stood for *Torpedonosets* ('Torpedo-carrier' in Russian), and it became the first mass-produced Soviet torpedo bomber. The internal Ilyushin designation was 'TsKB-53'. The M-85-powered prototype first flew in 1938. On production DB-3Ts, the M-85 was replaced with the more powerful M-86 engine. Some DB-3Ts were later retrofitted with the M-87 engine.

A torpedo bomber, of course, needs a torpedo; in the case of the DB-3T, this was the '45-36' torpedo, which was developed from the Italian *Fiume* torpedo. The 45-36 torpedo came in several variants. The 45-36 AN was equipped to be released at a low altitude ('AN' stood for *Aviatsionnaya Nizkovysotnaya* or 'Aerial Low-altitude'), being released at 98 feet (30 m). The 45-36 AM was equipped for operation in shallow waters, and the 45-36 AV was equipped to be released at relatively high altitudes ('AV' stood for *Aviatsionnaya Vysotnaya* or 'Aerial High-altitude'), being dropped from 820 to 1,312 feet (250 to 400 m) above the water. These torpedoes weighed 2,072 lb (940 kg) with a 441-lb (200-kg) high-explosive warhead.

In addition to being able to carry torpedoes, the DB-3T could also carry air-dropped sea mines. These included the 2,205-lb (1,000-kg) *Geyro* anchored mine, the 1,984-lb (900-kg) AMG-1, or two of the 1,102-lb (500-kg) MDM-500, which were designed to sit on the seafloor. The AMG-1 was characterised by a conical nose cone that streamlined the mine in flight and tail fins that stabilised it upon being dropped. Both of these detached when the mine entered the water.

With the advent of Operation Barbarossa and the rapid advance of the German forces, the AVMF's DB-3Ts were pressed into service as conventional bombers, even raiding Berlin in 1941. The DB-3Ts continued to be used mainly in conventional-level bombing missions against the Axis until the summer of 1942 when more attacks against Axis shipping were launched. The DB-3T continued in its combat role until the end of the Great Patriotic War, and even beyond, as some DB-3Ts took part in the campaign against Japan in Manchuria in August 1945.

DB-3 2M-88

The last of the DB-3s produced with the original airframe were fitted with the M-88 engine. This occurred in the second half of 1940. With the 1,100-hp M-88 engine, these DB-3s had a top speed of 267 mph (429 kph) at 23,310 feet (6,800 m). These aircraft were superseded on the assembly line by the redesigned DB-3F with the last of the original airframe DB-3s being built in the first quarter of 1941 at Z.126. Some 1,103–1,108 DB-3s of all types were constructed (as distinct from the extensively redesigned DB-3F/Il-4), although one source has 1,528 DB-3s being built.

DB-3M

The DB-3M designation was sometimes used for those aircraft that were basically the DB-3F design (see below), but still powered by the M-87 as opposed to the M-88 that was intended to be used by the 'true' DB-3F. This was how these aircraft were supposed to be designated, but it does not appear to have been mandatory and some DB-3s of the new design were produced with the M-87 engine and designated as 'DB-3F', not 'DB-3M'. I have seen at least one source use the 'DB-3M' designation to refer to a modernised version of the basic DB-3 with the old construction, but this appears to be inaccurate.

DB-3F (Il-4, TsKB-30F)

Although the DB-3 had given the Red Air Force a modern, all-metal long-range bomber, it was complicated and difficult to build, also being somewhat unreliable. The DB-3F was an extensively redesigned aircraft in an attempt to make it both easier to build and more reliable. As such, while remaining very similar to the earlier DB-3s in general appearance, the main external difference being the extended nose, the DB-3F differed a great deal in its construction, which was comprehensively simplified. The internal OKB designation for the DB-3F was 'TsKB-30F'. This redesigned aircraft may have gained the name 'DB-3F' because the 'F' signified *Forsirovanniy* ('Uprated'), referring to the engine, or the 'F' may have referred to *Fonar* ('Canopy'), referring to the new, extensively glazed nose. The new nose increased the fuselage length from 46.65 feet (14.22 m) to 48.52 feet (14.79 m).

An Il-4 (DB-3F) in flight. Note the white surrounds around the stars. (*Viktor Kulikov's collection*)

Construction was greatly simplified to make building the DB-3F easier, quicker, and cheaper. The template assembly (or loft and pattern) technique was used, which had been observed by Boris Lisunov and other Soviet designers and engineers when they had visited the United States as part of their mission to learn about the DC-3. This mission had been part of the Soviet Union's licence-building of the DC-3 (which became the Li-2, described further on). This new technique replaced the old 'cut-and-fit' technique, which had been used on the DB-3s. As part of this new technique, labour-intensive items—such as steel tubular construction, U-profiles, and welding—were replaced by pressed aluminium and open two-sided riveted items. These open-riveted joints were also easier to inspect. The tubular wing spars, which had to be x-rayed to properly inspect them (the x-rays often showing defects), were replaced by I-beams, which were easier to build and inspect. The time to construct a DB-3F/Il-4 as compared to the previous DB-3 version fell from 30,301 hours to 14,331 hours. This was reduced even further to 12,500 hours by 1943, which was less than that needed to construct the smaller Pe-2. This enabled up to forty Il-4s to be produced every month.

In addition to the changes in construction, the wing was also redesigned. Although of the same basic planform and basic aerofoil of the DB-3, the wing of the DB-3F was thinner and had 118.4 sq. feet (11 sq. m) more area than the DB-3's wing. The extra wing area came from larger flaps, as the wingspan remained the same at 70.34 feet (21.44 m).

The DB-3 M-88 (as it was known at the time) began factory tests on 21 May 1939, being flown by chief Ilyushin test pilot V. K. Kokkinaki. During testing, the DB-3F

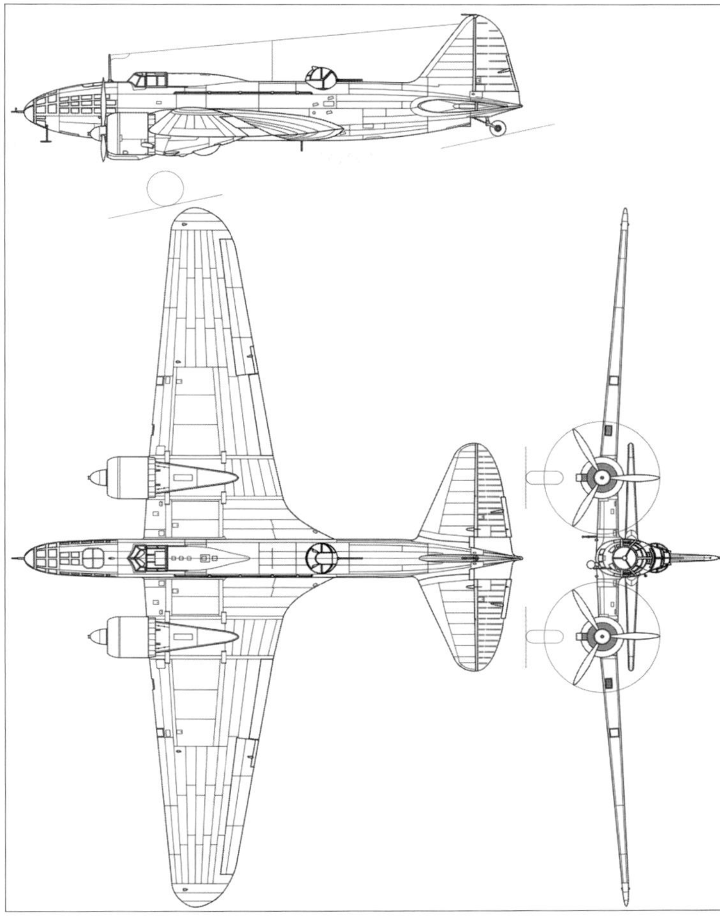

Three-view drawing of a DB-3F/Il-4. (*By Kaboldy. Wikimedia*)

exhibited a top speed of 277 mph (445 kph) at 17,717 feet (5,400 m). Its maximum range with a load of 2,205 lb (1,000 kg) was 2,175 miles (3,500 km). The landing characteristics were found to be better than that on the earlier DB-3s and the braking was improved. The testing took three months and despite some improvements over the earlier DB-3s still revealed many defects. Most of these were centred on the new engine and its installation. The VISh-23 propeller did not perform properly, and the nacelle did not allow sufficient air cooling for the M-88, which led to overheating. During state tests, the DB-3F was re-equipped with the M-87 engine because of problems with the M-88.

The problems with the M-88 installation were such that some aircraft with the new DB-3F construction were fitted with the M-87 engine instead, being designated as the 'DB-3M' (see previous entry). However, it was not all bad news for the redesigned DB-3. The new nose was found to be superior to the old nose and gave the navigator much more room to operate in and improved the bombing capability of the aircraft, besides giving the aircraft better streamlining. The new gun position for the navigator was also found to be an improvement. The provision for the neutral gas system for the fuel tanks improved the survivability of the redesigned aircraft.

It was for these reasons that it was decided to manufacture the intermediate DB-3M, while the problems with the M-88 were worked out. As mentioned previously, some of these intermediate DB-3s with the M-87 were nonetheless referred to as DB-3Fs and production of both the M-87 and M-88-powered DB-3Fs was done simultaneously for a time. In December 1939, for example, when production of the DB-3F began, twenty-five were built with the M-87 engine and twenty-four were built with the M-88.

The Winter War with Finland in 1939–40 highlighted problems with the DB-3, such as difficulty in heating the engines and the deficiency of the defensive armament. These were taken into account in the development of the DB-3F. For example, a fourth crew member was added to act as the ventral gunner, allowing the radio operator/gunner to concentrate on using the dorsal turret.

Meanwhile work continued on improving the M-88 engine, as this was the preferred engine for the DB-3F. The first series of M-88s installed on the DB-3Fs suffered from various problems, including disintegration of the connecting rods, overheating of the cylinder heads, oil leakage, and problems with production standards that adversely affected the interchangeability of engine parts. Some of these problems were so serious that they caused accidents. One change that was made to alleviate these problems was to enlarge the cowling opening, which allowed more cooling air to pass over the cylinders to prevent overheating. The cowling lips were shorter than those originally used on the DB-3F, which had been longer and more tapered (like the cowling lips used with the M-87A engines which had admitted less cooling air).

One notable difference between the prototype DB-3F and most of the production versions was the replacement of the flat-topped SU turret of the DB-3F prototype with the ball-shaped MV-3 turret, although it still mounted the ShKAS machine gun. The new turret gave the gunner more room to operate, although it did slow the aircraft down because of the additional drag.

DB-3F: 1940

Despite the intention to standardise on the M-88 engine for the DB-3F, most of the aircraft produced in 1940 still featured the M-87A engines. In addition to its other defects, the M-88 had a higher fuel consumption than the M-87A, resulting in a reduced range. In the fall of 1940, ribbed wheel discs were applied to the DB-3F. These discs were copied from those of a Ju 88 and a Do 215 the Soviets had purchased from Germany, another instance of the Soviets using technology from the modern aircraft that Germany had unwisely sold them during the brief German–Soviet thaw. 1,006 DB-3Fs were produced in 1940 (one source has 1,106).

Il-4 (DB-3F) 1941–42

In April 1941, production of the Il-4 was stopped at Z.18 at Voronezh so that the factory could concentrate on producing the Il-2. Production of the Il-4 was stopped at Z.39 soon afterwards, which left Z.126 as the sole factory producing the Il-4.

As mentioned previously, enlarged diameter cowlings were fitted to the Il-4 to allow more cooling air to pass over the engines. This was done in 1941. In the second half of 1941, the glazing behind the pilot's sliding canopy was replaced by metal. The large tailwheel fairing that had characterised the DB-3F was replaced by a small fairing in late 1941 (similar to that fitted to some Il-2s). Due to a shortage of metal caused by the German invasion, from the autumn of 1941, Il-4s were built with wooden cockpit floors, navigator station framework, and tail cones.

Most of the 757 DB-3Fs that were completed in 1941 were built by Z.126, which by the end of the year was the only *zavod* still producing the aircraft.

A persistent complaint about the DB-3 was its weak defensive armament of three rifle-calibre guns. A partial attempt to rectify this was made in the spring of 1942 with the replacement of the ShKAS-armed MV-3 turret with the UBT 12.7-mm machine gun-armed UTK-1 turret. The turrets were similar in size and appearance, with the main difference being the guns.

In the fall of 1942, the VISh-3 propellers were replaced by AV-5F-158 units, and the flap area was increased by 21.53 sq. feet (2 sq. m). This improved the take-off and landing characteristics of the Il-4 (as it was now called). Some 858 Il-4s were built in 1942.

Il-4 With Increased Wing Sweepback: 1942–Unknown

In an attempt to deal with the change in the centre of gravity caused by the change in the weight distribution of the Il-4 created by the addition of the gunner and more armour, a revised wing was tested and produced from 1942. This wing featured outer

A captured DB-3F that has been repainted in Finnish markings. This aircraft appears to have a UBT machine gun in the dorsal turret, which would make it a UTK-1 turret. (*Viktor Kulikov's collection*)

Another view of the Finnish DB-3F. (*Viktor Kulikov's collection*)

A Great Patriotic War DB-3F (Il-4) being serviced. Note the camouflage netting. (*Viktor Kulikov's collection*)

A DB-3F being prepared for a winter mission. This must be early in the Great Patriotic War as this aircraft appears to still be in the overall green topside camouflage, without the black bands applied. (*Viktor Kulikov's collection*)

Il-4s during the winter, with one aircraft painted with the temporary white finish, and the other retaining its normal, 'summer' camouflage. Both aircraft have quilted covers over the engines to keep the winter cold out. The primitive nature of this airfield is apparent. Most Soviet Great Patriotic War aircraft were expected to be able to operate from rough, unprepared airfields. (*Viktor Kulikov's collection*)

Il-4 with swept-back wooden-covered wings. Notice the rib caps protruding out of the bottom skin of the wing. (*Viktor Kulikov's collection*)

wing portions with an increased wing sweep on the leading edges, wooden structure on these portions except for metal spars, and wooden ribs whose caps protruded through the wooden skin on the lower parts of the wings. Two additional fuel tanks were added to each wing, bringing the total to three per wing, and increasing the fuel load by 2,502 lb (1,135 kg). This gave a range of 2,228 miles (3,585 km) with a bomb load of 2,205 lb (1,000 kg) at a speed of 211 mph (340 kph). The aircraft was considered to be better handling with the new wing. It is not clear from the record how many of the Il-4s were built with these modified wings, nor how long they were in production.

Il-4: 1943–45

In contrast to the end of 1941, in which only one *zavod* (Z.126) was producing Il-4s (DB-3Fs), by the beginning of 1943, three *zavodi* were producing the aircraft: Z.23 in Fili (Moscow), Z.81 at Tushino (Moscow), and Z.126. In Irkutsk, Z.39 switched from producing the Pe-3 back to the Il-4 in March 1943. Some 1,558 Il-4s were built in 1943, which was nearly twice the number that were produced in 1942 (858).

One change introduced in 1943 to deal with the increasing weight of the Il-4 was the change in the size of the tailwheel from 400 × 150-mm to 470 × 210-mm. The main wheel was also strengthened to deal with the greater weight and enlarged to 1,100 × 400-mm in size.

Il-4: 1946

It is recorded that four Il-4s were constructed after the war, in 1946. What is not clear is if these aircraft were built completely new in 1946, or if they were built from wartime components. It is also not clear from the record what differences, if any, these post-war aircraft had with those Il-4s that were constructed during the Second World War. The Il-4 began to be retired from long-range bomber units in 1947.

Preserved R-5 at Monino. (*Taken by Alan Wilson. Wikimedia*)

Colour rendition of an R-Z in flight. (*Viktor Kulikov's collection*)

Su-2 replica at Pobeda Park (Poklannaya Gora). (*Viktor Kulikov's collection*)

Su-2 replica at Pobeda Park, from the back. (*Viktor Kulikov's collection*)

Il-2 two-seater at Monino. (*Taken by Weslam 123. Wikimedia*)

Flying Heritage Collection Il-2 on take-off. (*Taken by Alan Cagle*)

Flying Heritage Collection Il-2 in flight. (*Taken by Alan Cagle*)

Po-2 in Great Patriotic War colours in flight. (*Taken by Alan Wilson. Wikimedia*)

Po-2 on the ground. Note the Guards insignia on the nose and the bomb racks under the wings. (*Viktor Kulikov's collection*)

Colourised photograph of a crew and other airmen in front of a Pe-2, during the Great Patriotic War. (*Viktor Kulikov's collection*)

Preserved Pe-2 at Monino. (*Taken by Alan Wilson. Wikimedia*)

Side view of the Monino Pe-2. Note the exhaust stubs and the dive brakes. (*Taken by Alan Wilson. Wikimedia*)

Front view of the Monino Pe-2. Note the under-nose glazing and the UBK gun in the nose. (*Taken by Alan Wilson. Wikimedia*)

Pe-2 at the Polish Army Museum in Warsaw. The aircraft is finished in post-war Polish markings and camouflage. (*Taken by Bene Riobo. Wikimedia*)

SB 2M-100A at Monino. (Taken *by Gonzolito. Wikimedia*)

Tu-2S at Monino. (*Taken by Alan Wilson. Wikimedia*)

Tu-2S at the Polish Aviation Museum in Krakow. (*Taken by Michael Perala. Wikimedia)*

Polar aviation (Aviaarktika) Pe-8, probably taken post-war. (*Viktor Kulikov's collection*)

DB-3 at Monino. (*Taken by Clemens Vasters. Wikimedia*)

Il-4 (DB-3F) at Pobeda Park. (*Taken by Alan Wilson. Wikimedia*)

Il-4 at Pobeda Park. This photograph was taken before the previous photograph, when the aircraft did not have the roof over it. (*Taken by Mike1979 Russia. Wikimedia*)

Il-4 at Pobeda Park. (*Public Domain*)

Il-4 at Pobeda Park. (*Public Domain*)

Li-2NB at Pobeda Park in black/green camouflage. It appears to have 'bombs' fitted under the fuselage.

Li-2 at Monino. (*Taken by Clemens Vasters. Wikimedia*)

R-5 with the pre-war green over blue camouflage, but with a Great Patriotic War white-outlined star, 1941–1942.

R-Z with pre-war green over blue camouflage and black-outlined star as seen early in the Great Patriotic War, 1941.

Su-2 in pre-war green over blue scheme as seen early in the Great Patriotic War, 1941.

Il-2. All-metal production version of the single-seater. Note the 20-mm cannons in the wings and the aileron anti-flutter balances. Captured by the Germans in the summer of 1941.

Il-2. Wooden-winged version of the single-seater. Note the 23-mm cannons in the wings, 1942.

Il-2. Wooden-winged straight-winged two-seater. This aircraft carries the black/green camouflage typical for early examples of the straight-winged two-seater, 1942–1943.

Il-2-37 from the winter of 1943–1944. Underneath the winter camouflage was the three-colour scheme of tan, green, and dark grey.

Il-2 arrow, possibly with the 62nd ShAP, with a quick recognition marking in the form of a white tail. This Il-2 features a variation of the NKAP #1 pattern for the three-colour scheme, 1944–1945.

Il-2 arrow with elaborate quick recognition markings, including red aileron trim tabs. This Il-2 features the NKAP #2 pattern for the three-colour scheme, 1944–1945. The inscription reads, 'For Zhoru Shuvayeva'.

Profiles showing the evolution of the Il-2, from an early metal-fuselaged single-seater to a late Great Patriotic War arrow, 1941–1945.

Il-10 in Great Patriotic War three-colour scheme, 1945.

Yak-2 in pre-war green over blue scheme as seen early in the Great Patriotic War. Note the 1940-type red stars with the thin black outline, 1941.

Yak-4 in black/green scheme introduced early in the Great Patriotic War, 1941.

U-2LNB in black/green scheme, 1942.

U-2LNB in three-colour scheme from the port side, 1944.

U-2LNB in three-colour scheme from the starboard side.

Above left: U-2LNB in three-colour scheme from the topside.

Above right: U-2LNB in three-colour scheme from the underside.

UT-1B in black/green scheme.

Ar-2 in pre-war green over blue scheme as seen early in the Great Patriotic War, 1941.

Early Pe-2 in black/green scheme.

Turret-armed Pe-2 in three-colour scheme from the port side, 1944.

Turret-armed Pe-2 in three-colour scheme from the starboard side.

Above left: Turret-armed Pe-2 in three-colour scheme from the topside.

Above right: Turret-armed Pe-2 in three-colour scheme from the underside.

SB 2M-100A in pre-Great Patriotic War overall light grey scheme.

SB 2M-103A in green over blue scheme from the port side, 1941.

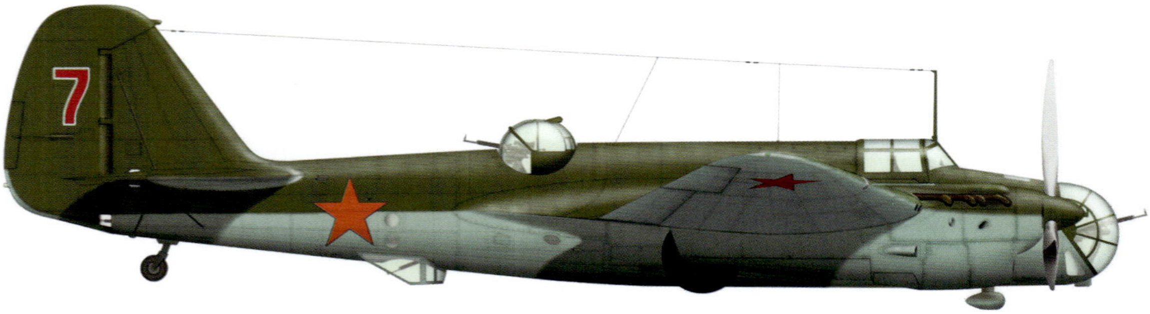

SB 2M-103A in green over blue scheme from the starboard side.

Above left: SB 2M-103A in green over blue scheme from the topside.

Above right: SB 2M-103A in green over blue scheme from the underside.

Early Tu-2 in black/green scheme from the port side, 1942.

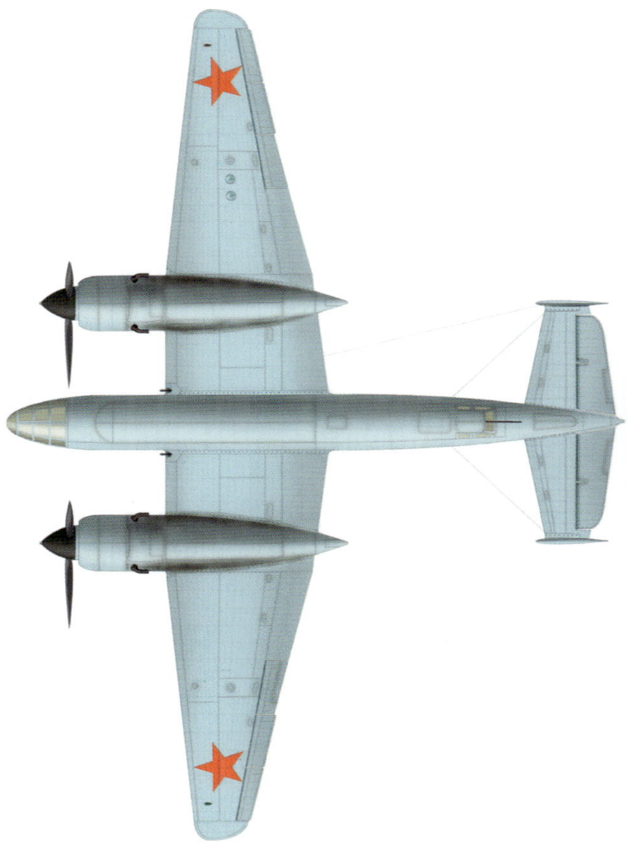

Above left: Early Tu-2 in black/green scheme from the topside.

Above right: Early Tu-2 in black/green scheme from the underside.

Tu-2S in three-colour scheme, 1944.

Tu-2T in three-colour scheme, 1944.

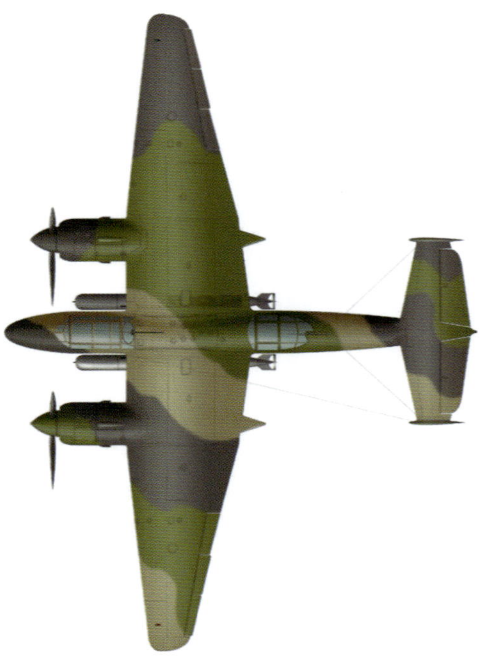

Above left: Tu-2T in three-colour scheme from the topside.

Above right: Tu-2T in three-colour scheme from the underside.

Tu-2S 'Moskva 32' from the port side.

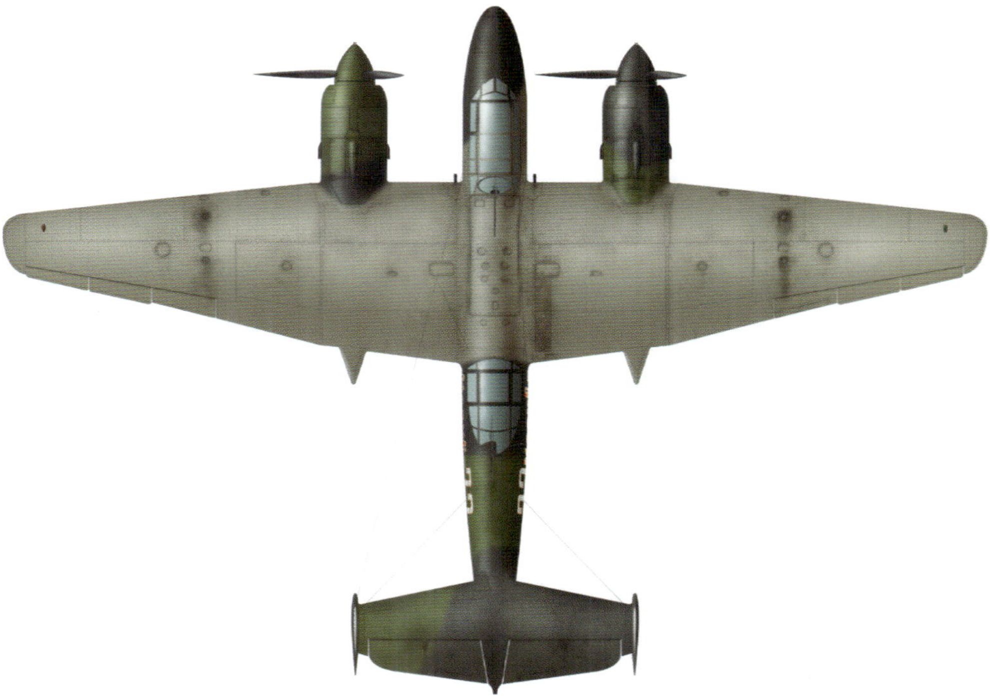

Tu-2S 'Moskva 32' from the topside. Note how extensive the A-21m Light Brown is on the wings. This was not uncommon on the Tu-2.

TB-3 4M-17 in green over blue pre-war (and early Great Patriotic War) scheme.

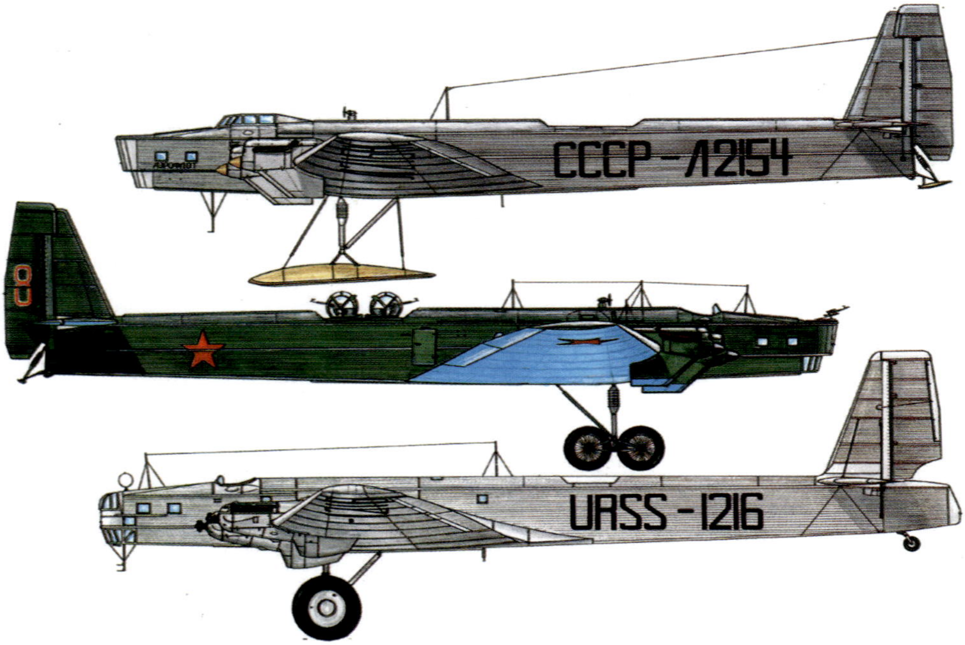

Side views of three different TB-3s; a ski-equipped civilian G-2, a Great Patriotic War TB-3 4M-17 with MV-3 turrets, and a civilian TB-3 equipped with AM-34FRNV engines. (*Viktor Kulikov's collection*)

Pe-8 AM-35A in black/green scheme, 1942.

Early DB-3 in pre-war overall silver scheme.

Early DB-3F (Il-4) in black/green scheme. Note that is still has the low-profile SU turret, 1941.

Il-4 (DB-3F) in three-colour scheme over black from the port side, 1944.

Il-4 (DB-3F) in three-colour scheme over black from the starboard side.

Above: Il-4 (DB-3F) in three-colour scheme over black from the topside.

Below: Il-4 (DB-3F) in three-colour scheme over black from the underside.

Li-2NB in black/green scheme, 1942.

Li-2NB in three-colour scheme over black from the port side, 1944.

Li-2NB in three-colour scheme over black from the starboard side.

Above left: Li-2NB in three-colour scheme over black from the top side.

Above right: Li-2NB in three-colour scheme over black from the underside.

Early Yer-2 in black/green scheme, 1942.

Late Yer-2 in two-grey scheme over black, 1945.

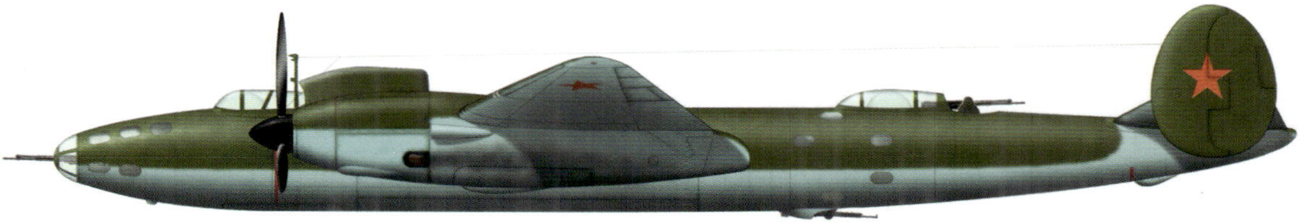

DVB-102, 1942.

Su-6 with rear-gunner and M-71F engine, 1943.

Su-8, 1944.

Scale profile of various Soviet bombers of the Second World War showing the relative sizes, 1939–45.

A Soviet DB-3F that has been painted in the Great Patriotic War scheme of black/green over a black underside, as befitted its role as a night bomber. (*Viktor Kulikov's collection*)

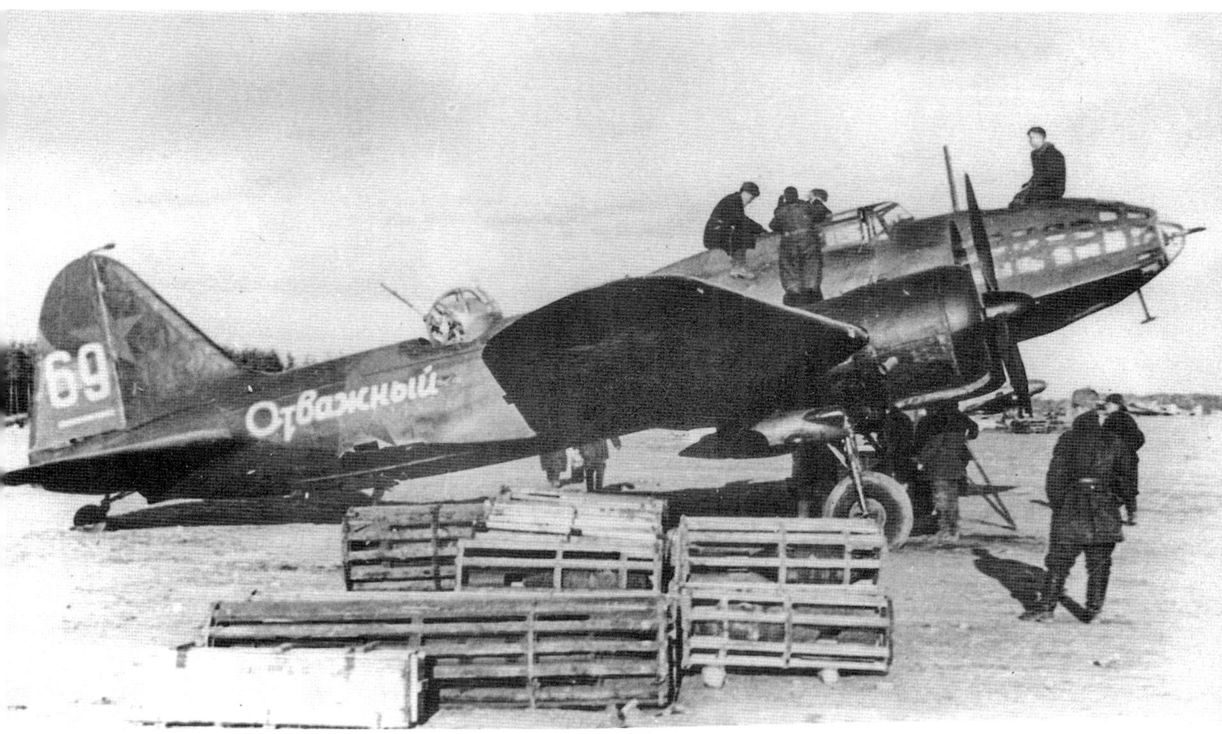

An Il-4 being prepared for a mission. The cylindrical wooden crates in the foreground were used to carry the bombs before they were loaded on to the aircraft. Some of the bombs are still present in these containers. (*Viktor Kulikov's collection*)

Il-4T

As with the earlier DB-3, the Il-4 was modified into a torpedo bomber version. As with the DB-3T, it was also designated with the 'T', for *Torpedonosets* or 'Torpedo-carrier'. Besides being able to carry two torpedoes in overload condition, some of the Il-4Ts differed from the standard bomber version in having extra windows in the nose to give the navigator a better view, which helped when launching the torpedoes. The Il-4T was modified in the same way and at the same time as the bomber version, so it mirrored the changes and modifications made to the bomber.

Like the DB-3Ts, the Il-4Ts, which first saw action on 25 June 1941 attacking Constanta in Romania, were primarily used on conventional level bombing raids until the middle of 1942. Il-4Ts were used to plant mines at the entrances to the ports of Helsinki, Finland and Tallinn, Estonia. These were mainly nocturnal missions. The Northern Fleet received its first Il-4Ts in September 1941. The 1st MTAP of the KBF did not undertake its initial torpedo bombing missions until mid-1942. The 1st MTAP claimed seventeen Axis vessels sunk during the summer, with another forty-three Axis vessels claimed sunk during 1943.

The wartime activities of the Il-4T did not stop with the end of the Great Patriotic War on 9 May 1945. Il-4Ts, along with DB-3Ts, saw action in the last great action of the Second World War, the Manchurian campaign. These actions are discussed in the section on the Manchurian campaign.

In comparison to the Il-4 bomber and the DB-3T torpedo bomber, which were quickly retired after the Second World War, the Il-4T continued in active service into 1952, before being replaced by the Tu-2T and the Ilyushin Il-28T Beagle jet torpedo bomber.

An Il-4T with an AN-45-36 torpedo loaded. The Il-4T could carry two torpedoes, but normally only one was carried, as here. (*Viktor Kulikov's collection*)

Combat Tactics

Like the SB, the DB-3 and the Il-4 were used as level bombers. They were neither equipped for nor stressed for dive bombing. In addition, their lack of strong forward-firing guns or (normally) rocket armament precluded their use as ground attack aircraft.

The DB-3s were used mostly for day missions during the Winter War. The DB-3s were also first used as day time bombers during the Great Patriotic War. On one occasion on 26 June 1941, when DB-3s attacked the Germans at low altitude without fighter escort, they suffered heavy losses from the German flak, forty-three DB-3 crew failing to return. Due to the losses it had sustained during day time missions, the DB-3s were moved to night-time operations, which were safer because of the general lack of Axis night fighters, and the greater inaccuracy of night-time flak. This move to the night, of course, affected bombing accuracy, but for bombing large fortifications and troop concentrations, this was not a great concern whereas survivability of the aircraft was. From 1942 on, the DB-3s and Il-4s were mainly used as nocturnal level bombers by the ADD.

Both the DB-3T and the Il-4T were used by AVMF MTAP torpedo bomber units, where their usage differed greatly from the level bomber versions. Because the torpedoes could only be dropped close to the water, the DB-3T and the Il-4T had to operate at low altitudes, much lower than those normally used by their level bomber counterparts. For example, the 45-36 AN was equipped to be dropped at a very low altitude, being released at 98 feet (30 m). The 45-36 AV was equipped to be dropped at higher altitudes, being dropped from 820 to 1,312 feet (250 to 400 m) above the water.

Experimental Versions

Below are some of the most interesting experimental examples of the Il-4/DB-3.

Long-Range Record Aircraft: the Moskva and the Ukraina

The long-range capabilities of the new bomber were obvious, so the Soviet Union decided to modify two aircraft for civilian long-range record flights. These aircraft were the *Moskva* and the *Ukraina*.

In early 1938, it was decided to construct a long-range record-breaking aircraft based upon the DB-3. The aircraft had no armament and fuel tanks were installed in the bomb bay and the rear fuselage. On 29 April 1939, chief Ilyushin test pilot V. K. Kokkinaki set out on a non-stop flight from Moscow to New York. Due to bad weather, the aircraft was forced to make a wheels-up landing at New Brunswick in Canada, but the aircraft had still flown nearly 4,971 miles (8,000 km) and set a new world's distance record. One notable feature of the *Moskva* was a taller canopy for the pilot, which was adopted on the DB-3.

Not content with the *Moskva*, the Soviet Union decided to create another long-range record aircraft in the *Ukraina*, which was notable in having an all-female crew. Like the *Moskva*, the *Ukraina* was based upon the DB-3. The *Ukraina* took off from Moscow for its record flight on 27 July 1940. Like the *Moskva*, the *Ukraina* encountered bad weather on its record-setting flight, force-landing in the Kirov region, but it had still flown nearly 4,350 miles (7,000 km), which was a record at the time for an all-female crew.

DB-3TP (TsKB-51)

One DB-3 was tested with two floats in 1938, the floats replacing the landing gear. This version was designated as the 'DB-3TP', the 'TP' standing for *Torpedonosets Poplavkoviy* ('Torpedo-carrier Floatplane'). The Ilyushin OKB's designation for it was the 'TsKB-51'. This version remained an experimental one-off version, as the tests revealed shortcomings, such as an inevitable decrease in the top speed as compared to the wheeled version, caused by the drag and weight of the large floats. In addition, it was difficult to maintain and to arm this float-equipped version, as the floats obstructed servicing the aircraft when it was in the water.

TsKB-54

One of the problems with long-range bombers was providing for protection on their long-range missions. The bombers possessed defensive armament, but this was often found lacking in combat. Normal fighters did not possess the range to escort the bombers to and from their targets. A seemingly obvious solution was to modify some of the long-range bombers into heavily armed escort fighters (a type of aeroplane which before the war had been called a 'cruiser').

Armed with more defensive weapons than the normal bomber versions, these aircraft would have the range to keep up with and the armament to protect the bombers from attacks by enemy fighters. That was the theory, anyway, and Ilyushin tried out this concept with the TsKB-54, a modification of the DB-3. Interestingly, this idea was also tried out by the USAAF in the form of the YB-40, a modified B-17 Flying Fortress that featured even more heavy armament than that already heavily armed aeroplane. Unfortunately for the USAAF, it met with the same problems and had the same success (or lack thereof) as the TsKB-54.

TsKB-54-I

This first heavy escort version was modified from one of the first DB-3s from Z.18 in Voronezh. One of its interesting features was the provision for a remote-controlled ShKAS machine gun mounted in a streamlined pod on a pylon under the fuselage, which had a 240-degree range of movement in the horizontal plane. The normal ventral position was also retained. The nose and dorsal turret now featured ShVAK 20-mm cannons.

TsKB-54-II

This was an improved escort version, modified from a newer airframe from the 1939 production run. One difference between it and the TsKB-54-I was the installation of gun blisters on each side of the fuselage, the blisters featuring ShKAS machine guns. Unlike the TsKB-54-I, it did not feature the remote-controlled gun installation under the fuselage, which had been found to cause handling problems when moved. The standard ventral position was also removed. The dorsal turret and nose installations were given new gun sights.

Due to the added weight of the additional gun armament, the TsKB-54-II was actually heavier than the bomber version, and slower. Due to this, it could not keep up with the bomber version in flight, which made it useless as an escort fighter. The concept was thereby dropped.

Il-4TK (IL-4K)

This heavily modified version of the Il-4 was intended to serve as a high-altitude bomber. As such, it was equipped with turbo-supercharged engines and a pressurised cabin for the two-man crew. No gun armament was included as it was supposed that the aircraft would be immune from interception due to its operating at high altitudes. The nose was completely different from the other DB-3s and Il-4s with a faceted, hemispherical, glazed step-less nose replacing the conventional stepped canopies of the other variants. The M-88B engines were equipped with TK-3 superchargers, which fed air to the pressurised cabin, in addition to providing compressed air to the engines.

The Il-4TK was first flown on 16 March 1943 by now Major-General Vladimir K. Kokkinaki (by this time, he had become the chief inspector of the Soviet Aviation industry). The aircraft was found to be lacking in power. During testing, it reached a maximum ceiling of only 30,512 feet (9,300 m). This was 5,577 feet (1,700 m) lower than the specification called for. In addition, the engine and supercharger combination were troublesome.

By 1943, the VVS had achieved air superiority on the Eastern Front, which would only increase with time, and as it was found that the Il-4 was adequate for the level bombing duties assigned to it, there was no longer any need for a high-altitude bomber capable of avoiding interception and work on the Il-4TK ceased.

Il-4 2M-82

The evacuation of Z.39, which produced the M-88 engines, caused concerns about the availability of these engines for the Il-4. This led to testing the Shvetsov M-82 engine on an Il-4. This engine had a rating of 1,300 hp at altitude compared to the 1,100 hp of the M-88. This first Il-4 with M-82s was tested at Z.126 starting in February 1942. It was heavier than the M-88 equipped DB-3F of 1940 and had a top speed of 272 mph (437 kph). This was quite a bit less than the 292 mph (470 kph) that had been anticipated because of the greater horsepower. The M-82 at this stage in its development was an immature engine. The Il-4 2M-82 also had a shorter range than the M-88 powered example because of the higher fuel consumption of the M-82 engine.

This was not the end of the Il-4 2M-82, however. An example was built in the spring of 1943 with M-82NV engines (this engine featured direct fuel injection). This aircraft further differed from the M-88-powered Il-4s by featuring a much heavier armament of five UBT machine guns, disposed of in the normal three positions of the standard Il-4, but with two beam positions added. The aircraft also featured many wooden components. During testing, one of the engines went out, with no spare engine readily available and because by now the M-88B was being produced in satisfactory quantities it was decided to stop testing on this M-82-powered Il-4.

Il-6

A last effort by Ilyushin to update and continue the Il-4 line, this aircraft was almost a new aeroplane, with different wings, new engines, revised armament, and a longer fuselage based upon the Il-4's fuselage.

The longer fuselage had a completely revised defensive armament, with five ShVAK 20-mm cannons placed in five positions: one in the nose, two in beam positions on the sides of the fuselage, one under the aft fuselage, and one in a dorsal turret. This very considerably improved upon the defensive firepower of the Il-4, with its two ShKAS and one UBT machine guns.

This aircraft first flew on 7 August 1943, piloted by Ilyushin's chief test pilot V. K. Kokkinaki. Although initially intended to be fitted with M-71 radial engines, the prototype featured Charomskiy ACh-30B diesels. At 1,500 hp, the engines were found to be inadequate in power, so the armour was reduced, the crew reduced from six to five, and some of the armament removed in the form of the beam positions. In the summer of 1944, new ACh-30BF engines of 1,900 hp were installed which enabled the aircraft to fly with its full complement of armour, armament, and crew. During factory tests, the Il-6 achieved a maximum speed of 288 mph (464 kph).

The high wing loading with the new wing necessitated long landing strips and there continued to be problems with the diesel engines, such as the long time it took the engines to achieve their maximum RPM. To make the Il-6 an acceptable warplane would have required a change in engine type, which would have taken some time, and with the end of the war with Germany looming, development of the Il-6 was ended and plans to produce it were dropped.

The Il-4 in Detail

As the previous descriptions indicate, there were several different production versions of the Il-4/DB-3 bomber. The description below will deal mainly with the definitive Great Patriotic War version, an Il-4 from 1944, with some comments relating to the earlier versions. It should be remembered that the Il-4 differed greatly in construction from the earlier versions (pre-DB-3F).

The Il-6, as it appeared in 1944. (*Viktor Kulikov's collection*)

General Description

The Il-4 was usually of mainly all-metal construction, a mid-winged, twin-engined cantilever monoplane with a retractable main landing gear and a fixed tailwheel. The pilot sat in a fully enclosed cockpit, the bombardier was seated in the nose, and the radio operator/rear gunner was accommodated in the rear fuselage, where he could operate the fully rotating dorsal (mid-upper) turret, while a dedicated gunner operated the ventral gun. The tail unit was composed of a single vertical tail with the horizontal tail planes mounted on either side.

Fuselage

The fuselage cross-section was oval in shape and was constructed as an all-metal semi-monocoque structure. On a handful of Il-4s, the rear fuselage was entirely wooden in structure. From the autumn of 1941, Il-4s were built with wooden cockpit floors, navigator station framework, and tail cones. It is not clear from the record if all Il-4s built subsequently had these features or if they were replaced with metal items as the aluminium shortage lessened later in the war, in part due to Lend-Lease supplies of aluminium from the United States.

Handrails were present on the port side of the fuselage. DB-3Fs produced in 1942 had external stiffeners on the upper sides of the fuselage and above the stabilisers, but these were deleted on the Il-4 as the new construction gave it sufficient strength without the stiffeners.

Armour Protection

The pilot was provided with an armoured seat and an armoured bulkhead of 13-mm steel armour. The navigator had an armoured head rest of 8-mm steel.

Wings

The wings were cantilever, mid-mounted, and were of two-spar and (normally) all-metal construction. The leading edges of the wings were smooth, with no air inlets, as there were no radiators to cool, the engines on the Il-4 being air-cooled radials. The trailing edge of the wings carried ailerons on the outer portions and flaps on the inner portions. I-beam spars replaced the labour-intensive welded tubular chrome/molybdenum steel spars used on previous versions. The wings were also slightly thinner and had a greater surface area than those used on earlier DB-3s, carrying larger area flaps. Some Il-4s had outer wings of mainly wooden construction with metal spars and swept-back leading edges, but it is unclear how many Il-4s were built with these redesigned wings.

Tail planes

The tail planes consisted of a single fin and rudder with the horizontal tail planes being parallel to the ground. The tail planes' construction was of metal, with the stabilisers having two metal spars, with a metal covering except for the rudders and elevators, which were of a metal structure with fabric covering.

The navigator/bombardier's position on an Il-4, complete with a rather grim-faced navigator/bombardier. (*Viktor Kulikov's collection*)

Control Surfaces

The ailerons, rudder, and elevators were all made of a dural structure, covered by fabric. The Schrenk-type flaps were all-metal, split, and hydraulically operated. The flaps were larger in area than the flaps of the DB-3s. The rudder had a mass balance on top, as with the Il-2.

Engine

The engine for most of the production Il-4s was the M-88B fourteen-cylinder twin-row air-cooled radial engine of 1,100 hp and later 1,250 hp on take-off. This engine could trace its ancestry all the way back to the Gnome-Rhone fourteen-cylinder Mistral Kdrs engine, which along with the Hispano-Suiza Ydrs and the Wright Cyclone R-1820 helped jump-start the Soviet aero-engine industry in the mid-1930s. Some of the early Il-4/DB-3Fs ('DB-3M') carried the M-87A engine, which had 950 hp on take-off.

Landing Gear

The main landing gear were retractable, retracting aft into the engine nacelles, and was enclosed by doors when retracted, with a small portion of the tyre protruding, which provided some protection in the event of the aircraft crash-landing. The main wheel was 'trapped' between two main oleo struts, with 'X' shaped struts that connected the

An M-88B engine on an Il-4 with the cowling panels off, showing the engine details. (*Viktor Kulikov's collection*)

oleo struts, very similar to the landing gear on the Il-2. This replaced the weaker single struts of earlier DB-3s. The main wheels were 1,100 × 400-mm in diameter on the Il-4. The forked tailwheel was fixed, but was at first protected by a fairing attached to the front of the tailwheel strut that helped keep dirt and mud out of the tailwheel recess. This fairing was sometimes removed and was separate from the small streamlined fairing that was in front of the tailwheel and was part of the fuselage, replacing the longer fairing of earlier versions. In 1943, to deal with the increasing weight of the Il-4, the tailwheel was changed in size from 400 × 150-mm to 470 × 210-mm.

Fuel System

The fuel system on the Il-4 consisted of six fuel tanks, with four tanks located in the inboard wing sections and two located in the outboard wing sections. This replaced the ten fuel tanks of earlier versions, which simplified the system considerably.

Hydraulic System

On the early DB-3s, the landing gear were retracted hydraulically. This was changed with the Il-4, where the landing gear were retracted pneumatically.

Oxygen/Pneumatic System

As mentioned above, with the Il-4, the landing gear were retracted pneumatically, in place of the hydraulic system that had been used previously.

Electronic Equipment

A RSB-3bis radio was fitted for communications purposes and comprised a receiver and a transmitter. From the middle of 1943, an APG-1 ADF (Aerial Direction Finder) was fitted to every second Il-4. The earlier SPU-3 intercom was replaced by the SPU-4F, and UV lights were used for the instrument panel for night-time flying.

Moveable Armament

The moveable armament consisted for the Il-4 of one Berezin UBT 12.7-mm (50-calibre) heavy machine gun mounted in a UTK-1 turret (some of the earlier Il-4s had the smaller ShKAS 7.62-mm (30-calibre) machine gun mounted in a MV-3 turret, which was similar to the UTK-1 except for the lighter calibre gun). Early versions of the Il-4 and all versions of the DB-3 featured the low-profile SU turret with the ShKAS machine gun. The navigator was equipped with a ShKAS machine gun on a rotatable ball mounting in the extreme nose, which replaced the TUR-8 mount of the earlier DB-3s. Another ShKAS machine gun fired through the bottom of the aft fuselage from a retractable MV-2 mount, this replacing the less effective LU mount of earlier DB-3s. The Il-4 featured a fourth crew member, as a dedicated gunner to man the ventral gun position. In the DB-3s, the radio operator was supposed to man both the dorsal turret and the ventral gun position, which obviously could not be done at the same time, thus decreasing the effective defensive firepower of the aircraft.

Disposable Armament

The bomb armament of the Il-4 was accommodated in an internal bomb bay located amidships. The maximum bomb load was 5,512 lb (2,500 kg). In addition to bombs being carried in the internal bomb bay, large-calibre bombs of up to 2,205 lb (1,000 kg) could be carried on external bomb racks. Some Il-4s may have been equipped to carry RS-82 rockets under the wings, although the record is not very clear on this.

Conclusion

The Il-4 was produced in the thousands from 1936 to 1946 (6,784) and contributed greatly to the Soviet war effort against the Germans. Yet it still remains an enigma, never having gained the accolades that other heavily produced Soviet aircraft of the Great Patriotic War have, such as the Il-2 and the Yakovlev fighters, or the Pe-2. Not even in Soviet post-war propaganda was it lauded as other Soviet Great Patriotic War aircraft were, especially the Il-2. The main reason may be that the basic design never quite seemed to live up to the initial promise and potential shown by the TsKB-26 and TsKB-30 prototypes.

Throughout its production run, it was continuously modified in a not entirely successful effort to cure its various defects and keep it from becoming obsolete. Some of these problems stemmed from its engines, which were never too powerful nor too reliable. Its defensive armament was found wanting on day missions. Since there was no co-pilot, it was also a taxing aircraft for the lone pilot to fly, especially on long-range missions. Nonetheless, whatever its defects, it gave the Soviets a long-range bomber and torpedo bomber at a time when they needed them, and it served throughout the Second World War and continued in use as a torpedo bomber in the Soviet Union until 1952.

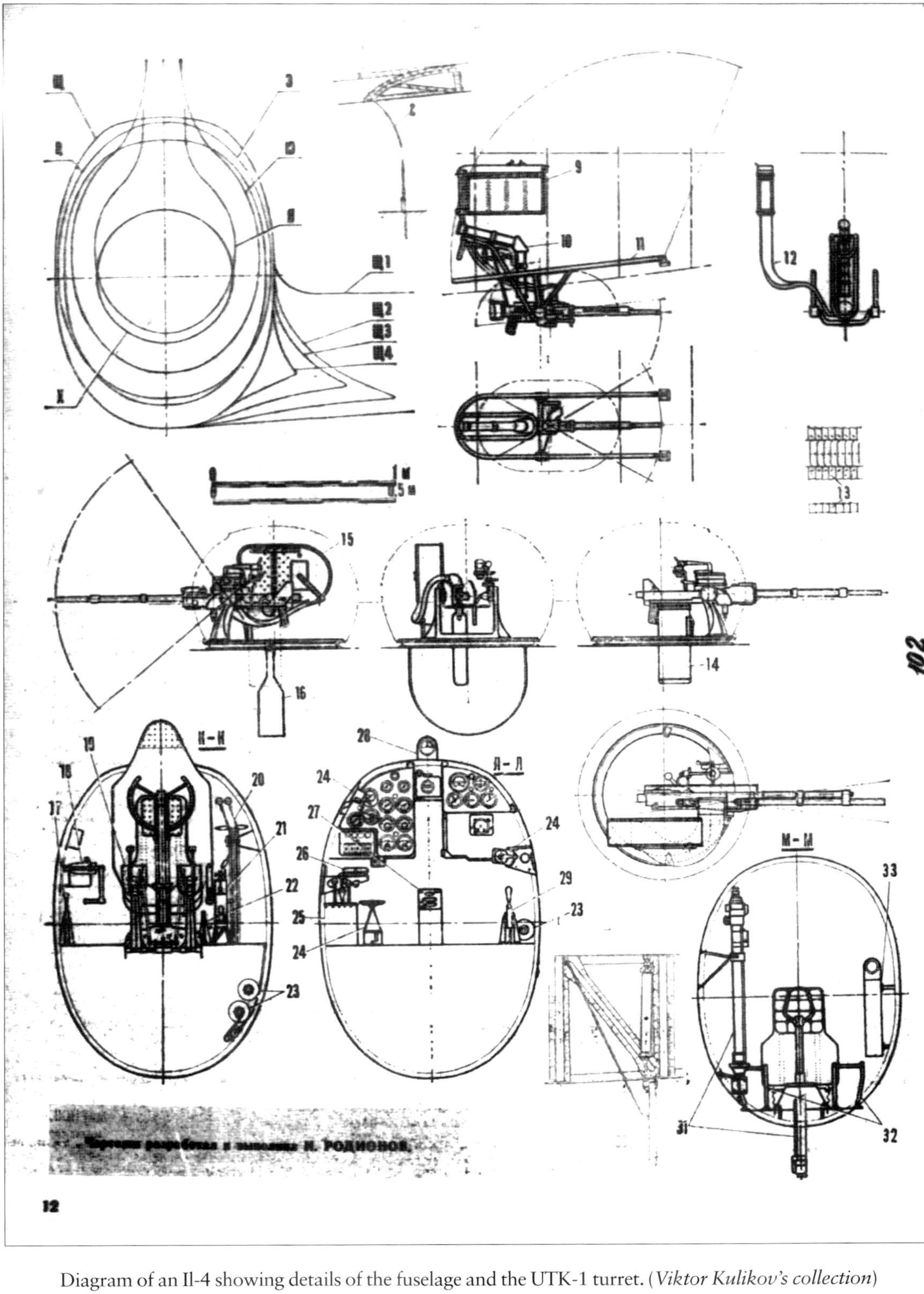

Diagram of an Il-4 showing details of the fuselage and the UTK-1 turret. (*Viktor Kulikov's collection*)

Above left: Dorsal turret on a DB-3. The turret mounts a single ShKAS machine gun. (*Viktor Kulikov's collection*)

Above right: Dorsal turret on an Il-4. This turret is mounting a UBT machine gun, which would make this a UTK-1. Notice how the turret top opens up, and the twin wind vanes. (*Viktor Kulikov's collection*)

A UTK-1 being rearmed. (*Viktor Kulikov's collection*)

Right: The bomb load of an Il-4 laid out to the side of the bomber. These bombs are relatively small FAB-100 100 kg (221 lb) bombs. This Il-4 belongs to the 5th Guards MTAB. (*Viktor Kulikov's collection*)

Below: A 45-36AVA torpedo. Note the Il-4Ts in the background. (*Viktor Kulikov's collection*)

DB-3/Il-4 Specification Table

Specifications	TsKB-26	TsKB-30	DB-3 (DB-3S)	DB-3A	DB-3B (DB-3 2M-87A)	Il-4 (DB-3F)	Il-4 (DB-3F)	Il-4	Il-4	Il-6
Year	1935	1936	1937	1938	1939	1940	1941	1942	1944	1944
Maximum Speed: mph (kph)	242 (390)	249 (400)	236 (380)	245 (395)	273 (439)	270 (435)	262 (422)	247 (398)		288 (464)
Range: miles (km)	2,485 (4,000)	2,485 (4,000)	2,485 (4,000)	1,988 (3,200)	2,361 (3,800)	2,361 (3,800)	2,361 (3,800)	2,228 (3,585)		3,418 (5,500)
Service Ceiling: feet (m)	32,808 (10,000)	27,559 (8,400)	27,559 (8,400)	27,231 (8,300)	31,496 (9,600)	32,808 (10,000)	29,199 (8,900)	27,231 (8,300)		22,966 (7,000)
Defensive Armament	N/A	3 × ShKAS 7.62-mm machine guns	3 × ShKAS 7.62-mm machine guns	3 × ShKAS 7.62-mm machine guns	3 × ShKAS 7.62-mm machine guns	3 × ShKAS 7.62-mm machine guns	3 × ShKAS 7.62-mm machine guns	1 × Berezin UBT 12.7-mm machine gun, 2 × ShKAS 7.62-mm machine guns	1 × Berezin UBT 12.7-mm machine gun, 2 × ShKAS 7.62-mm machine guns	5 × ShVAK 20.-mm cannons
Rocket Armament	N/A	N/A	N/A	N/A	N/A	2 BETAB-750DS 305-mm				N/A
Maximum Bomb Load: lb (kg)	2,205 (1,000)	5,512 (2,500)	5,512 (2,500)	5,512 (2,500)	5,512 (2,500)	5,512 (2,500)	5,512 (2,500)	5,512 (2,500)	5,512 (2,500)	11,023 (5,000)
Empty Weight: lb (kg)	8,818 (4,000)	10,534 (4,778)			11,089 (5,030)	12,787 (5,800)	15,939 (7,230)?	14,156 (6,421)?		26,301 (11,930)
All-up Weight: lb (kg)	13,228 (6,000)		15,128 (6,862)	14,551 (6,600)	16,424 (7,450)	17,710 (8,033)	20,878 (9,470)	22,167 (10,055)		35,494 (16,100)

Maximum Weight: lb (kg)			18,739 (8,500)	18,739 (8,500)	20,834 (9,450)	22,384 (10,153)	25,507 (11,570)	26,720 (12,120)		43,211 (19,600)
Engines/ take-off hp per	2 × Tumansky M-85 765	2 × Tumansky M-85 765	2 × Tumansky M-85 765	2 × Tumansky M-86 950	2 × Tumansky M-87A 950	2 × Tumansky M-88 1,100	2 × Tumansky M-88B 1,100	2 × Tumansky M-88B 1,100	2 × Tumansky M-88B 1,250	2 × Charomskiy ACh-30BF 1,900
Crew	2 (3)	3	3	3	3	3	4	4	4	6
Length: feet (m)	44.95 (13.7)	46.66 (14.223)	46.66 (14.223)	46.66 (14.223)	46.66 (14.223)	48.43 (14.76)	48.52 (14.788)	48.52 (14.788)	48.52 (14.788)	57.01 (17.378)
Wingspan: feet (m)	70.21 (21.4)	70.21 (21.4)	70.21 (21.4)	70.34 (21.44)	70.34 (21.44)	70.34 (21.44)	70.34 (21.44)	70.34 (21.44)	70.34 (21.44)	85.53 (26.07)

Li-2NB

The Li-2 was a licence-built version of the famous Douglas DC-3/C-47 redesigned for Soviet production by the Lisunov OKB (and initially known as the 'PS-84'). It was built in considerable numbers (3,000 or so at least, perhaps many more; production estimates vary a great deal even for a Soviet-built aircraft, for example, one source has 4,937 having been built). The aircraft was initially built at Z.84 in Khimki (Moscow), before the production facilities were evacuated to Tashkent, in Soviet Central Asia (Uzbekistan), where it continued to be produced by Z.33. It served throughout the Great Patriotic War as a transport. Vladimir Myasishchev, of M-4/3M 'Bison' jet bomber fame, helped in the redesign and preparation for licence-production. In addition to being used as a passenger and cargo transport, it was also used as a night bomber throughout most of the Great Patriotic War; a specialised variant, the Li-2NB was even produced for this role. The 'NB' in its name stood for *Nochnoiy Bombardirovshchik* ('Night Bomber' in Russian).

Although no longer used as a bomber, the Li-2 continued to serve for long after the war in its original transport role, and it received the NATO reporting name of 'Cab'. It was used by various Communist bloc countries; it continued in use with the Chinese into the 1980s (the last was retired in 1986). It is even possible that North Korea may still be using some as of the time of writing (2019), although these may just be derelict aircraft seen at air bases. At least one Li-2 is still flying as of 2019 on the warbird circuit in Europe (the DC-3/C-47 itself rather amazingly continues in service as a transport and freighter with civilian operators and even some air forces).

An Li-2NB from the side, showing the UTK-1 dorsal turret and the under fuselage mounted bomb load. (*Viktor Kulikov's collection*)

Development

PS-84 (Li-2)

In November 1936, Soviet aviation engineer Boris Pavlovich Lisunov (1898–1946), along with other Soviet designers and technicians was sent to the Douglas factory at Long Beach, California to learn about construction techniques, especially in regards to the DC-3, which the Soviet Union was scheduled to produce under licence. It was while in the United States that the Soviet designers and technicians learned about modern construction methods such as the template assembly technique, which were then applied to their own indigenously designed and produced aircraft, such as the Il-4.

The Soviet 'DC-3' was not a straight copy of the American machine as for example everything had to be converted from imperial measurements into metric measurements. In some places the skinning was thicker and, in some places, it was thinner than on the DC-3, although generally, it was thicker since the closest metric skinning was thicker. The engines were not American R-1820s nor Pratt & Whitney R-1830s, but Soviet Shvetsov M-62s (licence-built copies of the R-1820 Wright Cyclone). The engines were equipped with shutters in the front of the cowlings (similar to those fitted to the similarly powered I-16 fighter) to deal with the cold climate. The wings were slightly shorter in span than the DC-3, and a freight door was fitted to the port side of the fuselage, the passenger door being moved to the starboard side.

The resulting aircraft was heavier and the engines less powerful with the result that the 'PS-84', as the aircraft was now designated, was slower than the DC-3 (the 'PS' stood for *Passazhirskiy Samolyot*, 'Passenger Aeroplane', with the '84' standing for the factory where they were initially built: *Zavod* 84). The PS-84 of 1940 had a top speed of 204 mph (329 kph) as compared to 230 mph (370 kph) for a DC-3. The name was eventually changed from 'PS-84' to 'Li-2', to recognise the name of the chief designer of the Lisunov OKB, Boris Lisunov. A few Li-2s were fitted with the 1,100-hp M-88 engine.

Li-2NB (Li-2VP)

The ADD was established in 1942 as a long-range strategic bomber force, equipped with Il-4s, Pe-8s, TB-3s, and American Lend-Lease B-25s. During 1942, due to heavy losses and the evacuation eastward of aircraft factories, a need grew for additional long-range bombers, a need that could not be met by the available bombers. The decision was made to convert the Li-2 into a bomber. Some passenger Li-2s were converted in the field to be able to carry four FAB-250 551-lb (250-kg) bombs externally. In April 1942, the first Li-2s were incorporated into the ADD. Apparently, these were initially equipped as transports, but they were soon converted into bombers with the addition of external bomb racks.

Unlike other versions of the Li-2 that were converted from transports into bombers during the Great Patriotic War, the Li-2NB was a purpose-built night bomber version of the Li-2, where, as noted previously, the 'NB' in the name stood for *Nochnoiy Bombardirovshchik* ('Night Bomber'). It was capable of carrying up to 4,409 lb (2,000 kg) of bombs for short distances and 2,205 lb (1,000 kg) for longer missions, with the bombs being loaded on racks under the wings, there being no internal bomb bay, except for a container for small fragmentation bombs. It was used quite heavily as a bomber during the war and supplemented the Il-4s and the Lend-Lease B-25s in their night bombing duties with the ADD.

Like many of the military transport versions, the bomber version featured defensive armament in the form of a UTK-1 dorsal turret (like the one used on the Il-4), armed with a 12.7-mm (50-calibre) UBT heavy machine gun (some aircraft may have had the ShKAS gun in the similar MV-3 turret). In addition, it had up to three ShKAS 7.62-mm (30-calibre) rapid-fire machine guns, one fixed in the nose (which gun was sometimes removed as being of dubious utility) and two in moveable beam positions in the aft fuselage, the beam positions being enclosed by metal panels. The Li-2 bombers were used for the most part to re-equip units that still operated the obsolete TB-3 in the bomber role, but new bomber units equipped with the Li-2NBs were also established.

Since it was not a purpose-designed bomber, but a conversion of a passenger aircraft, the Li-2NB was not optimal for its bomber role. Due to the structure of its low-mounted wing, it lacked an internal bomb bay, which would have reduced the drag of its bomb load, which mounted externally further reduced its rather low top speed. This low speed made it more vulnerable to ground fire than other night bombers such as the Il-4 and the B-25, which were purpose-built bombers with internal bomb bays. It also lacked a bombsight in the nose, the bombsight instead being mounted to look through the bulged port entry door to the cockpit. This limited its ability to track targets, as it could only effectively follow targets on the port side of the aircraft.

Conversely, because of its transport heritage, the Li-2NB also had some advantages over completely purpose-built bombers. Its capacious fuselage gave the crew much more room to operate in, and it was equipped with a galley and toilet, luxuries other bomber crews could only dream of. Due to this, it was a much more comfortable bomber to fly in than other bombers, and its crews appreciated these rare amenities, proving popular in service. In addition, it was a multi-role aircraft, as the bomber versions were also utilised as transports.

Bombs being loaded on to the under-fuselage bomb racks on an Li-2NB. (*Viktor Kulikov's collection*)

An Li-2 taking off with what appear to be smoke-generators mounted under the fuselage, instead of bombs. (*Viktor Kulikov's collection*)

An Li-2 preparing to take-off, while an Il-4 in the background has already taken off. (*Viktor Kulikov's collection*)

An Li-2NB from the front, showing the bombs off to good advantage. This aircraft has the normal bomb load of four FAB-250 250-kg (552-lb) bombs. Note the ShKAS machine gun mounted in the nose. Note also how the engines have louvres mounted in the front of the cowlings, which in this case are closed off in the cold weather. (*Viktor Kulikov's collection*)

The MV-3 dorsal turret of an Li-2NB. Some Li-2s had the MV-3 with the ShKAS gun instead of the UTK-1 with the heavier UBT machine gun. (*Viktor Kulikov's collection*)

A close-up of the ShKAS mounted in the beam position and closed off by metal. These guns were present on both sides of the fuselage in the Li-2. (*Viktor Kulikov's collection*)

The Li-2NB was used heavily as a night bomber, flying missions for example at Stalingrad in 1942, and in January 1944 at Leningrad, during the successful effort of the Soviets to completely break the siege of that city. It was used in raids against Helsinki in February 1944. In addition to its usage as a night bomber, the Li-2NB was also used as a transport. In the Manchurian campaign, because there were enough purpose-built bombers such as the Il-4, the Li-2s were used exclusively as transports, with three divisions serving. The Li-2NB served as a bomber until the end of the Great Patriotic War, ending up with the 18th Air Army (the successor of the ADD), and on 10 May 1945, there were 593 Li-2s still in service with the 18th Air Force, although some of these may have been the transport variant. The Li-2 was returned completely to its transport duties after the end of the Second World War. During the war, long-range aviation (the ADD and its successor the 18th Air Army) received some 1,214 Li-2s, not all of which were the bomber version. It is unclear from the record how many Li-2NBs were produced during the war, or how many transports may have been converted to the bomber configuration.

Conclusion

Although not originally conceived of as a bomber but as a passenger aircraft (the PS-84), despite its limitations, the Li-2 bomber aided the ADD in its efforts to combat the Axis. It helped to fill a gap in the long-range bomber force that the Il-4 and B-25 alone could not; as such, it can be seen as a successful wartime adaptation (or improvisation) of a very successful transport into a useful bomber.

Li-2NB Specification Table

Version	DC-3A	PS-84	Li-2	Li-2NB
Year	1939	1940	1944	1944
Maximum Speed: mph (kph)	230 (370)	204 (329)	189 (304)	186 (300)
Range: miles (km)	1,495 (2,406)	1,653 (2,660)	1,330 (2,140)	1,553 (2,500)
Service Ceiling: feet (m)	23,200 (7,071)	18,766 (5,720)	17,060 (5,200)	34,449 (10,500)
Defensive Armament	N/A	N/A	1 × Berezin UBT 12.7-mm machine gun or (ShKAS), 3 × ShKAS 7.62-mm machine guns	1 × Berezin UBT 12.7-mm machine gun, 3 × ShKAS 7.62-mm machine guns

Maximum Bomb Load: lb (kg)	N/A	N/A	N/A	4,409 (2,000), 2,205 (1,000) normal bomb load
Empty Weight: lb (kg)	16,865 (7,650)	15,565 (7,060)	16,094 (7,300)	17,086 (7,750)
All-up Weight: lb (kg)		24,030 (10,900)	23,149 (10,500)	23,589 (10,700)
Maximum Weight: lb (kg)	25,199 (11,430)		25,353 (11,500)	24,868 (11,280)
Engines/ take-off hp per	2 × Pratt & Whitney R-1830 1,200	2 × M-62 (ASh-62) 1,000	2 × M-62IR (ASh-62IR) 1,000	2 × M-62IR (ASh-62IR) 1,000
Crew	2	5–6	5–6	5–6
Length: feet (m)	64.75 (19.74)	64.47 (19.65)	64.47 (19.65)	64.47 (19.65)
Wingspan: feet (m)	95.17 (29.01)	94.52 (28.81)	94.52 (28.81)	94.52 (28.81)

Yer-2 (Er-2)

Although not nearly as well-known or as widely produced as the Il-4, the Yermolayev (sometimes spelled 'Ermolaev' or 'Ermolayev' due to incorrect transliteration from the Cyrillic) Yer-2 (Er-2) also served in the Great Patriotic War as a long-range bomber. It was developed by Vladimir Grigoryevich Yermolayev (1909–44) from the civilian transport, the Stal-7, designed by the Italian-Soviet designer Robert Ludvigovich Bartini (1897–1974). Around fifty aircraft had been handed over to the VVS by the time the Germans invaded on 22 June 1941. As with the Tu-2, production was halted, this time in 1941, so Il-2 ground attack aircraft could be produced at its factory (Z.18), and production was not resumed until late 1943, this time with an improved version (again as with the Tu-2).

It was built in two main versions: the first version with two Klimov M-105 engines and an asymmetrical cockpit arrangement with the pilot seated on the port side of the aircraft; and the second version with two of the Charomskiy ACh-30B diesel engines, which proved rather troublesome (as seemingly with all Soviet diesel aero-engines), but which gave it increased range and power. This second version also featured a rearranged cockpit configuration, which was symmetrical and housed two pilots seated side-by-side, larger vertical tail planes, a larger tailwheel, and a wing with increased area. These improved Yer-2s served until the end of the Second World War and participated in operations very late in the Great Patriotic War. The Yer-2 was not retired until the late 1940s. Somewhat fewer than 400 were built in total, perhaps 371.

Although it served into the post-war period, it does not appear to have been given a NATO reporting name.

Development

Stal-7

This aircraft was designed by Robert Bartini as a modern all-metal twelve-seat passenger aeroplane and first flew in the spring of 1937. It was characterised by its reverse gull-wing design. Despite good qualities, like long-range and a high speed, the Stal-7 never went into production as the chief designer, Bartini, was arrested (like so many of his contemporary aircraft designers) on trumped-up charges in 1938. The Stal-7 had crashed, so Bartini was charged with sabotage. The idea that a designer would deliberately make his own aircraft crash is, of course, patently ludicrous, but by 1938, any semblance of reason in the Stalinist purges had long since disappeared, if it had ever existed. However, the good properties of the aircraft were still recognised, and it was decided that a long-range bomber should be developed out of it, this design effort to be led by V. G. Yermolayev, one of the leading designers at the Bartini OKB, and who had the additional advantage of not being charged with any crime.

This redeveloped aircraft was designed to meet a 1939 specification calling for a long-range bomber with a top speed of 342 mph (550 kph), which was capable of carrying 2,205 lb (1,000 kg) of bombs 2,485 miles (4,000 km). Tupolev developed the 103D (which was a variant of what became the Tu-2), Ilyushin developed the DB-4, and Myasishchev developed the DVB-102 to meet these requirements (the DB-4 and DVB-102 are described further on). In the end, Yermolayev's design, the DB-240, won out over these aircraft.

DB-240

The DB-240 was powered by two Klimov M-105 engines. It had been intended for Klimov M-106 engines to be fitted, but problems with this engine delayed its development and the M-105s were installed instead. This installation reduced the projected speed and altitude of the DB-240, which was to have included a top speed of 311 mph (500 kph) at an altitude of 19,685 feet (6,000 m) and a range of 3,107 miles (5,000 km).

The DB-240 was an all-metal cantilever monoplane with distinctive reverse gull-winged main planes, which had been inherited from the Stal-7. The fuselage was of a triangular cross-section with rounded corners. The crew consisted of four members: the pilot, the navigator, and two gunners. A fuel tank could be fitted into the bomb bay to increase the range. The pilot's cockpit was located on the port side of the fuselage to give the pilot a good view downward, which gave the DB-240 and the early version of the Yer-2 their distinctive asymmetrical appearance. The tail planes consisted of twin fins and rudders mounted at the end of the cantilever horizontal tail planes, unlike the Stal-7, which had featured conventional tail planes. The large dorsal turret was semi-retractable.

Also distinct from the Stal-7 was the design of the engine radiators, which on the DB-240 were now located in the leading edge of the wings, while on the Stal-7

The DB-240, the prototype of the Yer-2, in 1940. Note the silver finish. (*Viktor Kulikov's collection*)

they had been located in the front of the engines, somewhat in the style of the early SBs. The DB-240 also featured stub exhausts which provided a small amount of thrust.

The DB-240 flew for the first time on 14 May 1940, in a natural metal or silver finish. State testing began in September 1940. Due to the less powerful M-105 engines (as compared to the intended M-106 engines), the performance of the DB-240 was less than originally projected. The aircraft had a top speed of 277 mph (445 kph) at 13,944 feet (4,250 m). As mentioned earlier, the aircraft was projected to have a top speed of 311 mph (500 kph) at an altitude of 19,685 feet (6,000 m). The aircraft was also found wanting in terms of defensive armament (a common complaint with Soviet bombers), engine defects, and a long take-off. However, the aircraft was found to have a good range, being capable of carrying 2,205 lb (1,000 kg) of bombs over a distance of 2,548 miles (4,100 km). Due to this good long-range performance, the aircraft was released for production at Z.18 in Voronezh.

Yer-2 M-105 (Initial Production Version)

Based upon the DB-240, the Yer-2, as it was redesignated for its production version, was manufactured starting from March 1941. The first production Yer-2 flew in May 1941. Fifty aircraft had been delivered by 22 June 1941 to the 420th and 421st DBAPs, but these regiments did not become operational with the Yer-2 until late in the summer of 1941. It does not appear that the Yer-2 participated in any action in the very first month or so of the Great Patriotic War. However, on 11 August 1941, three Yer-2s took part in an attack on Berlin. They also took part in the Battle for Moscow, in which they took serious losses. The losses were also compounded by operational

An early version Yer-2 (Yer-2 M-105), with the asymmetrical cockpit. Although some of the early Yer-2s featured a small tail wheel, this example features a larger tail wheel similar to that fitted to the later version of the Yer-2 (Yer-2 ACh-30B). (*Viktor Kulikov's collection*)

losses occasioned by continued 'teething' problems with the Yer-2. By the end of the year, only twenty Yer-2s remained operational.

The aircraft was armed with a ShKAS machine gun in the nose for the navigator/bombardier, with another ShKAS gun in the ventral position. An UBT heavy machine gun was fitted to the large dorsal (mid-upper) turret. Due to a greater weight, the all-up weight increasing from 24,912 lb (11,300 kg) for the DB-240 to 27,602 lb (12,520 kg) for the Yer-2, it was slower by 3–5 mph (5–8 kph) than the DB-240. From photographs, it appears that sometimes the ventral ShKAS machine gun was replaced by the heavier UBT machine gun.

Compared to the DB-3F (Il-4), the Yer-2 had a higher top speed at low and medium altitudes. With the same bomb load, the range of the Yer-2 was 20 per cent more than the DB-3F, and this was at a higher cruising speed of 245 mph (395 kph) against the 211 mph (340 kph) cruising speed of the DB-3F. The Yer-2 was also easier to pilot. However, in the DB-3F's favour, the DB-3F flew its missions at higher altitudes because of the better high-altitude performance of its engines, which allowed it to be out of the reach of most flak, and harder to intercept by enemy fighters.

In all, 128 (one source states seventy-one) of the first version of the Yer-2 were produced before production ended in August 1941 as Z.18 switched production to the desperately needed Il-2. This original version of the Yer-2 served in ever-diminishing numbers until 1943, when the few that survived were sent to training schools. The last combat sortie, performed by three Yer-2s, occurred on 8 August 1943.

Yer-2 ACh-30B (Second Production Version)

The ending of production of the Yer-2 at Z.18 and the evacuation of the Yermolayev OKB to Kazan' in the eastern part of the European portion of the Soviet Union prevented Yermolayev from even working on improving the bomber. In 1942, the OKB moved to Moscow, but even then, work was impossible as its former facilities had been taken over by the Ilyushin OKB. It was another year before the improved Yer-2 was ready, in 1943.

A Yer-2 ACh-30B in flight in 1944 or 1945. It is possible that this aircraft is painted in a two-grey over black camouflage. (*Viktor Kulikov's collection*)

A Yer-2 ACh-30B on the ground, showing the reverse gull-wing configuration, which put the nose quite a distance off the ground. The nose position is mounting a ShKAS machine gun. As with all Yer-2 ACh-30B, this aircraft is fitted with the symmetrical canopy, which accommodated a pilot and co-pilot seated side-by-side. (*Viktor Kulikov's collection*)

When production started up again on the Yer-2 in late 1943, the aircraft was not produced without modifications and an improved version went into production. There were two obvious modifications; the Klimov M-105 engines of the initial version had been replaced by Charomskiy ACh-30B diesel engines (developed from the M-30) in revised nacelles, and the asymmetrical cockpit was replaced with a wider symmetrical cockpit, now accommodating a pilot and a co-pilot in side-by-side seating. This new arrangement gave the pilot a better all-around view, more room, and was easier to produce (both sides of the fuselage, port and starboard, were now the same). The vertical tail planes were made larger, and the tailwheel was larger than that found on the first examples of the initial Yer-2 aircraft (some later versions of the aircraft with the asymmetrical cockpit appear to have been equipped with the larger tailwheels).

The diesels were considered desirable since they gave the aircraft a greater range, as the engines were more fuel-efficient when operating at constant RPMs than gasoline-powered aero-engines. This gave the Yer-2 an improved range. The engines were equipped with geared, centrifugal-type superchargers. The engines also had the added benefit of not being as flammable as gasoline-powered engines, an important consideration for any warplane. However, they were heavier than and not as reliable as the gasoline engines.

The modified Yer-2 was tested with the M-30B (this designation was eventually changed to 'ACh-30B' to honour the designer, A. Charomskiy); by the end of 1943, it had passed its state tests. The aircraft was released for production at Z.39 in Irkutsk (Z.39 had been moved from Moscow-Khodynka to Irkutsk in Siberia with the nearing of the Germans forces to Moscow in 1941).

In addition to the above changes, the aircraft featured an improved defensive armament consisting of a UBT machine gun in the ventral position (some of the early versions were already equipped with this gun), and a ShVAK 20-mm cannon in the dorsal (mid-upper) turret. Despite claims in some sources that the nose gun was a UBT gun, photographs appear to show this as a ShKAS gun on most Yer-2 ACh-30Bs. In some Yer-2 ACh-30Bs, this gun does indeed appear to be a UBT, but it is unclear from the record how many aircraft were so equipped.

Units of the improved Yer-2 starting forming in spring 1944. It was introduced into service in mid-summer 1944, then went to ADD units, where it supplemented the Il-4, the Li-2NB, and the B-25. By mid-summer 1944, seven regiments were at least partially equipped with Yer-2s, but continuing problems with the engines kept these from seeing combat service. By the end of 1944, only forty had been delivered. It did see combat during the final stages of the Great Patriotic War, after the ADD had become the 18th Air Army of the VVS, with two regiments of the 18th Air Division seeing action in April 1945 when they were used against Königsberg and Berlin. It was not used in the Manchurian campaign.

Despite the continued unreliability of the ACh-30B engines, the excellent range of 3,418 miles (5,500 km) and the heavy maximum bomb load of 11,023 lb (5,000 kg) of the Yer-2 made it a valuable bomber. After the Second World War, it continued in active service until as late as 1949, when it was replaced by the Tu-4.

Conclusion

Much like the Tu-2, which the Yer-2 mirrored in some ways, if the production of this aircraft had not been stopped prematurely (in this case, in 1941), only to be restarted in 1943, it would have played a much greater part in the war effort. Despite its relatively small production run (around 360-370 aircraft, although one source gives 391 aircraft as being produced, and another 462), it saw heavy use in the first year of the war for both strategic and tactical targets. In the final stages of the Great Patriotic War, it saw use in the night bomber role and gave the Soviets a useful long-range bomber with an excellent range and bomb load, greater in both respects than those of the Il-4. If not for the unreliability of its diesel engines in its second version, which delayed its service introduction, its effect would have been greater still.

Yer-2 Specification Table

Version	Stal-7 (M-103)	DB-240	Yer-2 (M-105)	Yer-2 (ACh-30B)
Year	1939	1940	1941	1944
Maximum Speed: mph (kph)	280 (450)	277 (455)	272 (437)	261 (420)
Range: miles (km)	3,107 (5,000)	2,548 (4,100)	2,485 (4,000)	3,418 (5,500)
Service Ceiling: feet (m)	32,808 (10,000)	25,250 (7,700)	25,250 (7,700)	23,622 (7,200)
Defensive Armament	N/A	2 × Berezin UBT 12.7-mm machine gun, 1 × ShKAS 7.62-mm machine gun	1 × Berezin UBT 12.7-mm machine gun, 2 × ShKAS 7.62-mm machine guns (ventral ShKAS gun sometimes replaced with UBT)	2 × Berezin UBT 12.7-mm machine guns (sometimes nose gun remained a ShKAS), 1 × ShVAK 20-mm cannon
Maximum Bomb Load: lb (kg)	N/A	8,818 (4,000)	8,818 (4,000)	11,023 (5,000)
Empty Weight: lb (kg)	10,582 (4,800)	15,600 (7,076)	16,535 (7,500)	23,027 (10,445)
All-up Weight: lb (kg)	13,228 (6,000)	24,912 (11,300)	27,602 (12,520)	32,739 (14,850)
Maximum Weight: lb (kg)	24,251 (11,000)	29,886 (13,556)	31,195 (14,150)	40,962 (18,580)

Engines/ take-off hp per	2 × M-103 860	2 × Klimov M-105 1,100	2 × Klimov M-105 1,100	2 × Charomskiy ACh-30B 1,500
Crew	2	4	4	4
Length: feet (m)	52.49 (16)	53.48 (16.3)	53.81 (16.42)	53.81 (16.4)
Wingspan: feet (m)	75.46 (23)	75.46 (23)	75.46 (23)	75.46 (23)

9
Torpedo Bombers

Unlike the United States, the United Kingdom, and Japan, the Soviet Union did not employ any purpose-built aircraft for torpedo-bombing during the Second World War. This was probably due to the lack of Soviet aircraft carriers and the generally land-based character of the fighting, as opposed to the marine nature of much of the fighting in the Pacific War, for example. The aircraft used by the Soviets for torpedo-bombing were either variants of level bombers, such as the Il-4T, or modified Lend-Lease aircraft, such as the A-20 Boston.

DB-3T

A torpedo-carrying variant of the DB-3 bomber, this aircraft is described in detail previously in the section on the Il-4/DB-3.

Il-4T

This was the torpedo bomber variant of the Il-4 twin-engined medium bomber, which is described in more detail previously in the section on the Il-4/DB-3.

10
Flying Boat and Seaplane Bombers

Not only were land-based aircraft used as bombers, but so were flying boats and float-equipped aircraft. Below, I shall briefly describe a few of these aircraft.

Be-2 (KOR-1)

This single-float single-engined biplane was the product of the Beriev OKB, headed by Georgy Mikhailovich Beriev (1903–79), based at Taganrog on the Sea of Azov, which specialised in marine aircraft (and still does to the present day).

The prototype of this all-metal single-bay biplane floatplane first flew in April 1936. It was equipped with an M-25 engine of 700 hp and had a top speed of 152 mph (245 kph). In service, the aircraft suffered from handling problems and was not a success. Nonetheless, such was the need for combat aircraft during the early part of the Great Patriotic War that some Be-2s, equipped with normal fixed landing gear (sometimes with skis instead of wheels), were used as attack aircraft during the Battle for Sevastopol. Some 300 aircraft were produced in total and it was retired from service in 1942.

Be-4 (KOR-2)

As a replacement for the rather unsuccessful Be-2/KOR-1, this much more advanced aircraft was developed and produced. It was a fairly clean monoplane, with strut-braced monoplane wings, but a cantilever tail plane, and the pilot and the observer/gunner sat in enclosed cockpits. It was a true flying boat, unlike the Be-2/KOR-1 floatplane, and had a boat-hulled fuselage. It was equipped with a single M-62 engine of 1,000 hp and had a top speed of 221 mph (356 kph).

The aircraft first flew on 21 October 1940 at Taganrog. The Be-4 saw service with the Black Sea Fleet from 1942 to the end of the war as an anti-submarine aircraft, a light transport, and a reconnaissance aircraft. It was produced until 1945, but only forty-seven were built.

MBR-2

Another product of the Beriev OKB, this aircraft was the main flying boat of the AVMF during the Second World War and saw use throughout the Soviet Union's part in that conflict. The MBR-2 was a cantilever monoplane flying boat of wooden construction which first flew in 1931, powered by a single pusher BMW VI engine. The tail planes were braced, and the aircraft could be fitted with fixed wheeled or ski undercarriage for use from land. The MBR-2 entered service in 1934.

The first versions of the MBR-2 featured the M-17B (a licence-built version of the BMW VI) of 680 hp and had open cockpits, but the MBR-2bis, which first flew in 1935, changed the powerplant to the more powerful AM-34N of 750 hp. It provided the pilot with an enclosed cockpit and the dorsal gunner with an enclosed turret (the front gunner still had an open position). This version of the MBR-2 had a top speed of 171 mph (275 kph) and remained in production until 1941, with a total of 1,365 of all versions being produced. It carried two 7.62-mm machine guns for defence and could carry 661 lb (300 kg) of droppable ordnance. It was used in service as a patrol, or maritime reconnaissance aircraft, and was used to attack surface ships, submarines, and port facilities, dropping bombs or depth charges as appropriate.

11
Autogyros

TsAGI A-7

Probably the most singular Soviet aircraft to be equipped with bombs during the Second World War was the TsAGI A-7 autogyro. The autogyro was the ancestor of the helicopter, but instead of having the rotors providing the propulsive power and lift, a conventionally mounted engine and propeller provided the propulsion for the autogyro, with the freely rotating (and unpowered) rotors providing most of the lift. The advantage was that although the aircraft was not capable of vertical take-offs and landings, or hovering, it still had excellent STOL (short take-off and landing) characteristics. This was balanced by a low top speed—137 mph (221 kph) for the A-7 due to the drag of the rotors.

The TsAGI A-7 was designed by Nikolay Ilyich Kamov (1902–73), whose OKB went on to become one of the pre-eminent helicopter design bureaux in the Soviet Union, along with the Mil OKB. The A-7 first flew on 20 September 1934, and it was in service at the start of the Great Patriotic War. It was a two-seater, equipped with fixed tricycle landing gear, and had a rear gun for use by the observer in his rear cockpit. In addition, the aircraft could carry up to 882 lb (400 kg: four FAB-100s) of bombs under its small auxiliary wings (these wings contributed some lift, although the main lift came from the auto-rotating rotor blades) and carried a PV-1 machine gun in each auxiliary wing. It could also carry six RS-82 rockets under the wings. Apparently, these aircraft were mainly used for artillery correction (reconnaissance), both during the day, and at night, not dedicated bombing missions, but it is likely that they did carry out some attack missions, given the dire situation in 1941. Apparently, only five A-7s were produced, and these were soon out of service; with the evacuation of Kamov's OKB from the factory, it was working at in Moscow, work on the A-7 ended. These were evidently the first rotary-winged aircraft to see any combat service anywhere.

12
Fighter-Bombers

Just about any aeroplane can have bombs or other disposable ordnance attached to it, becoming in effect a bomber. Even without bombs, aircraft can use guns and rockets to attack ground targets. The use of fighter aircraft as bombers—or fighter-bombers—was widespread throughout all the air forces of the combatants of the Second World War, and the Soviet Union was no exception. Everything from obsolete biplane fighters, such as the Polikarpov I-5, to the best and most modern Soviet fighters, such as the La-7, were used at some point as fighter-bombers during the Second World War. Indeed, such was the importance that the Soviets attached to supporting their ground forces that it was inevitable that fighters would be used as fighter-bombers in the ground support role. Below, I shall briefly describe their usage as bombers. I shall not go into detail regarding their development and usage as fighters, as that lies outside the scope of this book and will be dealt with in detail in the companion book to this reference, *Soviet Fighters of the Second World War*. The Lavochkin fighters have already been described in detail in a previous book of mine, *Lavochkin Fighters of the Second World War*. Please refer to that work if you wish to know more about the Lavochkin fighters in particular.

Polikarpov I-5

Designed by the Polikarpov Bureau in the early 1930s, this was the first in a line of biplane fighters that ultimately led to the I-153, the I-153 seeing heavy usage during the Second World War, especially during its initial phases. By the beginning of the Great Patriotic War, the I-5 was still in use as an advanced trainer. Amazingly, during the Battle of Moscow, so desperate was the situation that it was used as a night bomber, carrying small bombs under the wings. The I-5 was out of front-line service by February 1942. It is not clear from the record how much action it saw during the defence of Moscow. Similar units were raised in the Crimea and by the Black Sea Fleet in September 1941; they also saw service until February 1942.

Polikarpov I-15

The basic I-5 design was further developed into the I-15, with a more powerful engine, heavier armament, and a gull-winged upper wing. Despite the heavy use it saw during the Spanish Civil War, surprisingly, the I-15 does not appear to have been used during the Great Patriotic War, even as a trainer. By the time of the Great Patriotic War, it had been replaced by further developments of the basic design, the I-15bis and the I-153 (I-15ter). In Spanish service, where it was known as the *Chato* ('Flat-nose' in Spanish due to its blunt profile), the I-15 continued in use during and after the Second World War. Its rapid disappearance from Soviet service may have been partly due to the purportedly disliked gull wing, which restricted the pilot's view downwards.

Polikarpov I-15bis ('I-152')

Dispensing with the gull wing of the earlier I-15 (apparently disliked by some pilots) in place of a conventional upper wing braced to the fuselage by struts, the I-15bis (sometimes referred to as the 'I-152') also featured a more streamlined, fully cowled radial engine. Although it was used as a fighter in the Spanish Civil War (as the *Super Chato*, the I-15 being the *Chato*), pre-war border incidents with the Japanese, the Winter War, and in the initial part of the Great Patriotic War, the I-15bis saw most usage during the Great Patriotic War as a fighter-bomber, utilising small bombs and RS-82 rockets installed under the lower wings. In the western part of the Soviet Union, it was used until 1943 as a fighter-bomber. Although it saw no action in the Manchurian campaign, it was apparently still in front-line service in the Soviet Far East until just before that offensive, when it was finally retired from front-line Soviet use.

Polikarpov I-153

The last in the series of I-5/I-15 biplane fighters, the I-153 (or rarely, the I-15ter) was notable in featuring a fully retractable (although manually operated) main landing gear in a concession to modernity. Unlike the I-15bis, it returned to the gull wing of the I-15, which earned it the nickname of *Chaika* ('Seagull'). This was an interesting development as the pilots had supposedly disliked the gull wing of the original I-15. However, speed considerations (dispensing with the wing-to-fuselage struts of the I-15bis made it more streamlined) may have overcome any objections pilots might have had, at least as far as head designer Nikolaiy Polikarpov was concerned. Along with the I-16 monoplane, despite its obsolescence, it was numerically the most important VVS fighter at the start of Operation Barbarossa.

Its superb manoeuvrability was no match for the superior speed of the Luftwaffe fighters and it was soon being operated mainly as a fighter-bomber. Although hundreds were destroyed on the ground in the opening days of Operation Barbarossa, enough survived for it to see substantial use in the early part of the Great Patriotic War. Equipped with small bombs and RS-82 rockets fitted underwing, the I-153 saw heavy use as a fighter-bomber and proved especially valuable in the Caucasus region, where its manoeuvrability allowed it to operate with ease in the tortuous valleys of that mountainous area. It was used as a fighter-bomber by the VVS until as late as February 1944 (or even 1945 in northern Russia), apparently outlasting the I-16 monoplane in front-line Soviet service (see below).

Polikarpov I-16

The first single-seat cantilever monoplane fighter with fully retractable landing gear to go into service anywhere in the world (1934), the I-16 was still in widespread use as a fighter at the start of the Great Patriotic War. Very manoeuvrable, it was still outclassed by German fighters such as the Bf 109F, so after the first year or so of the Great Patriotic War the I-16 found itself mainly relegated to lesser fronts or for use as a fighter-bomber, often equipped with underwing rockets such as the RS-82, or small bombs. In this guise, it continued in use with the VVS until late 1943, after which it continued in use as a trainer.

LaGG-3

One of the trio of modern fighters that appeared just before the Great Patriotic War (along with the MiG-1/3 and the Yak-1), the LaGG-3 entered service in 1941. Although it was a streamlined aircraft, with fully retractable main landing gear, it was under-powered because of its heavy if strong wooden structure, and it was not overly successful as a fighter, being outclassed by the German fighters such as the Bf 109 and the Fw 190. However, such was the need for ground support aircraft that it saw use as early as the summer of 1941 as a fighter-bomber, equipped with rockets.

As the LaGG-3-37, equipped with a 37-mm cannon firing through the spinner, the LaGG-3 found use as an attack aircraft during 1942, including at the Battle of Stalingrad, where its large cannon could be used with some effect against ground targets, including tanks. This version was only built in small numbers.

Despite its mediocrity, the LaGG-3 served until the end of the Second World War, even seeing service in the Manchurian campaign, and although the record is silent on this, it may have still been used in the ground attack role, equipped with underwing rockets.

La-5, La-5F, La-5FN

The La-5 was a radial-engined development of the less than successful inline-engined LaGG-3 design. With the M-82 (ASh-82) fourteen-cylinder radial engine fitted, the basic LaGG-3 design was transformed from a mediocre (at best) fighter into a good fighter, able in its later versions (La-5F, La-5FN) to go head-to-head at low altitudes on at least equal terms with the German Bf 109 and Fw 190 fighters. As with the LaGG-3, it was also used as a fighter-bomber. Unlike the LaGG-3, it does not appear to have been equipped with rockets, but only with small bombs, which were attached to underwing racks, one under each wing. It saw heavy use as a fighter-bomber during the Slovak Uprising of 1944, supporting the Slovak ground forces in their unsuccessful bid to break free of German control.

La-7

A development of the La-5, the La-7 was a faster, more streamlined version, which proved to be a superb fighter—one of the best fighters of the Second World War, especially at low altitudes. However, even an excellent air superiority fighter such as the La-7 could not escape usage as a ground support aircraft with the Soviets, and it saw use as a fighter-bomber, equipped with small bombs under the wings as with the La-5. Indeed, with the increasing disappearance of the Luftwaffe from the Eastern Front in the final year of the war, sometimes the paucity of aerial targets necessitated the use of the La-7 as a fighter-bomber, as despite the lack of aerial targets, there was never any lack of ground targets. Like the La-5, it does not appear to have ever been equipped operationally with rockets, but instead only utilised bombs and its cannons in the ground attack role.

MiG-1

Along with the LaGG-3 and the Yak-1, the MiG-1 was one of the new breed of monoplane fighters just entering service with the VVS when the Great Patriotic War began. Unfortunately for the MiG-1, it had been designed as a high-altitude interceptor, and although it was the fastest fighter in the world when it was introduced into service in 1940, it was not a good low-altitude fighter, and most of the aerial combat on the Eastern Front took place at low altitudes. It was quickly replaced by the improved MiG-3, so it is not clear how much use, if any, was made of the MiG-1 as a fighter-bomber.

MiG-3

An improved version of the MiG-1, the MiG-3 was heavily used in the first year of the Great Patriotic War in its role as a fighter. Equipped with rockets, it also saw use as a ground attack fighter-bomber. Although production ended in 1942 in favour of the Lavochkin and Yakovlev fighters, some MiG-3s soldiered on until 1945, some with PVO units, where the MiG-3's good high-altitude performance could be put to suitable use. The MiG-3's generally rugged and simple construction enabled it to continue in use long after its production had ended, as it was relatively easy to maintain and repair.

Yak-1

The Yak-1 was the best of the new monoplane fighters that were entering service with the VVS in 1940–41, better than the comparable LaGG-3 and MiG-1/3. Still, it was inferior to the Bf 109F, the main German fighter at the start of Operation Barbarossa. Nonetheless, the Yak-1 saw heavy use, both as a fighter and, out of necessity, as a fighter-bomber. As a fighter-bomber, it was equipped with RS-82 rockets, although it does not appear to have been equipped with bombs.

Yak-3

In an effort to make the Yak-1 an even better dogfighter, a lightened version of the Yak-1, the Yak-1M, was developed; this became the Yak-3. It is unclear from the record how much the Yak-3 was used as a ground attack aircraft, but being a VVS aircraft, it is hard to see how it would have avoided this duty.

Yak-7

It was felt that a two-seat trainer for the Yakovlev fighters was needed, so the Yak-7 was designed. It was basically a two-seat version of the Yak-1, with the second seat being occupied by the instructor-pilot, with the trainee-pilot in the original seat. Surprisingly, the modifications made to make it into a trainer also made it a better fighter than the Yak-1, as the Yak-7 had better handling characteristics. As with the Yak-3, it is unclear from the record how much use the Yak-7 saw as an attack aircraft, but it was undoubtedly used as one. As should be clear by now, any aircraft that could be used by the Red Air Force in the ground attack role was so used at some point.

Yak-9

Developed from the Yak-7, the Yak-9 became one of the best Soviet fighters of the war and, in its later incarnations, such as the Yak-9U, one of the best piston-engined fighters of the war in use by any country.

Yak-9B

Remarkably, given the small size of the Yak-9, a dedicated bomber version, complete with an internal bomb bay was developed, the Yak-9B (with the 'B' standing for

Bombardirovshchik, or 'Bomber'). The bombs were located in a small compartment behind the cockpit, in what had originally been the rear pilot's compartment in the Yak-7, of which the Yak-9 was a development. Only a small batch of Yak-9Bs was built, but it did see operational use as a fighter-bomber and could carry up to 882 lb (400 kg) of bombs internally.

Yak-9T

Some 37-mm cannons had already been fitted to fighters before the Yak-9, such as the LaGG-3-37, which had achieved some success with them in the ground attack role. In this version of the Yak-9, an NS-37 (Nudelman-Suranov) 37-mm cannon was fitted between the cylinder banks to fire through the propeller shaft and spinner. The 'T' in the name stood for *Tankoviy* or 'Tank(-buster)'. State trials began on 15 February 1943, and the Yak-9T was tested operationally at Kursk, where it proved to be a potent air-to-air weapon. Despite some common misconceptions, the Yak-9T actually found more use as a fighter than as a tank-busting aircraft, where its powerful cannon could destroy or severely damage an enemy aircraft with one hit.

Although not primarily used as a ground attack aircraft, Yak-9Ts were employed in this role during Operation Kutuzov, the attack on Oryol as a follow-up to the Battle of Kursk in 1943. This was necessitated by the lack of Il-2s. The Yak-9T proved successful in whichever role it was used in, and 2,748 were produced from March 1943 to June 1945.

Yak-9K

Despite the small size of the Yak-9, large cannons were fitted to the Yak-9 operationally, first 37-mm cannons on the Yak-9T (see above), then a 45-mm cannon on the Yak-9K. Evidently not content with the extremely powerful NS-37 of the Yak-9T, the VVS and the Yakovlev OKB decided to supply the Yak-9 with the NS-45 45-mm cannon. The 37-mm cannon used by the Yak-9T had caused some problems due to its powerful recoil (mostly rectified), but these problems were magnified with the even more powerful NS-45, which caused the aircraft to buffet when fired, caused lines and hoses to burst, damaged the radiators, and damaged the engine itself. It worked best when fired at high speed, as the inertia of the aircraft helped to balance out the powerful recoil of the weapon. To help deal with the recoil, a large muzzle brake was fitted to the end of the cannon, which projected some way in front of the spinner and was an identifying mark for this Yak-9 version. This muzzle brake helped, but did not completely ameliorate the effects of the powerful recoil.

The first Yak-9K ('K' for *Krupnokaliberniy* or 'Large-Calibre (Cannon)') was submitted for state trials on 12 January 1944. A small production run of fifty-three Yak-9Ks was recommended, and these aircraft saw service from August 1944. As the twin-engined and other bombers that were supposed to be the Yak-9K's main aerial quarry had nearly disappeared from the Eastern Front by this time, it was mainly used as a ground-attack aeroplane, where its large cannon proved very effective indeed. Despite this, the Yak-9K did not go into large-scale production, as the war was winding down, and the later Yak-9s and the Yak-3 were superior fighters, and the Il-10 was a superior ground attack aircraft.

13

Soviet Multi-Engined Bomber Specification Table

Type	TB-3 (ANT-6) with M-17F Engines	SB-2M-103A	Ar-2	Il-4 (DB-3F)	Pe-8
Year	1933	1939	1939	1940	1941
Maximum Speed: mph (kph)	110 (177)	280 (450)	298 (480)	255 (410)	276 (443)
Range: miles (km)	838 (1,350)	1,180 (1,900)	932 (1,500)	2,361 (3,800)	2,299 (3,700)
Service Ceiling: feet (m)	12,500 (3,800)	30,500 (9,300)	33,100 (10,100)	28,543 (8,700)	30,500 (9,300)
Offensive Armament	N/A	N/A	N/A	N/A	N/A
Defensive Armament	6 × DA 7.62-mm machine guns	4 × ShKAS 7.62-mm machine guns	4 × ShKAS 7.62-mm machine guns	1 × Berezin UBT 12.7-mm machine gun, 2 × ShKAS 7.62-mm machine guns	1 × ShVAK 20-mm cannon, 6 × ShKAS 7.62-mm machine guns
Rocket Armament	N/A	?	N/A	2 BETAB-750DS 305-mm	N/A
Maximum Bomb Load: lb (kg)	4,409 (2,000)	3,306 (1,500)	3,306 (1,500)	6,000 (2,700)	8,818 (4,000)
Empty Weight: lb (kg)	24,177 (10,967)	10,511 (4,768)	9,766 (4,430)	12,787 (5,800)	40,941 (18,571)
All-up Weight: lb (kg)	37,918 (17,200)	14,065 (6,380)	14,660 (6,650)		73,853 (33,500)

Yer-2 (M-105)	Pe-2 (series 205)	Li-2NB	Yer-2 (ACh-30B)	Tu-2S
1941	1943	1944	1944	1944
272 (437)	324 (521)	186 (300)	261 (420)	340 (547)
2,485 (4,000)	870 (1,400)	1,553 (2,500)	3,418 (5,500)	1,305 (2,100)
25,250 (7,700)	26,247 (8,000)	34,449 (10,500)	23,622 (7,200)	31,168 (9,500)
N/A	1 × Berezin UBT 12.7-mm machine gun, 1 × ShKAS 7.62-mm machine gun	N/A	N/A	2 × ShVAK 20-mm cannon
1 × Berezin UBT 12.7-mm machine gun, 2 × ShKAS 7.62-mm machine guns	2 × Berezin UBT 12.7-mm machine guns, 1 × ShKAS 7.62-mm machine gun	1 × Berezin UBT 12.7-mm machine gun, 3 × ShKAS 7.62-mm machine guns	2 × Berezin UBT 12.7-mm machine guns (sometimes nose gun remained a ShKAS), 1 × ShVAK 20-mm cannon	3 × Berezin UBT 12.7-mm machine guns
N/A	10 RS-82 or RS-132	N/A	N/A	N/A
8,818 (4,000)	2,205 (1,000)	4,409 (2,000)	11,023 (5,000)	6,614 (3,000)
	13,669 (6,200)	17,086 (7,750)	23,027 (10,445)	16,477 (7,474)
24,911 (11,300		23,589 (10,700)	32,739 (14,850)	22,839 (10,360)

Maximum Weight: lb (kg)				20,878 (9,470)	
Engines/ take-off hp per	4 × Mikulin M-17F 715	2 × Klimov M-103 960	2 × Klimov M-105R 1,100	2 × Tumansky M-88B 1,100	4 × Mikulin AM-35A 1,350
Crew	11	3	3	4	10
Length: feet (m)	80.05 (24.4)	40.26 (12.27)	41 (12.5)	48.43 (14.76)	76.12 (23.2)
Wingspan: feet (m)	129.6 (39.5)	66.70 (20.33)	60.7 (18.5)	70.34 (21.44)	128.38 (39.13)

	18,783 (8,520)	24,868 (11,280)	40,962 (18,580)	25,044 (11,360)
2 × Klimov M-105 1,100	2 × Klimov M-105PF 1,260	2 × M-62IR (ASh-62IR) 1,000	2 × Charomskiy ACh-30B 1,500	2 × Shvetsov ASh-82FN (M-82FN) 1,850
4	3	5-6	4	4
53.81 (16.4)	41.93 (12.78)	64.47 (19.65)	53.81 (16.4)	45.28 (13.8)
75.46 (23)	56.14 (17.11)	94.52 (28.81)	75.46 (23)	61.88 (18.86)

14
Soviet Bomber Doctrine During the Second World War

The main duty of Red Air Force bombers, such as the Il-2 and Pe-2, was to support Red Army ground forces. As such, these aircraft were based near the front line (as part of 'Frontal Aviation'). They were used on relatively short-ranged missions, either directly supporting the Soviet ground forces by strafing, rocketing, and bombing German front-line troops, vehicles and defences, or attacking troop concentrations, supply columns, and supply trains and train stations behind the front lines. In addition, they were used to attack German airfields, especially those near the front lines, and these were always dangerous targets due to patrolling fighters and heavy concentrations of flak. These missions were normally flown at low altitudes, below 15,000 feet (4,572 m), and the main task of the Soviet fighters was to protect these aircraft on their missions.

Although the long-range bombers of the ADD had been intended as a strategic bomber force, they flew relatively few of what would be considered missions against strategic targets, such as enemy factories, or enemy cities such as Berlin or Budapest. Aircraft like the four-engined TB-3 and Pe-8, and twin-engined bombers such as the Il-4, SB, Yer-2, and the American B-25 Mitchell were mainly used in interdiction missions against logistical targets such as troop concentrations and railroad yards that were beyond the reach of the shorter-ranged Il-2 and Pe-2, or tactical targets such as front-line fortifications. This is discussed in more detail further on.

15

Soviet Bomber Organisation During the Second World War

Reorganisation During 1941

Insufficiencies in the organisation of short-range bomber and shturmovik units showed themselves during the early stages of Barbarossa. Due to these deficiencies, these units were reorganised. This reorganisation was adopted on 10–12 August 1941. Short-range bomber regiments were to consist of two bomber squadrons and one fighter squadron, with two aircraft held by the commander in reserve, for a total of thirty-two aircraft in the regiment. ShAPs were organised with two Il-2 squadrons, one fighter squadron, and a Su-2 flight, with two aircraft in reserve for a total of thirty-three aircraft.

From 20 August 1941, polks with aircraft such as Il-2s and Pe-2s started being organised as single aircraft polks, not composite polks. These consisted of two squadrons with two command aircraft for a total of twenty aircraft. With increased production and an increase in the number of aircraft available, by 1943, the number of aircraft in a bomber and shturmovik polk was eventually increased to thirty-two aircraft, with three ten-aircraft squadrons and two aircraft assigned to regimental headquarters. Three of these polks then comprised an attack air division, with an additional penal squadron attached, staffed with air personnel who had committed various offences. In addition, mixed air divisions were changed into uniform units (only fighters, bombers, shturmoviks, etc.), simplifying maintenance.

Eventually, by 1944, the shturmovik polks were increased to forty aircraft, composed of three squadrons with four aircraft assigned to the command reserve for a total of forty aircraft (or forty-four or even forty-five; sources differ).

Reorganisation During 1942 (The Novikov Reforms)

General (Marshal from 1943) Aleksandr Novikov, who had replaced Pavel Zhigarev in April 1942 as head of the VVS, initiated far-reaching reforms during the spring of

1942, utilising the lessons learned during the hard fighting against the Germans. Far from moving away from the long-standing mission of the VVS to support the Red Army, the VVS was reorganised to become even more efficient and responsive to the needs of the Red Army's ground forces.

A very important reform effected by General Novikov was the creation of 'Air Armies' (or *VA* for *Vozdushnaya Armiya* or 'Air Army' in Russian). The aerial forces under the command of the Western Front were grouped together and became the 1st Air Army on 5 May 1942. The advantage of the air armies was that they were under centralised VVS control and could be switched quickly from one front to the other, as needed, thus giving the VVS operational flexibility in countering the Germans. This was more effective than sending smaller units piecemeal to different areas of the front.

The air army's commander worked in close concert with the frontal commander of whichever front they were assigned to. This enabled the resources of the air army, or VA, to be used wherever the frontal commander needed them and ensured good cooperation between the air units and the ground units they were supporting. This lessened the risk of bombing one's own troops. At the air division and air regiment (polk) level, the units were homogeneous, comprised of one aircraft, such as the Pe-2. This improved efficiency in the supply and maintenance of these units, as only one type of aircraft now had to be supplied and maintained.

At first, the VAs had only five to eight air divisions attached to them. This was increased to eighteen air divisions, although some VAs had only thirteen air divisions attached. By late 1944, there were sixteen VAs, with thirty-seven air corps and 170 air divisions comprised of sixty-three fighter, fifty-five bomber, fifty shturmovik, and two composite air divisions.

An air corps comprised two air divisions, with 120–170 aircraft per corp. Initially, in 1942, some of the air divisions consisted of two polks per division, while the shturmovik air divisions consisted of three to four polks per division, for up to eighty aircraft (showing the importance of the shturmovik polks). By late 1943, the air divisions had switched to three polks, with 100–120 aircraft.

The air armies proved to be so effective that by 1945 there were seventeen of these air armies on the Eastern Front, composed of 175 air divisions.

One improvement to Soviet aircraft in general was the provision of two-way radios for all aircraft as the war progressed (in the early part of the Second World War, only some aircraft were fitted with this equipment, and some aircraft lacked radios altogether). This enabled the aircraft to keep in close contact with the ground forces (and with each other in the air, an important consideration with the increasingly large formations the Soviets flew in). Although the larger bombers such as the Il-4 and the Tu-2 were always equipped with two-way radios, until 1943 not all of the Il-2s were equipped with these radios. Their incorporation in all the Il-2s built from 1943 on increased the Il-2's effectiveness, as it could now more quickly respond to the ever-changing situation on the ground, following the commands of the ground-based forward air controllers, and its formations could be better controlled in the air.

16
Long-Range Aviation: The ADD

Formation in 1942

By the mid-1930s, the Soviet Union possessed the most formidable strategic bombing force in the world, with hundreds of the huge long-range four-engined all-metal monoplane TB-3 bombers in service. Indeed, long-range strategic bombing capability was a key part of Soviet aerial doctrine at the time. This changed with experiences gained during the Spanish Civil War, which led the Soviets to believe that level bombers were of relatively limited usefulness, and the real key to victory lay in close support of the ground forces. This led to a de-emphasis on long-range strategic bombers (only a handful of the TB-3's four-engined successor, the TB-7/Pe-8 were ever built) and to a greater emphasis on tactical bombers and ground attack aircraft. However, during the Great Patriotic War, with the necessity of attacking the Nazi assets far to the rear of the front lines, in part to disrupt supply efforts, the idea of long-range bombing was resurrected. This resulted in the establishment of the ADD—*Aviatsiya Dal'nevo Deystviya* ('Long-range Aviation').

The GKO issued a decree on 5 March 1942 that established the ADD. Major-General Alexander Yevgeniyevich Golovanov (1904–75) was appointed as its commander. The ADD was under the direct control of the *Stavka*, the Soviet High Command. The number of aircraft in the ADD rose from 329 (114 heavy bombers) in May 1942 to 479 (sixty-three heavy) in November 1942. The loss of heavy bombers such as the TB-3 was compensated for by the arrival of Lend-Lease B-25 Mitchell bombers in the summer of 1942. The B-25s continued to be delivered and used throughout the rest of the war.

Although not often used for attacking strategic targets such as cities, the ADD was used for medium and long-range missions against targets sometimes far to the rear of the front lines. Despite supposedly being the strategic arm of the Soviet military, most of the bombers were twin-engined medium bombers such as the Soviet Il-4, the American Lend-Lease B-25 Mitchell, and the Soviet Li-2NB; they were used mainly on nocturnal level bombing missions against operational (logistical) objectives such as railway targets and against tactical targets such as Wehrmacht troop concentrations and front-line fortifications. In addition to its use as a level bomber, the B-25 Mitchell was used for low-level intruder missions, attacking German airfields at night, which included downing German bombers during take-off and landing.

The ADD saw heavy use in these missions throughout 1943 and 1944 in such operations as the Battle of Kursk and Operation Bagration. The missions behind the front lines against supply and support targets (operational or logistical targets) such as the railways could best be characterised as interdiction missions. The few four-engined Pe-8s in service were also used by the ADD, as well as the four-engined TB-3s, which were used through the middle of 1943 in the night bomber role. In addition to the B-25 Mitchell, the American-built Lend-Lease A-20 Boston (Havoc) light bomber was also used by the ADD as a night intruder, attacking enemy airfields at night.

At first, there was little or no German fighter opposition to the ADD or VVS night missions. However, German night fighters made their first appearance on the Eastern Front by early 1943; by the end of that year, there were approximately sixty. The Germans claimed 129 aircraft downed, including four Pe-8s, by the end of the year. German night fighters claimed 328 aircraft in 1944 and fifty-five in 1945, although no Po-2s were downed that year, indicating the difficulty the Germans had in intercepting these small VVS nuisance bombers.

By 1 June 1944, the ADD had 1,195 aircraft, including 413 Li-2s and three Mitchell intruder units. During the course of 1944, the ADD flew 48,097 operational level missions with 696 aircraft lost, including 410 bombers (the remainder were presumably transports).

Dissolution in 1944

The ADD was formally dissolved as a separate service on 6 December 1944 and its aircraft absorbed into the Red Air Force (VVS) as the 18th Air Army (18th VA). It retained the same aircraft, such as the Il-4, the Li-2NB, and the B-25 that it had used as the ADD; by this time, it had seven regiments of the Yer-2 ACh-30B, although these were neither fully equipped nor operational. By the time the ADD was absorbed into the Red Air Force, the TB-3s and the Pe-8s were no longer used as bombers, but some were still retained as non-combat aircraft, such as transports. As of 1 January 1945, the 18th Air Army had 1,186 aircraft, including 407 Li-2s, and an increasing number of Yer-2s were being used (although they did not see combat action until April 1945). As the 18th Air Army, it continued to see heavy usage, for example flying 5,126 missions in March 1945 alone. It was a key element in the Red Air Force's contribution to the final assault on Berlin, where the Tu-2 medium bombers now served as a major component of the 18th Air Army. On 10 May 1945, the 18th Air Army had seventy-three regiments with 1,675 bombers in total, of which 553 were Il-4s and 593 were Li-2s.

17

Soviet Bomber Usage During the Second World War

The following section will describe the combat use of Soviet-built bombers during the Second World War and will be mainly concerned with their usage during the Great Patriotic War. In addition to Soviet-built bombers, Lend-Lease bombers such as the B-25 Mitchell will of necessity also be mentioned, although these are not covered in detail in this book. Since the Red Air Force was tied to and indeed a part of the Red Army, the major ground actions are described in some detail as the main duty of the Red Air Force was to support the Red Army ground forces. The bombing activities of the AVMF, or the Naval Air Forces, will also be described where appropriate.

Battle of the Khalkhin-Gol (Nomonhan Incident)

Although not strictly a part of the Second World War, this battle—actually a small, undeclared war between the Soviet Union and Imperial Japan—will be discussed here briefly because it did overlap the beginning of the Second World War and because of its overall importance and influence on the Great Patriotic War.

The conflict itself arose out of a border dispute between Japanese-controlled Manchukuo (Manchuria) and the Soviet ally, Mongolia. The origins of the dispute lie outside the scope of this book, but suffice it to say that the semi-autonomous Japanese Kwantung Army took it upon themselves to try and enforce Japan's claim on the disputed territory. The battle takes its name from the Khalkhin-Gol River, which ran through the disputed region (the name 'Khalkhin-Gol River' is somewhat redundant, since *Gol* means 'river' in Mongolian). The name 'Nomonhan Incident' takes its name from the largest village in the disputed area.

It was during the Battle of the Khalkhin-Gol that General Georgy Konstantinovich Zhukov (1896–1974) first showed his military capabilities as a general, especially in the tight coordination he demanded between the infantry, armoured forces, and the VVS. This combined-arms experience would prove to be very useful in the Great Patriotic War, in which General (later Marshal) Zhukov was to become the pre-eminent Soviet military commander.

The main bomber used during the Khalkhin-Gol conflict was the Tupolev SB medium bomber, although the TB-3 heavy bomber also saw use as both a bomber and a transport. In addition to the SB and the TB-3, the R-5 also saw use as the Red Air Force's main reconnaissance aircraft and light bomber. It appears that neither the R-Z nor the R-10 were used during the conflict, probably because the R-5s were already in theatre and at hand. The DB-3 also played no role in the conflict.

It was in this war that aerial rockets, in the form of RS-82s, first made their combat appearance for the Red Air Force, in August 1939. The RS-82, the '82' referring to its diameter in millimetres, would be heavily used in the Great Patriotic War by both fighters and bombers, such as the Il-2 and the Pe-2. They were not used for ground attack in the Khalkhin-Gol conflict, but for air-to-air combat, in which the Soviets claimed nineteen aircraft downed. Although they were quite inaccurate, it was thought that firing them would help to break up enemy formations of aircraft. In addition, a lucky hit would be enough to bring down any aeroplane, even a multi-engined bomber.

In May 1939, there were twenty-nine SBs in the area; by June, there were 116, and by July, there were 181. Besides bombing Japanese positions, the SBs also conducted reconnaissance missions. By the beginning of Zhukov's counteroffensive, launched on 20 August 1939, all the operational SBs carried out attacks against various Japanese targets and flew nearly 300 missions. By this time, Zhukov had a superiority in aircraft of two-to-one (and four-to-one in tanks) over the Japanese. When the fighting ended, the SBs had suffered a loss of fifty-two aircraft, with seven being lost in accidents and forty-five due to enemy action (thirty-four of which were shot down by Japanese fighters).

Despite the fact that the Soviets suffered heavier casualties than the Japanese during the conflict, the Japanese forces were routed and an entire division surrounded and destroyed near the Khalkhin-Gol River. It would not be the last time that Soviet forces would suffer greater casualties than their enemies yet still emerge victorious.

Due to Japan's resounding defeat at the Khalkhin-Gol, Japan accepted the Soviet and Mongolian interpretation of the border between Mongolia and Manchukuo (Manchuria). In addition, Japan sought and received a signed non-aggression pact with the Soviet Union, which both sides adhered to until the Soviets launched their Manchurian campaign in August 1945. Also because of this defeat, Japan was persuaded to pursue its territorial interests southward, towards southern Asia and the Pacific (there was a faction in the Japanese military that had looked towards the eastern Soviet Union for territorial expansion). This move southward removed the possibility for the Soviet Union becoming involved in a two-front war with Germany and Japan and allowed the Soviet Union to shift much of its military resources from the east to the war in the west against Germany.

Invasion of Poland

The Soviet Union had never been satisfied with the Bolshevik peace treaty with Poland after the First World War, which gave to Poland large areas that had not been a part of the Grand Duchy of Poland under the Russian Empire. The Soviets wanted these largely non-Polish areas back and waited for their opportunity. That opportunity presented itself in the form of the Non-Aggression Pact between Germany and the Soviet Union, signed on 23 August 1939.

The most sinister part (certainly for the Polish) of the Non-Aggression Pact between Germany and the Soviet Union was a secret protocol that divided Eastern Europe between the two nations by delineating their 'zones of influence'. The Soviet zone of influence included the Baltic states of Estonia and Latvia, although not Lithuania, which was to be in the German zone of influence. Unfortunately for Poland, this zone of influence ran down the middle of their country, with the western half going to Nazi Germany and the eastern half going to the Soviet Union.

On 17 September 1939, as Poland was desperately fighting the Germans, the Soviet Union invaded Poland from the east, to claim their portion of the country as laid out in the secret protocol of the Non-Aggression Pact. Despite the fact that most of their forces were engaged against the Germans, the Polish did put up some resistance to the Soviet takeover of the eastern half of their country and the VVS was involved in some combat. The Di-6Sh, for example, saw the only combat use of its relatively short service life fighting against the Polish. The DI-6Sh was used by the 14th ShAP to support the Horse-Mechanised Group of the Byelorussian Front. SBs were also used in the invasion of Poland.

Since the conflict was so short-lived, and the combat activity of the VVS so limited, there were no great lessons to be learned from this 'war'; the VVS did not change its tactics or aircraft usage as a result. The next conflict the VVS found itself involved in would be a bit more intense, however.

The Winter War

With the decline of the Kingdom of Sweden's power in the Baltic region during the eighteenth and nineteenth centuries, Finland had passed from Swedish control to the control of Russia in 1809, when it became a Grand Duchy in the Russian Empire. However, this changed in 1917 in the aftermath of the Second Russian Revolution, when the Russian Bolshevik Party formally recognised Finnish independence from Russia. The Bolsheviks soon regretted this quick recognition of Finnish independence as the expected 'Red' Finnish takeover of Finland never materialised, and the 'White' Finnish forces, under Baron Carl Gustaf Emil von Mannerheim (1867–1951), triumphed.

With an independent non-Communist Finland so close to their second largest city, Leningrad, the Soviets grew concerned about the safety of this important population centre and industrial base. They were worried about Finland falling under the influence of a hostile power such as Nazi Germany (which indeed became a self-fulfilling prophecy). Accordingly, in 1939, the Soviet Union demanded border territories from the Finnish, including those north of Leningrad, and also demanded a lease of the strategic Hanko Peninsula on the Gulf of Finland. In return, the Soviets offered to cede territory to the Finnish, territory however that consisted mainly of dense forests and swamps. The Finnish government refused these demands and prepared for war as best it could.

During this war, which began on 30 November 1939, both the SB and the DB-3 saw heavy action. On this first day of the war, there were 580 SBs available on the front for the VVS, with another 51 available for the Red Banner Fleet (Baltic Fleet). The largest bombing raid of the Winter War was against Helsinki, the Finnish capital, during the first day of the war. By 1 January 1940, there were 739 SBs in theatre, which was nearly one-third of all aircraft available. By February 1940, the SBs were bombing the fortifications of the Mannerheim line. By the time the fighting stopped, there were 1,244 SBs available. It was this sort of numerical advantage that enabled the Soviets to triumph over the Finnish.

During these actions, the SB suffered substantial casualties, with more than 100 lost, revealing the deficiencies of its defensive armament. It was in this war that the RS-82 rockets were first used in the air-to-ground role, by Tupolev SB bombers. Like the SB, the DB-3 revealed its shortcomings, resulting in changes to its design which found their way into the extensively redesigned DB-3F (Il-4). R-5s also saw action during the Winter War, and the fighters used were the I-15bis, the I-153, and the I-16 Polikarpov fighters.

On 30 November 1940, the first day of the war, DB-3s were in action. Aircraft from the 1st MTAP of the Red Banner Fleet attacked installations in Helsinki and Hanko. Most of the DB-3 missions took place during the day, with only the 85th BAP undertaking night missions. The DB-3s usually carried from 2,205 to 2,425 lb (1,000 to 1,100 kg) of bombs on their missions. On 14 February 1940, ninety-five DB-3s attacked Viipuri (Vyborg). The DB-3s used during the Winter War were the DB-3As with the M-86 engine, and the DB-3B with the M-87 engine, with most of the aircraft being DB-3Bs. The VVS lost seventy-four DB-3s during the war.

TB-3s were used as night bombers for attacking targets behind the Finnish front lines. During the attack on the Finnish defensive Mannerheim Line, the TB-3s were used to bomb its fortifications. The TB-3 was invaluable as it was the only Soviet aircraft that could carry the large 4,009-lb (2,000-kg) bomb. It also used 551-lb (250-kg) and 1,102-lb (500-kg) bombs in its attacks. In addition to their use as bombers, TB-3s were used as transports. Two TB-3s were shot down by Finnish forces, one by flak and another by Finnish fighters. Interestingly, one civilian ANT-6A arctic aircraft was modified for use as a bomber; it was used as a night bomber in the Winter War.

Out of a total of some 2,500 aircraft used in the war, the Soviets lost approximately 500 aircraft to Finnish military action, in addition to 400 lost to other causes during 44,000 sorties flown.

Although they suffered heavy casualties in the air and on the ground, the Soviets were able to overwhelm the Finnish defences by sheer force of numbers and by a reorganisation of their forces and better tactics. On 13 March 1940, the Moscow Peace Treaty was signed. This treaty not only granted to the Soviet Union those territories they had demanded before the war, but additional territory, including the city of Viipuri (Vyborg). It was Finnish resentment over these territorial concessions that led Finland to ally itself with the Germans during the Great Patriotic War.

Incorporation of the Baltic States

Just as the Soviet Union regretted the Bolsheviks' recognition of Finnish independence, they regretted their recognition of the independence of the Baltic states of Estonia, Latvia, and Lithuania. They desired to regain these outlets to the Baltic Sea, and the preoccupation of the West with German actions in Poland and then Western Europe gave them the opportunity to incorporate these states into the Soviet Union.

In 1939, the Baltic States were forced by the Soviet Union to accept the basing of Soviet forces on their territory, with Estonia agreeing to this in September 1939, then Latvia and Lithuania following suit in October.

In 1940, the Communists of the Baltic States, who had won control of the governments in rigged elections, asked for incorporation into the Soviet Union, which was, of course, granted, in early August 1940, and the Baltic States now became Soviet Republics. Although Lithuania was supposed to have been a part of the German 'sphere of influence' laid out in the secret protocol of the Non-Aggression Pact, the Germans did not seem to be overly concerned about its incorporation into the Soviet Union. This was no doubt because they intended to not only invade Lithuania shortly, but the entire western portion of the Soviet Union.

Since the incorporation of Estonia, Latvia, and Lithuania was accomplished without any major combat and only a few minor ground skirmishes, bombers saw no combat use, although some Soviet bombers were now based in these annexed countries.

Incorporation of Bessarabia and Northern Bucovina

In addition to their territorial ambitions in Poland and the Baltic States, the Soviet Union also cast a covetous eye on Romania, where they wished to reincorporate former Russian imperial territory that had been lost due to the First World War. On 26 June 1940, the Soviet Union demanded that Romania hand over Bessarabia and northern Bucovina, territories in the eastern part of Romania. There was little resistance to the subsequent Soviet occupation, and no aerial combat took place.

As had been the case with Finland, Romanian bitterness over the incorporation of its territory into the Soviet Union persuaded the Romanians to attack the Soviet Union when the Germans did, to further cement their alliance with Nazi Germany.

The Great Patriotic War (GPW)

That portion of the Second World War that involved the conflict between Nazi Germany and the Soviet Union (from 22 June 1941 to 9 May 1945) is known in Soviet (and Russian) history as the Great Patriotic War. It was the most important part of the war in Europe, and the Wehrmacht was largely defeated during this conflict even before the Western Allies landed in Normandy (75 to 80 per cent of all Wehrmacht casualties occurred on the Eastern Front). Soviet bombers of all types, from the small single-engined U-2 nuisance bombers to the huge four-engined TB-3s and Pe-8s, saw heavy usage during this conflict.

Battle of the Frontiers (Operation Barbarossa)

Despite the signing of the Non-Aggression Pact between Germany and the Soviet Union on 23 August 1939, it was probably inevitable that the two nations would eventually go to war. Adolf Hitler's (1889–1945) own personal views, his *Weltanschauung* (or 'World View' in German), included the necessity of incorporating at the very least the western portions of the Soviet Union as *Lebensraum*, literally 'Living Room' or area necessary for the survival of the *Volk*, the German people. Not only was this area to be colonised and exploited by the Germans in the long term, but in the short term, the factories and resources of the western Soviet Union were considered essential if Germany was to become completely self-sufficient, with no need for overseas resources or trade. This was especially important as long as the British Empire remained hostile and controlled the seas; before, during, and after the Battle of Britain, the United Kingdom had shown no willingness to negotiate with the Nazi government.

Accordingly, plans were drawn up for the invasion of the Soviet Union, the largest invasion in history; these plans were ultimately named *Unternehmen Barbarossa* ('Operation Barbarossa'), in honour of a twelfth-century German emperor who had travelled to the Holy Land as part of the Third Crusade.

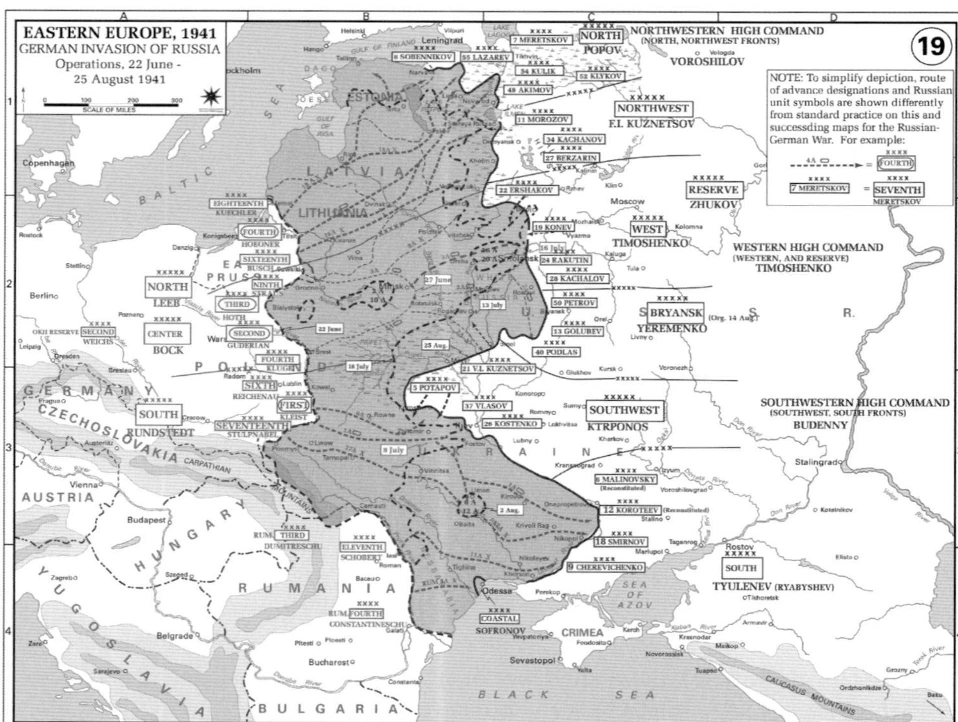

The Battle of the Frontiers. (*History Department of the United States Military Academy*)

At the beginning of Operation Barbarossa, the Germans had 3.8 million troops, 4,300 tanks, and 4,300 aircraft on the German–Soviet border. They opposed Soviet forces consisting of 5.5 million troops (2.68 million in theatre), up to 25,000 tanks (most of them obsolete, or light tanks), and 9,917 aircraft (most of them obsolete) in the western part of the country.

At the start of Barbarossa, the Germans had 4,300 aircraft, as mentioned previously. The Soviets had nearly 10,000 aircraft; however, many of these were obsolete and outdated biplanes, such as the I-15bis and I-153, still formed a major part of the fighter force, along with the I-16 monoplane fighter, a trendsetter in its day, but obsolescent by 1941. Although figures differ, it is clear that in the first few days of the war the VVS suffered tremendous losses, mostly on the ground. One Soviet account admits that 1,500 aircraft were destroyed on the first day of the war. Whatever the exact number, it was very significant, including large numbers of the Soviet's main medium bomber at that time (the SB) and crippled the Red Air Force's efforts to combat the German invasion. On 22 June 1941, the SB comprised over 90 per cent of the front-line medium bomber force of the VVS. There were more than 1,500 in the western districts, disposed of in 24 BAPs and 4 reconnaissance regiments. There were around 550 long-range DB-3s in the western districts, most of these being DB-3As and DB-3Bs, with a few being the M-85-equipped DB-3. There were also some 243 DB-3s in service with the AVMF. There were 1,122 DB-3Fs (Il-4s) in service with long-range bomber regiments in the western Soviet Union at the start of the Great Patriotic War.

On the opening day of Barbarossa, 22 June 1941, the Luftwaffe attacked sixty-six airfields in the western military districts. At the beginning of Barbarossa, the VVS had a numerical advantage over the Luftwaffe; eighteen days later the ratio was 1:2 in favour of the Luftwaffe such were the VVS' losses. Around 400 of the SBs alone were lost in the first two days of fighting (22–23 June 1941). Nonetheless, the SBs were able to attack Axis positions from the first day, attacking Königsberg and Memel on the first day of Barbarossa. SBs of the AVMF, from the Black Sea Fleet, attacked the Romanian port of Constanta on 23–25 June; they then attacked Romanian shipping on 26 and 29 June in the Tulcea area. AVMF SBs of the Red Banner Fleet attacked crossings over the Dvina River on 30 June. These attacks and others, often undertaken during the day and without fighter escort, took their toll; by 1 October 1941, there were only 130 SBs at the front, of which only eighty-three were operational. Production of the SB had already been stopped, so there were no replacements at hand.

The Pe-2 dive bomber had been introduced recently, the first examples leaving the factory by the end of 1940. By the start of Operation Barbarossa around 450 had been produced (464 by 30 June), not all of which had made their way to front-line units. 391 Pe-2s were recorded as being in service by 22 June, with 180 of these being in the front-line western border districts. The first action for the Pe-2 dive bomber took place on the opening day of Barbarossa, when the 95th SBAP, the first VVS unit to operate the Pe-2, sent seventeen of its aircraft to bomb the Galitskiy Bridge over the Prut River.

The first action for the newly introduced Il-2 Shturmovik took place on 27 June 1941 near Bobruisk in Byelorussia, when five Il-2s from the 4th ShAP attacked a

A Barbarossa victim SB 2M-103A in 1941. This aircraft appears to be painted in a fairly dark colour, but that may just be an artefact of the photography. The colour was probably a light grey. Note the ladder leading up to the nose position through the open hatch. (*Author's collection*)

German armoured convoy. From this point on, like the Pe-2, the Shturmovik found itself used continuously on the Eastern Front in support of the Soviet ground forces.

The Il-2 was not as successful as it could have been in this initial stage of the war due to the use of outdated tactics that had been developed for different aircraft (there being no combat manual specifically for the Il-2), the lack of coordination with ground forces (not helped by a lack of two-way radios in the Il-2), and the air superiority of the Luftwaffe. Greater success would come with time, but the Il-2 paid a heavy price in the interim.

Likewise, the Pe-2 suffered from not being used to its full potential, being used as a level bomber instead of a dive bomber due to their crew not being trained in dive bombing. As a result, the Pe-2 suffered both from the inaccuracy of level bombing, as opposed to the accuracy of dive bombing, and from heavier losses due to its greater vulnerability when level bombing as opposed to dive bombing. As with the Il-2, greater efficiency would come with time, especially from the work of the aviation tactician Ivan Polbin, but the Pe-2 suffered in the meantime.

The Il-2 and Pe-2 were lucky that they were new aircraft that were not available in greater quantities, as no doubt many of them would have been destroyed or captured in the first week on the ground, as indeed many were destroyed or captured in the coming weeks and months. For the TB-3, the situation was the opposite; as obsolete aircraft, they were no longer front-line equipment and had been withdrawn from the more exposed portions of the Soviet Union before the beginning of the Great Patriotic War and thus survived the initial attack.

This is an early Il-2 single-seater that was captured by German forces during the initial phases of the German invasion in 1941. Large numbers of Il-2s and other Soviet aircraft were captured in this way on the ground (such as the SB), basically intact, as their bases were overrun. Often, as here, the guns were removed, and the landing light covers were usually missing, as can also be seen here. This early example has the twin landing gear lights (or the holes where they would have been—only the starboard landing light is visible here, but the port landing light was always fitted) and the unpainted aluminium front blades of the propellers. (*Author's collection*)

The Germans gained ground quickly, trapping huge numbers of Soviet soldiers in gigantic battles of encirclement. Against this onslaught, the Red Army, including the Red Air Force, could only hope to slow down the Nazi juggernaut. The VVS suffered heavy casualties, like the rest of the Red Army, as they attacked the surging German forces. First Minsk, then Smolensk, and then Kiev fell, though none of these without a fight, especially around Smolensk, where the Soviets successfully counterattacked east of Smolensk at Yelnya beginning in August 1941, in the Soviet's first large scale successful counterattack against the Germans.

All available Soviet bombers, including the Il-2 and Pe-2, were in the thick of these fights, attacking German airfields, tanks, troop columns, truck convoys, and bridges—anything in a vain attempt to stop the Nazi *Blitzkrieg*. Despite their heavy losses, however, neither the Red Army as a whole, nor the Red Air Force stopped their counterattacks against the Germans, no matter how doomed these attacks were.

Due to the bomber losses in the first few days of Operation Barbarossa, the obsolete TB-3s were pressed back into front-line service; they even saw use as day time bombers, sometimes flying without fighter escorts. These types of missions proved nearly suicidal, and the TB-3s were soon relegated to mainly flying night-time missions. However, the TB-3s were also used in singular operations involving 'parasite' fighters. An operation on 1 August 1941 involved two TB-3 'mother ships', which each transported under their wings two bomb-carrying and piloted I-16 SPB (*Skorostnoiy Pikiruyushchiy Bombardirovshchik*: 'Fast Dive Bomber') fighters. The I-16s were successfully released and bombed oil tanks in Romania and then continued on to land at Soviet air bases. The *Zveno* operations were stopped in 1942 because of the vulnerability of the carriers, the TB-3.

AVMF DB-3Ts of the 1st MTAP (Mine and Bomb-layer Air Regiment) of the KBF (Red Banner Fleet: the Baltic Fleet) were the first Soviet aircraft to bomb Berlin. Taking off from an airfield on the Baltic island of Ösel off the coast of Estonia, fifteen DB-3Ts on 7 August 1941 attacked Berlin at night, dropping 220-lb (100-kg) bombs on Berlin's outskirts. The bombs caused little real damage but served to boost Soviet morale in this dark hour. In all, the DB-3Ts flew ten missions against Berlin in August 1941 and September 1941 before they were forced to give up their base on Ösel because of the German advance in the Baltics. Pe-8s and Yer-2s also flew missions against Berlin in this first part of the war, again for their morale-boosting effect, the Yer-2s of the 420th BAP flying against Berlin on 3 August. The 420th BAP Yer-2s also bombed Königsberg on 28 August and 1 September 1941. After losing thirty aircraft on 154 missions, by October, the ten remaining Yer-2s were handed over from the 420th BAP to the 412th BAP.

The DB-3Fs flew missions in the first few days of the war against targets in enemy territory, such as troop concentrations in the rear; aircraft of the 3rd BAK bombed targets in Poland and the Baltic States. The DB-3Fs also attacked river crossings. Because of losses during these actions, the number of DB-3Fs declined by the end of 1941.

A TB-3 *Aviamatka* with I-16 SPBs mounted under the wings. It was aircraft such as this that mounted attacks against the Axis early in the Great Patriotic War. (*Viktor Kulikov's collection*)

VVS and Red Army tactics were inadequate to the task of stopping the Germans. By October 1941, the Germans were ready for the assault on Moscow, the Soviet capital, having once again accomplished huge encirclements, this time at Bryansk and Vyazma. This operation against Moscow, known as *Unternehmen Taifun* ('Operation Typhoon' in German), started in October when the Germans had been able to retrieve some of their forces that had been sent south to help capture Kiev. On 2 October 1941, the 9th Army of Army Group Centre, under the overall command of Field Marshal Fedor von Bock (1880–1945), began the operation. The Battle of Moscow had begun.

Battle of Moscow

By the time of the Battle of Moscow, because of heavy losses and the cessation of production due to the evacuation of their factories to the East, there were only a few Il-2s still available. These few Il-2s were not alone, however, as the Soviets threw everything they had at the Germans during the Battle of Moscow. This included not only the Pe-2, but Yer-2 long-range bombers and even I-5 biplane fighters, which were taken from training units and equipped for ground attack duty carrying small bombs. Other fighter aeroplanes saw action during this battle, such as the LaGG-3, which although ill-suited to the role of a ground attack aircraft because of its vulnerable liquid-cooled inline engine, saw a great deal of use in the ground attack role, using rockets, cannons, and machine guns against the advancing Germans.

The Yer-2s performed their bombing attacks at low altitude, bombing railroads and troop concentrations. Due to the short ranges involved, the Yer-2s could carry heavy bomb loads on these missions. The attacks were often carried out without fighter escort in daylight, resulting in serious losses to the Yer-2s, which had never been intended to be used in low altitude attacks.

A description of a particularly brave mission executed by a pilot flying an Il-2 just after the official start of the Battle of Moscow is described in the book, *Famous Russian Aircraft, Ilyushin Il-2/Il-10* by Yefim Gordon, Sergey Komissarov, and Dmitriy Komissarov (p. 153):

> A heroic deed was performed by Lieutenant Senior Grade A. Novikov on 3rd October 1941. When strafing a troop convoy, his aircraft was hit by flak and caught fire; Novikov directed his blazing machine at the enemy troops he was attacking. In recognition of this and other heroic deeds the 215th ShAP was transformed into the 6th Guards Attack Air Regiment (GvShAP) and became the first among attack air units to be awarded this coveted title.

Although certainly not the norm, this type of action occurred often enough for the more reflective German officers and soldiers to realise that there was still quite a bit of fight left in the Red Army. The Red Army was far from finished, as would be shown in the coming Soviet counteroffensive.

SBs also contributed to the defence of Moscow, as their numbers had by now been somewhat replenished by aircraft from the eastern Soviet Union. They participated in actions against the 2nd Panzer Army under General Heinz Wilhelm Guderian

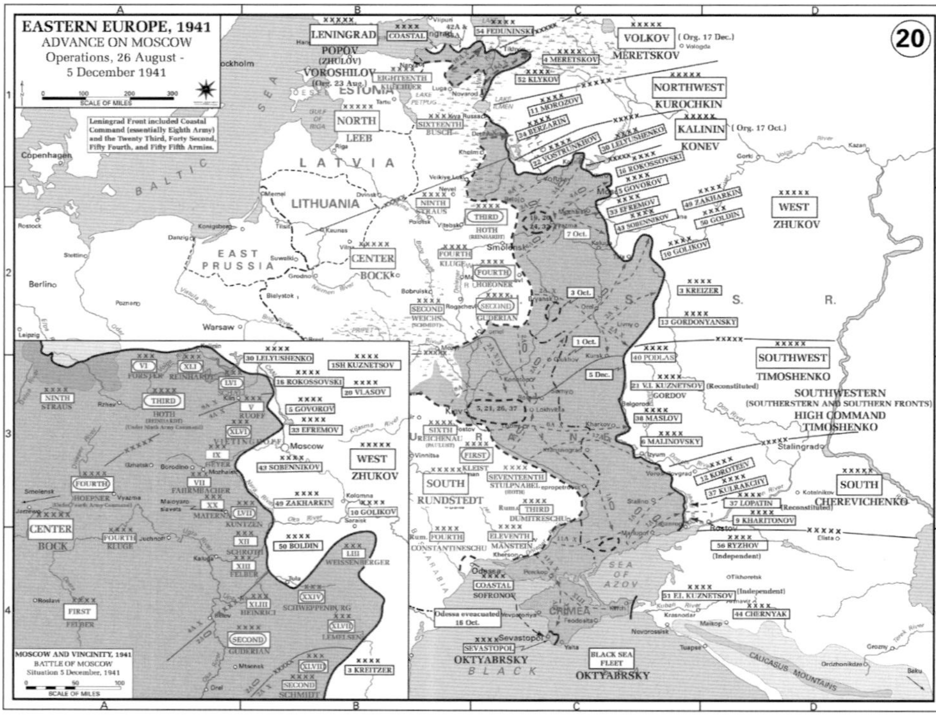

The German advance on Moscow. (*History Department of the United States Military Academy*)

(1888–1954), which slowed its advance towards Tula, southeast of Moscow. In November 1941, the 46th BAD arrived from Siberia, but despite this, by the time of the Soviet counteroffensive on 5 December 1941 (see below), there were only 111 SBs at the front, of which only sixty-eight were operational.

Soviet Winter Offensive

The Winter Offensive, the brainchild of General Zhukov (the hero of the Battle of the Khalkhin-Gol), commenced on 5 December 1941, coming as a complete and unpleasant surprise to the Germans, who had made the mistake of believing that the Red Army was on its last legs (this was certainly not the first time, nor would it be the last time that the Wehrmacht would make this grave and ultimately fatal mistake).

Far from being nearly defeated, the Red Army now had 4.2 million men on the entire front, 2,500 combat aircraft, 22,000 artillery pieces, and 1,730 tanks. The German forces, on the other hand, totalled around 2.5 million men. This numerical advantage in men showed just how much the Red Army had recovered from the terrible disasters of the summer. The Soviets attacked all along the front, first before Moscow, often with fresh and well-equipped troops. Some of these new troops had been drawn from Siberia and the Far East. Here, Soviet intelligence (from a Soviet spy, the German Communist Richard Sorge (1895–1944)) indicated that the Japanese Empire had no imminent plans to invade the Soviet Union, as they still remembered their defeat at the Khalkhin-Gol. This freed up these troops for use in the west. The Soviets were able to transfer eighteen divisions, 1,700 tanks, and 1,500 aircraft from Siberia and the Soviet Far East to the west.

Taken by utter surprise, and with only rudimentary defences in place in most areas, the Germans could not stop the onslaught and were splintered into hundreds of separate groups, all desperately fighting for survival in the intense cold of a winter that was bitter even by the harsh standards of Central Russia.

The Soviet attack consisted of massed formations of infantry, supported by tanks, including the fine T-34 medium tank and the formidable and heavily armoured KV-1 heavy tank. These formations were, in turn, supported by aircraft such as the Pe-2, large numbers of fighter-bombers, and the depleted ranks of the Il-2s. The German lines, especially in front of Moscow, were shattered, with parts of the front simply collapsing into chaos. It was Adolf Hitler's stubborn resistance to agree to a general withdrawal that may well have turned this very serious setback from becoming a headlong rout, albeit at the expense of heavy casualties and loss of materiel—losses that the Germans were ill-equipped to replace.

In the central area of the front, including that portion in front of Moscow, the German forces were thrown back in some cases more than 100 miles. Even in the south, the Soviets were able to establish themselves west of the Donets River, south of Kharkov at Izium. By the time the front stabilised in the spring of 1942, the Germans found themselves having lost hundreds of square miles of territory, but at least now they could rest, as the equally exhausted Soviets stopped their attacks with the onset of the *Rasputitsa* ('Rainy Season'), which made the roads nearly impassable.

In addition to its use as a night bomber against the Germans, the TB-3 was used in a large-scale operation dropping paratroopers behind the German lines, most notably in the area of Vyazma. This operation, occurring in January 1942, was a large action involving TB-3s and Li-2s of the ADD used as transports. The operation was not a success, however, with the paratroopers being scattered over too wide an area and with too little logistical support, the operation being poorly planned, and the Germans were able to surround and neutralise most of them.

One position where the Germans seemed in real danger of becoming encircled and captured was at Demyansk, where some 90,000 German soldiers, part of the 16th Army, were holding out against fierce Soviet attacks. Despite becoming surrounded, the Germans were just able to supply the besieged garrison by air (a somewhat Pyrrhic success that would later haunt them at Stalingrad as they became overly confident of the Luftwaffe's ability to supply an isolated army). It was here, where transports appeared daily over the front, that the ground attack Il-2 was first used deliberately in a role for which it had not been intended—that of a fighter.

Although not ordinarily manoeuvrable enough to oppose German fighters, the Il-2's heavy forward-firing armament and armour made it a good transport killer, as the weak rifle-calibre defensive armament of the transports was nearly useless against the heavily armoured Il-2. Despite the toll, the Il-2 and Soviet fighters took on transports such as the Ju 52, the Germans were eventually able to re-establish a land corridor to Demyansk and relieve and resupply the German forces there. Eventually,

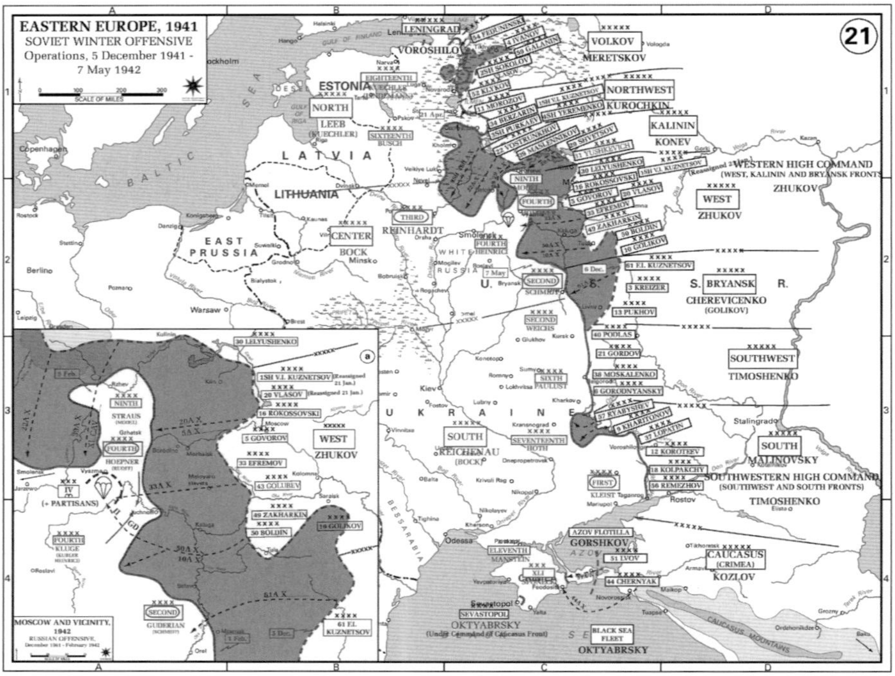

Above: The Soviet Winter Offensive. (*History Department of the United States Military Academy*)

Below: Close up of the Soviet Winter Offensive in the vicinity of Moscow. (*History Department of the United States Military Academy*)

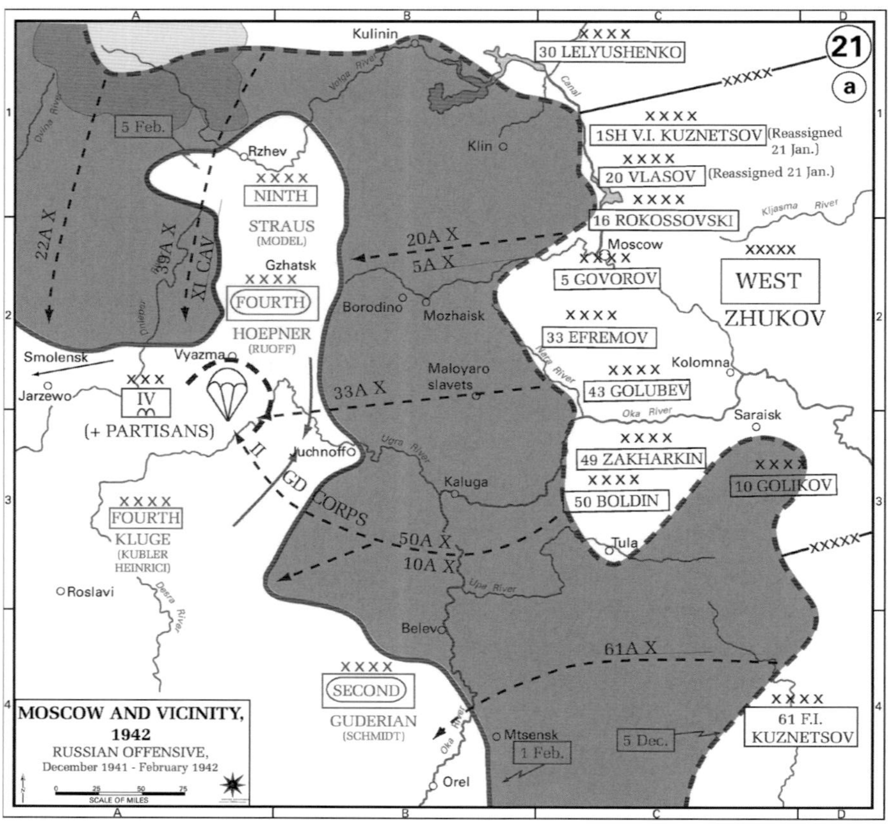

Not only were the TB-3 utilised as carriers for the I-16 SPBs, but they saw heavy usage throughout the war as a paratrooper carrier. It was TB-3s that carried out the dropping of paratroopers behind German lines during the Soviet winter offensive of 1941–42. (*Viktor Kulikov's collection*)

the situation stabilised here, as it did all along the entire Eastern Front, as both sides were exhausted by the struggle and paused to rest and replenish their depleted troops and war materiel.

This apparent stalemate might have continued for some time, but both the Germans and the Soviets had other plans. The Soviets wanted to continue their offensive against the Germans, and Hitler had not abandoned his hopes of securing both the industry and resources of the Don Basin (*Donbass*) and the oil of the Caucasus. These plans were to be dramatically put into effect in the summer of 1942 in a great offensive, called *Fall Blau* (German for 'Case Blue') that led the Germans deep into Southern Russia and the Caucasus region, and also eventually to the banks of the Volga, to a sprawling industrial city called Stalingrad.

Case Blue (Fall Blau: the 1942 German Summer Offensive)

By the spring of 1942, due to the loss of men and materiel in the course of Operation Barbarossa and the Soviet Winter Offensive, the Germans were no longer able to launch an offensive along the entire Eastern Front, nor could they rely solely upon German troops, so large numbers of troops from allied and satellite states were also used (nearly a million). Instead of attacking along the whole front, they chose to attack the southern half of the front, towards Voronezh on the Don, into that part of Ukraine east of the Donets still held by the Soviet Union, and on to the Volga and the

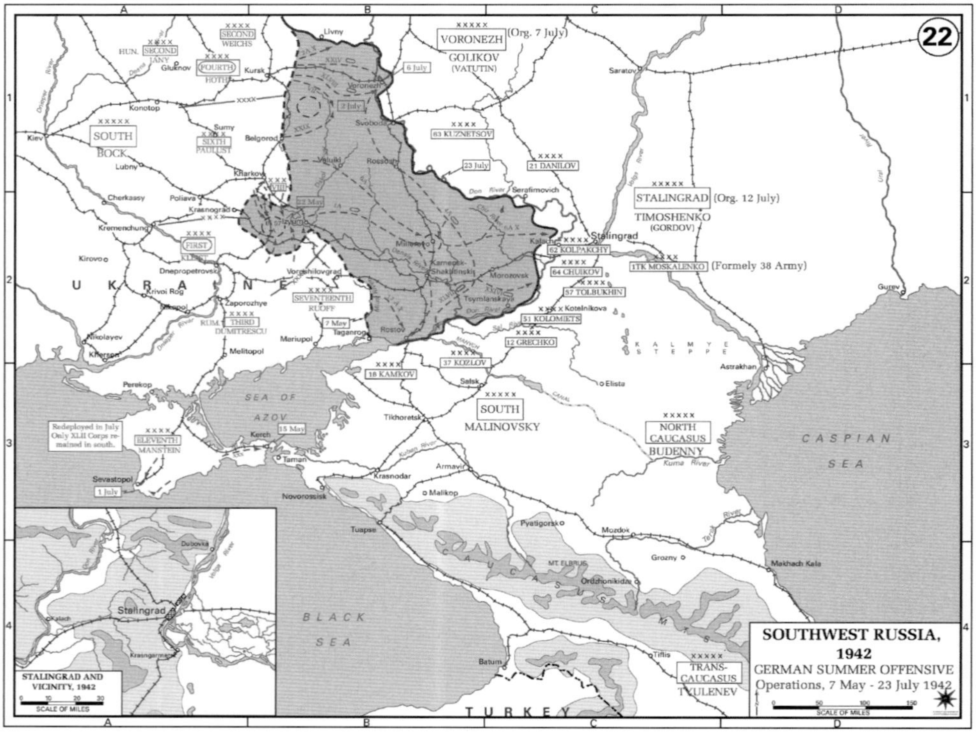

Above: Case Blue (*Fall Blau*), the German Summer Offensive in south-west Russia. (*History Department of the United States Military Academy*)

Below: The German advance to Stalingrad. (*History Department of the United States Military Academy*)

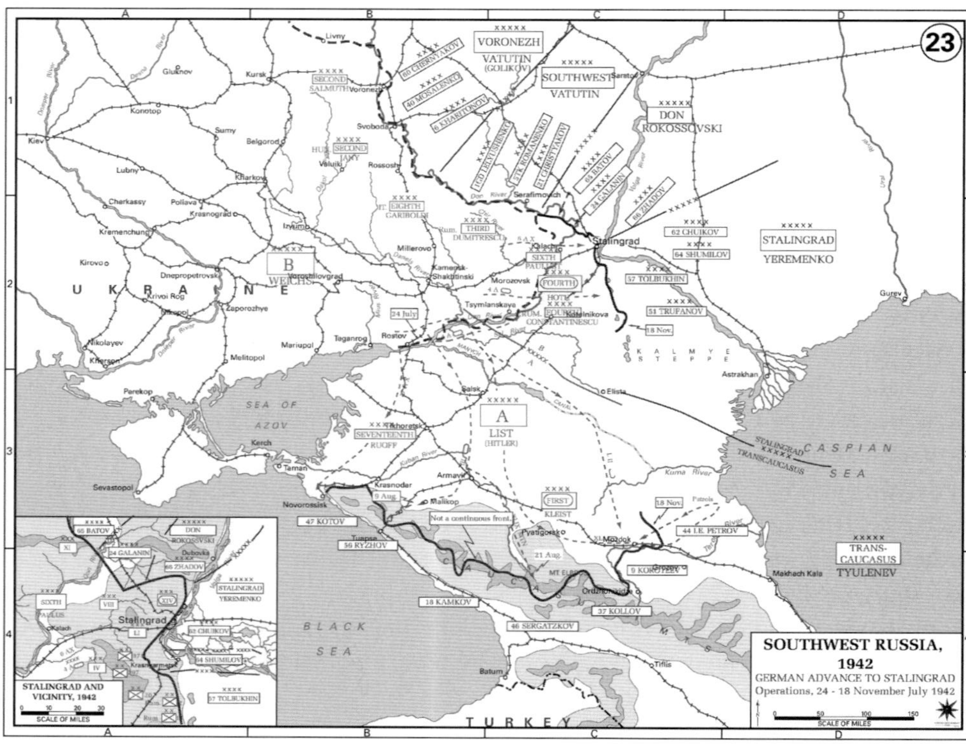

Caucasus region, with the intention of capturing the resources of the *Donbass* and ultimately the oil fields of the Caucasus. For Hitler, this oil was the real prize, as the Germans were chronically short of fuel for their war machine, and the resources at their disposal were barely sufficient to keep it running. Taking the Caucasus oil fields would also have the added benefit of depriving the Soviets of this precious and vital resource, as they received 80 per cent of their petroleum from these fields.

Army Group South, under the command of Field Marshal Fedor von Bock, who was now back in the Fuhrer's favour (for the moment; it would not last), was split into two groups, Army Groups 'A' and 'B'. Army Group 'A' was first under Field Marshal Wilhelm List (1880–1971), then General Ewald von Kleist (1881–1954) from 9 September 1942 and Army Group 'B' was under Colonel-General Maximilian von Weichs (1881–1954). Army Group 'A' was to penetrate into the Caucasus Mountains and take the oilfields in that area, then perhaps on to Baku, in addition to taking the Black Sea coast. Army Group 'B' was to take Soviet territory west of the Don from Voronezh to Stalingrad on the Volga (and from there along the Volga perhaps even to Astrakhan on the Caspian Sea at the mouth of the Volga) to protect the northern flank of Army Group 'A'. At this point, taking Stalingrad itself was not even an important objective, as just sealing it off and neutralising it was felt to be sufficient.

First, however, the important port city of Sevastopol in the Crimea, the home port of the Black Sea Fleet, had to be taken to clear the Germans' rear flank. The Soviets had withdrawn most of their aeroplanes from the Crimea before the Germans' final assault on this heavily fortified city, probably to use these resources in other threatened areas. As such, VVS aircraft did not participate in any great numbers in the defence of Sevastopol, which finally succumbed to Axis forces after a bitter nine-month siege. This absence of air cover was one of the reasons the city finally fell. Due to the lack of Soviet ground attack aircraft or other bombers, the Germans were able to use huge but vulnerable artillery, such as the self-propelled 600-mm siege mortars and the 800-mm *Schwerer Gustav* railway gun, which along with its 'twin', *Dora* was the most massive cannon ever built. These weapons would have proved easy prey to bombers and attack aircraft, such as the Il-4, Pe-2, and Il-2. In addition, fighter air cover would have enabled Soviet ships to resupply the besieged garrison. Without air cover, Soviet sea transports and other ships were easy targets for Ju 87 dive bombers. Sevastopol finally fell on 4 July 1942. With Sevastopol now in German hands, Case Blue could proceed as planned.

At first, the Germans made good progress, and it seemed like the *Blitzkrieg* was once again working to perfection as the Germans rolled across the steppes of Southern Ukraine and Southern Russia. Indeed, it appeared as if the initial stages of Operation Barbarossa were being repeated and it was the heady days of the early summer of 1941 all over again. The Soviets had exhausted themselves during the Winter Offensive and their disastrous offensive on the west bank of the Donets near Kharkov that followed in the spring. At first, they put up ineffective resistance to this new German advance, and west of the Donets River, the Germans were able to cut off the Soviet forces and capture some 200,000 prisoners. Although no one could have known it at the time, this was to be the Germans' last great encirclement victory of the war. There would

Two single-seaters from *Zavod* 30, characterised by the four-exhaust stacks and wooden-covered outer wings. Note that the nearest Il-2 is only equipped with two rockets on the four rocket rails under the port wing. (*G. F. Petrov photo archive*)

be further encirclements, but none would approach this number, as the Soviets learned to escape total encirclement.

As the offensive continued, the Soviets regained their balance and fought an aggressive and grudging retreat across Southern Russia, putting up fierce resistance particularly at Voronezh, at the northernmost point of Case Blue. The Soviets also resisted at Rostov, on the Don River (*Rostov na-Donu*: Rostov-on-Don), which was an essential acquisition for the Wehrmacht if the German invasion of the Caucasus region by Army Group 'A' was to proceed. In all these battles, the VVS was used extensively to try to slow down the German advance by attacking tanks, supply columns, and troop concentrations. During the day, Il-2s and Pe-2s saw the bulk of the action, with night actions being undertaken by nuisance bombers such as the U-2 and R-5, the larger bombers of the ADD, such as the Il-4, the Pe-8, the TB-3, and even the Lend-Lease B-25. Small groups of Il-4s even flew by day at low altitude to bomb the advancing Germans.

Stalingrad

As the Soviets executed their fighting retreat across the southern steppes of Ukraine and Russia, they eventually fell back upon Stalingrad (formerly known as Tsaritsyn), a long, narrow industrial city of 450,000 people on the west bank of the Volga. It was at this city, with their backs to the Volga, that the Soviets made their final stand. The defence fell mainly upon the 62nd Army, which was commanded by General

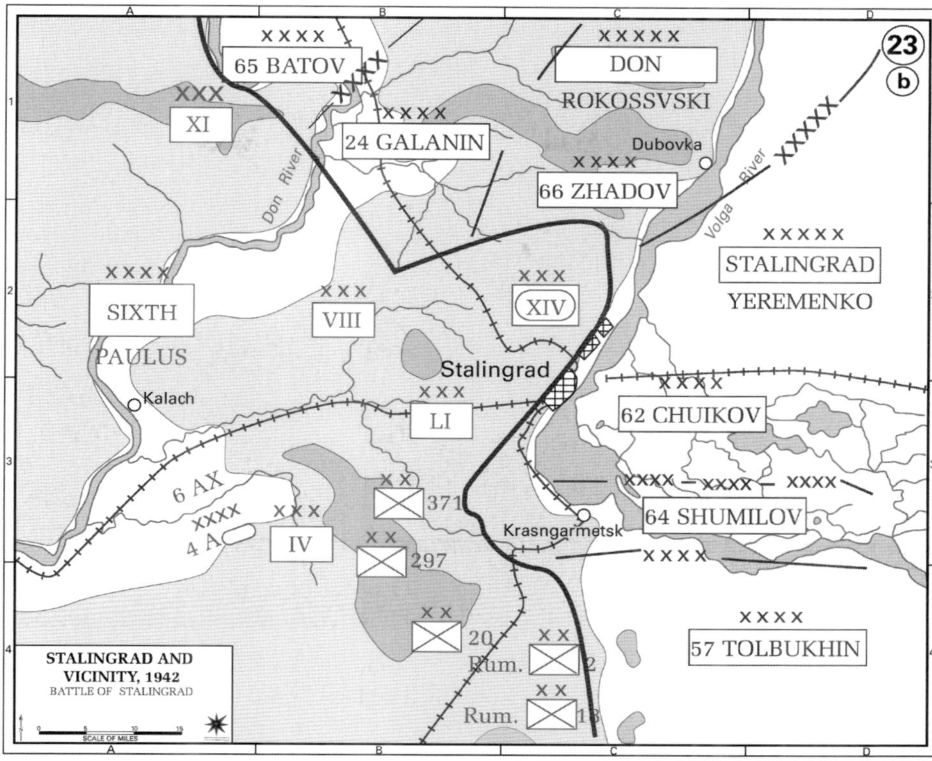

Stalingrad with German and Soviet dispositions. (*History Department of the United States Military Academy*)

Vasily Ivanovich Chuikov (1900–82) for most of the siege, although the 64th Army, commanded by General Mikhail Stepanovich Shumilov (1895–1975), to the south, was also heavily involved in the fight for the city. The German 6th Army, under General Friedrich Paulus (1890–1957) (not 'von' Paulus, as he is often erroneously referred to), opposed him, with assistance from elements of the 4th Panzer Army. It was here that the pivotal battle of the Great Patriotic War, and indeed the entire war in Europe, would be fought.

Regarding the fighting for the city itself, which consisted of hundreds of separate actions, it has become rather a cliché to talk about battles being fought over apartment buildings, floors of buildings, and even rooms. In this case, however, the clichés are true. Battles were fought not just above ground in the buildings or in the rubble-choked streets, but also below ground in the cellars and sewers of the destroyed city. The Germans had a name for this kind of war—*Rattenkrieg*, the 'Rat's War'. This kind of war was the antithesis of the *Blitzkrieg*, the 'Lightning War', the war of movement, of panzer formations driving across open ground supported by the Luftwaffe. In the ruins of Stalingrad, the German *Blitzkrieg* finally ground to a bloody, fatal halt.

The German aerial bombings of 23–24 August 1942 had destroyed much of the city. As many as 40,000 to 42,000 people may have been killed, although at least one source believes these numbers to be considerably inflated (I am inclined to agree—by comparison, the entire *Blitz* against London in 1940, which lasted months, killed some 50,000 people at the most). Whatever the actual number, civilian casualties were substantial, and much of the city, whose suburbs were largely constructed of wood, was left in ruins. The devastated city that resulted actually made it almost impossible for the Germans to execute the quick-striking mobile warfare that was their hallmark and greatest strength, as even their tracked vehicles found it rough going through (and over) the crumbled and crumbling buildings and rubble-strewn streets.

The Soviets, on the other hand, under General Chuikov developed tactics that took advantage of the cratered and wrecked terrain, whereby they were able to channel German assaults through the ruins into killing points, guarded by anti-tank rifles and cannons. In addition, the development of highly mobile and heavily armed assault teams allowed the Soviets to take back buildings that had been seized by the Germans. Instead of attacking through windows or doors, one tactic involved blowing holes in the sides of the buildings, creating unexpected openings that the Soviet assault teams would then rush into.

Sometimes, the Soviets would attack a building from two directions, with one team attacking from the ground level, while another team attacked from the roof. The Soviets also developed tactics whereby they moved into very close quarters with the German front lines, to 'hug' the Germans, sometimes closing to within 164 feet (50 m), such that German aircraft (even the highly accurate Ju 87s) were unable to offer ground support to the Wehrmacht, for fear of hitting their own troops. This eliminated some of the aerial advantage that the Germans enjoyed throughout most of the battle. Due to the cut-up and chaotic nature of the churned-up terrain, which was not particularly amenable to large formations, the Soviets often employed small squads to ambush equally small groups of Germans, operating as noted by the renowned Eastern Front historian Col. David Glantz as 'street gangs'.

Nonetheless, these Soviet measures were only able to slow down the inexorable advance of the Germans in Stalingrad, not stop it. More German troops were moved into the city, while the 62nd (and 64th) Army was given just enough troops to hold on to its tenuous and shrinking positions. By the time of the Soviet counteroffensive in November (Operation Uranus), the Germans controlled over 90 per cent of the city, with the Soviets clinging to just three precarious toeholds on the western banks of the Volga.

In their desperate and ultimately successful attempt to hold Stalingrad, the Soviets used every aeroplane at their disposal to combat the Germans, including, of course, the ubiquitous Il-2. Even a few Yer-2s were used briefly, and Li-2NBs were used to bomb crossings over the Don. At first, the Il-2s consisted completely of single-seaters, but by November 1942, as it was still undergoing service trials in the north near Smolensk, the first production two-seaters entered the battle.

As the battle for Stalingrad raged on, the Soviets gradually wrested control of the air away from the Luftwaffe, allowing the Il-2s and Pe-2s to operate with greater effectiveness during the day (the night belonged to the Soviet nuisance bombers and the bombers of the ADD). It was during the Battle for Stalingrad that the new turret-equipped Pe-2s, first introduced in June 1942, were used in number. The new Yak-9 (developed from the Yak-7) and La-5 fighters (a radial-engined development of the LaGG-3) saw their first action over Stalingrad, aircraft that helped the VVS to gain air superiority over Stalingrad and beyond. These were all aircraft that would see very heavy usage throughout the remainder of the Second World War and were instrumental in turning the tide of the aerial war against the Axis.

In addition to these new aircraft, older aircraft types—such as the U-2 and the R-5—continued to be used in night bombing missions. The U-2 was also used for propaganda purposes, equipped with a loudspeaker and distributing leaflets exhorting the Axis troops to surrender, especially after they had become surrounded in the *Kessel* (see further on).

Even the SB, flying with the 10th GvBAP, operating on average with only ten SBs, attacked German airfields at night (by 1942, the SB was limited to night operations). This unit continued to operate its SBs against the Germans at Stalingrad, attacking the encircled Axis forces after Operation Uranus (see further on) and did not finally relinquish its SBs until 1943, when it was rearmed with Lend-Lease A-20 Bostons.

Such was the intensity of the fighting over Stalingrad that the VVS suffered heavy losses. For example, the average number of sorties before loss for the Il-2 dropped to between ten and twelve sorties, down from twenty-four sorties in the spring and summer of 1942.

Pe-2s in flight over the Stalingrad front during summer 1942. (*Viktor Kulikov's collection*)

A turret-armed Pe-2 in flight. Note the roughly applied winter camouflage. (*Viktor Kulikov's collection*)

A U-2 before a night mission in 1942. (*Viktor Kulikov's collection*)

A ski-equipped SB 2M-100A (or early SB 2M-103A) runs up its engines prior to take-off. (*Viktor Kulikov's collection*)

An SB 2M-103A being prepared for a night-time mission. By the middle of the war, the SBs were only used on night-time missions due to their vulnerability during the day. (*Viktor Kulikov's collection*)

As the Germans threw more of their soldiers into the fight for Stalingrad, their flanks, especially the northern flank, became increasingly weakened as German troops were withdrawn for the struggle for Stalingrad itself. These flanks were now protected largely by Romanian troops, who were generally poorly equipped, especially in heavy weaponry; they were no match for the Red Army. The Soviets had retained or created large bridgeheads to the south and west of the Don River, at Serafimovich and Kletskaya, which the Axis forces were unable to dislodge them from. These proved to be excellent breakout points when the Soviet attack on the northern flank finally began in the middle of November.

Operation Uranus (The Encirclement of the 6th Army at Stalingrad)

When the Soviets started *Operatsiya Ooran* ('Operation Uranus' in Russian) on 19 November 1942, over 1,400 aircraft took part, with Shturmoviks being the most prominent aeroplane in this operation, flying over 1,000 sorties during the four days it took to completely encircle the Germans. The Pe-2 was an important component of this operation; as of 19 November 1942, there were 519 Pe-2s present at Stalingrad. The encirclement was completed on 23 November 1942 near Kalach (*Kalach-na-Donu*, 'Kalach-on-Don'). This encirclement resulted in the Stalingrad *Kessel* or 'Pocket' (literally 'Kettle' or 'Cauldron' in German), which contained some 250,000 to 330,000 German and Romanian troops, including the entire German 6th Army, much of the 4th Panzer Army, and the remnants of two Romanian divisions. From this point on, the only way to supply the entrapped soldiers was through the air, using transports taking off from the Germans' main airfields at Tatsinskaya and Morozovsk and landing at Pitomnik and Gumrak airfields inside the *Kessel*.

After the encirclement, not only were the Il-2s used in their normal ground attack role at Stalingrad, they were also used as *ad hoc* fighters (as at Demyansk) against the mixture of bombers and transports that the Germans used to supply the besieged 6th Army in the Stalingrad *Kessel*. In this role, they proved quite effective against the German bombers being used as transports (such as the He 111) and the Ju 52 transports, as the German aircrafts' generally weak defensive armament proved ineffective against the armour of the Il-2. The Il-2's heavy forward-firing armament allowed them to easily shoot down these aircraft.

It did not help the German resupply effort that the German transports had to fly in a narrow corridor that provided the quickest flight time to and from Stalingrad, thereby enabling flak, Soviet fighters, and Il-2s to lay in wait for them. In all, at least 467 transports were downed going to and from Stalingrad and the way was littered with the hulks of downed German aircraft. One German source admits that 488 aircraft were lost by the Fourth Air Fleet, while a Soviet account gives an undoubtedly inflated figure of 903 transports lost by the Germans. Whatever the exact figure, a substantial number of transports, as well as bombers used as transports, were lost in this unsuccessful resupply effort.

After the main German resupply airfields outside of the *Kessel* at Tatsinskaya and Morozovsk had been retaken by the Red Army, the airfield of Salsk now became the main airfield. This did not escape the attention of the Red Air Force which now

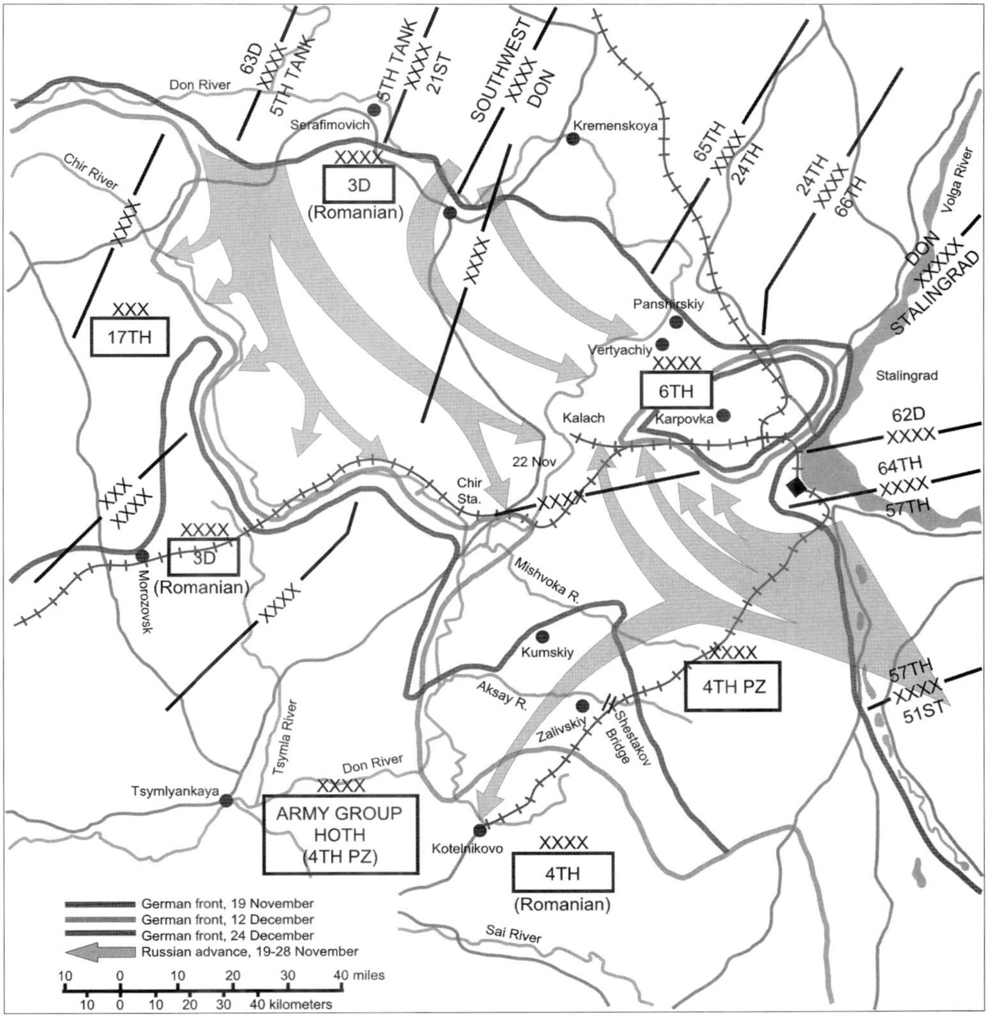

Operation Uranus and Operation Winter Storm. (*Wikimedia*)

launched an operation against this airfield. Oleg Rastrenin picks up the story in *Il-2 Shturmovik Guards Units of World War 2* (p. 48):

> The Il-2s made their first run over the target after diving from cloud cover, bombing and strafing German aircraft on the ground for 15 minutes from 1008 hrs to 1123 hrs. They expended a total of 26 FAB-100 bombs and 56 RS-82 rockets, together with 1386 VYa, 300 ShVAK, 120 UBT and 3820 ShKAS cannon and machine gun rounds. The anti-aircraft gunners failed to open fire until the Soviet attack aircraft had made their first pass.

The Soviets claimed that as many as seventy-six Ju 52 transports had been destroyed or damaged. Even given the tendency for all air forces to overestimate their effects upon the enemy (inflating their claims), this had been a very successful mission, with only two Il-2s and two Yak-1 fighters being lost to enemy action. The average Il-2 mission was usually not so successful, but this shows how effective it could be when handled with skill and good tactics were followed, with the addition of the element of surprise.

Despite the desperate attempts by the Germans to keep the *Kessel* supplied, the soldiers were doomed by a lack of food, ammunition, shelter, and warm clothing. Beginning on 12 December 1942, an attempt was made by the Germans under Field Marshal Erich von Manstein (born Erich von Lewinski, 1887–1973, the victor in the Battle of Sevastopol) to reach the *Kessel*, in an operation called *Unternehmen Winter Gewitter* ('Operation Winter Storm'). This operation failed, as the soldiers in Stalingrad were forbidden by Hitler to try and break out and reach von Manstein's troops; General Friedrich Paulus followed Hitler's orders and stayed where he was.

With his soldiers starving and freezing to death, Paulus, who had been newly promoted to Field Marshall, finally bowed to the inevitable and surrendered to the Soviets on 30 January 1943, with a smaller pocket to the north finally surrendering on 2 February 1943 (some small diehard groups of German soldiers were not to be finally eliminated until March). With this surrender, Stalingrad was now completely back in Soviet hands, and the German campaign, which had started out with such success in the summer of 1942, had ended in complete failure. Of the 300,000 or so Germans and Romanians who were originally encircled in the *Kessel*, only 90,000

A Pe-2 engaged in a dive over a target in winter 1942. (*Viktor Kulikov's collection*)

were left to surrender; of these, only 5,000 or so survived Soviet captivity to return home after the war.

Operation Mars (Second Rzhev-Sychevka Offensive Operation)

Concurrently with Operation Uranus, the Soviets attempted to reduce the Rzhev salient in an operation called Operation Mars. The Rzhev salient resulted from the stabilisation of the German lines after the Soviet Winter Offensive, anchored on the heavily fortified and defended town of Rzhev, an important rail junction, and it pointed like a dagger at Moscow. It had long been of concern to the *Stavka*, and the Soviets decided to take the opportunity of the assault to encircle the Germans at Stalingrad (Operation Uranus) to launch a simultaneous attack to reduce this salient and remove this potential threat to Moscow. General Zhukov was tasked by Stalin with the planning and execution of this operation.

As part of the operation, the ADD was called upon to bomb German airfields. VVS units flew ground attack missions in support of the ground forces that were attempting to penetrate the German defences. Zhukov partially attributed the failure of the Soviets to breach the German lines with the lack of aircraft, among other items.

Although Operation Mars was clearly a tactical disaster, with the loss of hundreds of thousands of Soviet casualties for minimal territorial gains in operations that were reminiscent of the Western Front operations of the First World War, its strategic impact was more favourable for the Soviets. As with the first Rzhev–Sychevka Offensive operation in July and August 1942, by attacking the Rzhev salient, the Soviets tied down thousands of German troops that could have been used to reinforce the Axis operations in the south, specifically at Stalingrad. In this respect, Operation Mars had some positive aspects to it. Whether it was worth the huge loss of men and materiel must remain outside the scope of this book.

After Stalingrad

After the defeat at Stalingrad, the Germans retreated from most of the territories they had conquered in the spring, summer, and autumn of 1942, including abandoning most of their gains east and south of the Don River, except for the Taman Peninsula, as described below. With the fall of Stalingrad, Army Group 'A' quickly retreated from its positions in the Caucasus to avoid being cut off by the Soviets. In addition, the Germans executed strategic retreats from the Rzhev salient (in *Unternehmen Bufel*, or 'Operation Buffalo') and the Demyansk Salient, both of which had been held since the Soviet Winter Offensive of 1941–42 (see map on page 286). These last manoeuvres were done at least partly to shorten the defensive lines and free up troops for use elsewhere (including for the upcoming *Unternehmen Zitadelle* or 'Operation Citadel' at Kursk, described further on).

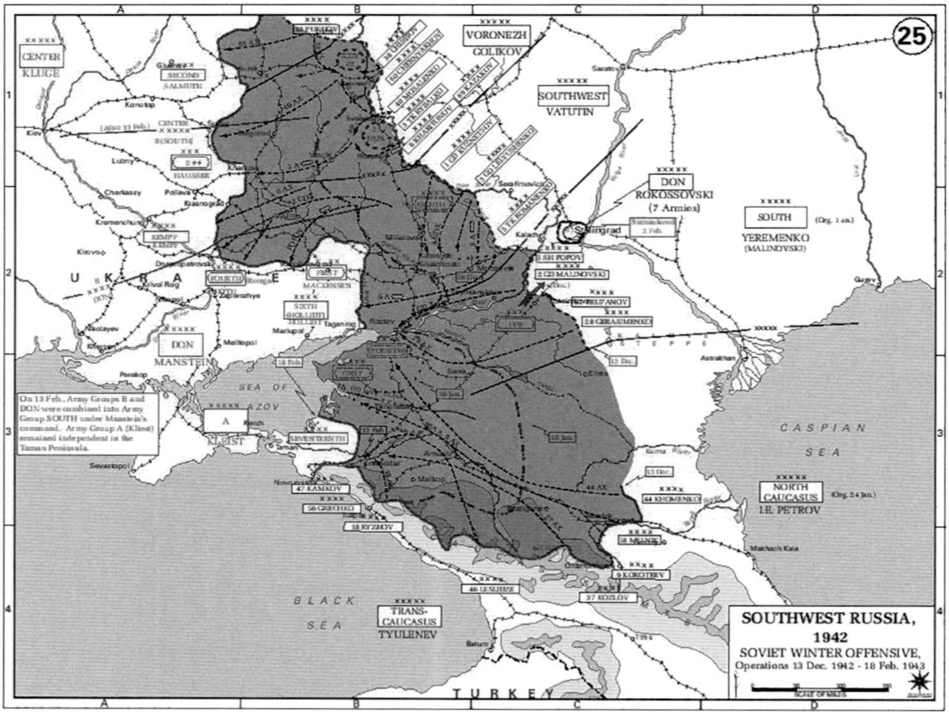

Operation Little Saturn and the German withdrawal from the Caucasus region. Note how the Germans still hold on to the Taman Peninsula opposite the Crimea. (*History Department of the United States Military Academy*)

The Kuban Bridgehead

After the defeat at Stalingrad, the Wehrmacht continued its retreat westwards across the steppes of Southern Russia, abandoning all of its captured territory south and east of the Don River, except for the Taman peninsula, opposite the Kerch peninsula of the eastern Crimea, where they established a defensive position called the Blue Line. The Taman peninsula was first held to allow German Army Group 'A' in the Caucasus to retreat, and then continued to be held as a launching point for a possible future offensive back into the Caucasus region and its oilfields, which Hitler still hoped to conquer. Here, on this peninsula, the fighting raged for much of 1943 (June–9 October), along and around the Kuban River, after which the fighting takes its name.

The Soviets attempted to strike behind the German defensive lines by launching an amphibious assault on the port of Novorossiysk on the Black Sea. Although the Soviets successfully landed and were able to create a beachhead, they were unable to break out from it due to successful German counterattacks. Likewise, the Germans were unable to dislodge the Soviets from their beachhead, and fierce fighting took place both on land and in the air. For the first time, large numbers of Lend-Lease fighters were thrown into the fray, including Supermarine Spitfire Mk Vbs from the United Kingdom and Bell P-39 Airacobras from the United States (which contrary to some accounts, were used not as ground attack aircraft but as air superiority fighters).

As was normally the case, the main role of these fighters was to escort and protect the Pe-2s and the Il-2s as they supported the Red Army troops. The P-39 was found to be very well suited to the fighting on the Eastern Front, where its low-altitude manoeuvrability, heavy nose cannon, and ability to operate from unprepared airstrips fit well into Red Air Force doctrine. The Spitfire Mk Vb was found to be lacking, however, as its somewhat fragile and narrow-track landing gear were not very suitable for the rough fields that Frontal Aviation units habitually operated from. By 1943, the German fighters, the Bf 109F, Bf 109G, and Fw 190 were all faster than the Spitfire Mk Vb and were considered superior aircraft. The Spitfire was also sometimes mistaken for the Bf 109 leading to friendly fire incidents, as it was not well known to the ordinary Soviet soldier and airman, and it was also very vulnerable to ground fire. Nonetheless, in the air, Soviet pilots found it to be an excellent aircraft to fly (as indeed most pilots did).

The new radial-engined Lavochkins (the La-5) were also used in large numbers, and finally provided the Red Air Force with a Soviet-built fighter that could fight the Luftwaffe fighters on something approaching equal terms, especially at lower altitudes where most air-to-air combat during the Great Patriotic War took place. In addition, improved versions of the Yakovlev fighters (the Yak-9, which had first seen limited use at Stalingrad) saw action and proved capable of engaging the Germans on more or less equal terms. These improved fighters enabled all the Soviet bombers to operate with greater efficiency and confidence.

Provision of adequate fighter escort in addition to better tactics enabled the Il-2s to operate with much lower losses than had been the norm earlier in the war; the number of sorties before the aircraft was irretrievably lost rose dramatically, from five to six sorties before loss in 1941, to twenty-six sorties before loss in 1943.

The ADD contributed to the fighting in the Kuban by flying from up to 186–217 miles (300–350 km) to their targets, which included airfields, enemy troops, and defences. Il-4s from the 50th BAD bombed airfields in the Crimea.

The fighting in the Kuban ended with the German withdrawal of forces from the Taman Peninsula, which was completed on 9 October 1943.

Before Kursk (von Manstein's Counteroffensive)

The German retreat after the defeat at Stalingrad was stopped only by Field Marshal Erich von Manstein's successful counterattack against the Soviets, when the Germans recaptured the city of Kharkov, which had just been retaken by the Soviets. It was this counterattack which established the huge Soviet-held salient in the German lines, centred around the city of Kursk, with the northern German lines anchored around Oryol (often spelled 'Orel', a poor transliteration of the Russian), and the southern lines anchored around Belgorod. This massive salient was the most distinctive feature of the Eastern Front at this time and was an obvious target for the Germans if they wished to stop the Soviet advance and regain the fighting initiative.

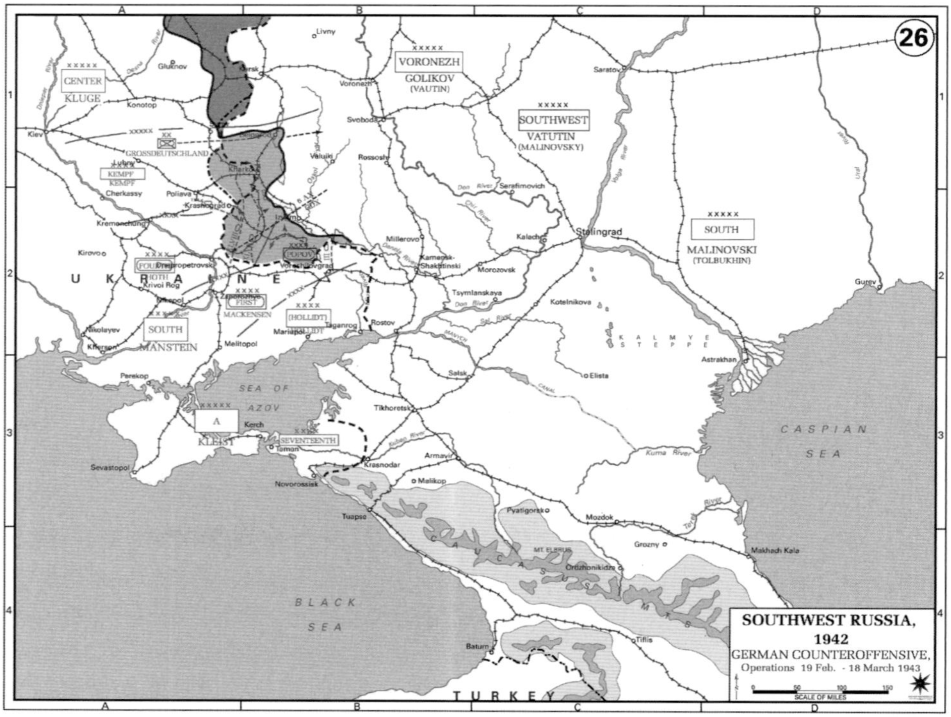

Von Manstein's counteroffensive at Kharkov. (*History Department of the United States Military Academy*)

Kursk

Both the German strategy for attacking the salient and the Soviet plan for defending it were simple: the Germans would attempt to pinch it off at its neck by simultaneous attacks from the north, under General Walther Model, and from the south, under Field Marshal Erich von Manstein. General Model was under the overall command of Field Marshal Gunther von Kluge (1882–1944), the commander of Army Group Centre, while the reorganised Army Group South was under Field Marshal von Manstein. If successful, this operation was expected to trap large numbers of Soviet troops and would shorten the German lines considerably, enabling the Wehrmacht to better defend these lines and use them as a launching point for further attacks against the Red Army, including possible future offensives against Moscow.

The Soviet plan was to use three concentric main lines of defence that would soak up the German attacks, and then when the German forces were exhausted, launch their own counterattacks in the north and the south against the weakened German forces. In addition to its defences, the Soviets had also amassed a large fleet of aircraft, of which from 800 to 950 were Il-2s (sources differ on the exact number). On 1 July 1943, 556 day bombers, mainly Pe-2s were stationed on the Kursk Front, along with the Il-2s. The ADD had from 500 to 740 bombers (mostly Il-4s), with the total Soviet aircraft strength being around 3,000 compared to the Luftwaffe strength in this

A straight-winged two-seater with metal wings and the black/green camouflage typical of the middle period of the Great Patriotic War (1943). The slogan on the fuselage means 'Death to Fascism!' (*G. F. Petrov photo archive*)

sector of 2,132 aircraft. This 2,132 was out of a total of 2,980 aircraft on the entire Eastern Front.

Aircraft of the ADD—such as the Il-4, the B-25, the Pe-8, and even the obsolete TB-3—saw heavy usage as they sought to disrupt the German build-up. The ADD flew 15,328 sorties from January to July 1943 to upset the German preparations for *Zitadelle*. The Battle of Kursk and its build-up saw the last heavy use of the TB-3 in the night bomber role. The Il-4s flew attacks on the railway junction of the city of Bryansk. Light night bombers—such as the U-2 and the R-5—were also used as the Soviets threw everything they had flying against the Germans. Although they suffered heavy losses, Il-2s were able to interdict and disrupt enemy road and rail traffic, which helped to slow down the build-up of German forces in the Kursk Salient, thereby giving the Soviets time to bolster their defences.

Stalin himself issued an order on 4 May 1943 that stressed the importance of attacking trains, convoys, and disrupting enemy traffic, all logistical or operational targets, as opposed to tactical targets. The ADD's long-range bombers—such as the Il-4, the B-25, the Pe-8, and the TB-3—saw heavy use in attacking these logistical targets. Night bombers—such as the R-5, SB, Ar-2, and Su-2—were used in spoiling attacks against the German build-up, as all these aircraft were still part of the VVS inventory as of 1 July 1943 and the Soviets were very keen to interrupt the German preparations for the coming offensive. There were still forty-one SBs on the front as of

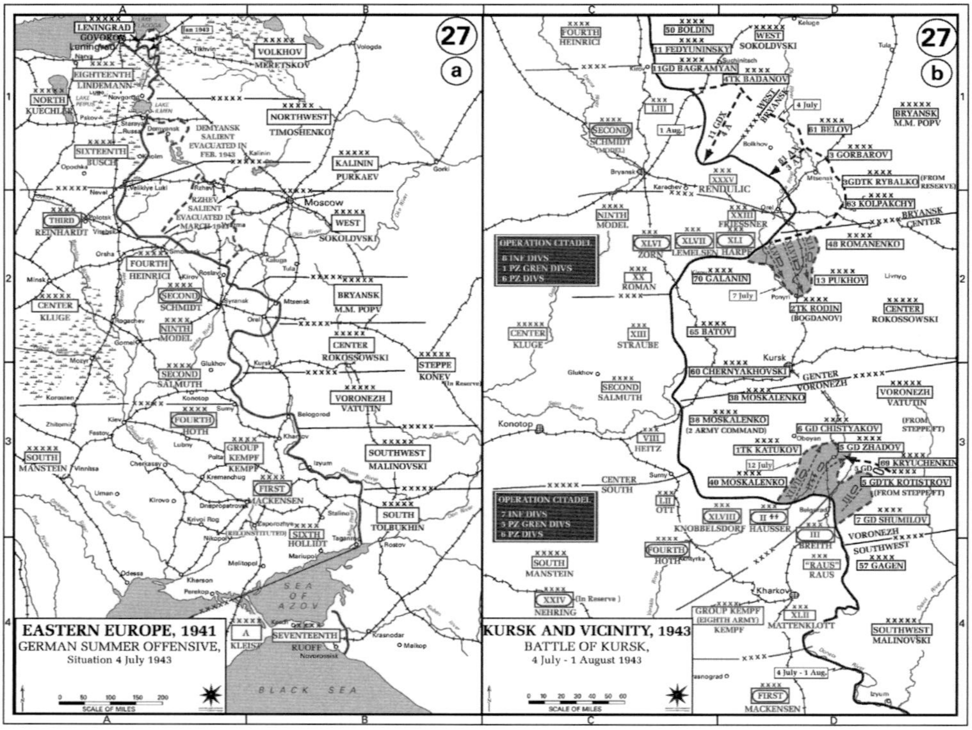

The Battle of Kursk. (*History Department of the United States Military Academy*)

1 July 1943, of which eighteen were operational, but after Kursk, the SB disappeared from front-line units on the Eastern Front.

Despite the disruptions caused by these Soviet attacks, the attack on the Kursk salient duly went ahead, opening on 5 July 1943. In the north, General Model was forced to attack the forces of Soviet General Konstantin Konstantinovich Rokossovsky (1896–1968) on a narrow front through the forest; the Germans soon became bogged down and were unable to penetrate the third Soviet defensive line, foundering on the Soviet defences around the towns of Olkhovatka and Ponyri. Field Marshal von Manstein, however, had much more success in the south, where the open steppe offered many possible lines of attack, thereby complicating the Red Army's defences considerably. It was here in the south that the most serious threat to the Soviets occurred.

In the south, against Soviet General Nikolai Fyodorovich Vatutin (1901–44), the main Soviet defensive lines were actually penetrated, and the Germans advanced as far as Prokhorovka, where a huge tank battle developed, generally considered to be the largest tank battle of all time. The Soviets had some 600 tanks, while the Germans had 300. Even though the Soviets suffered much heavier losses, the German advance was stopped on 12 July, just as the Soviet attack in the north towards Oryol was beginning. The Germans had lost the Battle of Kursk, and with that, they had permanently lost the initiative on the Eastern Front. From here on, the Germans would be in almost continuous retreat, all the way back to Berlin. That the fighting would last for nearly two more deadly years was due to the tactical ability of the German Army and the individual bravery of the German soldier, but after Kursk, there was no doubt about the Germans' ability to retrieve the situation on the Eastern Front. Nazi Germany would be defeated; it was only a matter of time.

Use of PTABs at Kursk

At the Battle of Kursk, the 37-mm-armed Il-2s saw widespread use for the first time. It was also during the Battle of Kursk that the Il-2 was equipped in combat for the first time with the PTAB bomblets, which greatly increased their tank-killing capability.

The PTABs (*Protivo Tankovaya Bomba*—'Anti-tank Bomb' in Russian) were small (5.5-lb) armour-piercing shaped-charge bomblets which were capable of penetrating the top armour on even the Panther and Tiger tanks. They were dropped from a height of 320 to 480 feet (100 to 150 m) and had a zone of destruction of 50 feet by 230 feet (15 m by 70 m). The Il-2s would fly straight or move in a shallow S-curve against columns of armour, dropping their PTAB anti-tank bombs. These bombs saw their initial combat use on the first day of Operation Citadel, 5 July, and because of their success saw increasing use as the battle went on.

After Kursk

After the defeat at Kursk, the German forces attempted to withdraw to a prepared defensive line on the Dnieper River called the 'Wotan Line' (in the north the defensive line, no longer located on the Dnieper River, was called the 'Panther Line'). However, the speed of the Soviet advance kept the Germans from regrouping and taking up all their defensive positions. Soon the Red Army had penetrated across the Dnieper River in multiple places and were able to regain Kiev.

Battle of Ukraine

The Battle of Ukraine occupied the Red Army after their victory at Kursk, starting in December 1943 and January 1944, when the four Ukrainian fronts were given the task of destroying Army Group South and Army Group 'A', late of the Caucasus. This action continued until May 1944, with the Germans being pushed out of Western Ukraine and the Crimea (where the German 17th Army was). In the battle to liberate the Crimea, ADD Il-4s attacked the Romanian ports of Constanta and Galati; they also attacked German positions near Sevastopol. The Soviets continued into northern Romania and those regions of south-eastern Poland that had been incorporated into the Soviet Union in 1939.

Pressing hard against the Germans, the Soviets were able to keep them from preparing adequate defences or even becoming established behind or holding on to existing defensive lines, such as the Wotan–Panther Line. The Il-2s harassed the retreating Germans by attacking tank and transport convoys, railway stations, and blowing up bridges, in what were logistical operations, as opposed to strict ground support.

Above: The German retreat after the Battle of Kursk. (*History Department of the United States Military Academy*)

Below: The Battle of Ukraine and the advance of the Red Army in the Baltics. (*History Department of the United States Military Academy*)

Leningrad—The Siege is Lifted

In January 1943, the siege of Leningrad was partially lifted by the opening of a narrow land corridor, the result of Operation *Iskra* ('Spark'). During this operation, AVMF bombers such as the MBR-2 flying boat, the SB, and the R-10 were used. Food and armament could now be supplied by land to Leningrad on a continuous basis. This corridor was only 10 miles (16 km) across, however, and was still subject to bombardment from the Germans to the south of this land bridge. The Soviets were unable at first to dislodge the Germans from their well-entrenched defensive positions. Leningrad itself was also still subjected to artillery bombardment and aerial bombardment from these and other positions ringing the city.

In December 1943 and January 1944, while operations in Ukraine were taking place, the Soviets launched an offensive that finally drove the Germans out of shelling range of Leningrad and finally and completely lifted the siege. The offensive was started on 15 January 1944 when 250 aerial sorties were flown against the Germans.

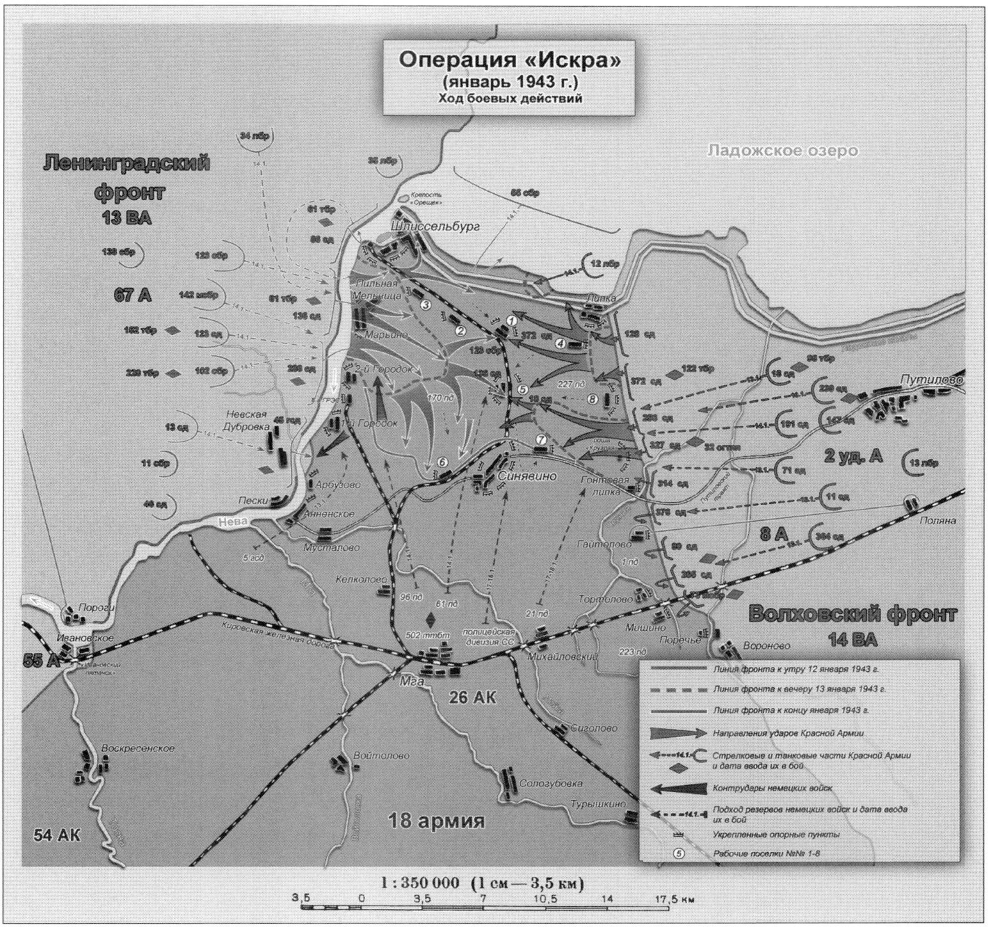

Operation Iskra (in Russian). (*Wikimedia*)

The ADD provided 442 bombers, consisting of Il-4s and Li-2NBs, for the offensive. The ADD was used to attack rail targets in the offensive. By the time this offensive ended, on 1 March 1944, the Germans had been driven back to Lake Peipus, on the border of Estonia. This operation, which started on 15 January 1944, involved 1,099 sorties by attack aircraft of the Red Banner (Baltic) Fleet.

Operation Bagration (Destruction of Army Group Centre and the Liberation of Byelorussia)

Once the Germans had been cleared from Western Ukraine and the area around Leningrad, the only substantial part of the Soviet Union still occupied by German forces was in Byelorussia, in a huge salient with its southern end resting on the Pripet Marshes, a large area of forests and swamps with few good roads. After the clearing of most of Ukraine, this so-called 'Byelorussian Balcony' was to be the next site of a large-scale Soviet attack. Although the Nazis were cognizant of the exposed nature of this sector of the front, they believed that the next big Soviet attack would be in Ukraine and disposed of their forces, both land (including most of their panzer forces) and aerial (including most of their remaining fighters), accordingly.

As partisan attacks against German supply lines such as railroads were an important part of the run-up to Bagration, the ADD flew missions to support them. In addition, from 13 June to 18 June 1944, the ADD flew 1,472 sorties against German airfields. Intruder polks (mainly B-25s) were also used to harass the airfields. By June 1944, the ADD had 1,195 bombers available, which included 30 Pe-8s and 212 B-25s. By July 1944, there were 1,226 bombers in the ADD, and their bombers attacked railway junctions as their main targets.

In a brilliant feat of deception, or *Maskirovka* ('Camouflage' or 'Deception') as the Soviets called it, the Red Army was able to hide their intentions from the Germans. So effective was this deception, that when the invasion commenced in full on 23 June 1944 (preliminary battalion-sized probing attacks had already started on 22 June 1944, the third anniversary of the opening of Operation Barbarossa), the Germans still thought it was only a diversionary attack, with the main attack yet to come in Ukraine. By the time they realised their mistake, it was far too late to do anything about it and their outnumbered forces were routed.

The main Red Air Force units that were involved in the operation were the 1st, 3rd, 4th, and 16th Air Armies in the opening phases, while the 6th Air Army took part in the second phase of the operation. This operation was named Operation Bagration after the Georgian-Russian General Pyotr Bagration (1765–1812), who had been killed at Borodino in the war against Napoleon (the Patriotic War); it was one of the biggest and best-planned set-piece operations of the war.

The total number of serviceable aircraft available for the operation included 637 day bombers, 435 night bombers, and 1,733 Il-2s. The Il-2s constituted 62 per cent of all serviceable bombers for the operation, indicating their importance. Il-2s from fifteen ShADs took part. The Il-2s continuously harassed the German forces, both at the front lines and behind the front lines, where they attacked troop and transport

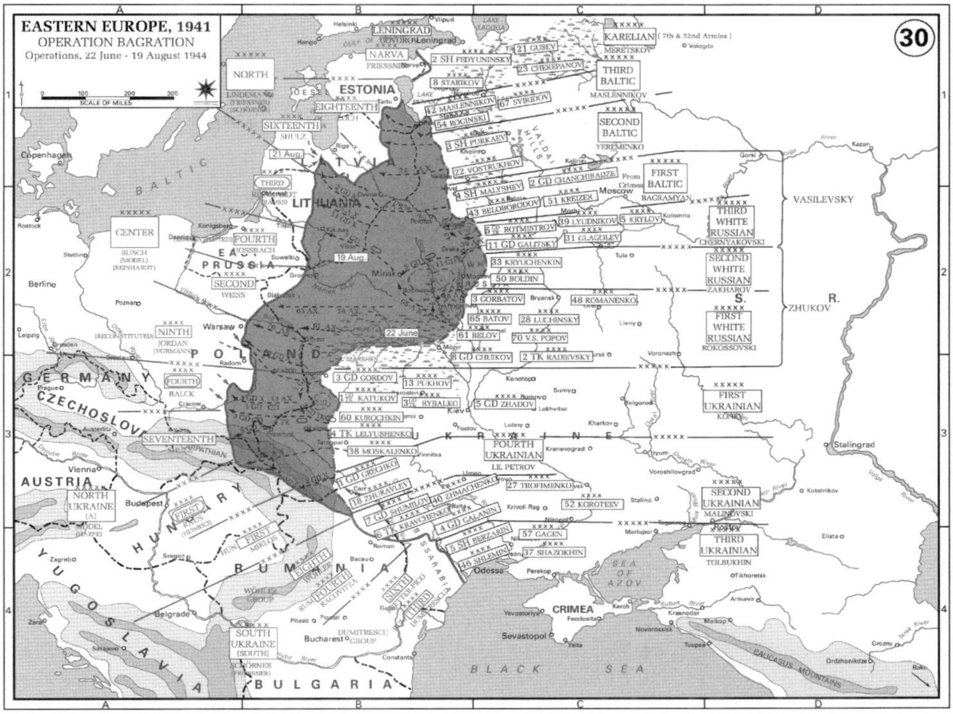

Operation Bagration. (*History Department of the United States Military Academy*)

convoys and destroyed locomotives and railroad cars, attacking railroad stations well behind the front lines. By now, the Luftwaffe had largely disappeared from the Eastern Front, so the Il-2s operated with little fear of aerial attack, although as always ground fire was a concern.

General of the 4th Army Kurt von Tippelskirch (1891–1957) noted that the 6th Air Fleet had only forty fighters operational because of a lack of fuel and spare parts. In addition, most of the fighters had been shifted to what were considered higher risk fronts, such as Ukraine (where the Germans expected the main Soviet assault) and the Western Front (Operation Overlord, the Anglo-American invasion of Normandy, had commenced on 6 June 1944). The German flak, however, continued to take a heavy toll of the low-flying Shturmoviks. Indeed, by now most of the combat losses were to German AA fire as opposed to fighters, even more so than had been the case at Kursk.

Most importantly, this concentrated strike had completely disrupted the German command and control system in the area, resulting in total defeat for the enemy. Soldiers simply threw away their weapons, abandoned their equipment and fled into the forest. Some tried to cross the River Berezina to reach Bobruisk, but units of the 65th Army had already secured its western bank. The demoralised German force was finished off by the 48th Army on 28 June. Bobruisk was liberated a day later.

Although not always to this degree, this scene was repeated over and over again during Operation Bagration, as the Il-2s helped sweep the battlefield of German soldiers and forced them to flee, abandoning most of their equipment. Operation Bagration was succeeding beyond even Soviet expectations, and the operations of the Il-2 helped in no small part with this success.

By 4 July, the ADD had flown 6,053 sorties in support of Bagration, including 3,200 sorties against rail targets in the salient (from 26 June to 4 July), and 2,646 sorties were flown against rail targets leading to the west. In mid-July, the Soviets attacked in southern Poland with 1,046 Il-2s, and three ADD divisions of Il-4s, B-25s, and Li-2NBs. In all of July, the ADD flew 5,590 sorties in Byelorussia and Poland, with 2,302 being against rail targets.

Interestingly, because of its relatively short range and the large distances the Red Army was now covering, by 1944, Pe-2 divisions usually had a regiment of the longer-ranged Boston attached to handle the longer-ranged missions.

Clearing of the Baltic States (Baltic Strategic Offensive Operation)

At the same time that the Soviets were breaking into Romania and the Balkans, they were pushing the Germans out of the Baltic states of Estonia, Latvia, and Lithuania. This operation, known to the Soviets as the Baltic Strategic Offensive Operation, lasted from 14 September to 24 November 1944. During this time, Soviet forces cleared the Germans completely out of Lithuania and Estonia, and out of most of Latvia (see map on page 312), where the Germans retained the Courland (Kurland) Peninsula, which they held on to until the end of the war. The Soviets deployed over 2,600 aircraft for the Baltic operation.

Summer 1944 Finnish Operation

The front against Finland had long been a backwater for the Soviets, as the Finnish had taken all the territory they had wanted and the Soviets were busy fighting elsewhere. Finland was not forgotten, however, and its day of reckoning came in the middle of 1944, after Soviet peace offers were refused (probably not to the surprise or even disappointment of the Soviets). Even before the Soviet offensive began, the ADD had conducted raids on Helsinki, in February, using Il-4s. Smaller raids were conducted on other cities and towns in Finland at this time and continued into March. These were all part of the Soviet effort to 'persuade' Finland to conclude its participation in the war, at least on the side of the Axis.

On 10 June 1944, the expected Soviet offensive began. Although the Finnish were forced back and Viipuri (Vyborg) was recaptured by the Soviets, the Germans assisted the Finnish with men and weapons and the Soviets were unable to penetrate the Finnish defensive VKT Line. With troops needed elsewhere against the Germans, the Soviets stopped their assault and the fighting ended on 9 August 1944. In September 1944, peace terms from the Soviet Union were accepted by the Finnish and the Continuation War ended. Part of the peace terms required the Finnish to turn against their one-time allies; therefore, with the Soviets, they fought against the Germans to push them out of Finland. The Soviets followed the retreating Germans into northern Norway, taking the Norwegian town of Kirkenes, which they departed from in late 1945 when they withdrew their forces back into the Soviet Union.

An Il-4 in flight during Operation Bagration in July 1944. (*Viktor Kulikov's collection*)

Pe-2s over the Karelian Isthmus during 1944. (*Viktor Kulikov's collection*)

Clearing of the Balkans

The operation to clear Western Ukraine had taken the Red Army to the border of Romania. From here, the Soviets were poised to break into the Balkans. Although Greece was to be liberated by the British, Prime Minister Sir Winston Leonard Spencer-Churchill (1874–1965) and Stalin made a deal to give the Soviets a free hand in the rest of the Balkans, which included the responsibility of clearing out the substantial Axis forces that still remained in the Balkan Peninsula. At any rate, there was little either the British or the Americans could have done militarily to stop the Soviets from taking most of the Balkans.

An example of the effect the Soviet aerial attacks had on Axis forces in the Balkans is provided by this testimony from a German officer, taken from *Il-2 Shturmovik Guards Units of World War 2* by Oleg Rastrenin (pp. 83-84):

> When the preparatory bombardment was over we thought we could recover and repulse the Russian infantry and tanks, but attack aircraft appeared overhead and gave us no chance to recover. They forced us to leave our equipment and run for it. The attack aircraft [Il-2s] were constantly wheeling overhead. It was horrible.

Romania and especially Bulgaria surrendered to the Soviets and changed sides fairly quickly, attacking their former allies, the Germans. Romania quit the Axis after

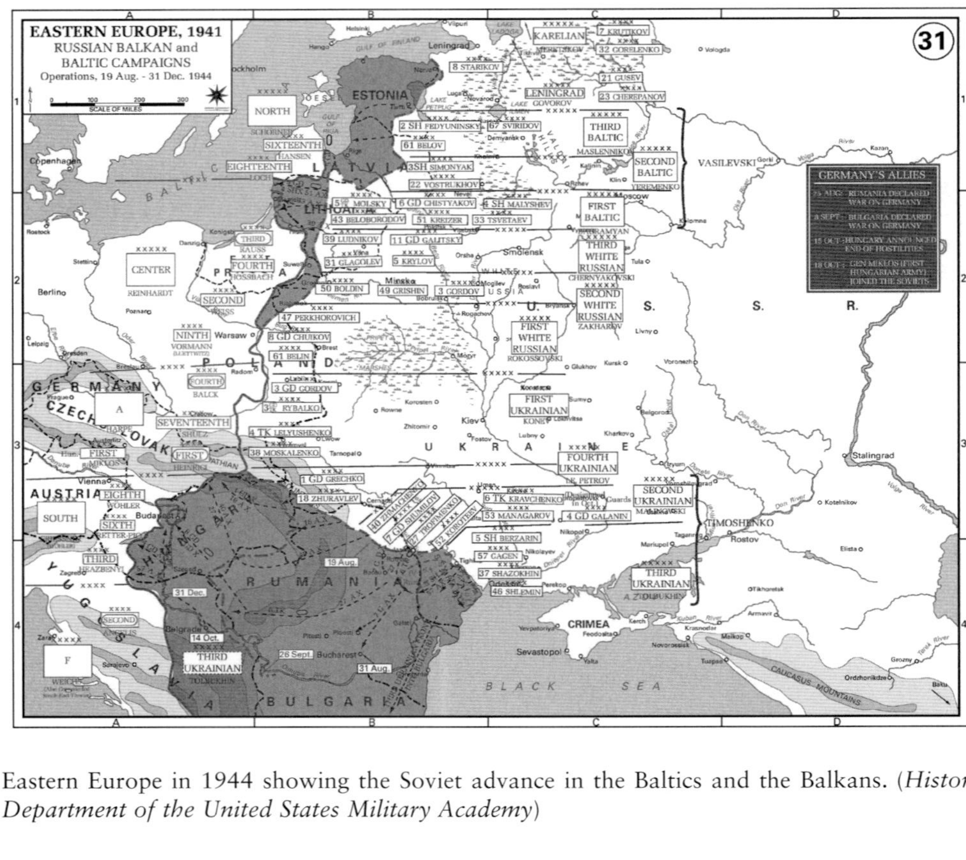

Eastern Europe in 1944 showing the Soviet advance in the Baltics and the Balkans. (*History Department of the United States Military Academy*)

a pro-monarchy coup toppled the pro-German Romanian dictator Marshal Ion Antonescu (1882–1946), with the Romanians declaring war on Germany on 24 August 1944, and Bulgaria, which had been neutral in the Great Patriotic War, quickly joined the Soviets when the Red Army appeared at their borders. Fighting, however, was very heavy in Hungary, where the Nazis had overthrown the Hungarian leader Adml Miklos Horthy (1868–1957) and taken control of the government, and Hitler was determined to hold on to his last supplier of natural petroleum. The fighting was especially intense in and around Budapest, which was surrounded by Soviet forces.

In the Battle of Budapest, such was the intensity of the fighting that some Il-2s flew up to five sorties a day. There was also at least one instance when Il-2s flew without gunners, to allow them to carry more bombs, while carrying out an attack against a bridgehead. The Il-2s were now able to fly without gunners because of the nearly complete absence of the Luftwaffe and the nearly complete air dominance that the Red Air Force had by now achieved.

Vistula to Oder Operation

The Vistula to Oder Operation was the follow-on to Operation Bagration and took the Soviets from Warsaw and the border of East Prussia to the Oder River, only 30 miles (48 km) from Berlin. This operation was not as straightforward as Operation

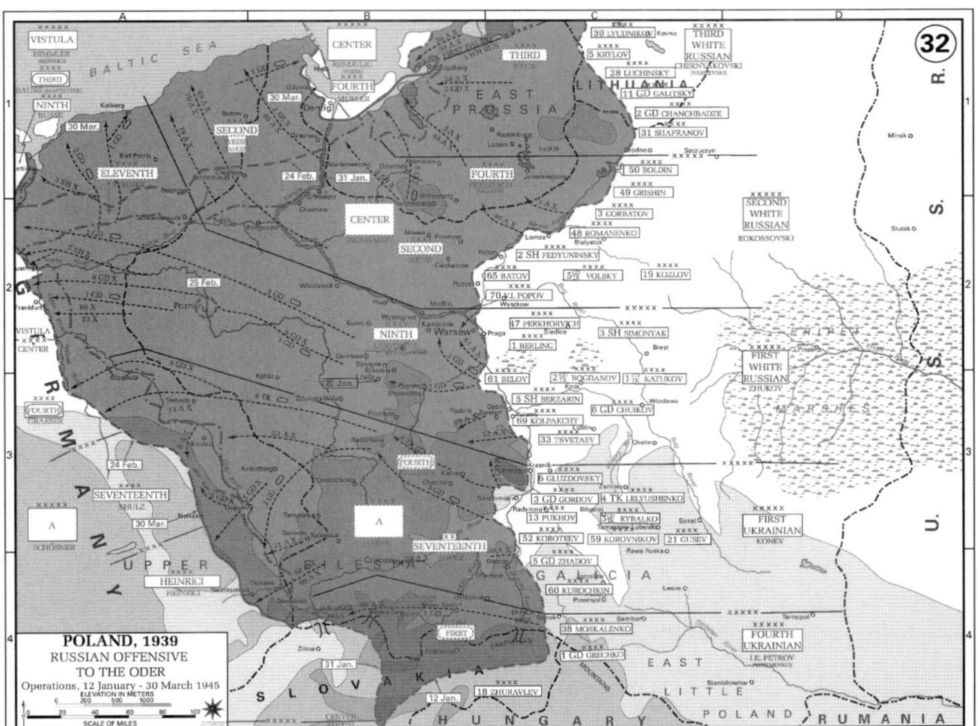

The Vistula to Oder Operation. (*History Department of the United States Military Academy*)

Bagration had been, as the closer the Soviets got to Berlin, the less room for manoeuvre they had, the fiercer the German resistance was, and the operation started in the dead of winter, beginning on 12 January 1945. Indeed, the start date of the operation had been moved forward due to a personal request from Winston Churchill to Josef Stalin. Churchill was concerned about Germany's initial success in the Ardennes Offensive (the Battle of the Bulge) and wanted pressure on the Germans from the Soviets to relieve the pressure on the Western Front. Stalin, perhaps surprisingly, obliged and moved the start date forwards.

By the beginning of 1945, there were 1,727 serviceable Pe-2s and Bostons, and 3,524 Il-2s available for operations. Based on airfields in Poland, Il-4s were able to bomb targets in Germany, including German cities, airfields, and ports.

As part of the effort to clear the northern flanks for the upcoming Berlin campaign, German defences in East Prussia were reduced, including the formidable fortress city of Königsberg. On 21 January 1945, Königsberg's airfields were bombed and strafed. On 7 April 1945, 246 Tu-2s with 236 fighter escorts attacked the city. Yer-2 ACh-30Bs also bombed Königsberg on 7–8 April 1945. By 9 April 1945, (the city surrendered on 10 April), 14,090 missions had been flown and 4,440 tons of bombs dropped.

Battle of Berlin (Berlin Strategic Offensive Operation)

From their positions on the Oder, the Soviets launched their last great operation of the Great Patriotic War, the Battle of Berlin or the Berlin Strategic Offensive Operation as they termed it. At the start of the Berlin operation, the Soviets had some 7,500 aircraft arrayed against the Germans, mainly from the 16th and 18th Air Armies (the 18th Air Army was the former ADD and had around 500 long-range bombers, many of which were Il-4s, for the Berlin operation), of which these air armies had 731 ground attack aircraft—most, if not all of which were Il-2s (a few might have been Il-10s). The commander of the VVS, Marshal Aleksandr A. Novikov, took direct command over these forces, such was the importance of this last great operation of the Great Patriotic War.

For the Soviets, the ground forces were composed of around 2½ million men and women (of which up to 200,000 were Polish troops), some 6,000 tanks and self-propelled guns, 75,000 guns and mortars, and 400 rocket launchers (Katyushas). Against them, the Germans were able to field between 750,000 and 1 million men (with the actual number probably being closer to the lower figure), around 500 tanks and 1,000 assault guns, over 9,000 artillery pieces, and 2,200 or so aircraft.

The battle itself opened in full on 16 April 1945, a day after the initiation of the battalion and smaller units' reconnaissance and probing attacks, as was normal with large Soviet operations. The Soviets moved out from their bridgehead at Küstrin and their bridgeheads on either side of Frankfurt-an-der-Oder. Il-2s led the way as they attacked the crumbling German defences and made low altitude attacks against the German armour. By the end of the first day of the operation, the VVS had flown 6,548 combat sorties, according to Soviet accounts. The Germans were able to slow the Soviet advance in the centre at the Seelow Heights for three days. The Soviets suffered considerable casualties despite massive bombings of the Heights, including Pe-2 and

Right: Tu-2S in flight, probably during 1945. (*Viktor Kulikov's collection*)

Below: Tu-2S in flight, probably during 1945. (*Viktor Kulikov's collection*)

The Berlin Strategic Offensive Operation (Berlin Operation or Battle of Berlin). (*Wikimedia*)

Yer-2 bombers, but there was nothing the Germans could do to stop the huge Soviet army facing them; by 25 April, Berlin itself was surrounded. It was also on this day that advance elements of the Red Army met up with their American counterparts at Torgau, on the Elbe River. Germany was now split in two.

On the approaches to Berlin, the density of Il-2s per kilometre of front was thirty to thirty-five aircraft, and, in some cases, sixty to eighty per kilometre. Such a concentration of force would have been almost unimaginable for the VVS early in the war; now it could be achieved with relative ease. This huge concentration enabled the Il-2s to smash the German defences, allowing the Soviet armour and soldiers to penetrate deeply into the collapsing German lines. This concentration was made possible not just by the improved coordination of large numbers of Il-2s, but by the increasing number of Il-2s in the Red Air Force. Although the relative number of Il-2s remained at about 30–32 per cent of all Red Air Force warplanes from 1942–45, the absolute numbers of Il-2s in frontline units increased, as the number of Red Air Force aircraft overall increased.

Pe-2s in force, preparing for take-off. This was a typical scene during the Battle for Berlin, when the Red Air Force unleashed huge aerial attacks against the German defences. (*Viktor Kulikov's collection*)

Il-2 arrows during flight, probably in 1945. Note the 'Kremlin' stars on the fuselage of the nearest aircraft. (*Viktor Kulikov's collection*)

Il-2 arrows taking off during the Berlin operation in 1945. Note the distinctive markings on the tail and fuselage. (*Viktor Kulikov's collection*)

Although it was normally used only in relatively small numbers in its operations, on the night of 20–21 April, 713 Po-2s (U-2s) of the VVS bombed Berlin, in another example of the large numbers of aircraft the VVS could now bring to bear on the battlefield. The former ADD, now the 18th VA, had by now switched its bombers to day operations because of Soviet air supremacy.

During the Battle of Berlin, a rather interesting incident occurred when Il-2s landed at Tempelhof airfield and positioned their aircraft in such a way that the rear gunners could train their guns and fire on the airfield's buildings, from which the German forces were still resisting. While this was happening, a tank unit advanced on the airfield and the airfield was taken. This action took place on 25 April 1945. By 2 May 1945, the German capital had surrendered, with Adolf Hitler having already taken his life on 30 April. The Third Reich itself survived only a week more until its unconditional surrender.

The last major action of the Great Patriotic War was the capture of Bohemia and Moravia, whose forces, under General Ferdinand Schörner (1897–1973), a fanatical Nazi, had refused to surrender on 9 May 1945, a day still celebrated in Russia as 'Victory Day', when all German forces were to have laid down their arms. The Soviet response lasted until 11 May, and Il-2s were the first Soviet aircraft to land in Prague, the Czech capital, on an airfield that had been captured by Czechoslovakian insurgents.

At the end of the Great Patriotic War, on 10 May 1945, the disposition of Il-2s in service was as follows: 3,075 Il-2s and Il-2Us, of which 450 were not airworthy; 214 Il-2KRs, of which seventeen were not airworthy; and 197 naval Il-2s, with an unknown number not airworthy, making a total of 3,486 Il-2s. This represents an airworthiness rate of over 86 per cent, a tribute to the Il-2 mechanics. The 18th VA, the former ADD, had 1,675 aircraft, which included 593 Li-2s and 553 Il-4s.

Manchurian Campaign (Manchurian Strategic Offensive Operation)

The Battle of Berlin was not the last operation of the war for the Soviet Union. Stalin had promised US President Franklin Delano Roosevelt (1882–1945) at the Yalta Conference in February 1945 that with the conclusion of the war in Europe, the Soviet Union would join the fight against the Japanese within three months. Thus the campaign against the Japanese forces in Manchuria (or the Kwantung Army as this army is often known) was born. The Soviet name for this campaign was the Manchurian Strategic Offensive Operation.

Although not a part of the Great Patriotic War, this campaign was not only the last campaign for Soviet forces in the Second World War, but the last major land campaign

The Manchurian Campaign (Manchurian Strategic Offensive Operation) (in Spanish). (*Wikimedia*)

for any side during the war, occurring during August 1945. Although the fighting was short, lasting only a couple of weeks, it was intense and saw combat usage of bombers such as the Pe-2, Il-4, DB-3, B-25, and both the Il-2 and its successor, the Il-10. By this time, the Pe-8 was no longer in use as a bomber. The Li-2NB likewise saw no use as a bomber in this campaign, although the Li-2 did see use in its original transport role. The Il-2s were used not just against ground targets, such as railway stations and enemy airfields, but they were also active in attacking Japanese shipping and other naval targets.

VVS Il-4s were used from the first day of the operation, flying missions on the night of 8–9 August 1945, with Il-4s of the 108th BAP bombing Harbin. On 9 August, the Il-4Ts of the 4th MTAP bombed the Korean port of Rashin (Rason). On 10 August, Il-4s once again bombed Harbin and also attacked Changchun. The Il-4s were used until 19 August to attack such Japanese targets as railways, enemy fortifications, and ports. Il-4s of the Pacific Fleet attacked ground targets and shipping.

Apparently, there were none of the 37-mm-armed Il-2s employed in Manchuria, and indeed, they would not have been greatly missed, as the Il-2's standard armament proved more than enough for the missions set for the Il-2s in this campaign. The Pe-2s, DB-3Ts, and Il-4Ts were capable of taking care of the shipping that the Il-2-37s were adept at attacking.

18 Colours and Markings

Pre-War

During the 1930s, Soviet aircraft were normally painted in light grey and/or silver, or in the case of all-metal aircraft, they were sometimes left in a natural metal finish. On those aircraft that had both metal and fabric-covering, such as the I-15bis, the metal areas were painted light grey and the fabric-covered areas were painted silver.

Khalkhin-Gol

An interesting exception to the normal pre-war paint schemes occurred in the Battle of the Khalkhin-Gol. In this conflict, some light grey, silver, or natural metal-finished aircraft, such as the I-153, the SB, and the Li-2 had green painted on to them in an *ad hoc* field-applied camouflage. This camouflage consisted of irregular markings, such as 'squiggles' of green paint applied directly to the light grey, silver, or metal finish of the topsides of these aircraft. The paint used was apparently the '3B' green paint. Some of these aircraft still retained this scheme into the early part of the Great Patriotic War.

Early Second World War

In May 1940, a directive ordered that Soviet military aircraft should be finished with a green topside over a blue underside. The red stars were to be black outlined and consisted of stars on the fuselage as well as the tops and bottoms of the wings. Instead of being repainted in blue, evidently, some aircraft retained the underside scheme they had originally been painted in, such as light grey and/or silver.

This directive was not followed immediately, and the pre-war schemes of light grey and aluminium continued to be used on some aircraft such as SBs and I-153s into the early period of the Great Patriotic War. As mentioned previously, some aircraft still retained their field-applied green mottling over light grey/silver camouflage from the Khalkhin-Gol conflict.

Great Patriotic War: Early to Mid-War

The standard early Great Patriotic War camouflage for wooden and mixed-construction aircraft was black (AMT-6 in Soviet parlance) and green (normally AMT-4, but also A-19f and AII 3) over blue (AMT-7 Blue, which seems to have been the standard underside paint for all Il-2 versions, for example, except for some early single-seaters, which would have used A-18f for the metal portions, and AII Sv.gol. for the wooden parts). These colours were applied to all Soviet combat aircraft. The topside was painted with alternating bands of black and green, although the application of these bands varied from aircraft type to aircraft type (and sometimes from aircraft to aircraft for a given type, especially early in the Great Patriotic War).

The brown and green schemes, seen in many colour profiles for Great Patriotic War aircraft, were actually black and green (AMT-6 Black and AMT-4 Green), and the brown colour that often appears in these colour profiles (and in plastic kit instructions) is a misinterpretation of wartime photographs. The AMT nitrocellulose lacquers were normally a matte to satin finish when first applied, which would have then weathered to a more matte finish.

After the initial part of the Great Patriotic War, when A-18f Blue and A-19f Green were utilised for the metal portions of aircraft, as well as AII Blue (Sv.gol.—*Svetlo Goluboi* or 'Light Blue' in Russian) and AII 3 (Green—where 'II' is the Roman numeral for '2' and the '3' is actually the Cyrillic letter representing 'Z' for *Zashchitniy* or 'Protective (Colour)' in Russian) for the wooden portions, all mixed-construction or wooden aircraft, such as the Il-2s and Su-2s used AMT lacquers such as AMT-6 Black and AMT-4 Green over AMT-7 Blue, as mentioned above. During the Great Patriotic War, 'A-xxm' enamels were used on all-metal (or nearly all-metal aircraft), such as the Il-4 and the Tu-2. A-26m corresponded to AMT-6 Black, A-24m to AMT-4 Green, and A-28m to AMT-7 Blue.

During the winter, a temporary white finish, called distemper paint (MK-7—which was normally a mixture of white chalk powder and casein glue), was sometimes applied over the normal or 'summer' camouflage (Russian historian Mikhail Orlov sometimes refers to this as 'spring' camouflage). Here is where the situation gets a bit more complicated. There seem to have been no real standards as to how the white was applied; it varied from aircraft to aircraft and regiment to regiment (and quite possibly within the regiment itself). Although it is common to see the white applied to the entire topside, especially with factory-applied winter camouflage, this was by no means always done in the field, and if done, it was done with varying results. Sometimes, the white was applied evenly (especially if it was applied at the factory with an airgun).

Sometimes you will see photographs of single-engined aircraft, such as the Il-2, with the white only applied to the rear fuselage, or the wings and rear fuselage but not the nose. This was apparently done because a tarpaulin often covered the nose while on the ground, so there was no need for camouflaging the nose. It is possible that the summer camouflage was left on the nose even when the aircraft was painted in the white winter scheme at the factory. Sometimes you will see a patchy white camouflage on the nose; in these instances, it is possible that the use of the tarpaulins may have worn off some of the temporary white finish. Sometimes white tarpaulins were also placed on the wings, which negated the need for MK-7 on the wings also, at least as far as camouflaging the aeroplane on the ground. Early in the war, with the very real threat of marauding German aircraft attacking airfields, the winter camouflage served not only to protect the aeroplane while flying at low altitudes, but also to provide camouflage when it was parked on the ground.

The white covering was applied evenly with an airgun at the factory, whereas at other times the white was applied roughly, sometimes with a brush, with the summer camouflage showing through in many places. It is also possible that when first applied the white overcoat was relatively pristine (again, especially with factory-applied winter camouflage), but the undercoat showed through more as time went on and the aircraft became more weathered, with the temporary white paint wearing off.

Great Patriotic War: Mid- to Late War

The black/green scheme was superseded by the 'three-colour' scheme (1943–45) (Order Number 389S/0133 NKAP and VVS RKKA, 3 July 1943, for the beginning of painting new aircraft at the aircraft factory, scheduled from 15 July 1943, and attack aircraft and bombers from 1 August). This scheme used AMT-12 Dark Grey (this was similar to the British Extra Dark Sea Grey), AMT-4 Green, AMT-1 Light Brown (actually a greyish-tan), and AMT-7 Blue underside. In addition, some bombers were to have been finished in 1944–45 in the two-grey 'fighter' scheme of AMT-11 and AMT-12 topside, and AMT-7 underside, according to Order Number 5590/0207, dated October 1944, and it appears that a few bombers, such as the Yer-2, were finished with these colours, or their A-xxm enamel analogues (see below), over a black underside. On some night bombers, such as the Il-4 and Li-2NB, black was used in place of the dark grey, and the undersides were painted in black.

White distemper paint (MK-7) was applied over the summer camouflage in the winters of 1941–42, 1942–43, and of 1943–44, but not the winter of 1944–45, when this practice seems to have been abandoned. The A-xxm analogues were A-32m for AMT-12 Dark Grey and A-21m for AMT-1 Light Brown. The analogues for AMT-4 Green and AMT-7 Blue remained A-24m and A-28m respectively. The A-xxm enamel analogue for the AMT-11 Grey Blue lacquer was A-33m, but the Grey Blue colour was almost exclusively used on fighter aircraft, which utilised the AMT-11 lacquer, as the Soviet-built fighters during the Second World War were of wooden construction (the Lavochkin fighters) or composite construction (the Yakovlev fighters).

As the concentration of Soviet aircraft grew, identification markings became more important to keep track of the aircraft from different units as they flew together in massed formations. Thus, for example, Il-2s sprouted stripes on the fuselage, the wings, coloured fins and rudders, and distinctively coloured spinners, all in an effort to distinguish their particular unit (or even place within that unit, such as which flight in a polk, with the different flights having differently coloured spinners, for example). As the Luftwaffe was scarcely to be seen anymore, attack while on the ground was no longer a concern for the Red Air Force, so the Soviet aircraft (including the fighters) became more colourful, as control and identification in the air increased in importance with the large formations that these aircraft were now flying in.

Insignia

The standard Red Air Force insignia was the red star, which had been in use since the Russian Civil War of 1918–22. According to a May 1940 directive (for aircraft with a green upper surface), red stars with a black outline were specified, to be applied in six positions—the fuselage and lower and upper wing surfaces. The usage of these black-outlined stars persisted long into the Great Patriotic War, especially on certain aircraft types such as the Lavochkin fighters, although no stars were applied to the upper wings after the beginning of the Great Patriotic War (those that were present would have been fairly quickly painted over).

A June 1941 directive (for aircraft with the black/green camouflage scheme) did not specify any border—stars were supposed to be borderless with this scheme. Factories did generally follow this as an instruction, but in operational units, white, black, or silver borders were added to make the stars more visible against the black/green background. Stars were not painted on the upper wings. In addition, there would normally be stars on the rudder and the fuselage.

From September 1943, for aircraft with the three-colour scheme, stars with a white border and a thin red outline around it were specified. This directive has been followed to the present day. These stars, called '1943' stars, since that is when they went into effect, still appear on modern Russian aircraft.

The so-called 'Kremlin Star' (a 'relief' star, in two shades of red to give it a three-dimensional effect, based on the stars mounted over the Kremlin, hence the name) was something of a decorative element applied by units to individual aeroplanes; it was like a personal marking. Strangely, the Kremlin Star was not necessarily applied to all the positions on a single aircraft; for example, it might be used only on the fuselage and not on the wings. The different types of stars can be seen on the aircraft portrayed in the colour plates section.

Aircraft (Tactical) Numbers

Most Soviet warplanes in the VVS, AVMF, and the ADD bore some sort of tactical or aircraft number, known as a bort, on the tail or fuselage, or much more rarely, both. The numbers were typically red, white, or blue (or a combination of these colours), were normally one or two digits, although three-digit borts were seen; the style and font varied from regiment to regiment. These were not applied at the factory, but in the field by the regiments. Although you may see it in colour profiles, yellow was rarely used during the Great Patriotic War, as this was the Axis identification colour. Yellow borts were seen applied on aircraft early in the Great Patriotic War, but this practice was soon discontinued because of the possibility of misidentification with Axis aircraft. Yellow, however, was commonly used before the Great Patriotic War for the borts, for example during the Winter War. Examples can be seen in the colour plates section.

Personal Markings

There doesn't seem to have been any specific official prohibition against the use of personal markings on VVS, AVMF, and ADD aircraft; these were common on Soviet bombers and other Soviet aircraft during the Second World War, especially during the Great Patriotic War. Animals such as lions and eagles were common. Erotic themes such as nude or semi-nude pinups were not used, and supernatural or religious themes do not seem to have been used either. One exception to this was the use of a coat of arms featuring St George slaying the dragon; this was the traditional coat of arms for Moscow and was no doubt also seen as an analogy for the Soviet Union (St George) defeating Nazi Germany (the dragon).

Common markings were patriotic slogans such as *Za Rodinu!* ('For the Motherland!') or *Za Stalina!* ('For Stalin!'), as examples. Some aircraft were presentation machines which were paid for by donations from various groups or even individuals, for example, with the name of the donating organisation or individual being painted on the side(s) of the aeroplane. Animals—such as lions, bears, and eagles—were common. Again, examples can be seen in the colour plates section.

This close-up of the nose of a turret-armed Pe-2 reveals some interesting details. Note the lion painted on the nose, and the lines on the side windscreen next to the pilot—probably sighting lines while diving. At the very rear of the photograph, one of the vanes for the turret can be made out. (*Viktor Kulikov's collection*)

19
Experimental Bombers

This section will describe some of the experimental bombers developed by the Soviet Union during the Second World War. It will not be all-encompassing, as that would entail a book in itself, but it will include some of those aircraft that were built and flown. Experimental versions of production aircraft are described in that aircraft's section; for example, the experimental wartime versions of the Tu-2 are described in the Tu-2 section.

Bolkhovitinov S (*Spartak*)

An unusual design, the Bolkhovitinov S or *Spartak* featured an interesting arrangement where two M-103 inline engines were mounted in the fuselage, to drive two counter-rotating propellers. This engine design was chosen to provide the maximum power combined with the minimum amount of drag.

The aircraft was built starting in 1938, and it was completed by winter of that year. Test flights started in the summer of 1939, piloted by Boris N. Kudrin on its first flight 29 January 1940. This aircraft had only one engine, and the maximum speed was only 249 mph (400 kph). The aircraft was of all-metal construction, with extensive use of electrically operated systems. It featured relatively short span wings and had twin tails. The two crew members sat underneath a greenhouse-type canopy enclosure.

The second prototype had two M-103 engines and was armed with a single ShKAS (later two UBTs) in the rear position and 882 lb (400 kg) of bombs. State testing started on 20 March 1940 and lasted until June 1940. A top speed of 354 mph (570 kph) was reached and the aircraft exhibited good handling except on take-off and landing because of the high wing-loading caused by its short wings. Ultimately, further development of this aircraft was abandoned.

DB-4

This development of the Il-4 differed by having a new, more streamlined fuselage combined with wings similar to those of the Il-4. Unlike the Il-4, the DB-4 featured a fully retractable tailwheel and twin fins and rudders mounted at the ends of the horizontal tail planes on the second prototype. The wing was high-mounted so a large bomb bay could be fitted.

This aircraft was designed to meet a 1939 specification calling for a long-range bomber with a top speed of 342 mph (550 kph), which was capable of carrying 2,205 lb (1,000 kg) of bombs over 2,485 miles (4,000 km). Tupolev developed the 103D (which was a variant of what became the Tu-2), Yermolayev developed the DB-240 (which became the Yer-2), and Myasishchev developed the DVB-102 to meet these requirements.

AM-37 engines, a development of the AM-35 engines, were fitted to the DB-4. These replaced the Klimov M-120 'Y' type engines that were to be fitted. The defensive armament of the first prototype was the same as that of the DB-3F, with three ShKAS guns, one being fitted to a MV-3 turret. As with the DB-3F, a fourth crew member was provided to man the ventral gun. The initial flight of the single-tailed first prototype was made on 15 October 1940, piloted by V. K. Kokkinaki. The second prototype, which featured twin fins, was completed in late November 1940 and flew on 20 February 1941, but flight testing ceased after the first flight. The DB-4 exhibited a top speed of 311 mph (500 kph), had a service ceiling of 32,808 feet (10,000 m) and had a maximum bomb load of 6,614 lb (3,000 kg).

It was felt that Ilyushin should concentrate on achieving production for the Il-2 and the DB-3F (Il-4), and since the DB-240 (Yer-2) was chosen for the long-range bomber, the DB-4 became redundant and development stopped. The two prototypes were used as testbeds by Ilyushin for improving the Il-4 and for development of the Il-6.

DVB-102

Although an experimental design that never went into production, this aircraft is interesting for two reasons, it was apparently the first aeroplane designed by Vladimir Myasishchev, and it was the most advanced Soviet long-range bomber design to fly during the war. He designed it while he was also assisting with the design (under NKVD detention) of what became the (Petlyakov) Pe-2 dive bomber.

First flying in 1942, the DVB-102 was a remarkably advanced design, especially compared to other Soviet bombers of the time. It was pressurised, had remote-controlled turrets, and a fully retractable tricycle landing gear, all features it shared in common with the American Boeing B-29 Superfortress, at which time (the early 1940s), the Soviets had no knowledge of. It was powered by two of the powerful experimental Shvetsov M-71 radial engines of 2,000 hp plus, which powered so many experimental Soviet designs.

The DVB-102's development was cancelled in 1946 due to the non-availability of its intended engines, as the M-71 never entered large-scale production, no doubt also due to the decision to go with the reverse-engineered B-29, which became the Tu-4 'Bull'. With its cancellation, the Myasishchev OKB was shut down, although it would be resurrected for the development of the first Soviet four-engined jet-powered strategic bomber, the M-4 'Bison'.

Polikarpov NB ('T')

This bomber, designed in 1941–42, then built in 1943, was intended to be a night bomber, hence the designation 'NB' for *Nochnoiy Bombardirovshchik* or 'Night Bomber'. The internal Polikarpov OKB designation was 'T'. The aircraft was a clean high-wing monoplane twin-engined aircraft of mixed metal and wooden construction and twin tails. All the landing gear units were retractable and the aircraft was powered by two ASh-82FN engines of the type which powered the La-5FN fighter. It carried three UB machine guns—one in a fixed mount for use by the pilot and two for use by gunners, one being mounted in a dorsal turret. The bomb bay could carry 4,409 lb (2,000 kg) of bombs, while an additional 6,614 lb (3,000 kg) could be mounted externally for an impressive total bomb load of 11,023 lb (5,000 kg).

The aircraft flew for the first time on 23 May 1944 and achieved a top speed of 317 mph (510 kph). Despite the promising performance, with the death of Nikolaiy Polikarpov in 1944 his OKB was shut down and work on the NB ('T') was discontinued.

Polikarpov SPB

Resembling a smaller version of the pre-war experimental VIT-2 bomber, the SPB (for *Skorostnoiy Pikiruyushchiy Bombardirovshchik* or 'Fast Dive Bomber') was powered by two Klimov M-105 engines and, like the VIT-2, featured twin fins and rudders and retractable landing gear, including the tailwheel. For protection, the aircraft had a UBT machine gun and a ShKAS firing rearward along with a single ShKAS firing forward. The aircraft was equipped to carry 1,764 lb (800 kg) of bombs in an internal bomb bay, and an additional 1,543 lb (700 kg) could be carried externally for a total bomb load of 3,307 lb (1,500 kg). This aircraft is sometimes referred to as the SPB (D), with the 'D' possibly standing for *Dalnost* or 'Distance', or perhaps the 'D' was just an internal designation given by the Polikarpov OKB. Besides the first prototype, an additional five aircraft were apparently built.

The first prototype initially flew on 18 February 1940, piloted by Boris N. Kudrin. In tests, a top speed of 323 mph (520 kph) was recorded. However, on 27 April 1940, the prototype crashed for unknown reasons, killing the pilot, Pavel Golovin. This was not the end of the SPB's problems as on 30 June 1940 the second prototype, flown by Mikhail Lipkin broke up in flight, killing him and his flight engineer. It was determined that the balance weights that should have been added to the leading edges of the ailerons were not fitted, causing catastrophic wing flutter. To add to the SPB's woes, the rudder trim tab broke off on the third prototype, but Boris Kudrin was able to land the aircraft safely. He refused to fly the fourth prototype. These problems, and the success of what became the Pe-2, spelled the end of the SPB programme; it was cancelled on 29 July 1940.

Su-6

First flown on 1 March 1941, this aeroplane became a rival to the Il-10 as the successor to the Il-2. Initially built as a single-seater, combat experience with the Il-2 had shown the need for a rear gunner for defence, so the Su-6 was suitably modified to accommodate this position. Unlike the Il-2, the Su-6 gunner enjoyed all-around armour protection in a fully enclosed position. Although a good design, the Su-6 lost out to the Il-10 as the Il-10 had generally superior performance, and the Su-6 remained in prototype form only. It was tested with both the powerful but problematic Shevtsov M-71 radial engine and the Mikulin AM-42 inline engine (which latter engine powered the Il-10), both engines developing around 2,000 hp.

Su-8

This formidable aeroplane was in a sense a 'super-shturmovik', carrying 3,706 lb (1,681 kg) of steel armour and having an extremely potent offensive firepower, consisting of eight 7.62-mm (30-calibre) ShKAS machine guns in the wings and in its ultimate configuration four of the very powerful NS-45 45-mm cannons under the fuselage. It was also equipped with a UBT 12.7-mm (50-calibre) gun in a turret and a ShKAS 7.62-mm (30-calibre) gun mounted ventrally for rear defence (the massive forward-firing armament would have been more than adequate for forward defence rendering attack from that quarter suicidal). It was larger than the Il-2, being a twin-engined design with similar dimensions to the Pe-2 dive bomber. It first flew on 11 March 1944. Two prototypes were built.

Powered by the Shvetsov M-71 radial engines, it did not go into production, as its troublesome engines and the impending end of the war rendered it unnecessary in the eyes of the VVS. The possibility of re-engining it with AM-42 engines was explored, but not proceeded with. If development and production had been proceeded with, using the AM-42 engines, the Su-8 might have proven a very powerful ground-attack weapon indeed in the closing months of both the Great Patriotic War and the Manchurian campaign.

Tomashevich *Pegas*

If the Il-2 was considered to be a fairly simple design, the *Pegas* ('Pegasus' in Russian) took this to an extreme. It was meant to occupy something of a middle ground between the Il-2 and the small U-2/Po-2 biplane. This experimental twin-engined single-seat cantilever monoplane attack aircraft was built almost entirely out of wood, with steel armour plating around the pilot's open cockpit and a fixed landing gear. It was powered by two M-11 five-cylinder radial engines (the same powerplant that drove the U-2/Po-2, even utilising the same type of propeller). The armament consisted of two VYa-23 23-mm cannons and one UBK 12.7-mm (50-calibre) machine gun in the nose, with 1,102 lb (500 kg) of bombs being carried in place of the cannons, if necessary. It was considered too slow and underpowered and was not put into production. It first flew in late 1942 and only four prototypes were built and it does not appear that they ever saw any service or action.

20
Experimental Soviet Bomber Specification Table

Type	Bolkhovitinov *Spartak* second prototype	DB-4	DVB-102	Polikarpov NB ('T')	Polikarpov SPB	Su-6 M-71	Su-8	Tomashevich *Pegas*
Year	1940	1940	1942	1944	1940	1943	1944	1942
Maximum Speed: mph (kph)	354 (570)	311 (500)	354 (570)	320 (515)	323 (520)	319 (514)	342 (550)	107 (172)
Range: miles (km)	435 (700)	2,485 (4,000)	2,324 (3,740)	1,883 (3,030)	1,367 (2,200)	605 (973)	901 (1,450)	249 (400)
Service Ceiling: feet (m)		32,808 (10,000)	35,269 (10,750)	20,177 (6,150)	29,528 (9,000)	26,575 (8,100)	29,528 (9,000)	8,596 (2,620)
Offensive Armament	N/A	N/A	N/A	1 × UBK 12.7-mm machine gun	N/A	2 × ShKAS 7.62-mm machine guns, 2 × NS-37 37-mm cannons	8 × ShKAS 7.62-mm machine guns, 4 × NS-45 45-mm cannons	1 × UBK 12.7-mm machine gun, 2 × VYa-23 23-mm cannons
Defensive Armament	2 × UBT 12.7-mm machine guns	4 × ShKAS 7.62-mm machine guns	1 × ShKAS 7.62-mm machine gun, 2 × UBT 12.7-mm machine guns, 3 × ShVAK 20-mm cannons	2 × UBT 12.7-mm machine guns	1 × ShKAS 7.62-mm machine gun, 2 × UBT 12.7-mm machine guns	1 × UBT 12.7-mm machine gun	1 × ShKAS 7.62-mm machine gun, 1 × UBT 12.7-mm machine gun	N/A

Maximum Bomb Load: lb (kg)	882 (400)	6,614 (3,000)	8,818 (4,000)	11,023 (5,000)	3,307 (1,500)	882 (400)	3,086 (1,400)	1,102 (500)
Empty Weight: lb (kg)		16,669 (7,561)	21,621 (9,807)	14,919 (6,767)	9,877 (4,480)	8,818 (4,000)	20,238 (9,180)	3,968 (1,800)
All-up Weight: lb (kg)	12,461 (5,652)	23,823 (10,806)	34,172 (15,500)	27,866 (12,640)	15,102 (6,850)	12,200 (5,534)	27,392 (12,425)	4,740 (2,150)
Maximum Weight: lb (kg)		28,673 (13,006)	39,683 (18,000)	40,896 (18,550)			29,498 (13,380)	6,217 (2,820)
Engines/ take-off hp per	2 × M-103 960	2 × AM-37 1,400	2 × M-71 2,200	2 × ASh-82FN 1,850	2 × M-105 1,100	1 × M-71 2,200	2 × M-71F 2,200	2 × M-11F 140
Crew	2	4	4	5	5	2	2	1
Length: feet (m)	43.31 (13.2)	58.56 (17.85)	65.29 (19.9)	50.16 (15.29)	36.75 (11.2)	30.31 (9.24)	44.29 (13.5)	28.61 (8.72)
Wingspan: feet (m)	45.28 (13.8)	85.53 (26.07)	82.58 (25.17)	70.6 (21.52)	55.77 (17)	44.29 (13.5)	67.26 (20.5)	54.56 (16.63)

21
Ordnance Used by Soviet Second World War Bombers

Bombers are rather useless machines without bombs to drop or guns to protect them (or be used offensively), so below I shall describe some of the armament that enabled the Soviet bombers to go about their deadly business. Rockets are also discussed as these were heavily used by the Soviets in ground attack missions.

Bombs

Typically, Soviet bombers carried high-explosive bombs of varying calibre. The FAB-250 (551-lb (250-kg)) bombs were often carried both internally and externally. The 'FAB' stood for *Fugasnaya Aviatsionnaya Bomba*: 'General Purpose Aviation Bomb' in Russian. The smaller FAB-100 (220-lb (100-kg)) bomb was also commonly used. The largest bomb carried during the war was the huge FAB-5000 11,023-lb (5,000-kg) bomb that could only be carried by some Pe-8s (the radial-engined Pe-8 M-82). Besides carrying the FAB high-explosive type bombs, bombers could also carry BRAB armour piercing bombs, PTAB anti-tank bomblets (described below), and fragmentation bombs.

In addition to large bombs, some aircraft, such as the Il-2 often carried PTABs, anti-tank shape-charged bomblets of around 5.5 lb (2.5 kg) apiece. The Il-2 carried 192 of them in its internal wing root bomb bays according to one source, although Dr Rastrenin states that up to 280 of these bomblets could be carried. These bomblets proved particularly effective against armour, even against heavily armoured tanks such as the Panther (Panzer Mk V) and the Tiger (Panzer Mk VI) tanks, as the tops of these tanks were not as heavily armoured as the front and sides.

Indeed, it was the success of the PTAB that rendered the 37-mm-armed Il-2 redundant. The PTABs were much easier to use, and even inexperienced pilots could use them with considerable success and without special training, in contrast to the expertise needed to gain the best results with the 37-mm cannons.

Regarding the PTABs, according to Dr Rastrenin in *Ijusin Il-2: Ilyushin Il-2 Attack Aircraft* (p. 60):

> Massive deployment of PTABs achieved a tactical surprise, dumbfounded the enemy, and undermined his morale significantly. Ex-chief of staff of the 48th Panzer Corps General Friedrich Mellenthin wrote later on: '…many tanks fell a victim to the Soviet Air Force.'

Dr Rastrenin goes on to say, on pp. 61–62 of the same book:

> Combat claims and high appreciation of active Air Force units allowed the authorities to arrive at the following conclusion: 'PTAB anti-tank air bombs solved the main problem, causing the low efficiency of aviation against enemy tanks, when using high-explosive and fragmentation bombs, namely, the low hit probability…'
>
> '…PTABs should be launched into mass production and be widely employed for delivering air strikes against enemy motorised and mechanised units, railway cars, river crossings, artillery firing positions, and similar targets, successfully destroyed by PTABs,' head of Operations Directorate of the Air Force Headquarters General Zhuravlev stated.

The Germans soon developed countermeasures to reduce the effectiveness of the PTABs, such as spreading out their armour formations (which lessened the efficiency of the PTABs by four to four-and-a-half times). However, this also lessened the effectiveness of the tank formations, as there was less cohesion and cooperation in these spread-out formations, and command and control became more difficult, increasing their deployment time. However, even with these German countermeasures, the PTABs still proved more successful at destroying tanks than any other weapons the Il-2s carried, being between two to three times more effective than high explosive and fragmentation bombs.

AZh-2 ampoules, with KS inflammable liquid, could be loaded into the bomb bays of Il-2s, with up to 216 being carried. These flammable ampoules proved to be effective even against tanks, with the flaming liquid covering vision ports and observation devices and the fire could not be suppressed. However, the effectiveness of this weapon depended on flammable objects near the target and the weather.

As related by Dr Rastrenin in his book, *Il-2 Shturmovik Guards Units of World War II* (p. 65), a military engineer had this to say about what happened when two Il-2s dropped AZh-2 clusters on to artillery:

> I saw several dozen bright-red explosions, and 20 seconds later the target area was covered with thick white smoke. Incendiary bottles, dropped on air defence artillery batteries, killed gun crews, and, as a result, enemy flak near Rzhavets decreased considerably.

In addition to using their own bombs, the Soviets increasingly used captured German bombs as the war progressed and they captured more German equipment.

Rockets

The Soviets first used aerial rockets as air-to-air weapons, seeing their first use in the Battle of the Khalkhin-Gol. The rockets used were RS-82 rockets. Being unguided, they were none too accurate, and they soon found use mainly as ground attack weapons, being fitted to many aircraft during the Second World War, such as fighter-bombers and the Il-2 and Pe-2 bombers. The larger RS-132 (the number referring to the diameter of the rocket in millimetres) was also used widely in the Great Patriotic War, being one of the Il-2's main weapons. The rockets were normally carried on unstreamlined RO-82 rocket rails. Some RS-82s were fitted experimentally to Il-2s and operationally to some Pe-2s to fire backwards for rear protection, reverting to their original air-to-air role.

The RS-82 and RS-132 rockets were armour-piercing projectiles, although these were supplemented from spring 1942 by the more effective armour-piercing RB-82 and RB-132 rockets. The ROFS-132s were also fitted, which were very powerful fragmentation-type rockets, and were longer than the RS-132s, although of the same diameter. From later in 1942, M-8 (82-mm) and M-13 (132-mm) rockets were also fitted, which were developments of the RS-82 and RS-132 rockets respectively.

Guns

The main rifle-calibre weapon used in the Soviet Union on aircraft during the Second World War was the Shpitalniy-Komaritskiy ShKAS 7.62-mm (30-calibre) rapid-fire machine gun, which featured a revolving magazine. These guns were used both in moveable and fixed installations. Although they sometimes jammed, they had an extremely high rate of fire, 1,800 rpm. An 'Ultra-ShKAS' was even developed, with a maximum rate of fire of 3,000 rpm, but this gun jammed too easily and did not go into large-scale use.

The main aerial heavy machine gun used by the Soviets during the war was the Berezin UB 12.7-mm (50-calibre) machine gun. Like the ShKAS, this gun was used in both moveable (the UBT) and fixed (the UBK and UBS, the UBS being synchronised to fire through the revolving propeller) installations.

There were two cannons that were widely used by the Soviets during the war: the Shpitalniy-Vladimirov ShVAK 20-mm cannon and the Volkov-Yartsev VYa-23 23-mm cannon. The ShVAK was used in both moveable and fixed installations, while the VYa-23 was used only in fixed installations. A few fighters were equipped with this weapon in the nose, such as a few LaGG-3s and a few Yak-9s, but the vast majority of VYa-23s were used as wing-mounted weapons on the majority of Il-2s. These proved to be the single most important weapon utilised by the Il-2 and were very effective against a variety of unarmoured and lightly armoured ground targets. The Tu-2 carried two of the ShVAK cannons in the wings; some of the early Il-2s also carried two in the wings.

22
Soviet Bomber Production Figures

Below are tables listing the production figures of the Soviet-built bombers used during the Second World War. Unfortunately, some of the production tables are not complete, as the wartime records are sometimes rather spotty when it comes to exactly how many aircraft were manufactured at each *zavod* during a particular year. I have endeavoured to be as complete as the record allows. Please note that I have not included production figures for the U-2 and Li-2, as I have been unable to find production tables that list the bomber versions separately or find information on the exact number of bomber versions produced for these aircraft.

Il-2

Zavod	**1941**	**1942**	**1943**	**1944**	**1945**	**Total by *Zavod***	**Percentage of Total Production**
1	5	2,991	4,257	3,719	957	11,929	33%
18	1,510	3,942	4,702	4,014	931	15,099	42%
30	0	1,053	2,234	3,377	2,201	8,865	25%
381	27	243	0	0	0	270	0.75%
Total by Year	1,542	8,229	11,193	11,110	4,089		
					Total	36,163	

Il-4/DB-3

Zavod	**1936**	**1937**	**1938**	**1939**	**1940**	**1941**	**1942**	**1943**	**1944**	**1945**	**1946**
18		12	204	555	808	328					
23							110	257			

39		3	165	279	198	44	53	698	118		
126			30	125	100	25 DB-3/360 DB-3F/Il-4	695	658	597	485	4
166											4
Unknown	8									Total	6,923 (some sources have 6,784)

Il-10 (1944-47)

Zavod	1944	1945	1946	1947
Type	Il-10	Il-10/Il-10U	Il-10/Il-10U	Il-10/Il-10U
1		893/228	2/41	
18	73	1,362	1,006/11	859
64				12
Total	73	2,255/228	1,008/52	871
			Total	4,207/280 (Does not include Il-10M or Czech-built B-33/CB-33)

Pe-2

Zavod	No. Built
22	10,058 (includes Pe-3s?)
39	896
124	104
125	144
Total	11,202

Pe-8

Zavod	1940	1941	1942	1943	1944
124	10	23			
22			22	29	5
				Total	93?

SB

Zavod	1936	1937	1938	1939	1940	1941
22	268	853	1,250	1,435	1,749	
125		73	177	343	375	24
					Total	6,547 (Soviet-built only; does not include 161 Czech-built B-71s)

TB-3 (Production Figures from NKAP)

Zavod/Type	1932	1933	1934	1935	1936	1937	1938
22							
TB-3 4M-17	155	200					
TB-3 4M-34		70	41				
TB-3 4M-34R			85	65			
TB-3 4M-34RB				8	15		
TB-3 4M-34RN				1	100	22	1
39							
TB-3 4M-17	5	37	8				
18							
TB-3 4M-17			5			1	
						Total	819

Tu-2

Zavod/Type	1941	1942	1943	1944	1945	1946	1947	1948	1949	1950	1951	1952	Total
23/Tu-2S			16	378	742	188	244	259	2				1,829
39/Tu-2S							5	48	161	4			218
82/(Tu-10											19	6	25
166/Tu-2/Tu-2S	1	79	1			2	48	62	110				81/222
381/UTB – apparently all converted aircraft							35	117	25				176
												Grand Total	2,551 (one source has 2,527) 2,375 without UTBs

Yer-2

Zavod/Type	1941	1942	1943	1944	1945
18/Yer-2 M-105	71	-			
39/Yer-2 ACh-30B		_	2	148	241
				Total	462

23
Survivors

As mentioned in the Preface, some of the aircraft described in this book do not exist today, such as the Pe-8 and the Yak-2/Yak-4. During the 1950s, an effort was made in the Soviet Union to dispose of obsolete Second World War aircraft, which effort was all too successful in some cases. For example, amazingly not a single Il-2 was set aside for preservation in the Soviet Union, although thankfully enough examples survived as well-preserved hulks so that there are now a few preserved in Russia (others are preserved elsewhere, such as the beautifully restored example at the Prague-Kbely Museum in the Czech Republic). Some aircraft, such as the Yak-2 and Yak-4, disappeared without a trace, having been completely used up during the Great Patriotic War. Nonetheless, some Soviet Second World War bombers have survived. Below, I shall list some of these survivors by country. In addition, photographs of some of these preserved aircraft also appear in the colour plates section.

Bulgaria

There is an Il-2 preserved at Plovdiv, on outside display. At one time in a rather parlous state, it was restored in the late 1990s and still appears to be in good condition, finished in post-war Bulgarian markings. In addition, Bulgaria has a preserved Tu-2, also on outside display at Plovdiv.

China

As the last users, by far, of such wartime Soviet bombers as the Il-10 and the Tu-2, China not surprisingly has several preserved examples of each on display, some at the PLAAF (People's Liberation Army Air Force) Museum at Datangshan near Beijing.

Czech Republic

It should come as no great surprise that the Czech Republic contains some preserved Soviet Second World War bombers as Czechoslovakian units operated under the VVS banner during the Great Patriotic War, and post-war, Soviet bombers served with the Czechoslovakian Air Force. Most notable among the Czechoslovakian survivors is the restored Il-2 (B-32) now present at the museum at Prague-Kbely airport, just outside of the Czech capital. This aircraft was completely restored by 2006. In addition, a preserved Il-10 (B-33) is also present at the museum, although it could use a bit of restoration work. This may be the Il-10 that was on outside display at Ostrava, but that aircraft was sent to France, for restoration work. It is not clear what its status is now, along with another Il-10 that was sent for restoration.

Poland

Several Soviet wartime bombers are on outside display at the Polish Army Museum in Warsaw. These include an Il-2, an Il-10, a Pe-2, and a Tu-2. The aircraft display some signs of having been displayed outside for quite some time, but they appear to be in generally good condition and are finished in post-war Polish markings. In addition, a well-preserved Tu-2 is on inside display in Krakow, next to a preserved Il-10 (a B-33, the Czech-built version). This Tu-2 was used for post-war ejection seat trials by the Polish.

Romania

Although Romania used several Soviet wartime bombers post-war such as the Il-10 and Tu-2, they have not gone to great lengths to preserve them. At least one Tu-2 is still preserved, however.

Russia

Not surprisingly, Russia contains the greatest number of different wartime Soviet bombers preserved, including the only examples of the Tupolev SB, DB-3, and Il-4 to have survived. In addition, some mock-ups have also been constructed, such as the reasonably good mock-up of the Su-2 displayed at Pobeda Park in Moscow.

The museum at Monino, located outside of Moscow, has the examples of the SB and the DB-3. The aircraft are currently displayed inside at Monino, although they may eventually be displayed inside at the new military park/museum in Moscow. An Il-2 and a Pe-2 are also displayed inside at Monino. Pobeda Park, located on Poklonnaya Gora (Hill) in Moscow, has fairly convincing mock-ups of the Di-6Sh and the Su-2, and has a restored Il-4, finished in Great Patriotic War night bomber markings, and an

Il-2, convincingly restored as a single-seater. Pobeda Park also has a Li-2 restored as a Li-2NB, complete with turret and in wartime markings. Once displayed completely in the open, these Pobeda Park aircraft are now displayed under a large roof open at the sides, which offers some protection from the elements. Photographs of some of these aircraft are in the colour plates section. There is an Il-4 on display at Komsomolsk-na-Amure, although it is hard to tell from the photographs how much is original and how much is a replica (the propellers are definitely not original, for example). It does not appear to be purely a mock-up.

In 2011, a straight-winged two-seater Il-2 with metal wings was recovered from a lake near Murmansk. The aircraft was preserved by the low oxygen content and cold water of the lake. This aircraft has now been completely restored to flying condition, flying for the first time on 16 June 2017. It apparently has an AM-38F engine powering it. An original single-seater is now reportedly being restored to flying status in Russia, apparently with a restored AM-38 engine to power it.

Although no TB-3s have been preserved, a wreck was found in 1992. I have been unable to determine the current status of this wreck, but it is possible it may be restored. If it is, it will be the only example of the TB-3 in the world.

United States

Perhaps surprisingly, the United States of America is home to one of the best-preserved Il-2s in the world. So well-preserved is this aircraft that it is one of only two examples of this famous warplane still flying in the world as of 2019. It first flew in its restored state on 27 September 2011. It is powered by an American Alison V-1710 engine, not the original AM-38F, but the engine's rotation has been reversed (the propeller rotates to the left) to match the rotation of the AM-38F. It resides at the Flying Heritage Museum at Everett in Washington State; the museum was owned by the late Paul Allen, one of the founders of Microsoft. This museum also houses a flyable U-2/Po-2, in Soviet wartime markings.

A Tu-2, obtained from China, is presently (2019) at the War Eagles Air Museum in Santa Teresa, New Mexico. This aircraft has apparently undergone some restoration.

Bibliography

Internet Resources

vvs.hobbyvista.com: Modelling the Aircraft of the Soviet VVS—this was a worthwhile site for making VVS models. It contains some useful information, although its articles on colour are controversial and should not be taken for gospel. This site is now moribund and the forum portion is no longer functioning, but the reference articles are still up as of the time of writing (2019).

www.airaces.ru: a very useful Russian language site that contains much information about Soviet aeroplanes, including production figures.

www.airpages.ru: This site is not specifically about Soviet aircraft, but as a Russian site, it does contain a great deal of material about Soviet aeroplanes of the Second World War. It has both a Russian language and an English language option, but the Russian language option is more exhaustive in its coverage. Still, the English language version contains some interesting information, such as drawings, photographs, and performance figures (as does the Russian language version).

www.airwar.ru: An excellent resource for aviation-related material of all eras, not just Soviet aircraft. It has much textual information on Great Patriotic War bombers and also has many plans, drawings, and photographs of these aircraft. It is in Russian, although an incomplete English version is available. Online translation is also available.

www.arcforums.com: Not specifically for the VVS, but contains threads and posts regarding VVS aircraft and colours.

www.aviapress.com: A good site for Soviet aircraft kits, accessories, and books. The prices are not cheap, however.

www.britmodeller.com: A good site for modelling in general, containing some threads and posts concerning Soviet aircraft and VVS colours, some by this very author.

www.hannants.co.uk: An excellent British online ordering house. They stock kits of Soviet wartime bombers and scale accessories.

www.hobbyterra.com: A good site for Soviet/Russian aviation subjects; it includes some kits and scale accessories of Soviet wartime bombers.

www.ilyushin.org: the Ilyushin Joint Stock Company's official website. It contains some interesting information about the Il-4, the Il-2, and the Il-10 in its historical section.

www.iremember.ru: A site that has interviews with veterans of the Great Patriotic War. The interviews are available in both Russian and English. This site is recommended not just for aviation historians, but also for anyone interested in the experiences of Soviet military men and women during the Great Patriotic War.

www.lindenhillimports.com: A good internet store for all things concerning Soviet/Russian aviation, including VVS subjects.

www.massimotessitori.altervista.org/sovietwarplanes/pages/: An excellent website for all things VVS and run by the illustrator of my books on the Il-2 Shturmovik and wartime Lavochkin fighters, Massimo Tessitori. Highly recommended for all those interested in Soviet Great Patriotic War aircraft and has accurate representations of the colour schemes that they wore. This site should also be of great interest for the plastic modeller of VVS aeroplanes. It includes low-resolution versions of some of the colour profiles in this book.

www.modelism.airforce.ru: An excellent site that describes and reviews various aircraft models and accessories. In Russian, but with plenty of helpful photographs.

www.redbanner.co.uk: The successor site to Modelling the Aircraft of the Soviet VVS. The same comments about the old site generally apply to this site.

www.ScaleModels.ru: A very good site for reference material on VVS aircraft, including the Soviet wartime bombers and kits. In Russian with automatic English translation available (with all the interesting translation artefacts and peculiarities that entails).

www.squadron.com: A very good online ordering house with a good selection of aeroplane kits, including VVS subjects such as Soviet wartime bombers. They offer quick delivery in the US.

www.tupolev.ru/en/aircrafts: Tupolev's own site; it has some interesting information about the Tu-2.

Further Reading

Note on literature: Although I have attempted to be as comprehensive as possible regarding good literature on Soviet wartime bombers, I have no doubt missed some worthy titles. Nevertheless, if you are able to obtain and read at least some of the following books and magazines, then you will have gained an even better understanding of the history and development of Soviet wartime bombers than can be contained in any one volume, even one as comprehensive as this book. In addition, since the Red Air Force was such an integral part of all the major Soviet battles and operations, I have also added some books that give more background on these battles, as my coverage of these actions has been somewhat cursory, this being a general reference work on the Soviet Second World War bombers and not a dedicated war history. These war histories are books that I have personally read and found to be both interesting and informative, and I hope that you will also find them to be so should you choose to read them. Please remember that these books are general military histories, not aviation histories, but for those who are interested in learning more about the battles that the Soviet bombers took part in (or even Eastern Front battles in general), these books can be recommended.

Note for modellers: An important item to remember is that much of the literature mentioned further on that have bomber profiles have colour inaccuracies in their profiles. Typically, they have profiles with the fictitious colour scheme of green and brown, which should either be green and black or dark grey, green, and tan, depending on the time period (mid-1941 to mid- to late 1943 for the black and green scheme, and mid- to late 1943–1945 for the dark grey (or black), green, and tan scheme). Sometimes they will also feature the equally spurious scheme of green and dark green, or overall green for a Great Patriotic War bomber (although some bombers did retain the pre-war overall green topside scheme for a time in the early part of the war). It is also not clear from the record when or if any bombers received the two-grey 'fighter' scheme, although it is possible that some Yer-2s were so finished, over a black underside. You should never rely only on profiles for your paint schemes for your models unless you have no photographs or other references. You will have to interpret whether to use the black with the green scheme, the dark grey (or black), green, and tan scheme, or the single overall topside colour schemes used post-war (and early in the Great Patriotic War), depending on the time period of your bomber, if the profiles show any of the spurious schemes mentioned previously.

Beevor, A., *The Fall of Berlin 1945*—A thorough and balanced account of the last great battle of the Great Patriotic War.

Buttar. P., *Battleground Prussia: The Assault on Germany's Eastern Front 1944–45*—An excellent account of the Soviet invasion of East Prussia and the terrible retribution that the Red Army exacted on the German soldiers and civilians there.

Clark, L., *The Battle of the Tanks: Kursk, 1943*—A good and detailed overview of this important battle, the last major German offensive in the Soviet Union.

Duffy, P. and Kandalov, A., *Tupolev: The Man and His Aircraft*—A book that is not specifically about the pre-war and wartime Tupolev bombers, but does contain some interesting information about these aircraft.

Glantz, D. M. and House, J. M., *Stalingrad*—The single most comprehensive operational overview of this critical battle of the Second World War that I have read, and I have read many.

Gordon, Y., *Soviet Air Power in World War 2*—This book contains a great deal of information about the Soviet bombers used during the Second World War, including experimental aircraft.

Gordon, Y. and Khazanov, D. with Medved', A., *Soviet Combat Aircraft of the Second World War: Volume Two—Twin-Engined Fighters, Attack Aircraft, and Bombers*—This book gives a good overview of the bombers used by the Soviet Union during the Second World War.

Gunston, B., *Tupolev Aircraft Since 1922*—This book contains some good information about the Tupolev bombers, such as the TB-1, TB-3, SB, and Tu-2 and its derivatives.

Hardesty, V. and Grinberg, I., *Red Phoenix Rising*—A general history of the VVS during the Great Patriotic War. Although not specifically about VVS bombers, it is the best reference in English of the VVS during the Great Patriotic War. Highly recommended if you wish to gain an overall understanding of the VVS and its strategy and tactics as used during the Great Patriotic War.

Hornat, J. and Migliardi, B., *Colours of the Falcons*—The best reference work for VVS colours in English. Recommended with reservations, as it does contain some inaccuracies, such as the spurious 'Southern Front' schemes. Note that this book only cover fighters, but the early black/green scheme is discussed, which was used on both fighters and bombers, such as the early versions of the Il-2, Il-4, and Pe-2, for example.

Jones, M., *The Retreat: Hitler's First Defeat*—A good account of the Battle of Moscow, in what was, after Stalingrad, the most important battle of the Great Patriotic War. This is a good book about the early part of the Great Patriotic War.

Jones, M. K., *Stalingrad: How the Red Army Triumphed*—An excellent and balanced look at what I believe to be the pivotal battle of not just the Great Patriotic War, but of the war in Europe.

Khazanov, D. B., *Air War Over Kursk: Turning Point in the East*—Besides containing a good account of the air war, which had an important impact on the ground fighting, this book contains many good colour profiles and tables of statistics dealing with the different units and aircraft that fought on both sides. This is a good book on the air battle over Kursk.

Lunde, H. O., *Finland's War of Choice: The Troubled German-Finnish Coalition in World War II*—This book gives a good and balanced insight into the complex relationship between the democratic Finnish and Nazi Germany, including their sometimes joint, but more often disjointed actions against the Soviet Union.

Merridale, C., *Ivan's War: Life and Death in the Red Army, 1939–1945*—This book tells the story of the common soldier in the Red Army. This book seems free of the prejudices and misconceptions, both flattering and unflattering, so common to popular accounts of the Red Army soldier. Highly recommended if you wish to know what it was like to be one small cog in the huge Soviet war machine during the Great Patriotic War.

Orlov, M., *Aviakollektsia: Soviet VVS Colours 1941–1945*—Contains colour profiles, photographs, and NKAP templates. Despite being a fairly short book, to date, this is the definitive work on Great Patriotic War VVS colours. It is highly recommended, though it is in Russian.

Salisbury, H. E., *The 900 Days: The Siege of Leningrad*—A fascinating book on the deadliest siege of all times.

Stahel, D., *Kiev 1941: Hitler's Battle for Supremacy in the East*—A book that explores an often-overlooked chapter of the war in 1941: the Battle for Kiev and how it derailed the German advance on Moscow. This book gives a fairly convincing argument that this battle was crucial in the failure of Operation Barbarossa, at least in its failure to capture the Soviet capital before the end of 1941 and possibly knock the Soviet Union out of the war.

Tu-2 Flight Manual. This is the original flight manual for the Tu-2S, published in 1945. It is recommended for its drawings and historical value and is in Russian.

Wagner, R. (ed. and annotations) and Fetzer, L. (trans.), *The Soviet Air Force in World War II, The Official History*—Originally published in the 1970s in the Soviet Union, this book is as propagandistic as one might expect from a Soviet-era book on the Great Patriotic War. Nonetheless, if one can look past the propaganda, there is interesting and generally accurate information about the evolution of the Red Air Force during the Second World War. Recommended if you can stand a fair helping of Soviet propaganda ('Socialist Heroes of the Motherland versus the Fascist Invaders', etc.).

Books

Bakurskiiy, V., *Shturmovik Il2* (Moscow: Mir Tekhniki, 2004)

Bergstrom, C., *Bagration to Berlin—The Final Air Battles in the East: 1944–1945* (Hersham; Ian Allen Publishing, 2008)

Chernikov, Y., АРМАДА № 4—БРОНИРОВАННЫЙ ШТУРМОВИК ИЛ-2—*(Armada No. 4—Bronirovanniy Shturmovik Il-2)* (Armada, 1995)

Denny, I., with Afterword by Dennis Showalter, *The Fall of Hitler's Fortress City: The Battle for Konigsberg, 1945* (New York City; Skyhorse Publishing, Inc., 2016)

Duffy, P., and Kandalov, A., *Tupolev: The Man and His Aircraft* (Warrendale: SAE International, 1996)

Fujita, K., Torikai, T., and Tamura, T., *Famous Airplanes of the World (FAOW) Il-2 Shturmovik No. 129* (Tokyo: Bunrindo Co., Ltd, 2008)

Glantz, D. M., and House, J. M., *Stalingrad* (Lawrence: University Press of Kansas, 2017)

Gordon, Y., and Khazanov, D., with Medved', A., *Soviet Combat Aircraft of the Second World War—Volume Two—Twin-Engined Fighters, Attack Aircraft, and Bombers* (The Hollow: Midland Publishing, 1999)

Gordon, Y., and Sergey K., *The Ilyushin Il-2 and Ilyushin Il-10 Shturmovik* (Ramsbury: The Crowood Press Ltd, 2004)

Gordon, Y., Komissarov, D., and Komissarov, S., *OKB Ilyushin: A History of the Design Bureau and its Aircraft* (London: Ian Allen, 2004); *Famous Russian Aircraft, Ilyushin Il-2/Il-10* (Hersham: Ian Allen Publishing, 2010); *Lisunov Li-2: The Soviet DC-3* (Hinckley: Midland Publishing, 2006)

Gordon, Y., *Soviet Air Power in World War 2* (Hinckley: Ian Allen Publishing Ltd, 2008)

Gordon, Yefim, and Rigmant, Vladimir, *OKB Tupolev: A History of the Design Bureau and its Aircraft* (Hinckley: Midland Publishing, 2005)

Gunston, B., and Gordon, Y., *Yakovlev Aircraft Since 1924* (London: Putnam Aeronautical Books, 1997)

Gunston, B., *The Osprey Encyclopedia of Russian Aircraft 1875–1995* (General Aviation) (London; Osprey, 1995); *Tupolev Aircraft Since 1922* (Naval Institute Press, 1995)

Hardesty, V., and Grinburg, I., *Red Phoenix Rising: The Soviet Air Force in World War II* (Lawrence: University Press of Kansas, 2012)

Hooton, E. R., *War Over the Steppes: The Air Campaigns on the Eastern Front 1941–45* (Oxford: Osprey Publishing, 2016)

Hornat, J. and Migliardi, B., *Colours of the Falcons* (Ottawa: Iliad Design, 2006)

Il-2 Flight Manual (Moscow: People's Commissariat of Defence, 1942)

Il-2 Technical Manual (Moscow: People's Commissariat of Defence, 1943)

Khazanov, D. and Medved', A., *Osprey Combat Aircraft 96: Pe-2 Guards Units of World War 2* (Oxford: Osprey Publishing Limited, 2013)

Kirilov, R., *Shturmovik Il-2, Chernata Sm'rt* (Sofia: Retro Salon, 1999)

Koran, F. and Ovcacik, M., *Il-2 Type 3 and Il-10/Avia B-33 in detail* (Hradec Kralove: Wings & Wheels Publications, 1997)

Kotel'nikov, V. R., *Air War Over Khalkhin Gol: The Nomonhan Incident* (Bedford: SAM Publications, 2010); *Il-4: Stalin's 'Armed Cruiser'* (Moscow: Yauza, Kollektsiya, Eksmo, 2009); *Bomber TB-3: Stalin's Aerial Superlinkor* (Moscow: Yauza, Kollektsiya, Eksmo, 2008); *Russian Piston Aero Engines* (Ramsbury: The Crowood Press Ltd, 2005)

Krolikiewicz, T., *Typy Broni i Uzbrojenia (TBiU)—Ilyushin Il-2 (Warsaw:* Wydawnictwo Minsterstwa Obrony Narodewej, 1971)

Kulikov, V., *Monografie Lotnicze 77: Tupolew Tu-2, Tu-1, Tu-6, Tu-8, Tu-10* (Gdansk; AJ-Press, 2001)

Kuznetsov, S., *Bronirovanniy Shturmovik Il-2* (Moscow: Eksprint, 2003); *M-Hobby: Seria 'Model' i Prototip', Shturmovik Il-2* (Moscow: Tseiykhgauz, 2003)

Legendariye Samolyeti Il-2 (Moscow: DeAgostini, 2009?)

Legendariye Samolyeti Il-2 KSS (Moscow: DeAgostini, 2011)

Liss, W., *Aircraft Profile 88* (Profile Publications Ltd., 1966)

Maslov, M., *Tupolev SB: Soviet High Speed Bomber* (Moscow: Icarus Aviation Press, 2004)

Matthews, R., *Kursk: The World's Greatest Tank Battle* (London: Arcturus Publishing Limited, 2016)

Michulec, R., *Monografie Lotnicze 22—Ilyushin Il-2, Il-10* (Gdansk: AJ Press, 1995)

Moore, J. N., *Il-2 Modelling Guide* (unpublished manuscript); *Il-2 Shturmovik: Red Avenger* (Stroud: Fonthill Media, 2015); *Lavochkin Fighters of the Second World War* (Stroud: Fonthill Media, 2016); *Soviet Fighters of the Second World War* (unpublished manuscript); *Soviet Strategic Bombers: The Hammer in the Hammer and the Sickle* (Stroud: Fonthill Media, 2018); *Tupolev Tu-2: The Forgotten Medium Bomber* (Stroud: Fonthill Media, 2016)

Noszczak, M., *Ilyushin Il-2 AM-38: All models* (Lublin: Kagero Publishing Sp. z. o.o., 2011)

Orlov, M., *Aviakollektsia—Soviet VVS Colours 1941-1945* (Moscow: Modelist-Konstruktor, 2008)

Ovcacik, M. and Susa, K., *4+ Publication. #022—Ilyushin Il-2 Shturmovik* (Prague: 4+ Publishing Co., 2006)

Perov, V. and Rastrenin, O., *Shturmovik Il-2* (Moscow: Aviatsiya i Kosmonauvtika, 2001)

Pilawskii, E., *Soviet Air Force Fighter Colours 1941–1945* (Ian Allen Publishing, 2004)

Povinsky, V., *Il-2 Shturmovik* (Sandomierz: STRATUS s.c., 2014); *Ilyushin Il-2 Shturmovik—Part 1. The single-seater (MaxiProfile No. 4) and Ilyushin Il-2 Shturmovik—Part 2. The two-seater versions (MaxiProfile No. 5)* (Viktor Publishing, 2010); *Ilyushin Il-2 Shturmovik: The single-seater* (Viktor Publishing, 2011)

Rastrenin, O., *Il-2 Shturmovik: 'Flying Tank'* (Moscow: Eksmo, 2007); *Il-2 Shturmovik Guards Units of WWII* (Botley: Osprey Publishing Limited, 2008); *Ilyushin Il-2: Ilyushin Il-2 Attack Aircraft* (Bucovice: Jakab, 2008)

Rigmant, V., *Bomber Tu-2* (Moscow; Aviatsiya i Kosmonavtika, 2015)

Saukke, M. B., and Kotel'nikov, V. R., *Bomber Tu-2: Part 1* (Moscow; Modelist-Konstructor, 2008); *Bomber Tu-2: Part 2* (Moscow; Modelist-Konstructor, 2008)

Spravochnik Pa Samolyetu Il-2 1944 (Reference (Parts List) of the Il-2 Aeroplane 1944) (Moscow: People's Commissariat of Defence, 1944)

Stapfer, H.-H., *Il-2 Stormovik in action* (Squadron/Signal Publications, 1978?); *Ilyushin Il-4 in action* (Carrollton: Squadron/Signal Publications, Inc., 2004); *Tupolev SB in action* (Carrollton: Squadron/Signal Publications, Inc., 2004)

Taller, A. I., *Il-2: Samolyot i Model* (Moscow: DOSAAF SSSR, 1978)

Tu-2 Flight Manual (Leningrad; Leningrad Military Aviation Academy of the Red Army, 1945)

Wagner, R. (ed.) and Fetzer, L. (trans.), *The Soviet Air Force in World War II, The Official History* (Garden City: Doubleday & Company, Inc., 1973)

Yakubovich, N., *Our Aviation and the Battle for Berlin: Victory 'Stalin's Falcons'* (Moscow: 'Yauza', 'EKSMO', 2015); *Tu-2: Light Bomber: Patriotic War* (Moscow: 'Yauza', 'EKSMO', 2010)

Magazines

Vakhlamov, V. and Orlov, M., *M-Hobby 1999, Vols 1–4, 6* (1999)

Voiyna V Vozdukhe Magazine, Vol. 7

Voiyna V Vozdukhe Magazine, Vol. 8

Voiyna V Vozdukhe Magazine, Vol. 66, Tu-2

Voiyna V Vozdukhe Magazine, Vol. 67, Tu-2

Voiyna V Vozdukhe Magazine, Vol. 126 (2005)

Index